LOVE ATTACK™

JUNAI TOKKO TAICHO!

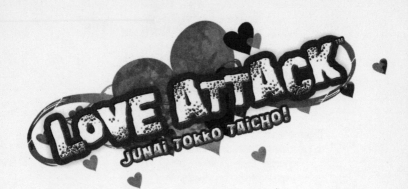

Vol. 1

by

Shizuru Seino

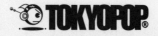

TOKYOPOP®

HAMBURG // LONDON // LOS ANGELES // TOKYO

Love Attack Vol. 1
Created by Shizuru Seino

Translation - Adrienne Beck
English Adaptation - Magdalena Sniegocki
Copy Editor - Reza Emaddudin
Retouch and Lettering - Star Print Brokers
Production Artist - Michael Paolilli
Graphic Designer - James Lee

Editor - Hyun Joo Kim
Digital Imaging Manager - Chris Buford
Pre-Production Supervisor - Erika Terriquez
Production Manager - Elisabeth Brizzi
Managing Editor - Vy Nguyen
Creative Director - Anne Marie Horne
Editor-in-Chief - Rob Tokar
Publisher - Mike Kiley
President and C.O.O. - John Parker
C.E.O. and Chief Creative Officer - Stuart Levy

A **TOKYOPOP** Manga

TOKYOPOP and 🌀 are trademarks or registered trademarks of TOKYOPOP Inc.

TOKYOPOP Inc.
5900 Wilshire Blvd. Suite 2000
Los Angeles, CA 90036

E-mail: info@TOKYOPOP.com
Come visit us online at www.TOKYOPOP.com

ISBN: 978-1-4278-0294-1

First TOKYOPOP printing: December 2007
10 9 8 7 6 5 4 3 2 1
Printed in the USA

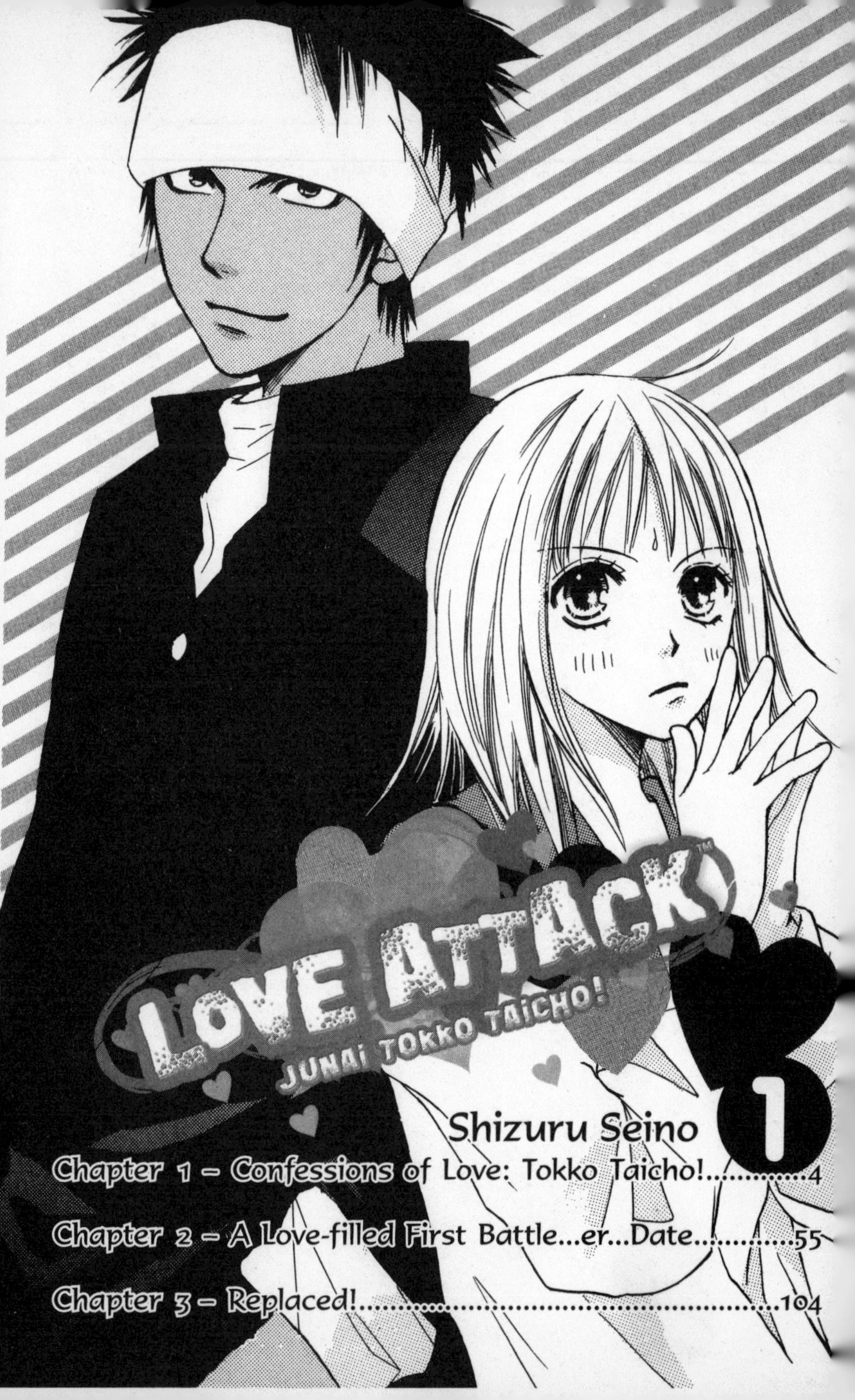

LOVE ATTACK™

JUNAI TOKKO TAICHO!

1

Shizuru Seino

Ch.1 Confessions of Love: Tokko Taicho!

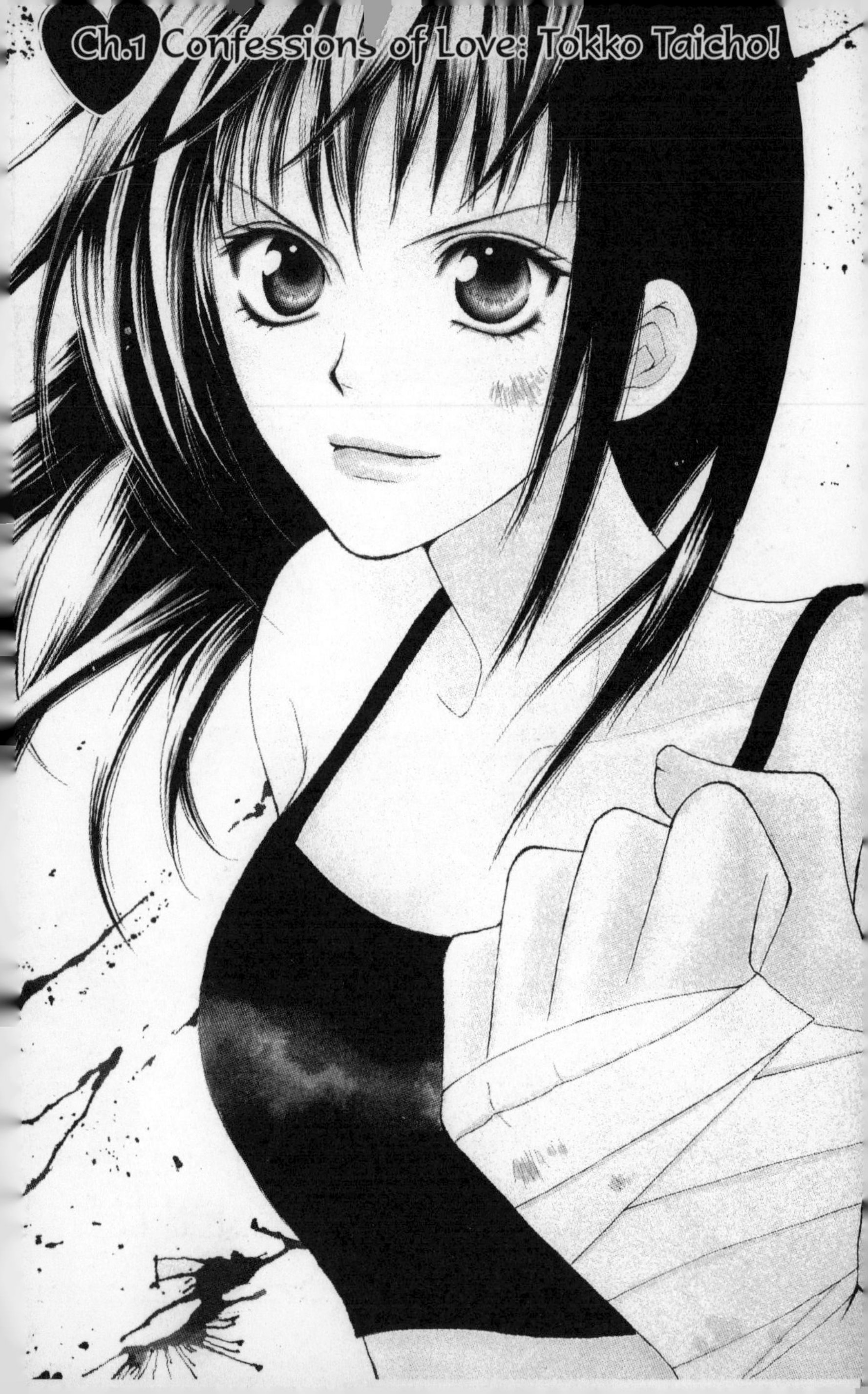

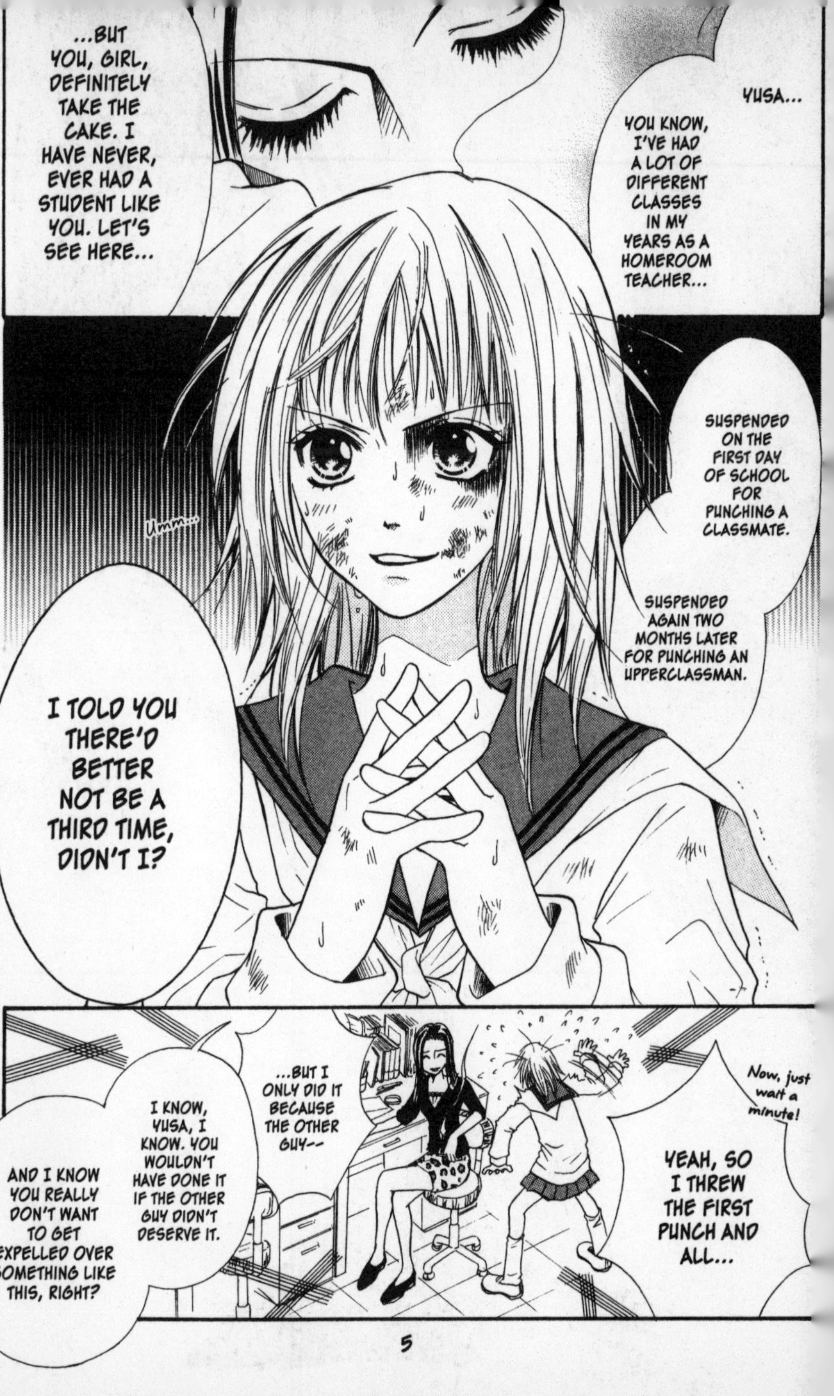
YUSA...
YOU KNOW, I'VE HAD A LOT OF DIFFERENT CLASSES IN MY YEARS AS A HOMEROOM TEACHER...
...BUT YOU, GIRL, DEFINITELY TAKE THE CAKE. I HAVE NEVER, EVER HAD A STUDENT LIKE YOU. LET'S SEE HERE...
SUSPENDED ON THE FIRST DAY OF SCHOOL FOR PUNCHING A CLASSMATE.
SUSPENDED AGAIN TWO MONTHS LATER FOR PUNCHING AN UPPERCLASSMAN.
Umm...
I TOLD YOU THERE'D BETTER NOT BE A THIRD TIME, DIDN'T I?
Now, just wait a minute!
YEAH, SO I THREW THE FIRST PUNCH AND ALL...
...BUT I ONLY DID IT BECAUSE THE OTHER GUY--
I KNOW, YUSA, I KNOW. YOU WOULDN'T HAVE DONE IT IF THE OTHER GUY DIDN'T DESERVE IT.
AND I KNOW YOU REALLY DON'T WANT TO GET EXPELLED OVER SOMETHING LIKE THIS, RIGHT?

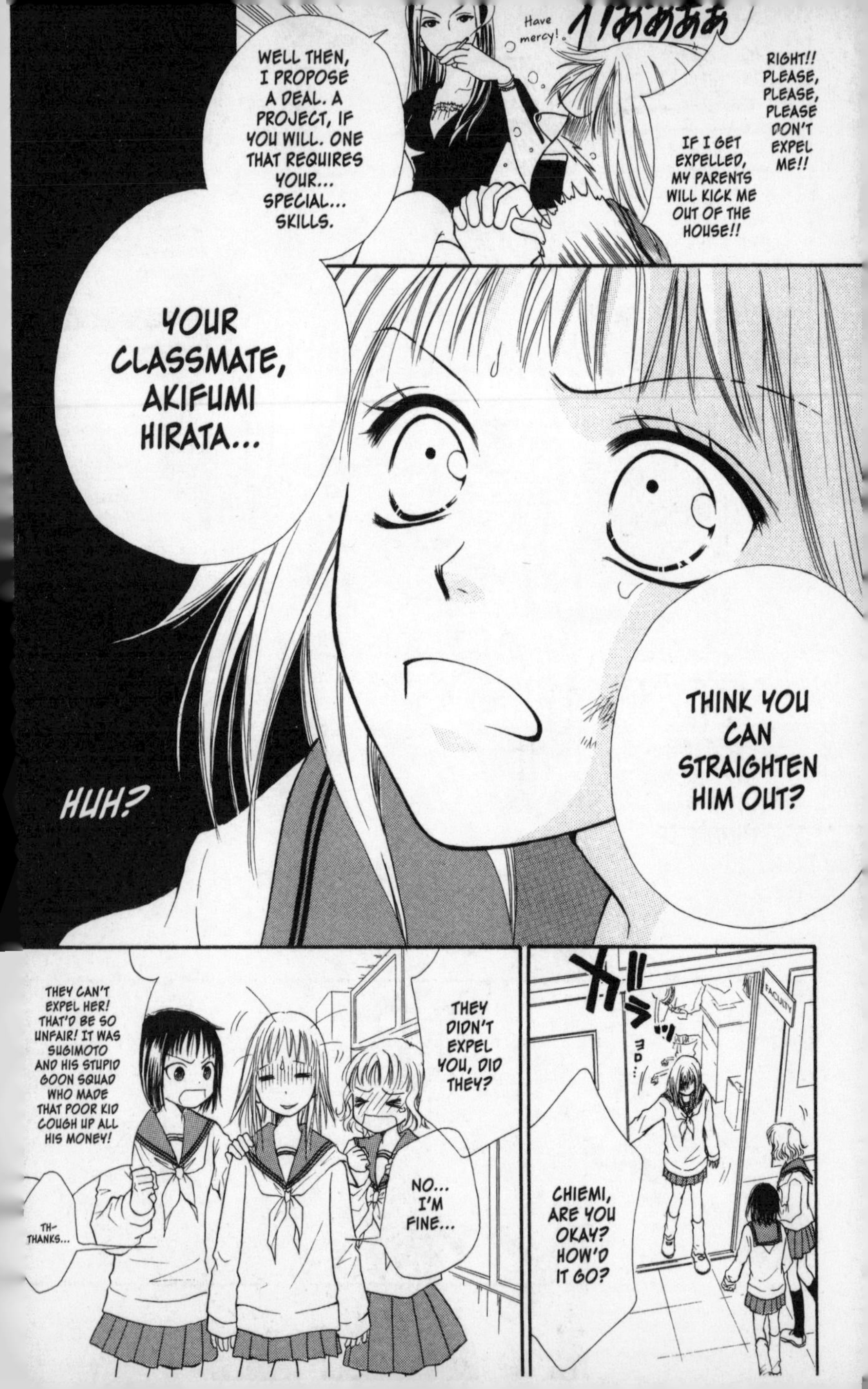
Have mercy!
RIGHT!! PLEASE, PLEASE, PLEASE DON'T EXPEL ME!!
IF I GET EXPELLED, MY PARENTS WILL KICK ME OUT OF THE HOUSE!!
WELL THEN, I PROPOSE A DEAL. A PROJECT, IF YOU WILL. ONE THAT REQUIRES YOUR... SPECIAL... SKILLS.
YOUR CLASSMATE, AKIFUMI HIRATA...
THINK YOU CAN STRAIGHTEN HIM OUT?
HUH?
FACULTY
CHIEMI, ARE YOU OKAY? HOW'D IT GO?
THEY DIDN'T EXPEL YOU, DID THEY?
NO... I'M FINE...
THEY CAN'T EXPEL HER! THAT'D BE SO UNFAIR! IT WAS SUGIMOTO AND HIS STUPID GOON SQUAD WHO MADE THAT POOR KID COUGH UP ALL HIS MONEY!
TH-THANKS...

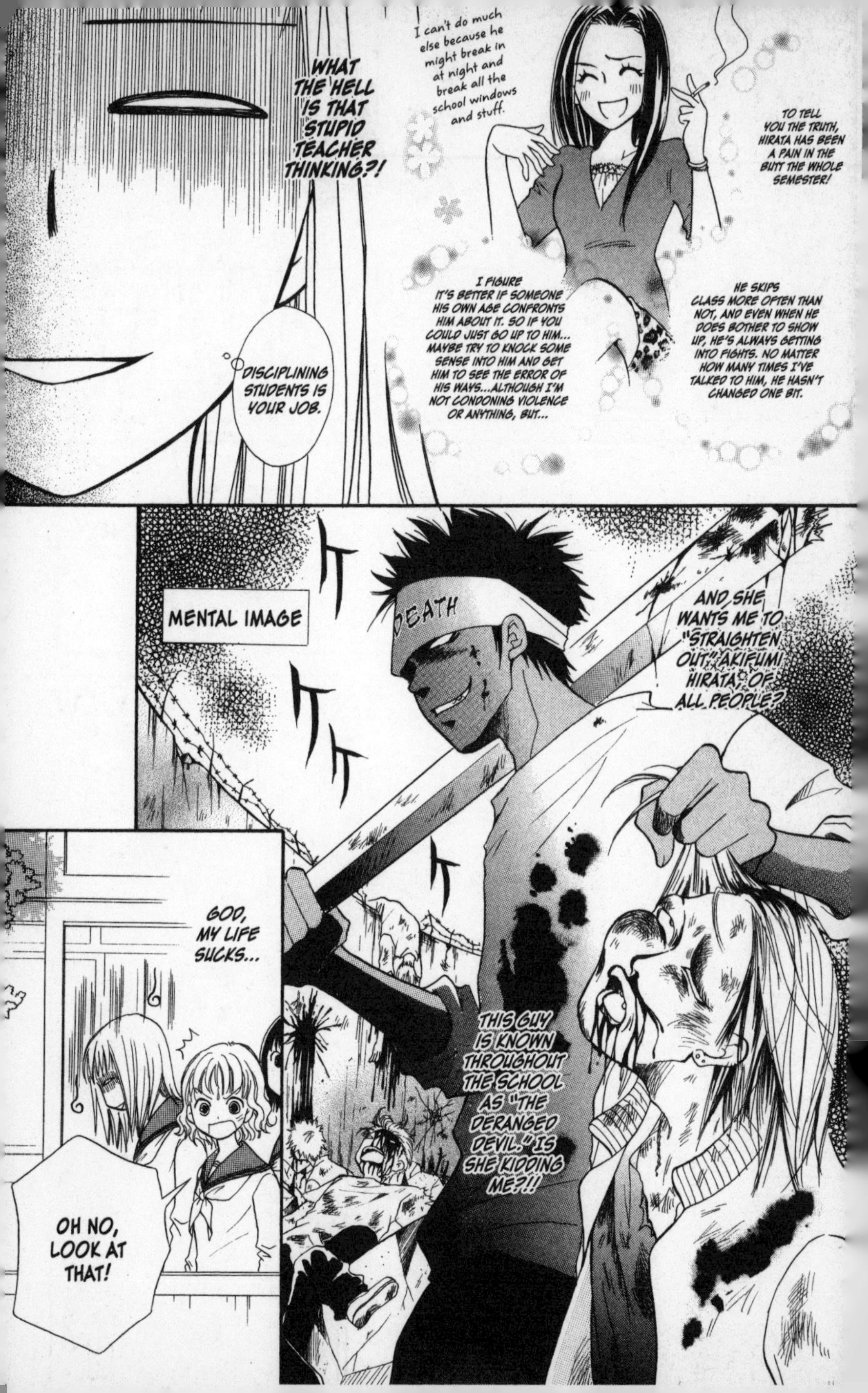
TO TELL YOU THE TRUTH, HIRATA HAS BEEN A PAIN IN THE BUTT THE WHOLE SEMESTER!
HE SKIPS CLASS MORE OFTEN THAN NOT, AND EVEN WHEN HE DOES BOTHER TO SHOW UP, HE'S ALWAYS GETTING INTO FIGHTS. NO MATTER HOW MANY TIMES I'VE TALKED TO HIM, HE HASN'T CHANGED ONE BIT.
I FIGURE IT'S BETTER IF SOMEONE HIS OWN AGE CONFRONTS HIM ABOUT IT. SO IF YOU COULD JUST GO UP TO HIM... MAYBE TRY TO KNOCK SOME SENSE INTO HIM AND GET HIM TO SEE THE ERROR OF HIS WAYS...ALTHOUGH I'M NOT CONDONING VIOLENCE OR ANYTHING, BUT...
I can't do much else because he might break in at night and break all the school windows and stuff.
DISCIPLINING STUDENTS IS YOUR JOB.
WHAT THE HELL IS THAT STUPID TEACHER THINKING?!
AND SHE WANTS ME TO "STRAIGHTEN OUT" AKIFUMI HIRATA, OF ALL PEOPLE?
DEATH
MENTAL IMAGE
THIS GUY IS KNOWN THROUGHOUT THE SCHOOL AS "THE DERANGED DEVIL." IS SHE KIDDING ME?!!
GOD, MY LIFE SUCKS...
OH NO, LOOK AT THAT!

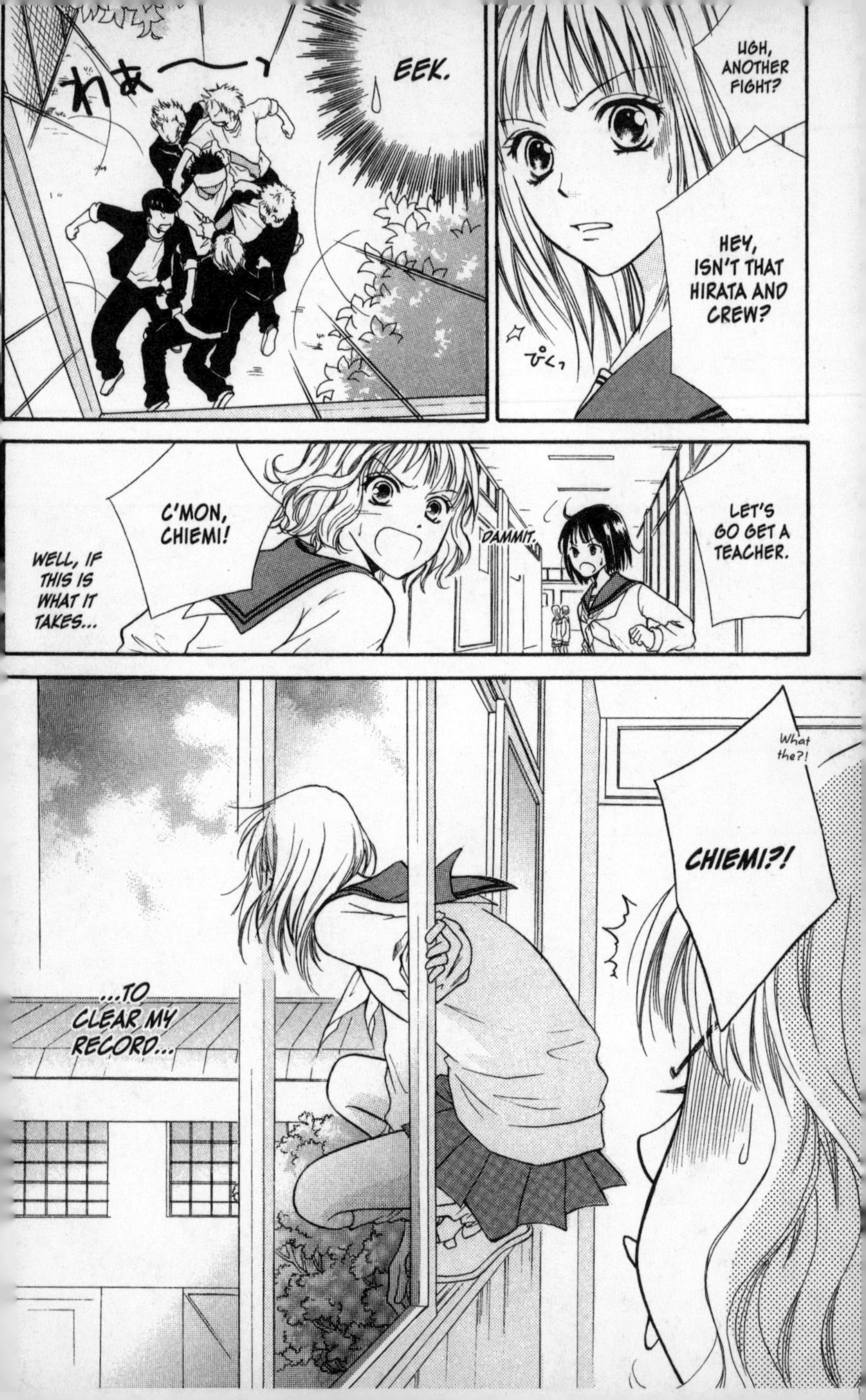
UGH, ANOTHER FIGHT?
HEY, ISN'T THAT HIRATA AND CREW?
ぴくっ
EEK.
わあ〜っ
LET'S GO GET A TEACHER.
DAMMIT.
C'MON, CHIEMI!
WELL, IF THIS IS WHAT IT TAKES...
What the?!
CHIEMI?!
...TO CLEAR MY RECORD...

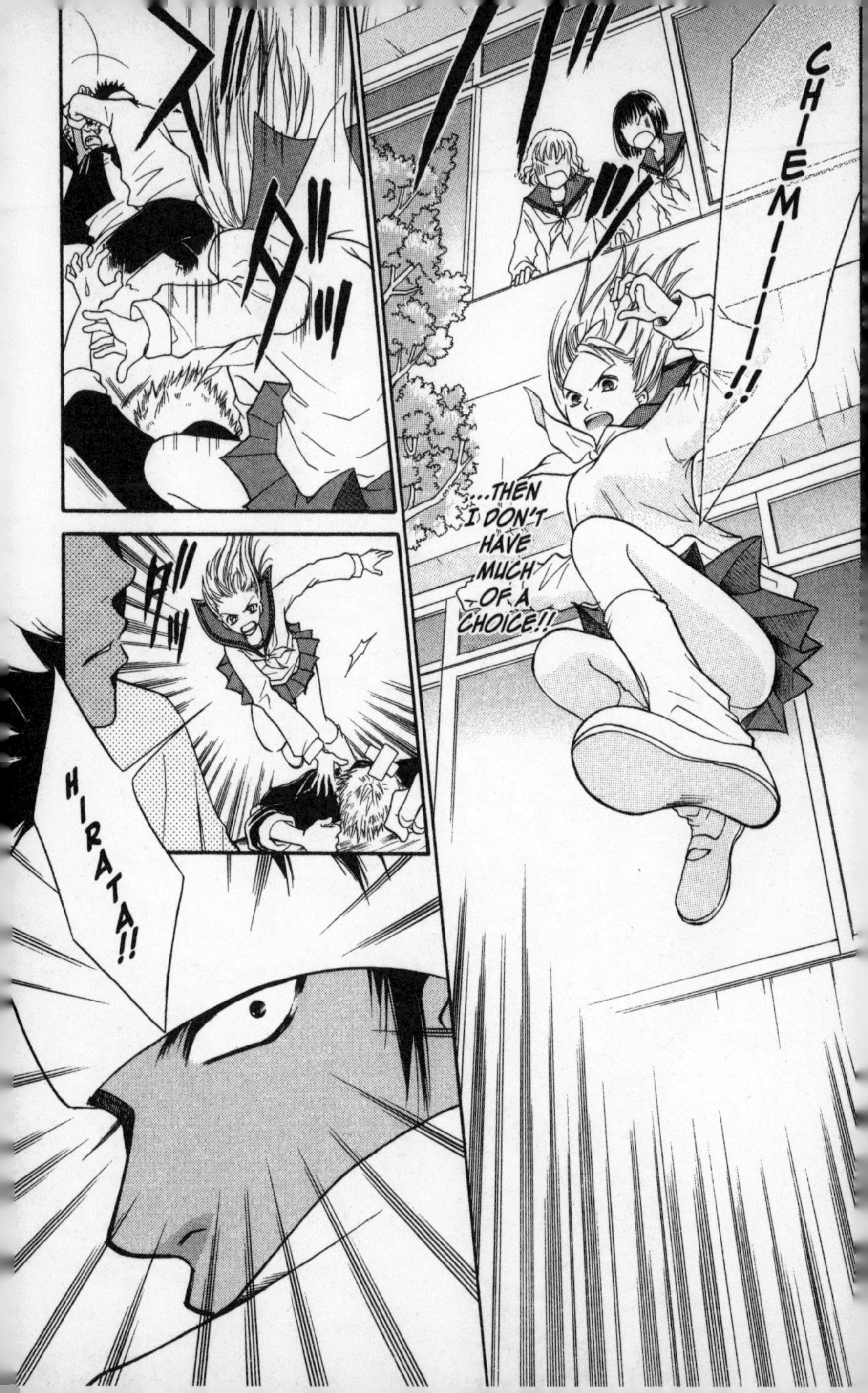
CHIEMIIIII!!
...THEN I DON'T HAVE MUCH OF A CHOICE!!
HIRATA!!

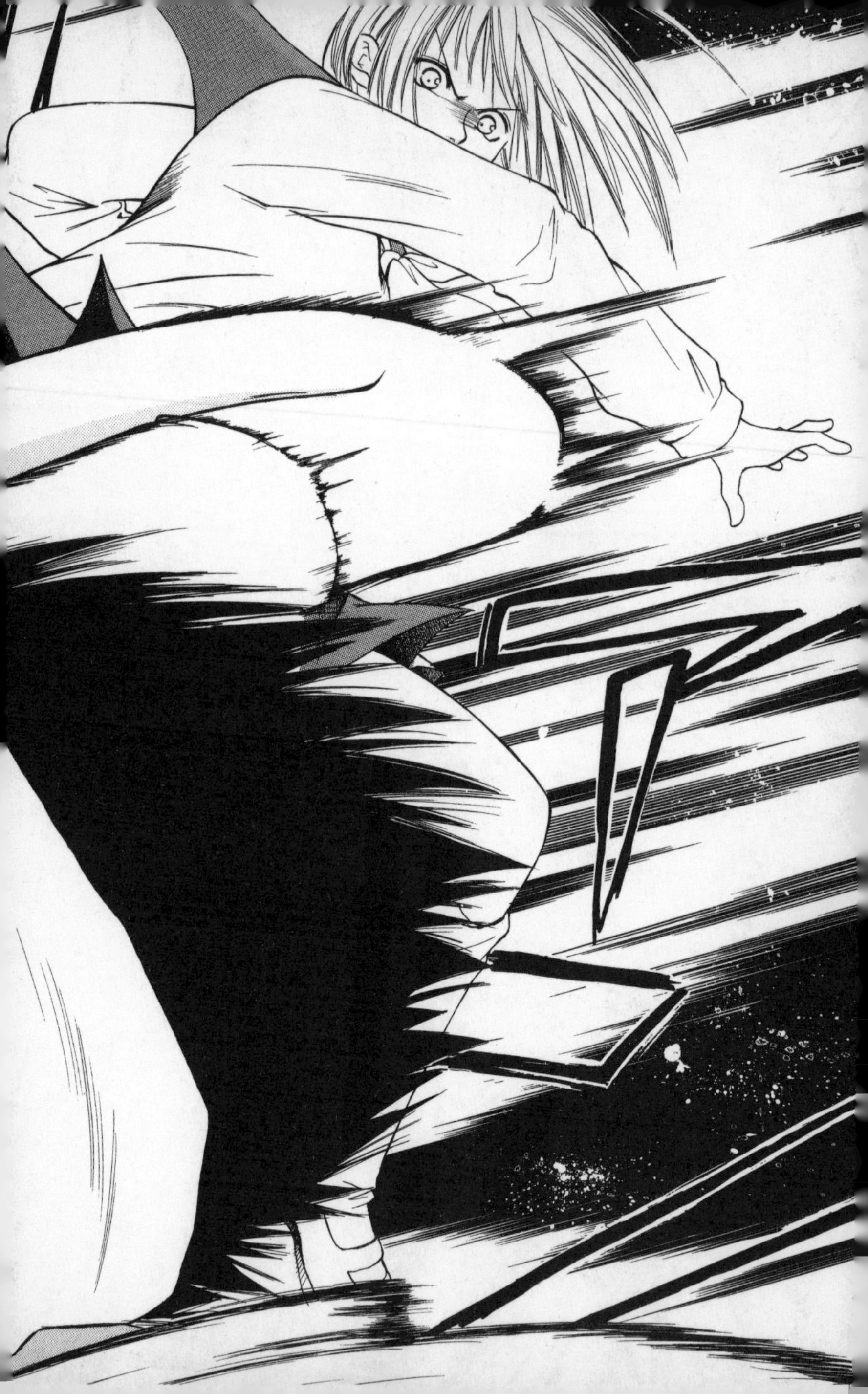

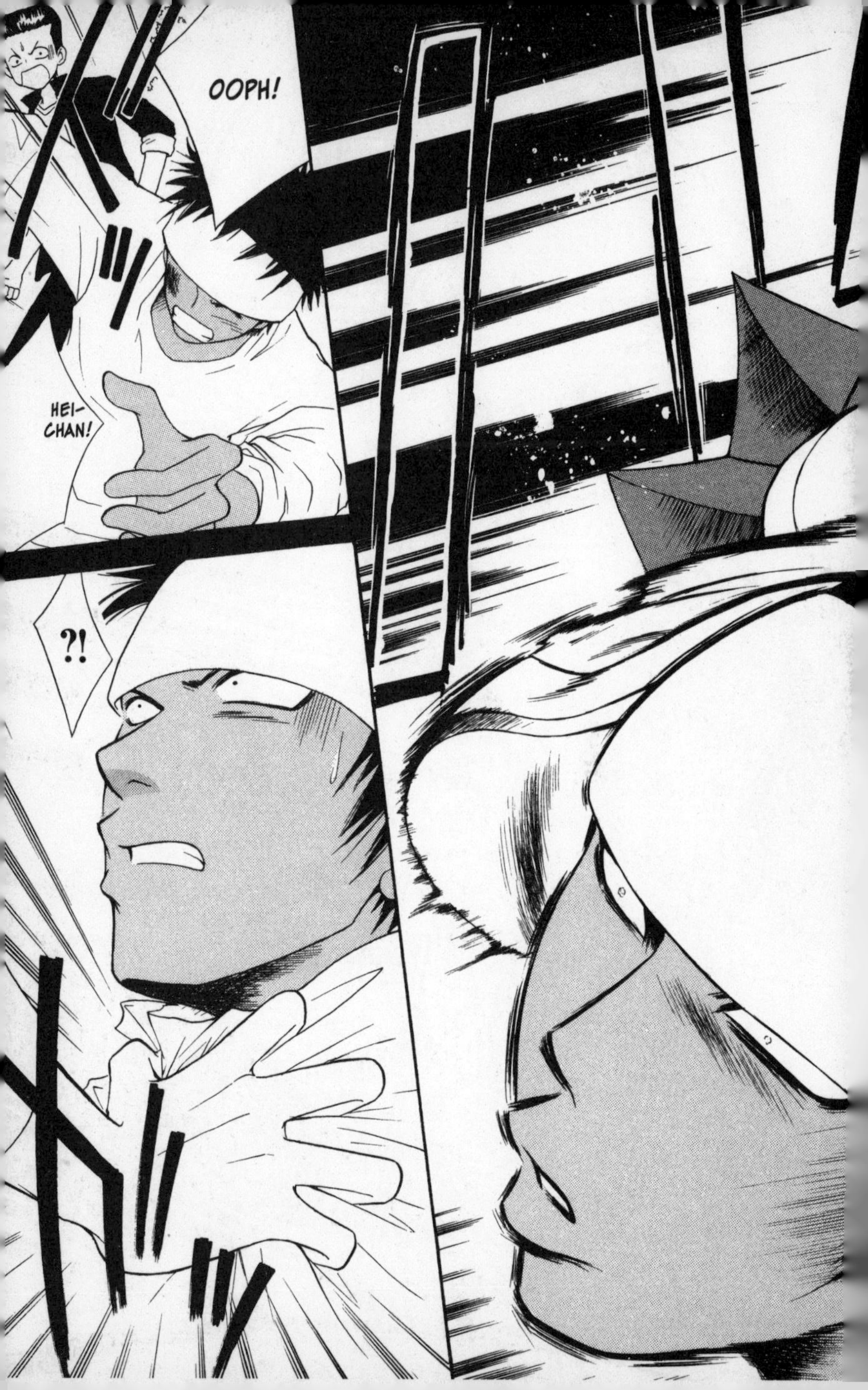
OOPH!
HEI-CHAN!
?!

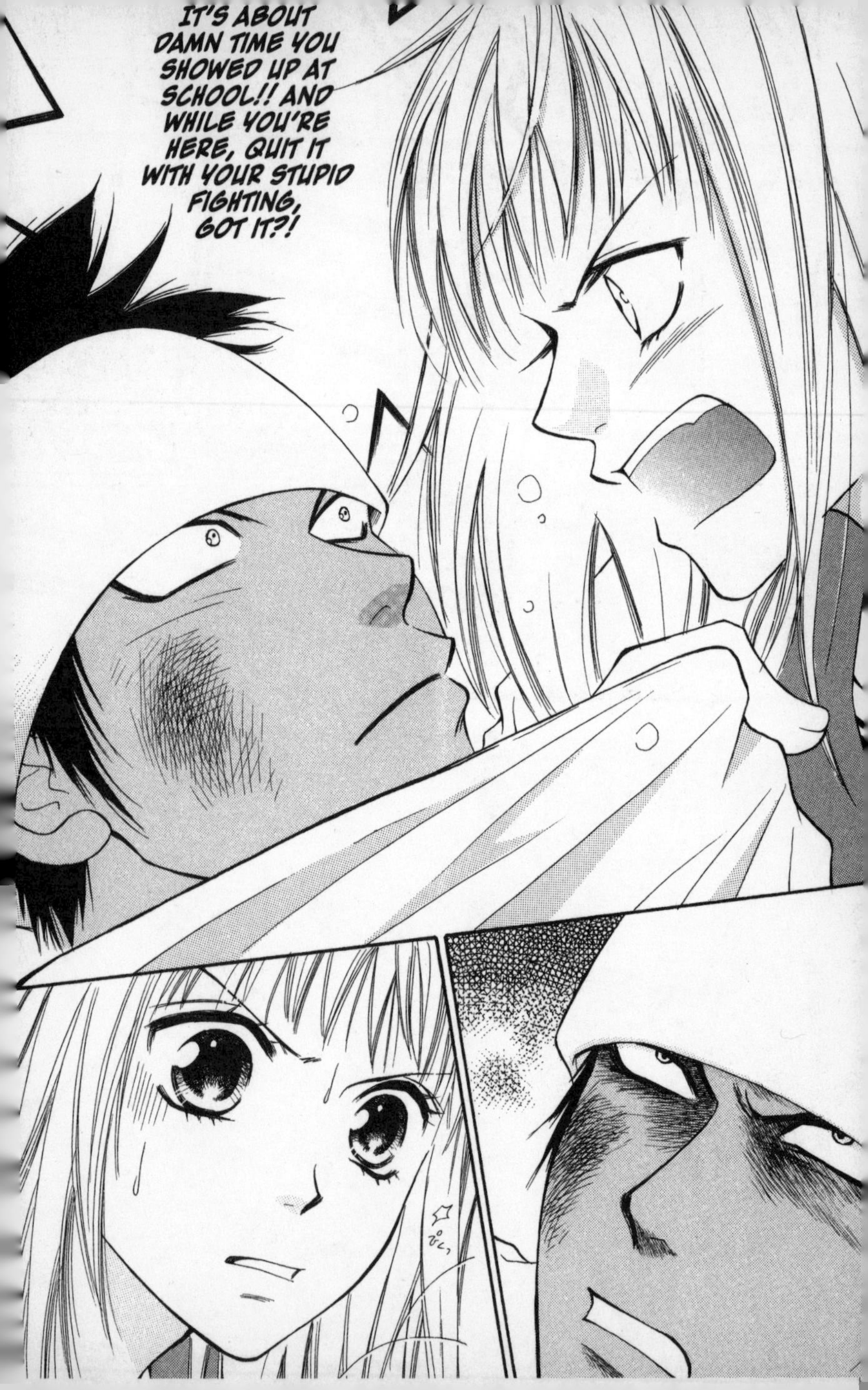
IT'S ABOUT DAMN TIME YOU SHOWED UP AT SCHOOL!! AND WHILE YOU'RE HERE, QUIT IT WITH YOUR STUPID FIGHTING, GOT IT?!

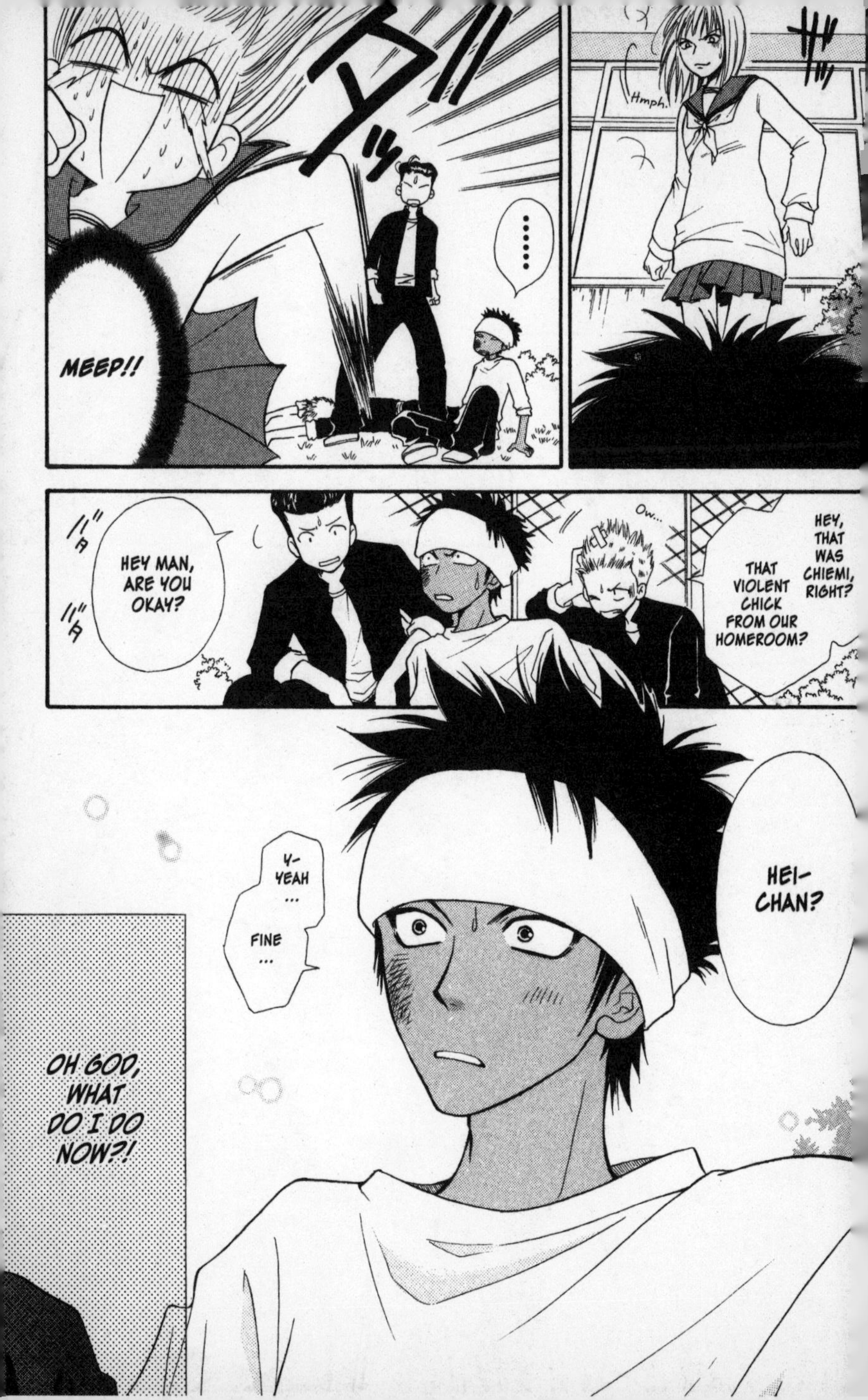
Hmph.
MEEP!!
......
HEY, THAT WAS CHIEMI, RIGHT?
THAT VIOLENT CHICK FROM OUR HOMEROOM?
Ow...
HEY MAN, ARE YOU OKAY?
HEI-CHAN?
Y-YEAH ... FINE ...
OH GOD, WHAT DO I DO NOW?!

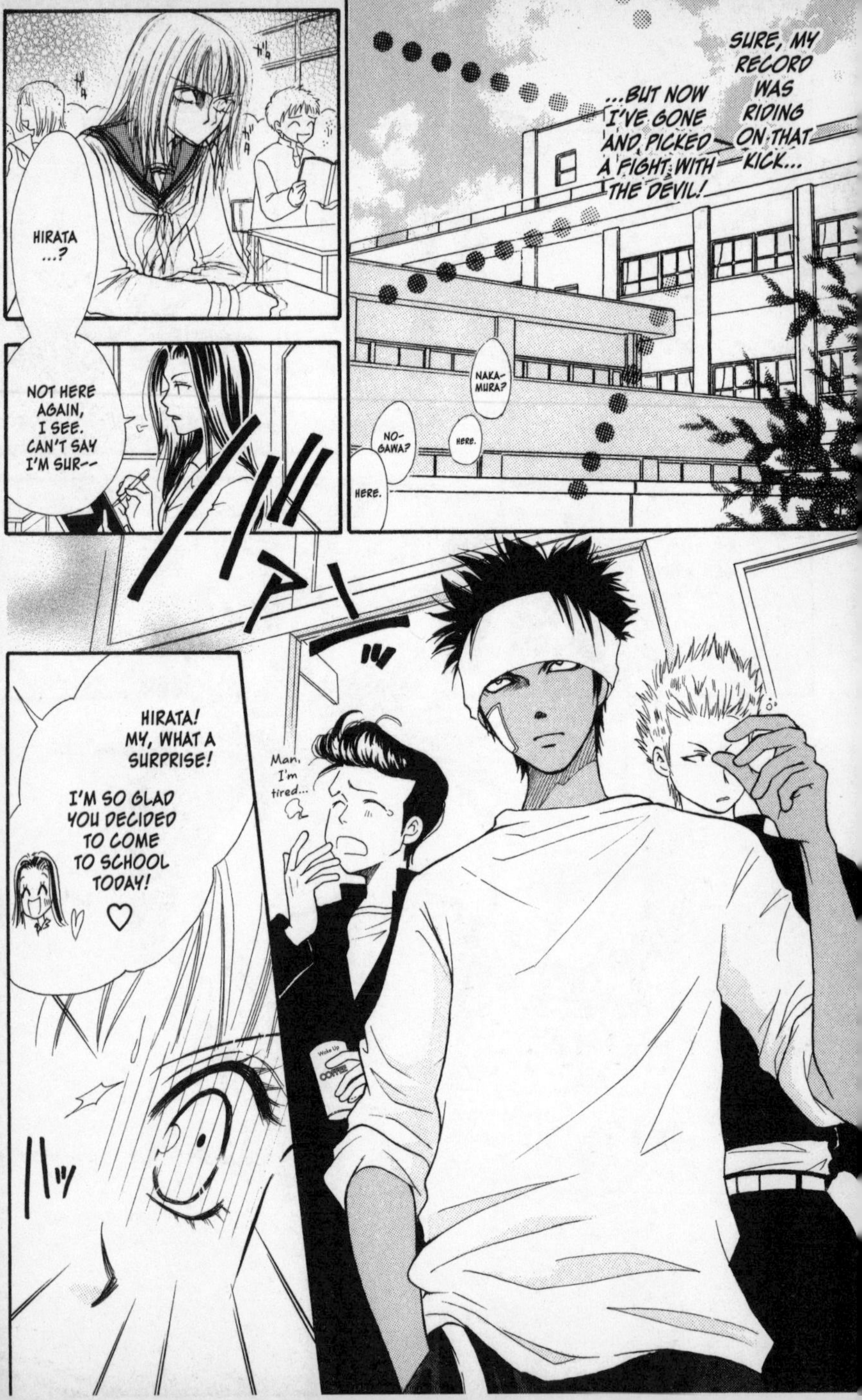
SURE, MY RECORD WAS RIDING ON THAT KICK...
...BUT NOW I'VE GONE AND PICKED A FIGHT WITH THE DEVIL!
NAKA-MURA?
HERE.
NO-GAWA?
HERE.
HIRATA ...?
NOT HERE AGAIN, I SEE. CAN'T SAY I'M SUR--
Man, I'm tired...
Wake Up COFFEE
HIRATA! MY, WHAT A SURPRISE!
I'M SO GLAD YOU DECIDED TO COME TO SCHOOL TODAY!

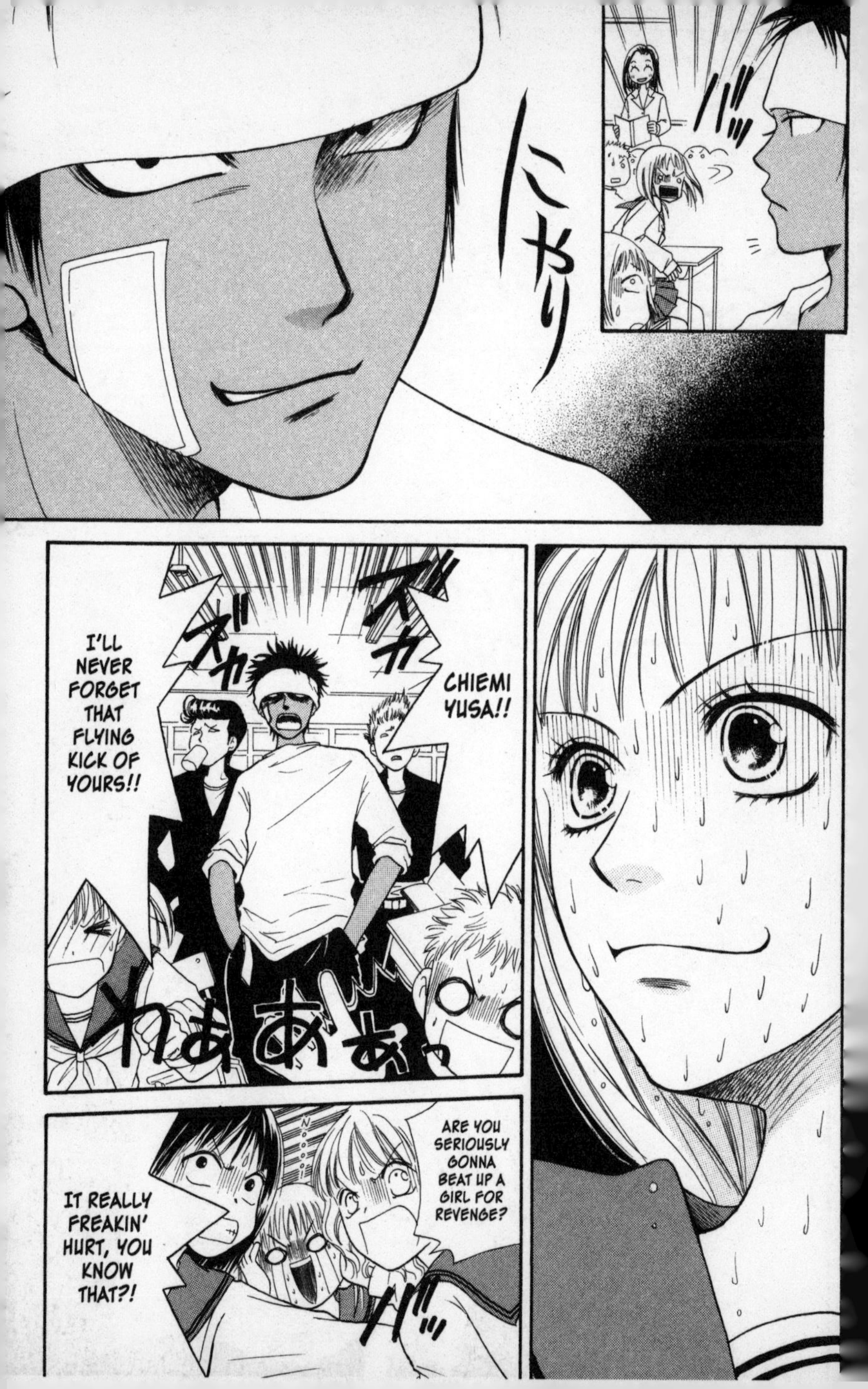

バッ
にやり
ズカ
ズカ
CHIEMI YUSA!!
I'LL NEVER FORGET THAT FLYING KICK OF YOURS!!
わあああっ
ARE YOU SERIOUSLY GONNA BEAT UP A GIRL FOR REVENGE?
IT REALLY FREAKIN' HURT, YOU KNOW THAT?!
バッ

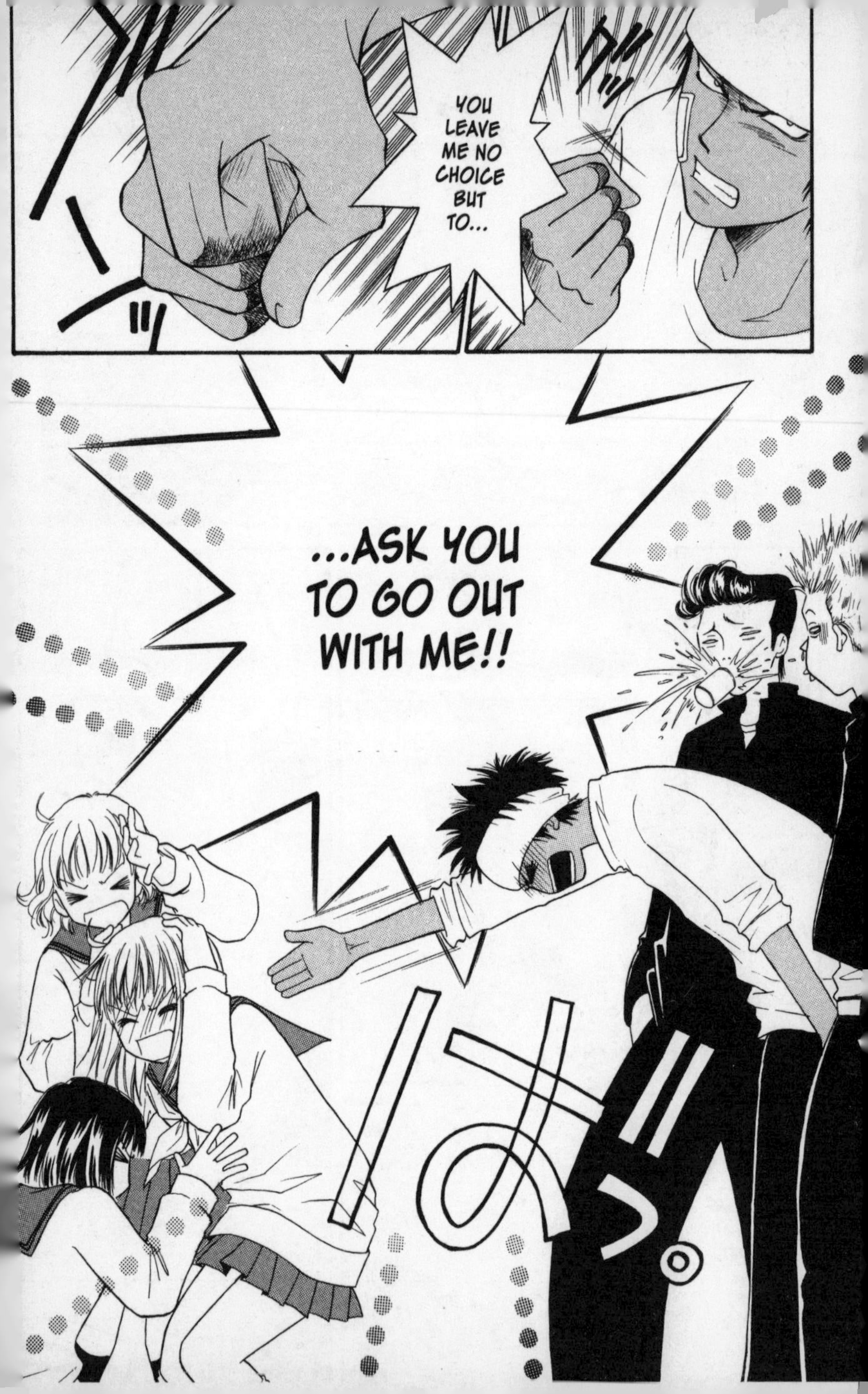
YOU LEAVE ME NO CHOICE BUT TO...
...ASK YOU TO GO OUT WITH ME!!

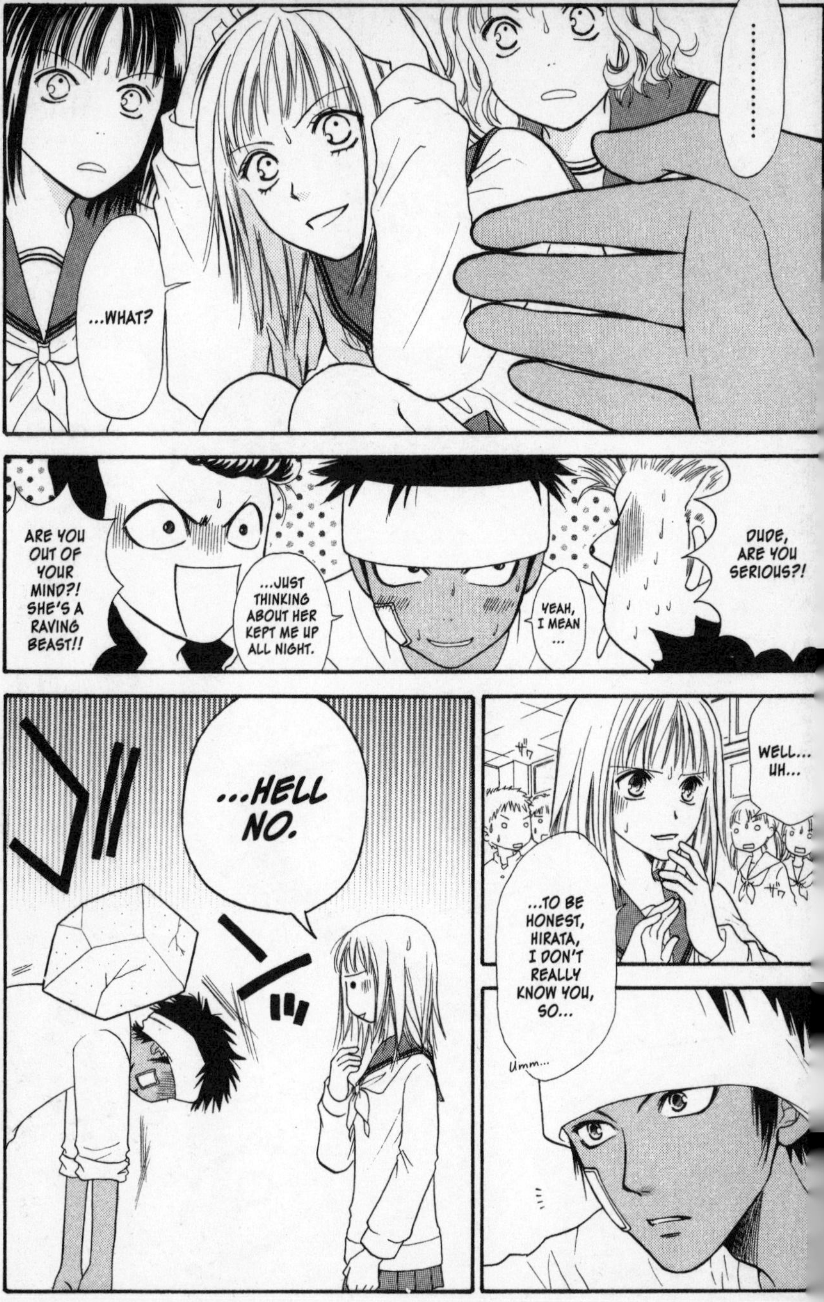
……
...WHAT?
DUDE, ARE YOU SERIOUS?!
YEAH, I MEAN ...
...JUST THINKING ABOUT HER KEPT ME UP ALL NIGHT.
ARE YOU OUT OF YOUR MIND?! SHE'S A RAVING BEAST!!
WELL... UH...
...TO BE HONEST, HIRATA, I DON'T REALLY KNOW YOU, SO...
Umm...
...HELL NO.

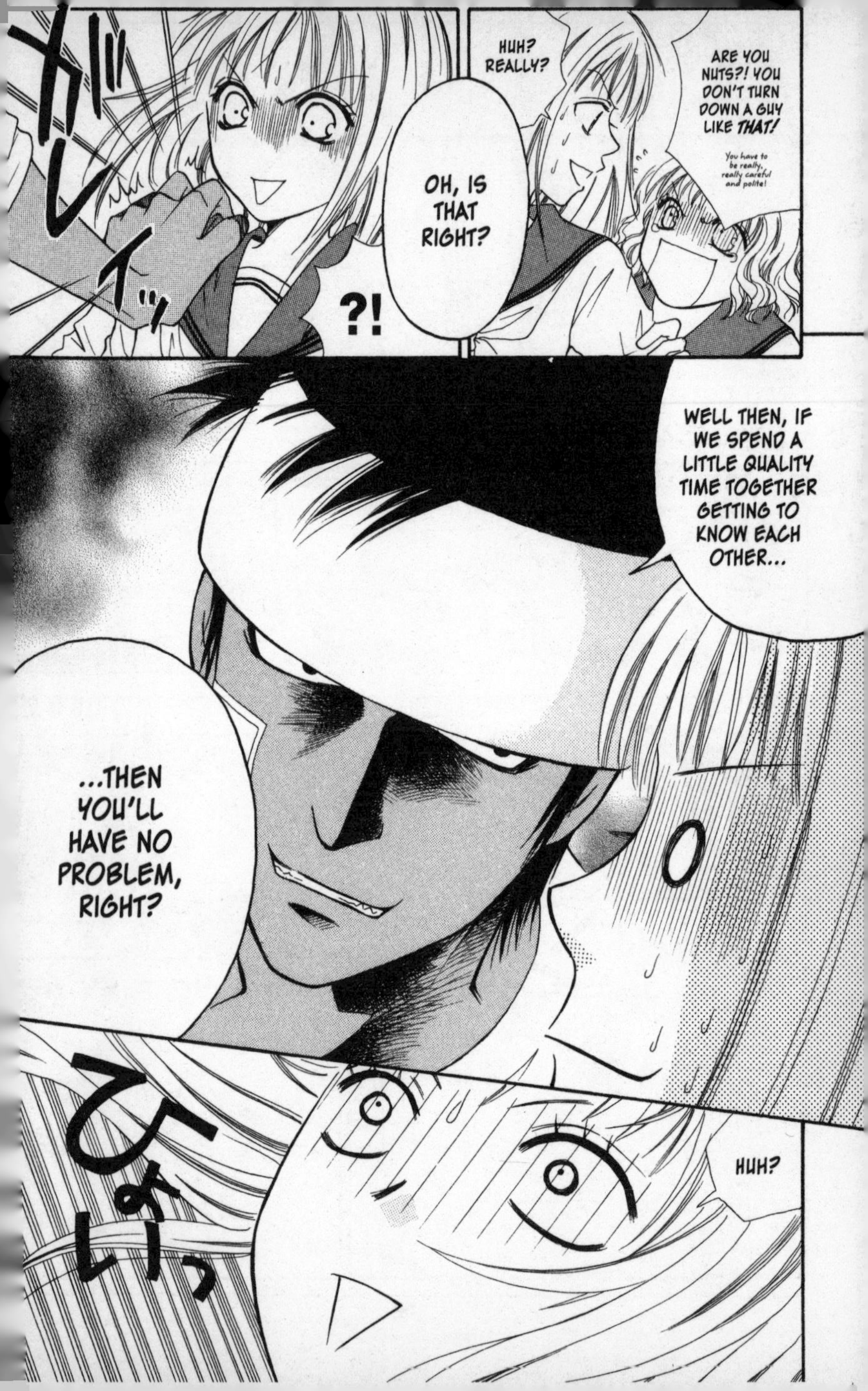
ARE YOU NUTS?! YOU DON'T TURN DOWN A GUY LIKE *THAT!*
You have to be really, really careful and polite!
HUH? REALLY?
OH, IS THAT RIGHT?
?!
WELL THEN, IF WE SPEND A LITTLE QUALITY TIME TOGETHER GETTING TO KNOW EACH OTHER...
...THEN YOU'LL HAVE NO PROBLEM, RIGHT?
HUH?

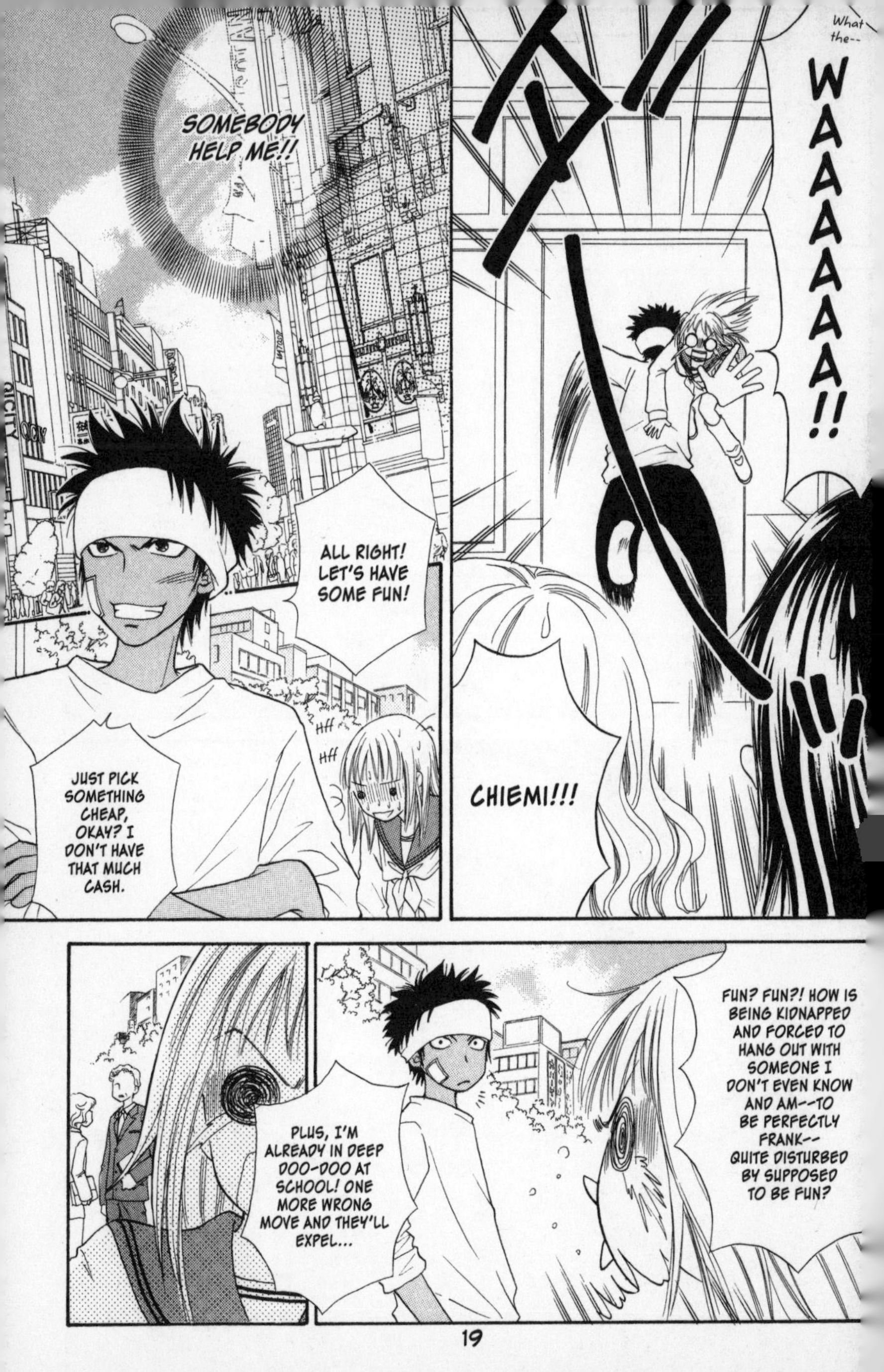
What the--
WAAAAAAA!!
CHIEMI!!!
SOMEBODY HELP ME!!
ALL RIGHT! LET'S HAVE SOME FUN!
Hff
Hff
JUST PICK SOMETHING CHEAP, OKAY? I DON'T HAVE THAT MUCH CASH.
FUN? FUN?! HOW IS BEING KIDNAPPED AND FORCED TO HANG OUT WITH SOMEONE I DON'T EVEN KNOW AND AM--TO BE PERFECTLY FRANK--QUITE DISTURBED BY SUPPOSED TO BE FUN?
PLUS, I'M ALREADY IN DEEP DOO-DOO AT SCHOOL! ONE MORE WRONG MOVE AND THEY'LL EXPEL...

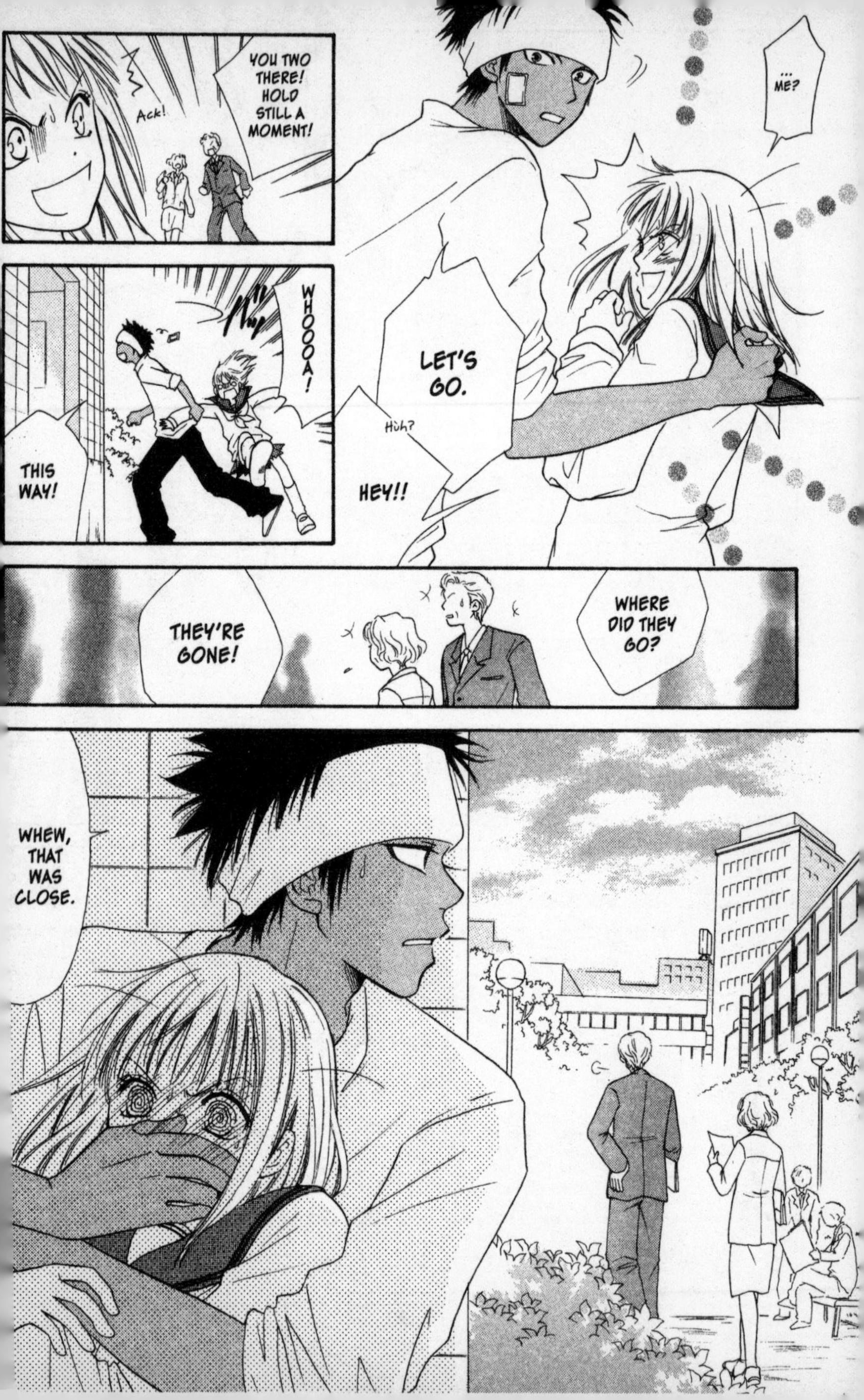

... ME?
LET'S GO.
Huh?
HEY!!
YOU TWO THERE! HOLD STILL A MOMENT!
Ack!
WHOOOA!
THIS WAY!
WHERE DID THEY GO?
THEY'RE GONE!
WHEW, THAT WAS CLOSE.

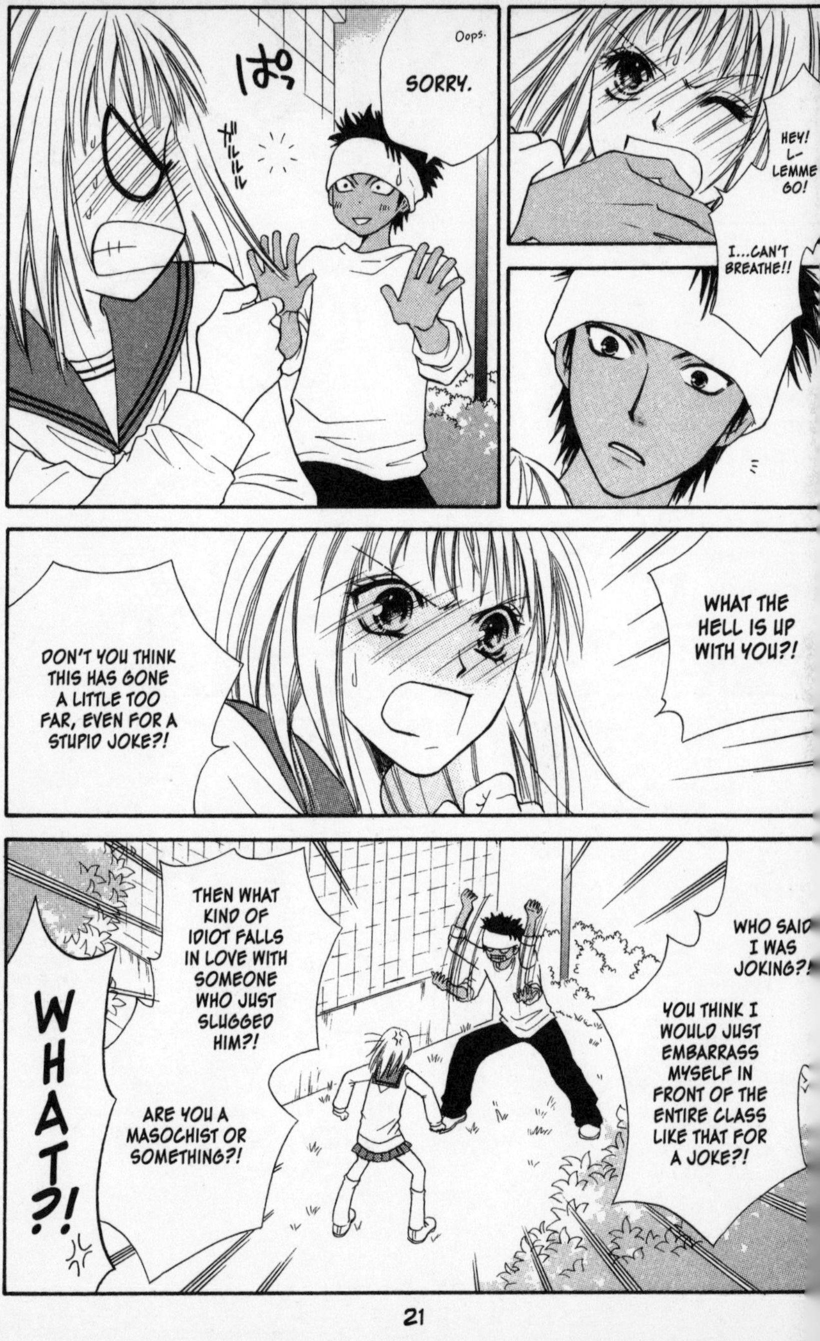

HEY! L-LEMME GO!
I...CAN'T BREATHE!!
Oops.
SORRY.
ぱっ
ガルルル
WHAT THE HELL IS UP WITH YOU?!
DON'T YOU THINK THIS HAS GONE A LITTLE TOO FAR, EVEN FOR A STUPID JOKE?!
WHO SAID I WAS JOKING?!
YOU THINK I WOULD JUST EMBARRASS MYSELF IN FRONT OF THE ENTIRE CLASS LIKE THAT FOR A JOKE?!
THEN WHAT KIND OF IDIOT FALLS IN LOVE WITH SOMEONE WHO JUST SLUGGED HIM?!
ARE YOU A MASOCHIST OR SOMETHING?!
WHAT?!

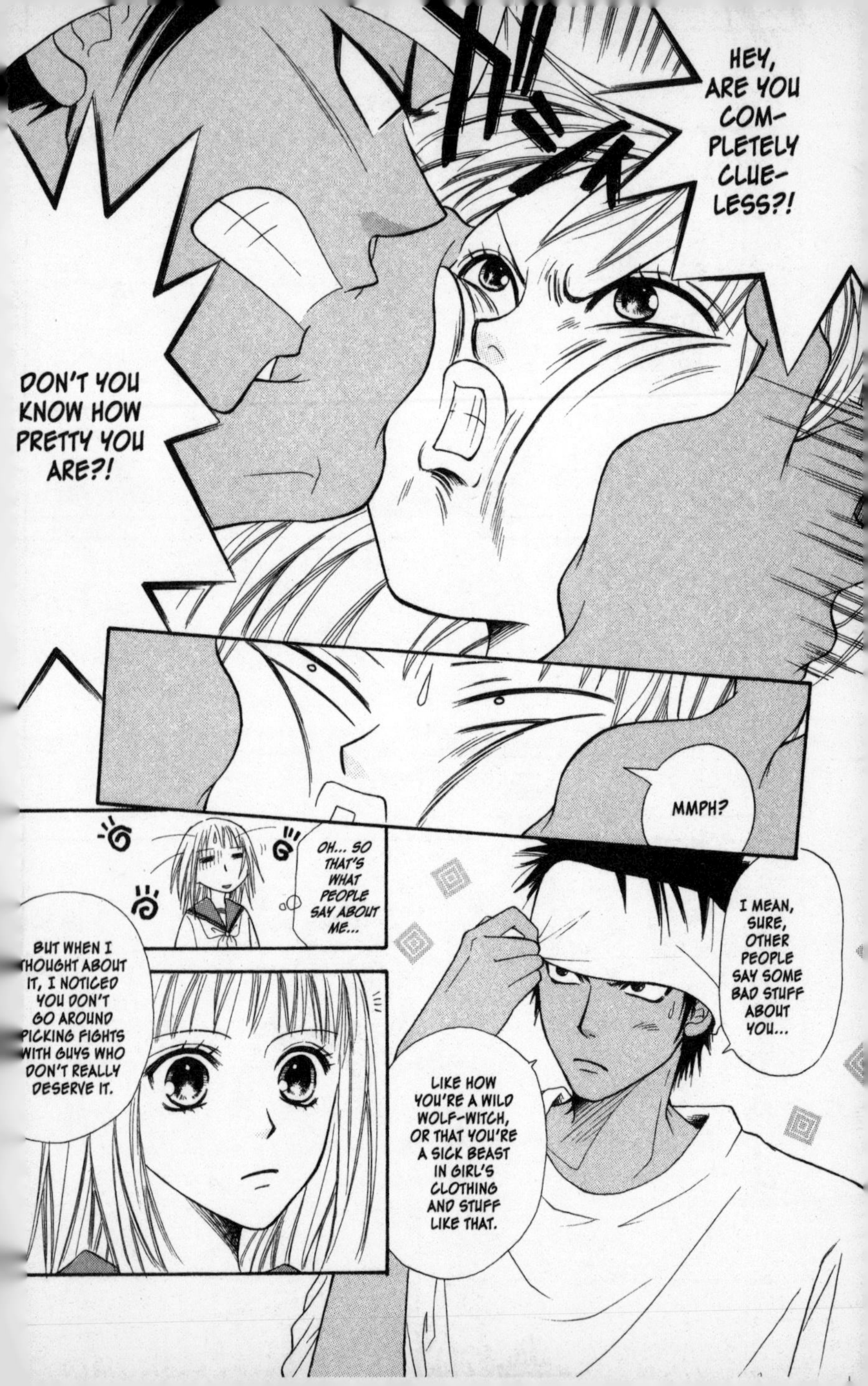
HEY, ARE YOU COMPLETELY CLUELESS?!
DON'T YOU KNOW HOW PRETTY YOU ARE?!
MMPH?
I MEAN, SURE, OTHER PEOPLE SAY SOME BAD STUFF ABOUT YOU...
LIKE HOW YOU'RE A WILD WOLF-WITCH, OR THAT YOU'RE A SICK BEAST IN GIRL'S CLOTHING AND STUFF LIKE THAT.
OH... SO THAT'S WHAT PEOPLE SAY ABOUT ME...
BUT WHEN I THOUGHT ABOUT IT, I NOTICED YOU DON'T GO AROUND PICKING FIGHTS WITH GUYS WHO DON'T REALLY DESERVE IT.

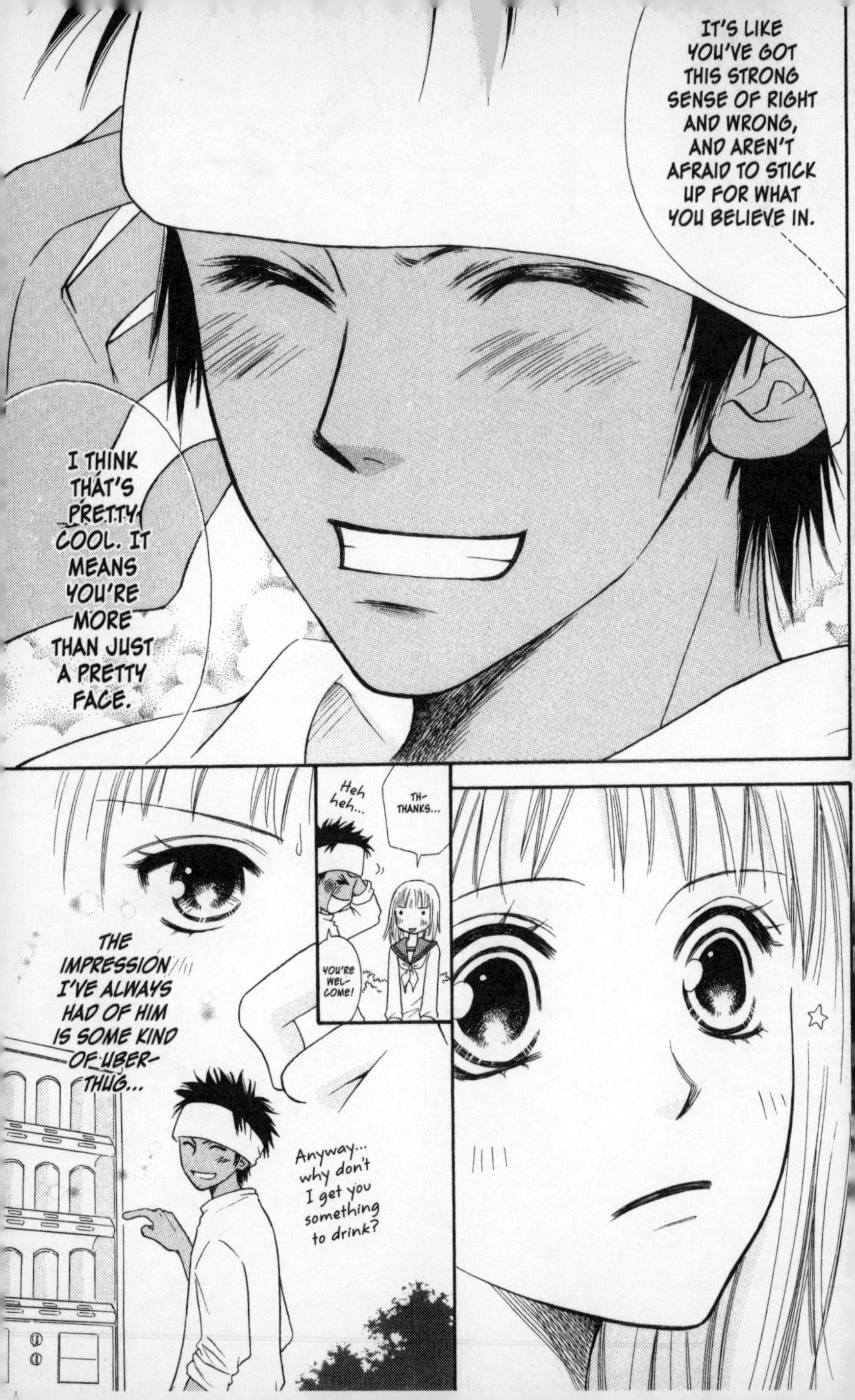
IT'S LIKE YOU'VE GOT THIS STRONG SENSE OF RIGHT AND WRONG, AND AREN'T AFRAID TO STICK UP FOR WHAT YOU BELIEVE IN.
I THINK THAT'S PRETTY COOL. IT MEANS YOU'RE MORE THAN JUST A PRETTY FACE.
TH-THANKS...
Heh heh...
YOU'RE WEL-COME!
THE IMPRESSION I'VE ALWAYS HAD OF HIM IS SOME KIND OF UBER-THUG...
Anyway... why don't I get you something to drink?

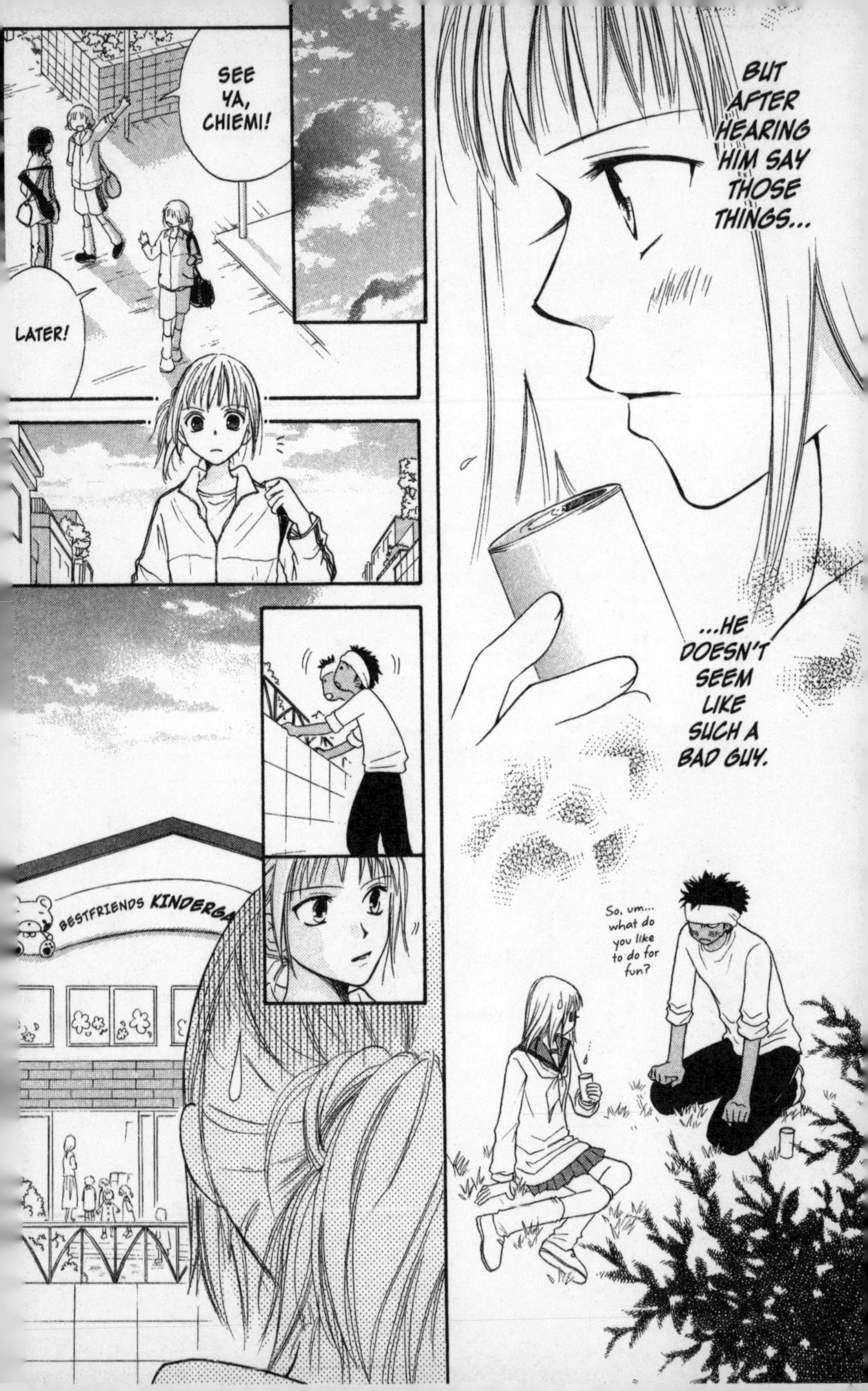
BUT AFTER HEARING HIM SAY THOSE THINGS...
...HE DOESN'T SEEM LIKE SUCH A BAD GUY.
So, um... what do you like to do for fun?
SEE YA, CHIEMI!
LATER!
BESTFRIENDS KINDERGA

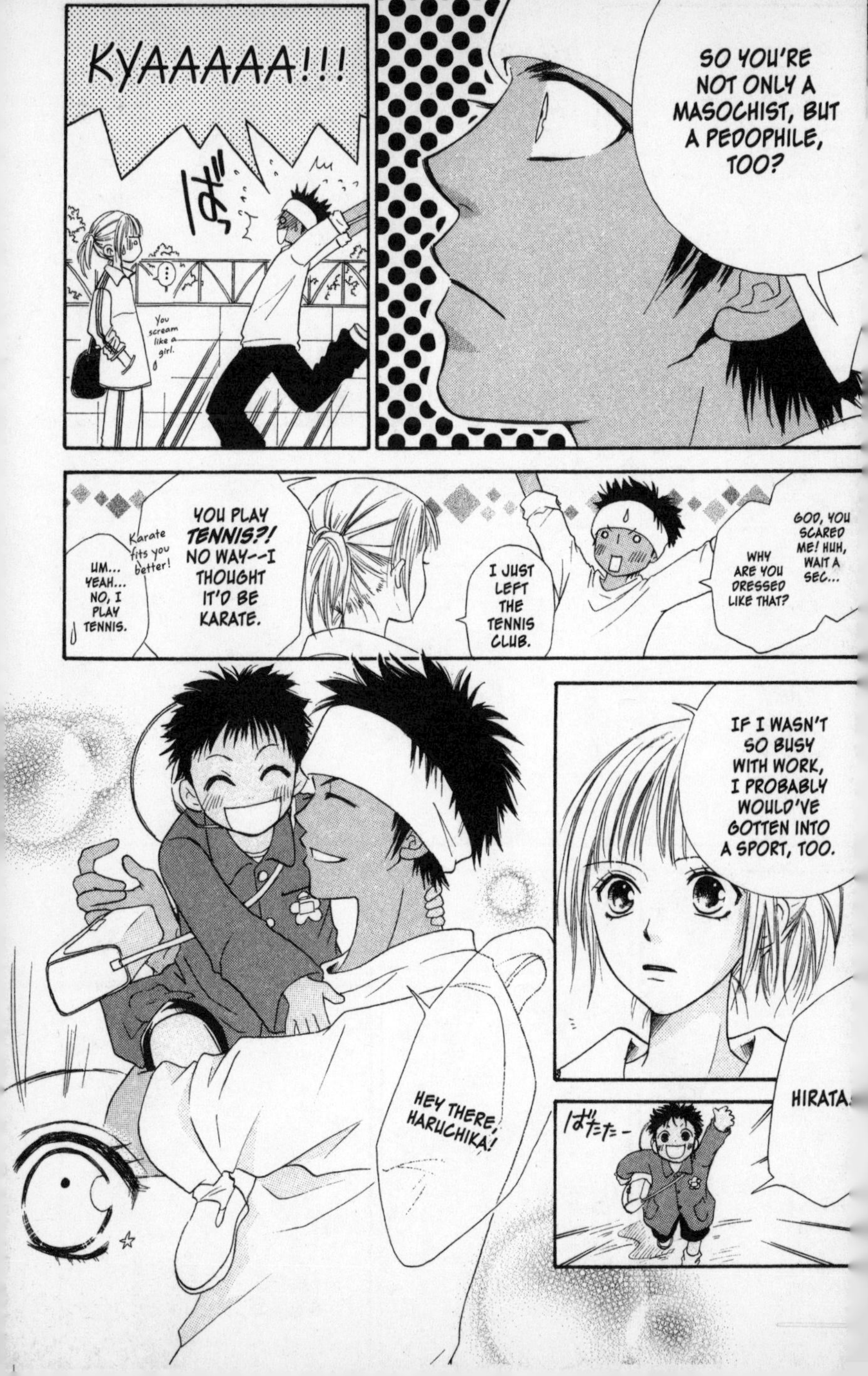
SO YOU'RE NOT ONLY A MASOCHIST, BUT A PEDOPHILE, TOO?
KYAAAAA!!!
You scream like a girl.
GOD, YOU SCARED ME! HUH, WAIT A SEC...
WHY ARE YOU DRESSED LIKE THAT?
I JUST LEFT THE TENNIS CLUB.
YOU PLAY TENNIS?! NO WAY--I THOUGHT IT'D BE KARATE.
Karate fits you better!
UM... YEAH... NO, I PLAY TENNIS.
IF I WASN'T SO BUSY WITH WORK, I PROBABLY WOULD'VE GOTTEN INTO A SPORT, TOO.
HIRATA!
ぱたたー
HEY THERE, HARUCHIKA!

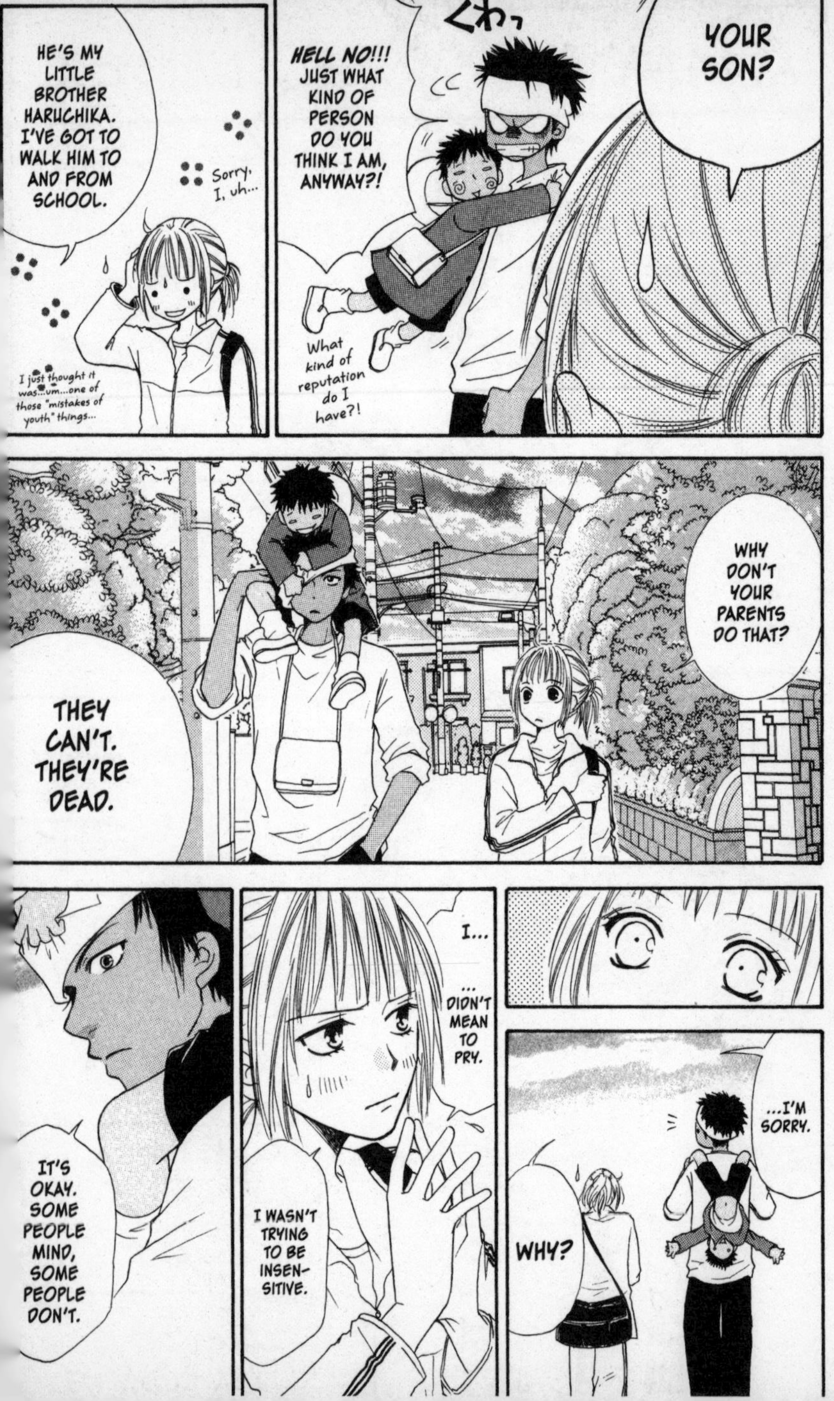
YOUR SON?
くわっ
HELL NO!!! JUST WHAT KIND OF PERSON DO YOU THINK I AM, ANYWAY?!
What kind of reputation do I have?!
HE'S MY LITTLE BROTHER HARUCHIKA. I'VE GOT TO WALK HIM TO AND FROM SCHOOL.
Sorry, I, uh...
I just thought it was...um...one of those "mistakes of youth" things...
WHY DON'T YOUR PARENTS DO THAT?
THEY CAN'T. THEY'RE DEAD.
...I'M SORRY.
WHY?
I...
...DIDN'T MEAN TO PRY.
I WASN'T TRYING TO BE INSENSITIVE.
IT'S OKAY. SOME PEOPLE MIND, SOME PEOPLE DON'T.

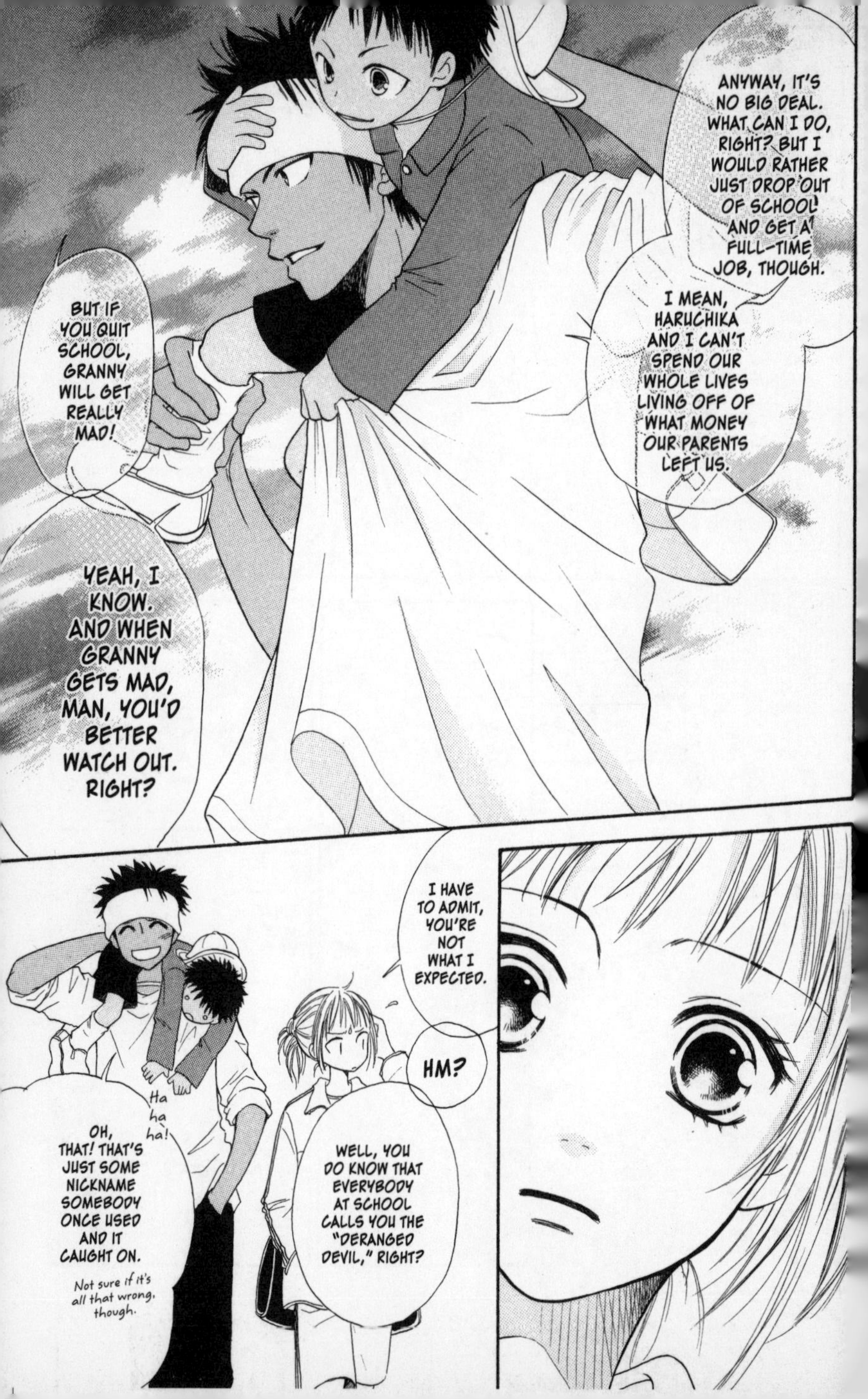
ANYWAY, IT'S NO BIG DEAL. WHAT CAN I DO, RIGHT? BUT I WOULD RATHER JUST DROP OUT OF SCHOOL AND GET A FULL-TIME JOB, THOUGH.
I MEAN, HARUCHIKA AND I CAN'T SPEND OUR WHOLE LIVES LIVING OFF OF WHAT MONEY OUR PARENTS LEFT US.
BUT IF YOU QUIT SCHOOL, GRANNY WILL GET REALLY MAD!
YEAH, I KNOW. AND WHEN GRANNY GETS MAD, MAN, YOU'D BETTER WATCH OUT. RIGHT?
I HAVE TO ADMIT, YOU'RE NOT WHAT I EXPECTED.
HM?
WELL, YOU DO KNOW THAT EVERYBODY AT SCHOOL CALLS YOU THE "DERANGED DEVIL," RIGHT?
Ha ha ha!
OH, THAT! THAT'S JUST SOME NICKNAME SOMEBODY ONCE USED AND IT CAUGHT ON.
Not sure if it's all that wrong, though.

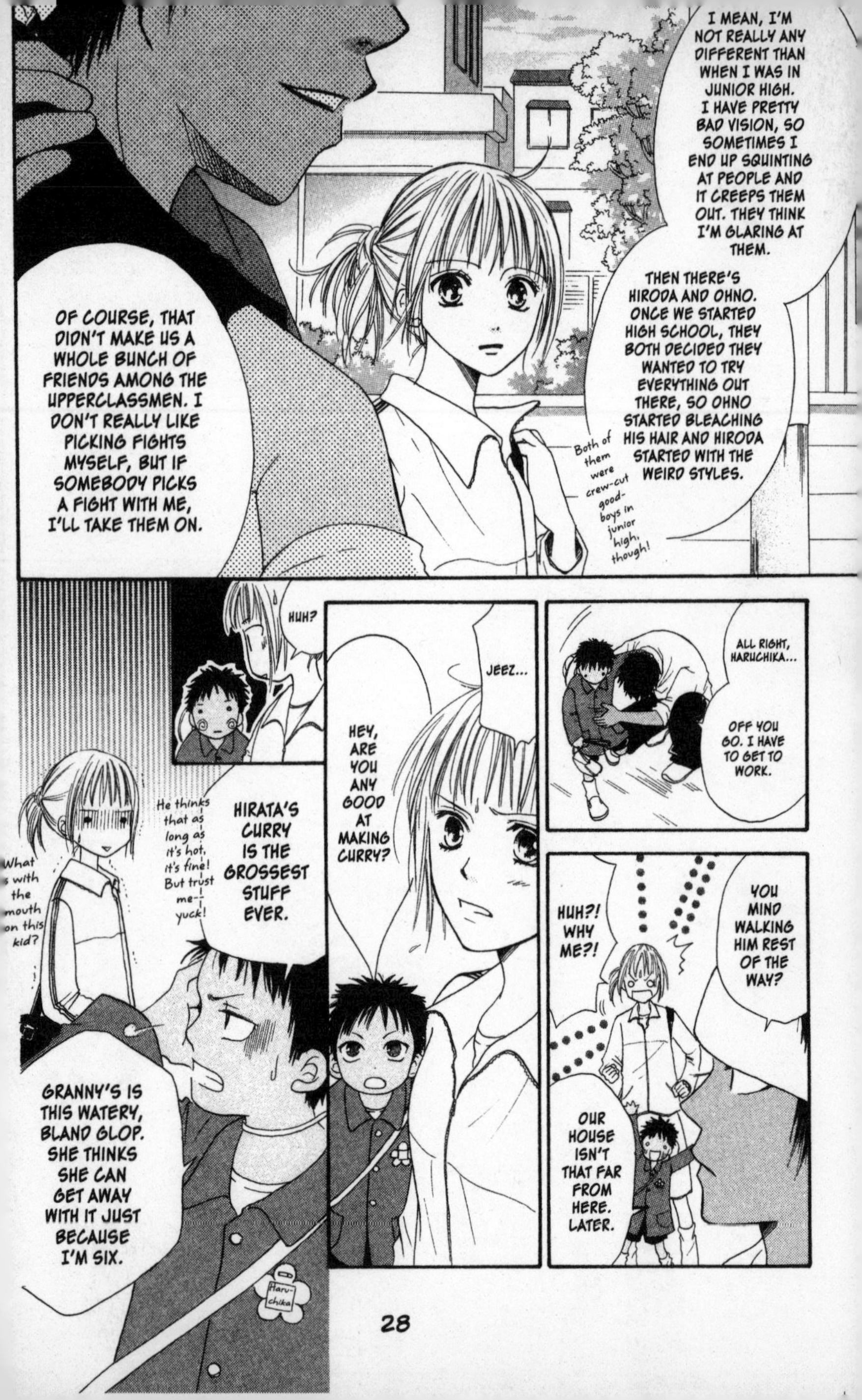
I MEAN, I'M NOT REALLY ANY DIFFERENT THAN WHEN I WAS IN JUNIOR HIGH. I HAVE PRETTY BAD VISION, SO SOMETIMES I END UP SQUINTING AT PEOPLE AND IT CREEPS THEM OUT. THEY THINK I'M GLARING AT THEM.
THEN THERE'S HIRODA AND OHNO. ONCE WE STARTED HIGH SCHOOL, THEY BOTH DECIDED THEY WANTED TO TRY EVERYTHING OUT THERE, SO OHNO STARTED BLEACHING HIS HAIR AND HIRODA STARTED WITH THE WEIRD STYLES.
Both of them were crew-cut good-boys in junior high, though!
OF COURSE, THAT DIDN'T MAKE US A WHOLE BUNCH OF FRIENDS AMONG THE UPPERCLASSMEN. I DON'T REALLY LIKE PICKING FIGHTS MYSELF, BUT IF SOMEBODY PICKS A FIGHT WITH ME, I'LL TAKE THEM ON.
ALL RIGHT, HARUCHIKA...
OFF YOU GO. I HAVE TO GET TO WORK.
YOU MIND WALKING HIM REST OF THE WAY?
HUH?! WHY ME?!
OUR HOUSE ISN'T THAT FAR FROM HERE. LATER.
JEEZ...
HEY, ARE YOU ANY GOOD AT MAKING CURRY?
HUH?
HIRATA'S CURRY IS THE GROSSEST STUFF EVER.
He thinks that as long as it's hot, it's fine! But trust me-- yuck!
GRANNY'S IS THIS WATERY, BLAND GLOP. SHE THINKS SHE CAN GET AWAY WITH IT JUST BECAUSE I'M SIX.
What's with the mouth on this kid?
Haru-chika

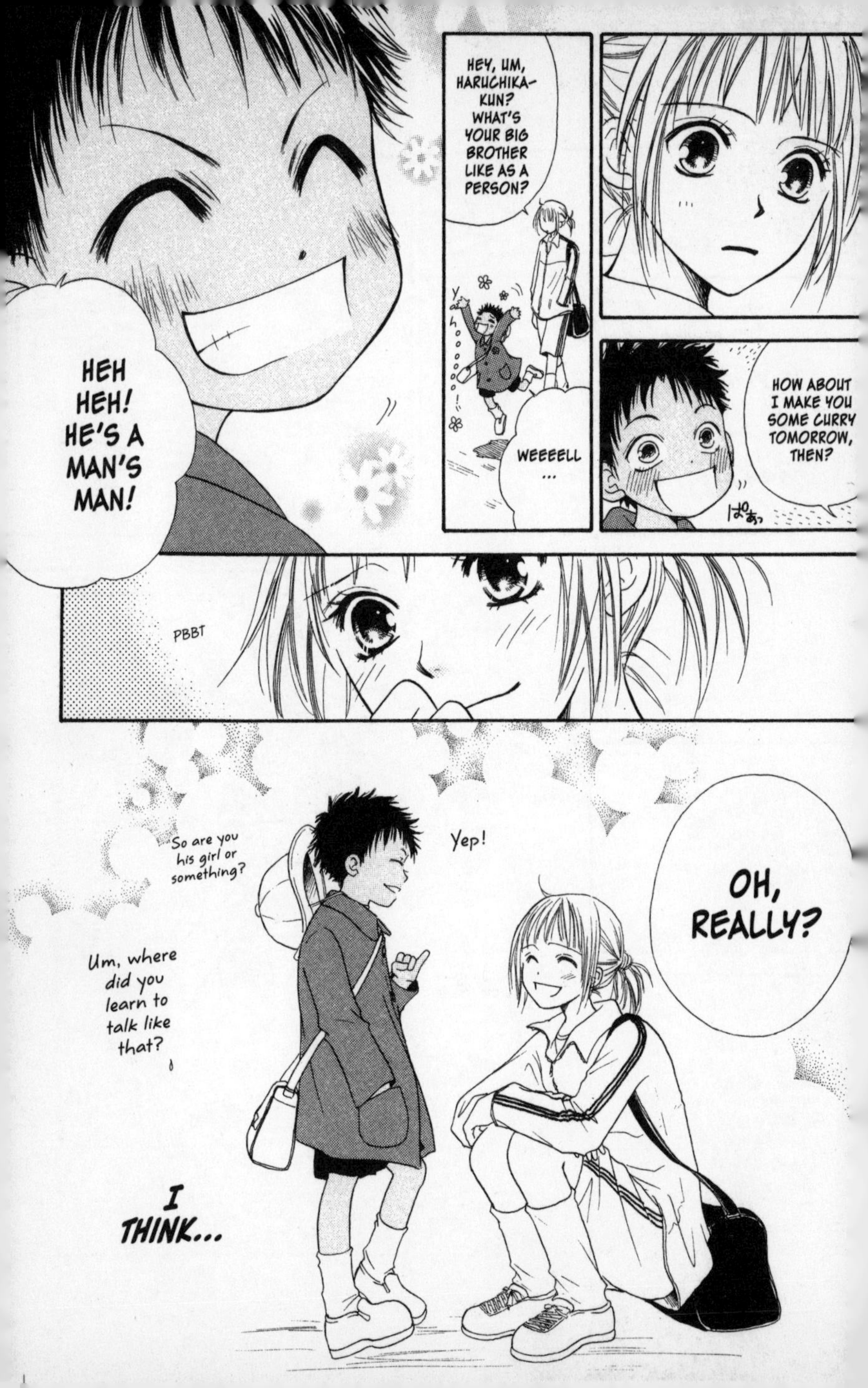

HOW ABOUT I MAKE YOU SOME CURRY TOMORROW, THEN?
ぱあっ
HEY, UM, HARUCHIKA-KUN? WHAT'S YOUR BIG BROTHER LIKE AS A PERSON?
yahoooooo!
WEEEELL ...
HEH HEH! HE'S A MAN'S MAN!
PBBT
OH, REALLY?
Yep!
So are you his girl or something?
Um, where did you learn to talk like that?
I THINK...

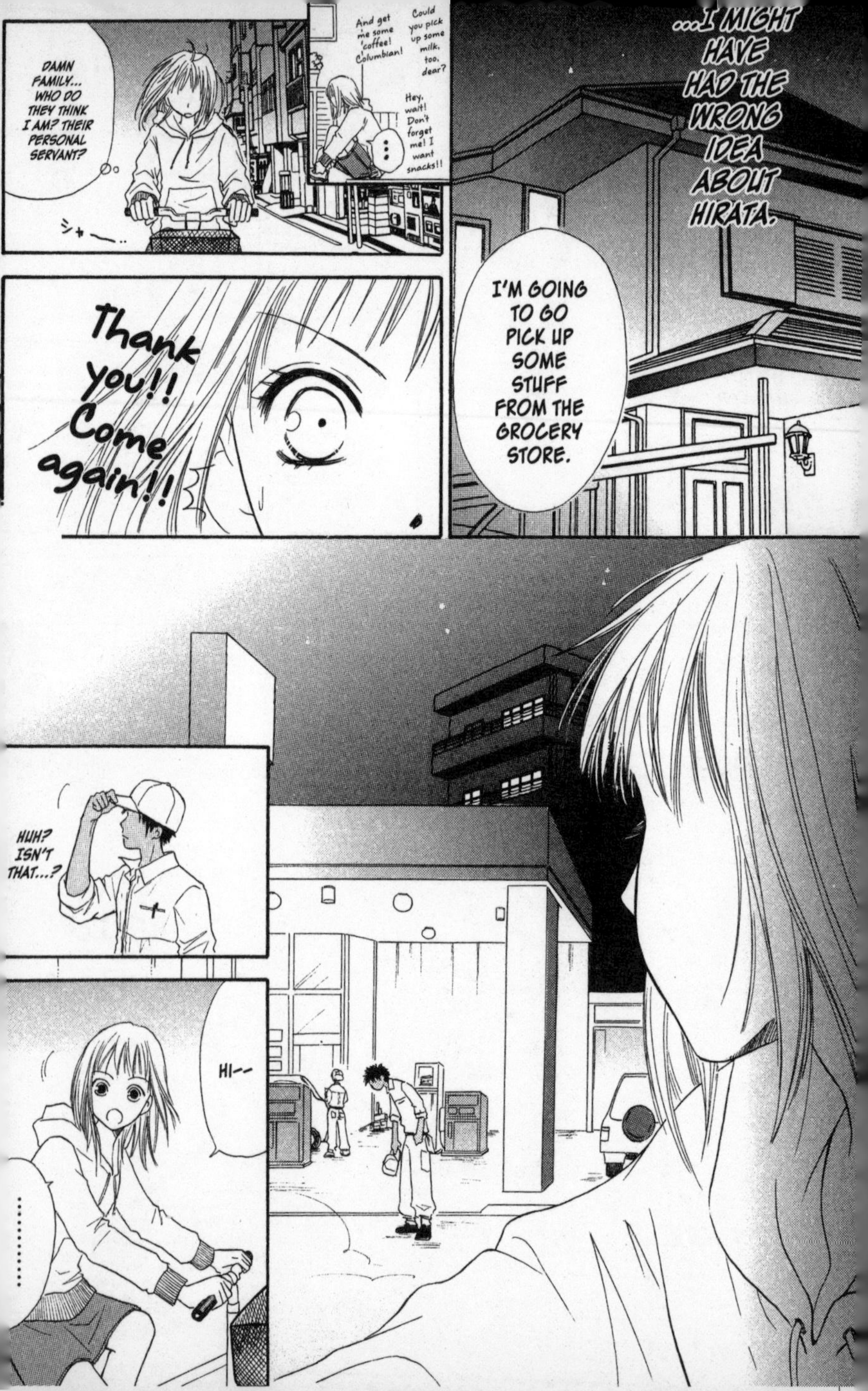
...I MIGHT HAVE HAD THE WRONG IDEA ABOUT HIRATA.
I'M GOING TO GO PICK UP SOME STUFF FROM THE GROCERY STORE.
Could you pick up some milk, too, dear?
And get me some 'coffee! Columbian!
Hey, wait! Don't forget me! I want snacks!!
...
DAMN FAMILY... WHO DO THEY THINK I AM? THEIR PERSONAL SERVANT?
シャー..
Thank you!! Come again!!
HUH? ISN'T THAT...?
HI--

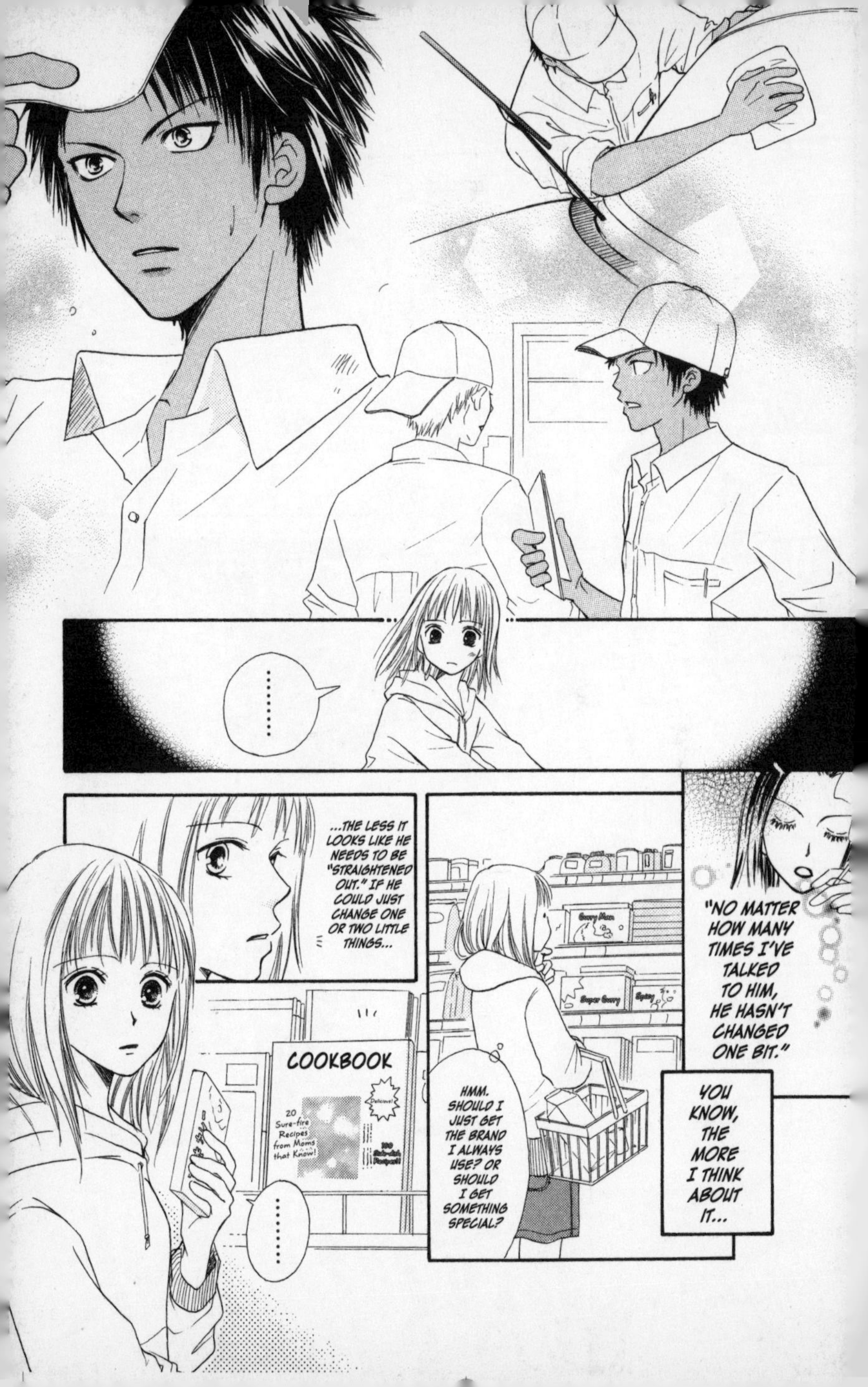
......
"NO MATTER HOW MANY TIMES I'VE TALKED TO HIM, HE HASN'T CHANGED ONE BIT."
YOU KNOW, THE MORE I THINK ABOUT IT...
HMM. SHOULD I JUST GET THE BRAND I ALWAYS USE? OR SHOULD I GET SOMETHING SPECIAL?
...THE LESS IT LOOKS LIKE HE NEEDS TO BE "STRAIGHTENED OUT." IF HE COULD JUST CHANGE ONE OR TWO LITTLE THINGS...
COOKBOOK
Delicious!
20 Sure-fire Recipes from Moms that Know!
......

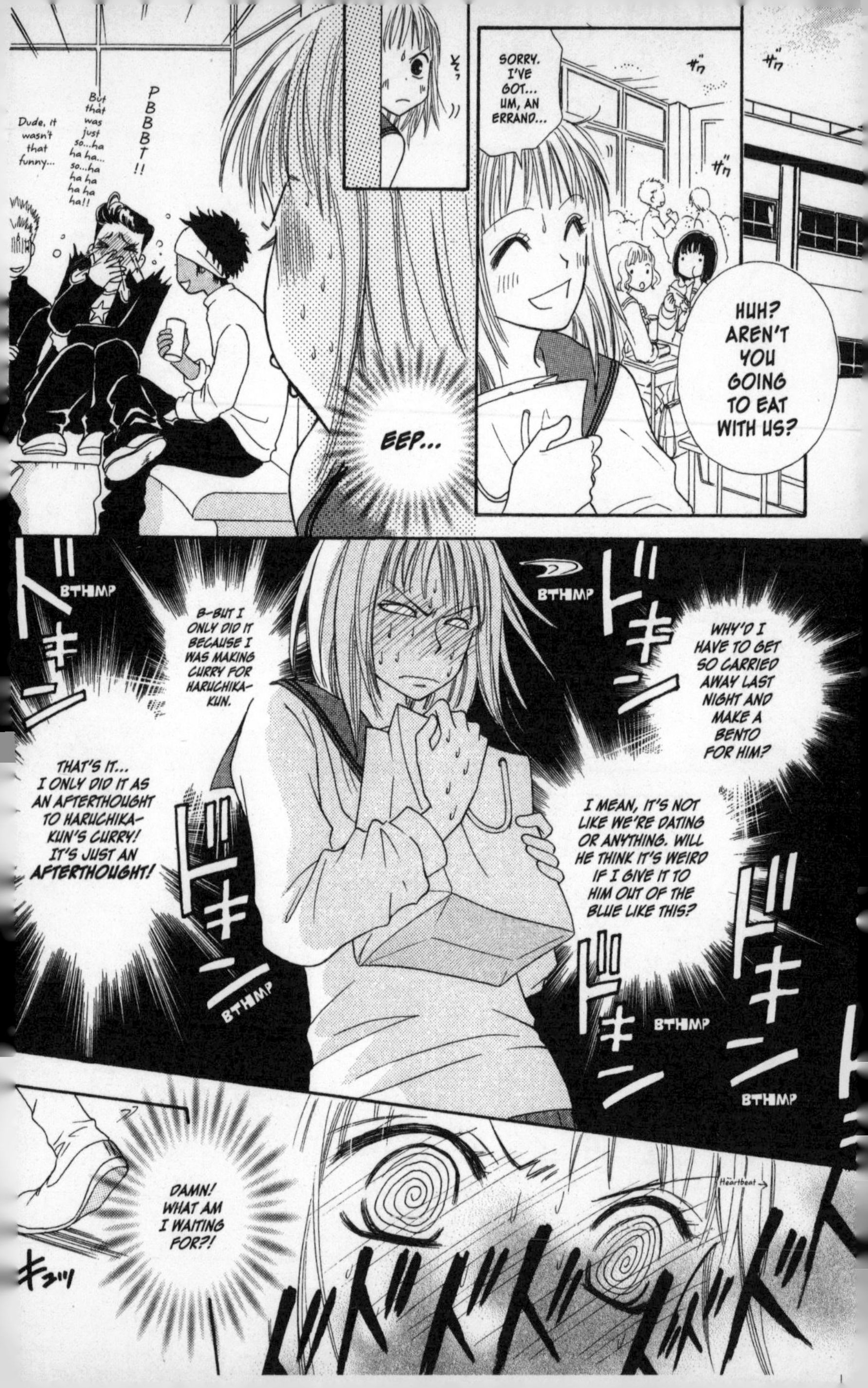
HUH? AREN'T YOU GOING TO EAT WITH US?
SORRY. I'VE GOT... UM, AN ERRAND...
PBBBT!!
But that was just so...ha ha ha... so...ha ha ha ha ha ha!!
Dude, it wasn't that funny...
EEP...
BTHMP
WHY'D I HAVE TO GET SO CARRIED AWAY LAST NIGHT AND MAKE A BENTO FOR HIM?
BTHMP
B-BUT I ONLY DID IT BECAUSE I WAS MAKING CURRY FOR HARUCHIKA-KUN.
I MEAN, IT'S NOT LIKE WE'RE DATING OR ANYTHING. WILL HE THINK IT'S WEIRD IF I GIVE IT TO HIM OUT OF THE BLUE LIKE THIS?
THAT'S IT... I ONLY DID IT AS AN AFTERTHOUGHT TO HARUCHIKA-KUN'S CURRY! IT'S JUST AN AFTERTHOUGHT!
BTHMP
BTHMP
BTHMP
Heartbeat
DAMN! WHAT AM I WAITING FOR?!

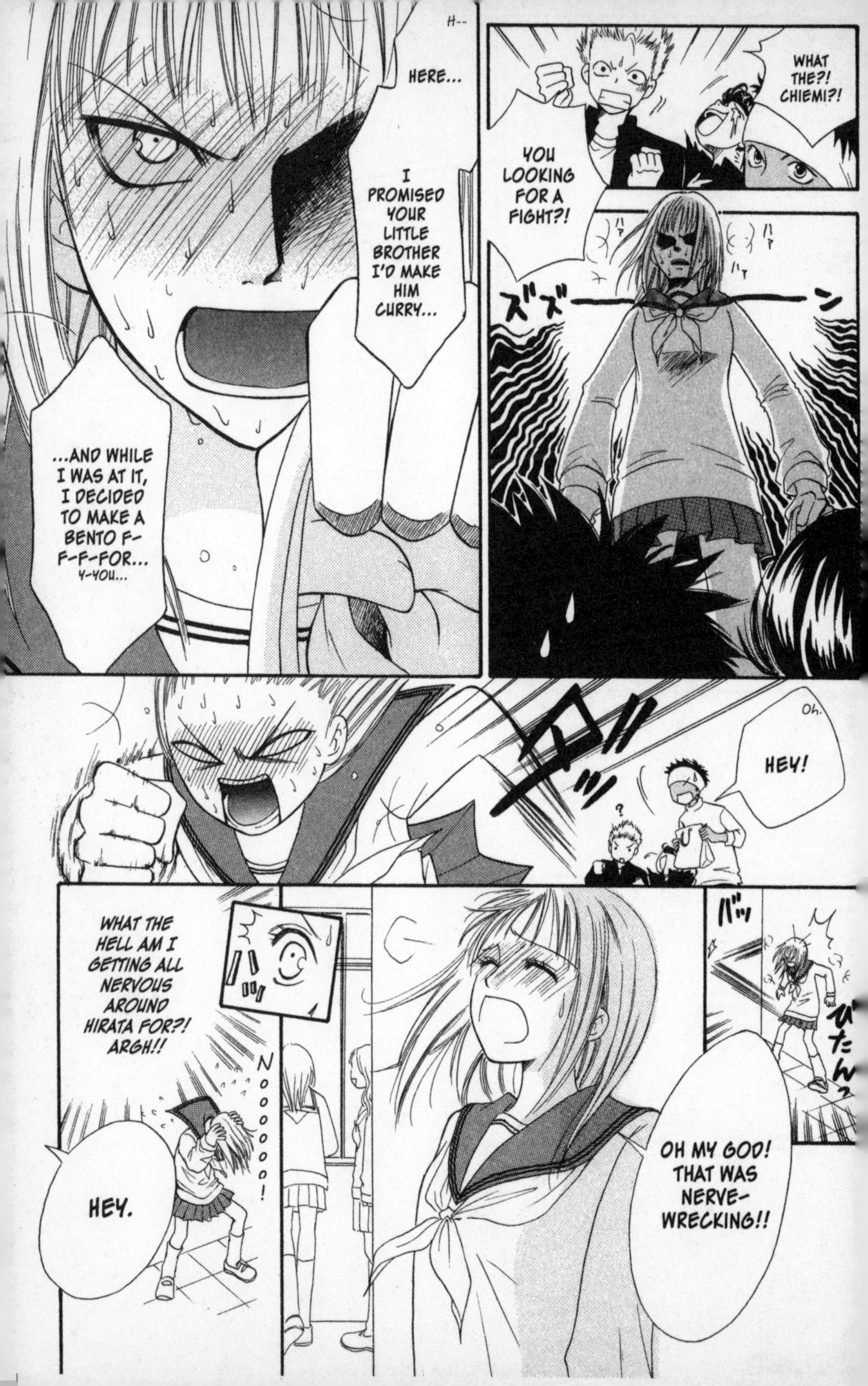
WHAT THE?! CHIEMI?!
YOU LOOKING FOR A FIGHT?!
H--
HERE...
I PROMISED YOUR LITTLE BROTHER I'D MAKE HIM CURRY...
...AND WHILE I WAS AT IT, I DECIDED TO MAKE A BENTO F-F-F-FOR... Y-YOU...
Oh.
HEY!
OH MY GOD! THAT WAS NERVE-WRECKING!!
WHAT THE HELL AM I GETTING ALL NERVOUS AROUND HIRATA FOR?! ARGH!!
Nooooooo!
HEY.

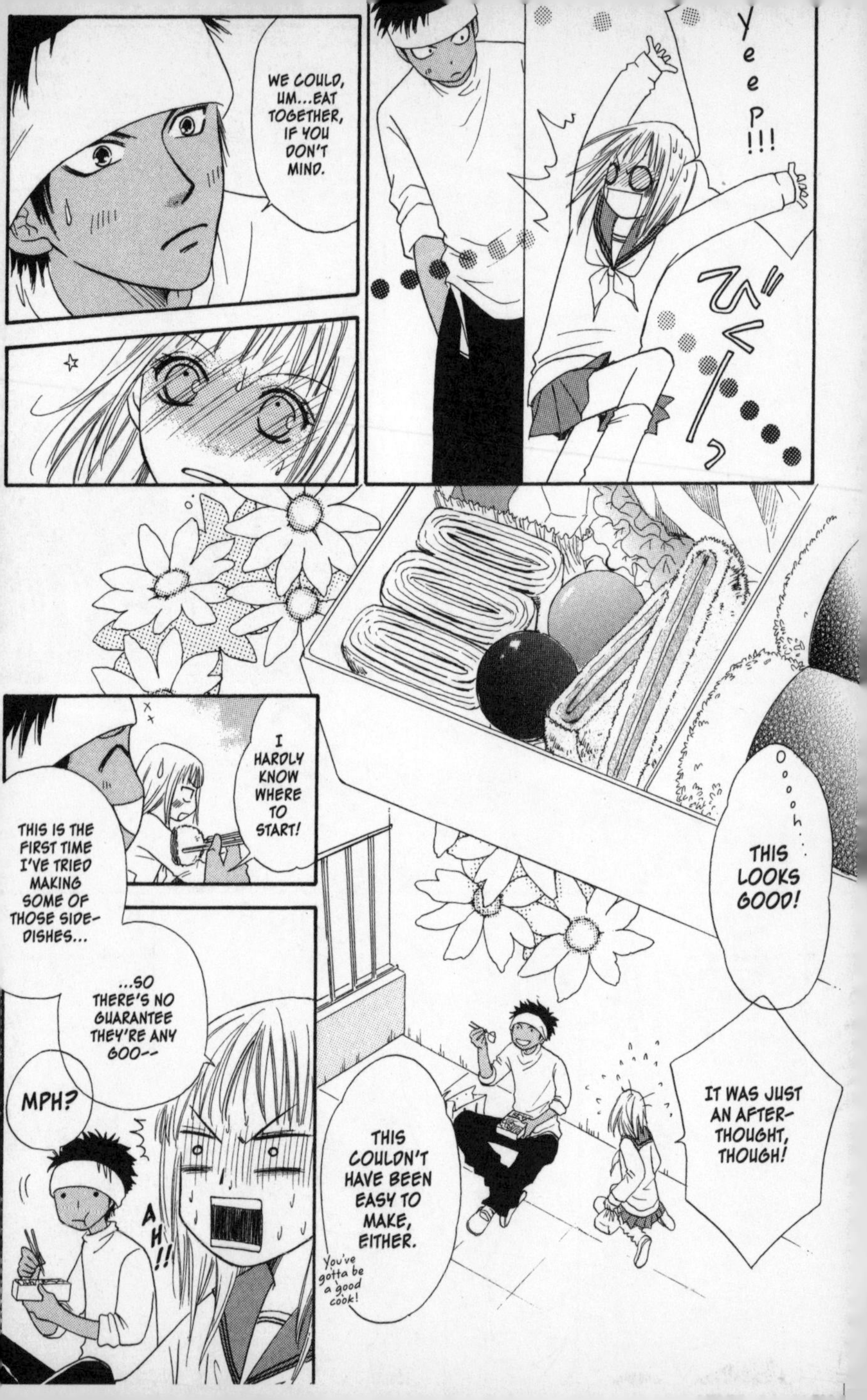
Yeep!!!
びくーっ
WE COULD, UM...EAT TOGETHER, IF YOU DON'T MIND.
Oooh...
THIS LOOKS GOOD!
I HARDLY KNOW WHERE TO START!
IT WAS JUST AN AFTER-THOUGHT, THOUGH!
THIS COULDN'T HAVE BEEN EASY TO MAKE, EITHER.
You've gotta be a good cook!
THIS IS THE FIRST TIME I'VE TRIED MAKING SOME OF THOSE SIDE-DISHES...
...SO THERE'S NO GUARANTEE THEY'RE ANY GOO--
MPH?
AH!!

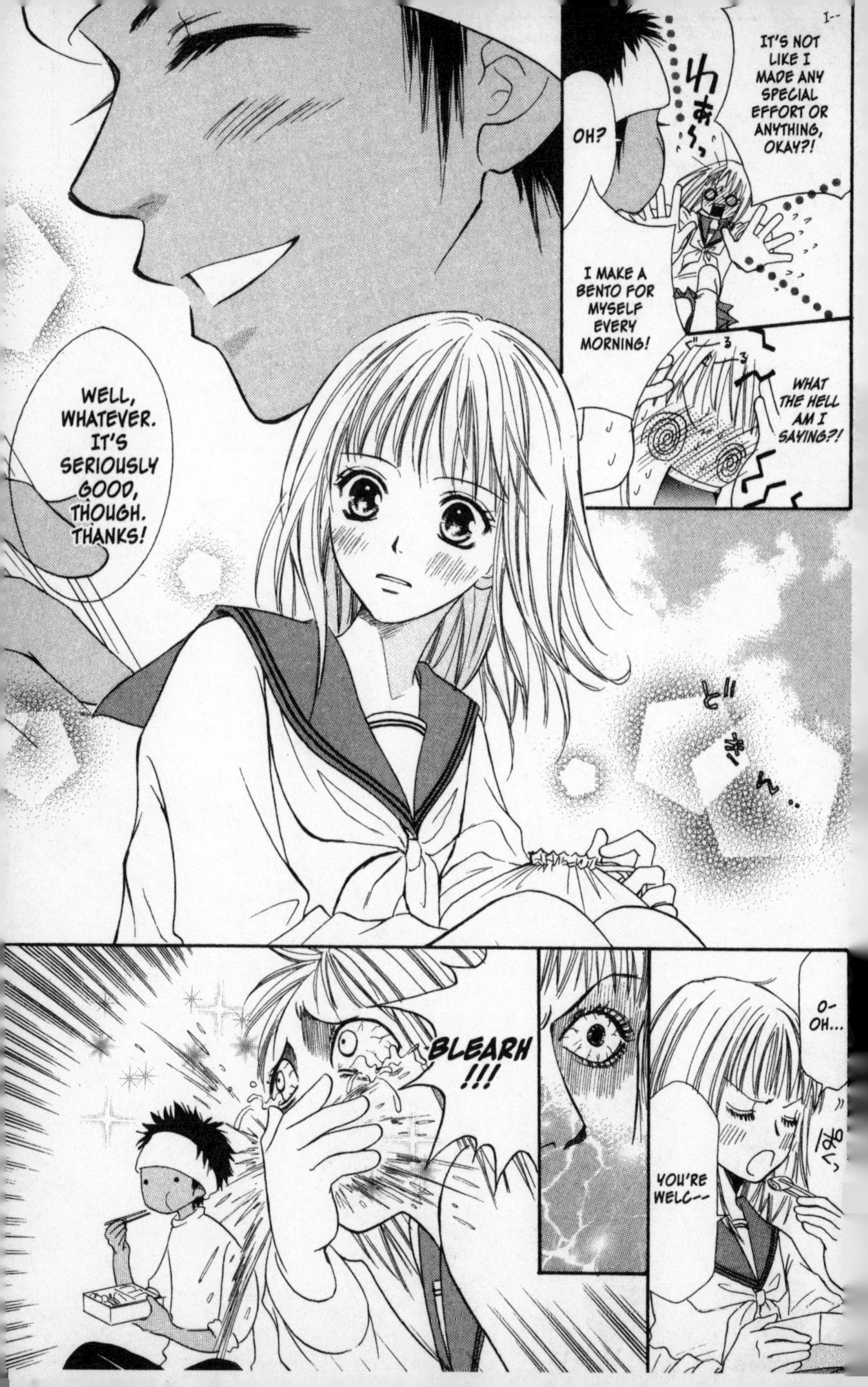
I--
IT'S NOT LIKE I MADE ANY SPECIAL EFFORT OR ANYTHING, OKAY?!
OH?
I MAKE A BENTO FOR MYSELF EVERY MORNING!
WHAT THE HELL AM I SAYING?!
WELL, WHATEVER. IT'S SERIOUSLY GOOD, THOUGH. THANKS!
O-OH...
YOU'RE WELC--
BLEARH!!!

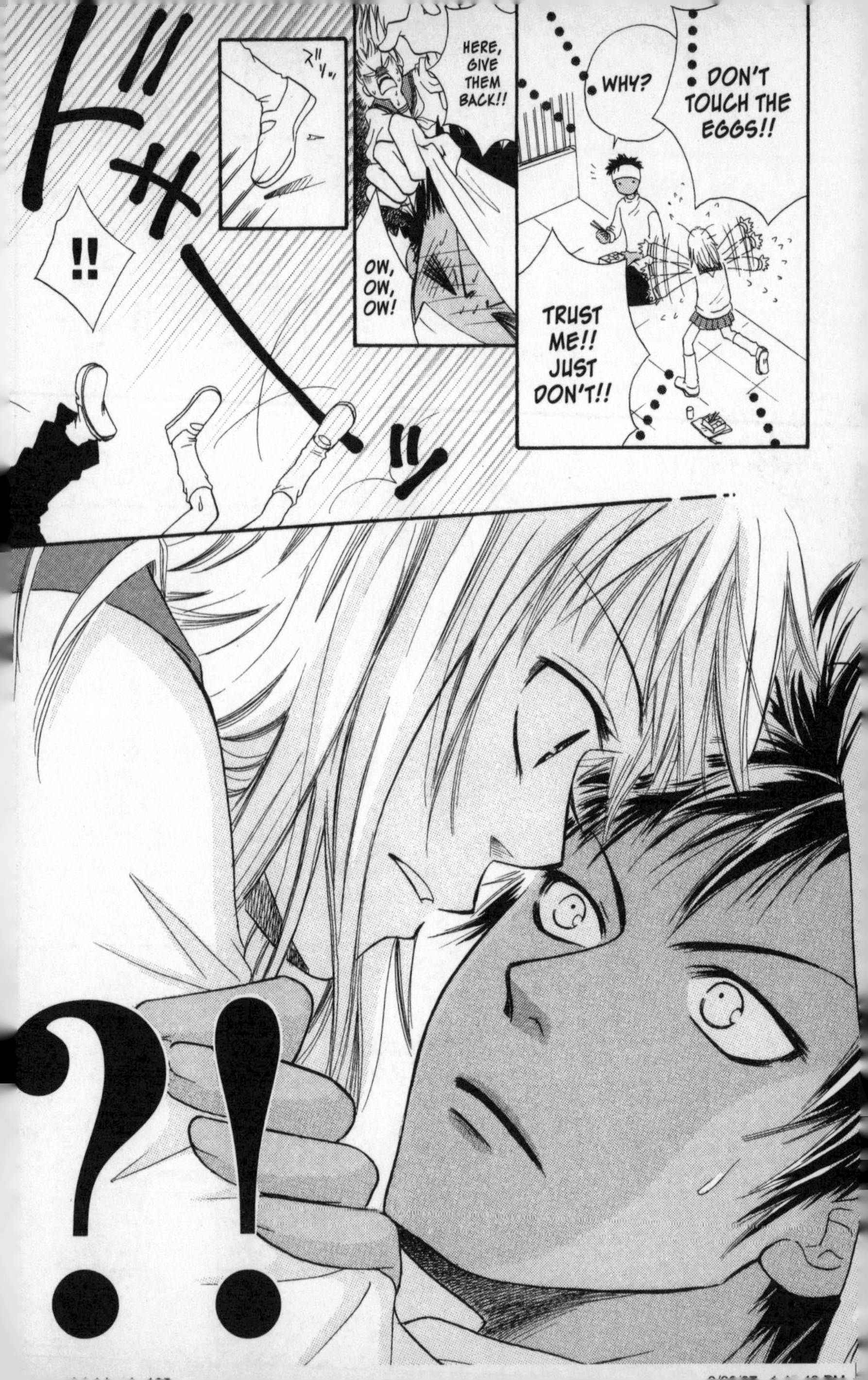
DON'T TOUCH THE EGGS!!
WHY?
TRUST ME!! JUST DON'T!!
HERE, GIVE THEM BACK!!
OW, OW, OW!
!!
?!

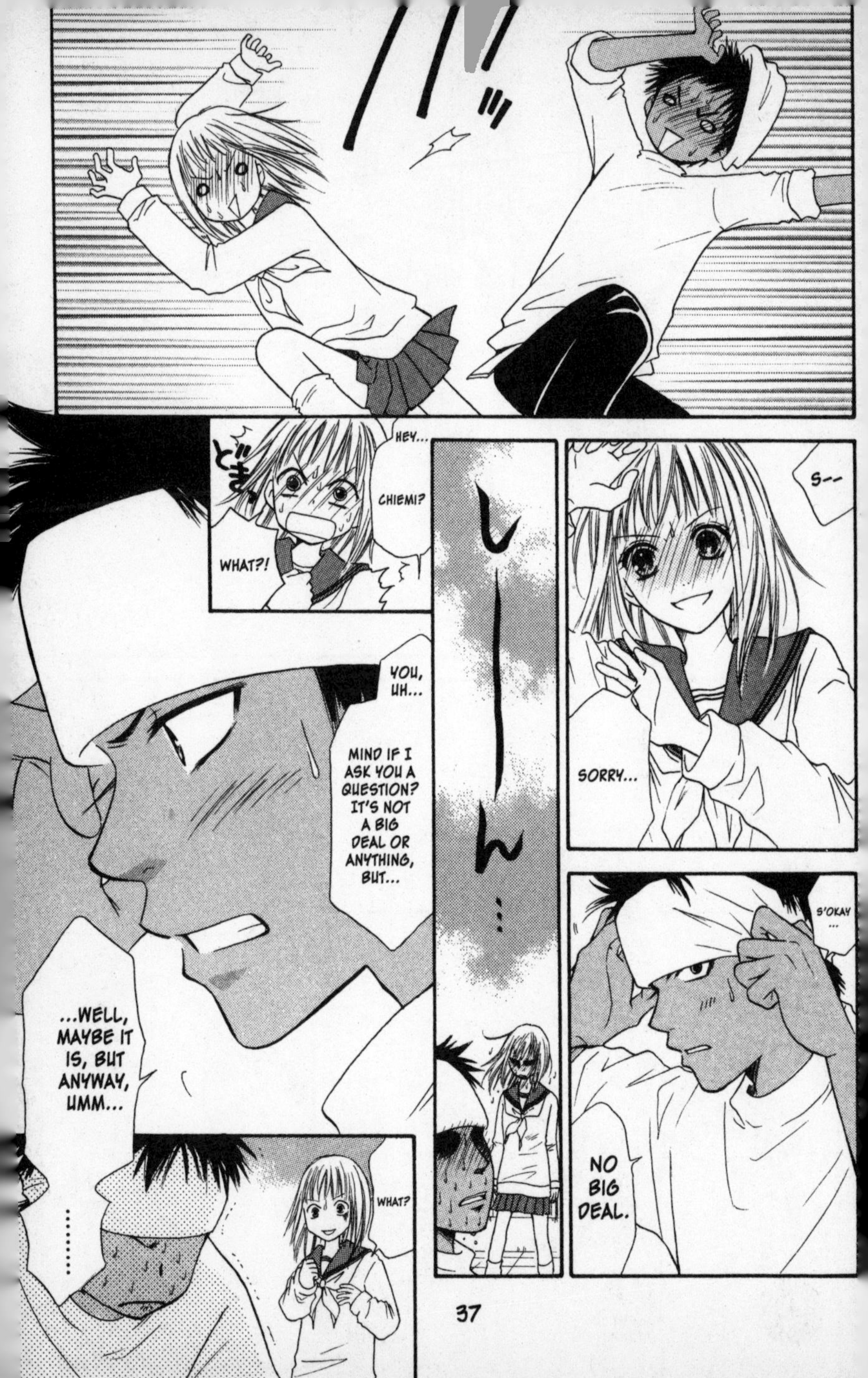
S--
SORRY...
S'OKAY...
NO BIG DEAL.
しーん…
HEY...
CHIEMI?
どきっ
WHAT?!
YOU, UH...
MIND IF I ASK YOU A QUESTION? IT'S NOT A BIG DEAL OR ANYTHING, BUT...
...WELL, MAYBE IT IS, BUT ANYWAY, UMM...
WHAT?
......

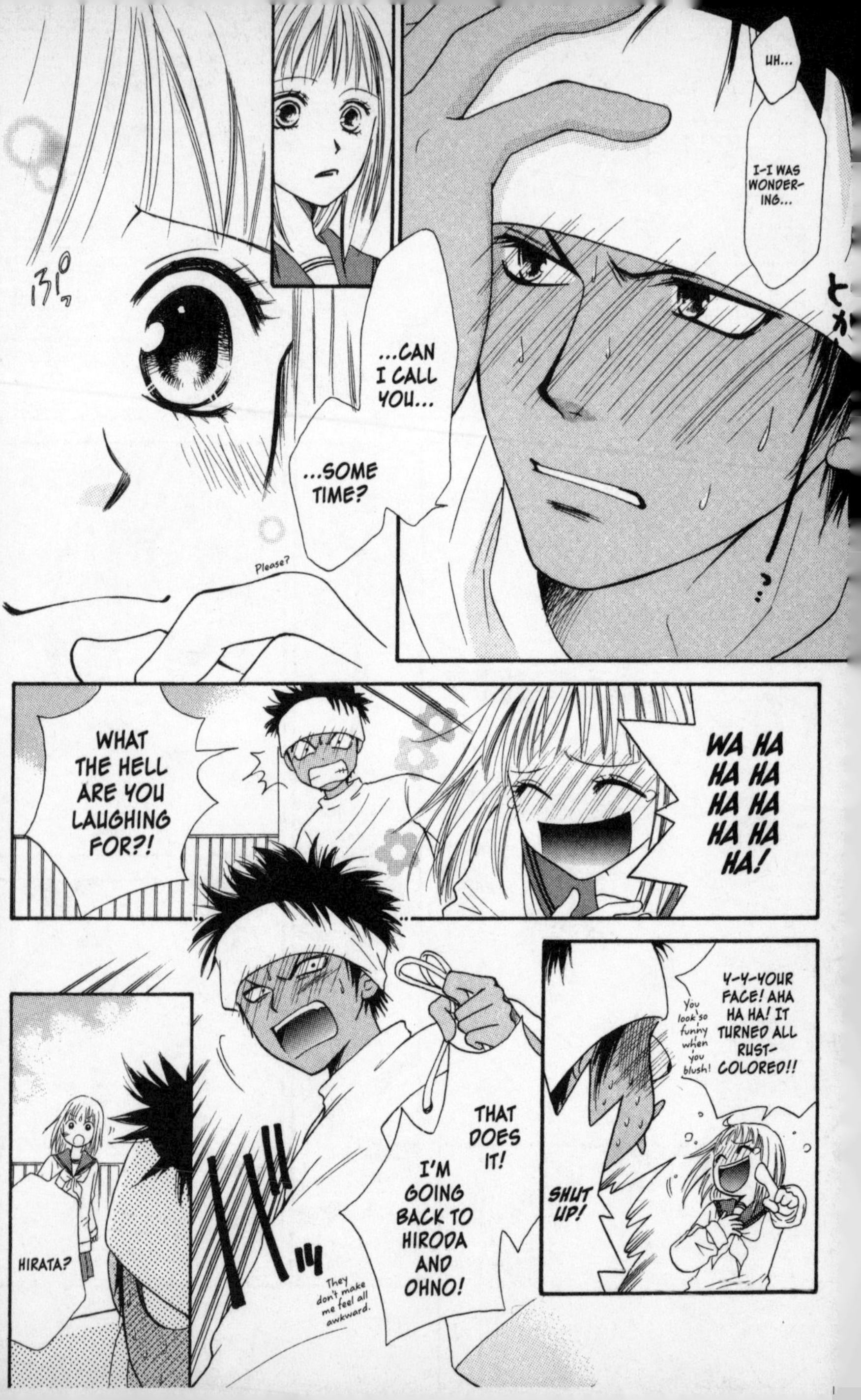
UH...
I-I WAS WONDER-ING...
...CAN I CALL YOU...
...SOME TIME?
Please?
WA HA HA HA HA HA HA HA HA!
WHAT THE HELL ARE YOU LAUGHING FOR?!
Y-Y-YOUR FACE! AHA HA HA! IT TURNED ALL RUST-COLORED!!
You look so funny when you blush!
SHUT UP!
THAT DOES IT!
I'M GOING BACK TO HIRODA AND OHNO!
They don't make me feel all awkward.
HIRATA?

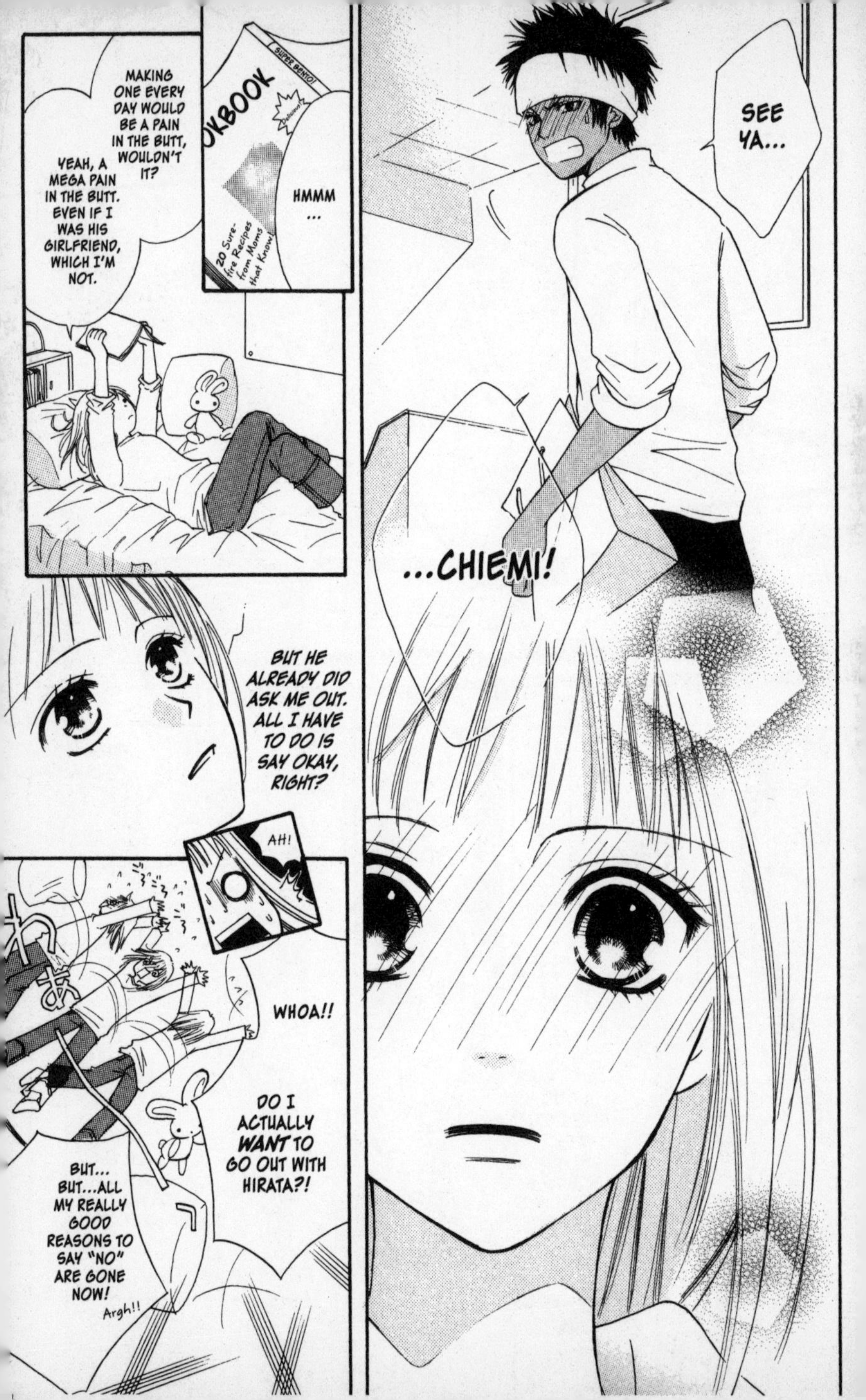
SEE YA...
...CHIEMI!
SUPER BENTO!
OKBOOK
20 Sure-fire Recipes from Moms that Know
HMMM...
MAKING ONE EVERY DAY WOULD BE A PAIN IN THE BUTT, WOULDN'T IT?
YEAH, A MEGA PAIN IN THE BUTT. EVEN IF I WAS HIS GIRLFRIEND, WHICH I'M NOT.
BUT HE ALREADY DID ASK ME OUT. ALL I HAVE TO DO IS SAY OKAY, RIGHT?
AH!
WHOA!!
DO I ACTUALLY WANT TO GO OUT WITH HIRATA?!
BUT... BUT...ALL MY REALLY GOOD REASONS TO SAY "NO" ARE GONE NOW!
Argh!!

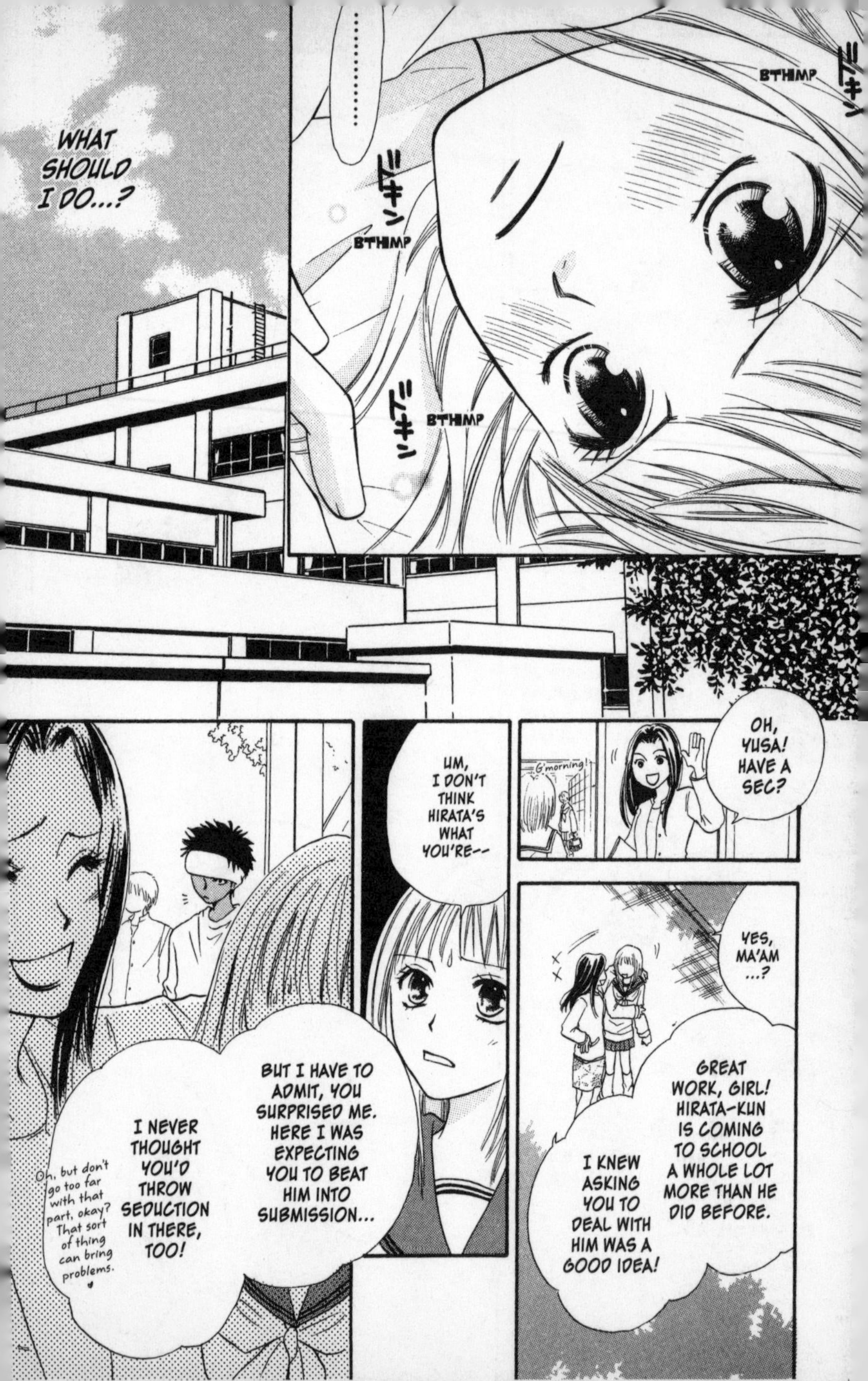
......
ドキン
BTHMP
ドキン
BTHMP
ドキン
BTHMP
WHAT SHOULD I DO...?
OH, YUSA! HAVE A SEC?
G'morning!
YES, MA'AM ...?
GREAT WORK, GIRL! HIRATA-KUN IS COMING TO SCHOOL A WHOLE LOT MORE THAN HE DID BEFORE.
I KNEW ASKING YOU TO DEAL WITH HIM WAS A GOOD IDEA!
UM, I DON'T THINK HIRATA'S WHAT YOU'RE--
BUT I HAVE TO ADMIT, YOU SURPRISED ME. HERE I WAS EXPECTING YOU TO BEAT HIM INTO SUBMISSION...
I NEVER THOUGHT YOU'D THROW SEDUCTION IN THERE, TOO!
Oh, but don't go too far with that part, okay? That sort of thing can bring problems. ♥

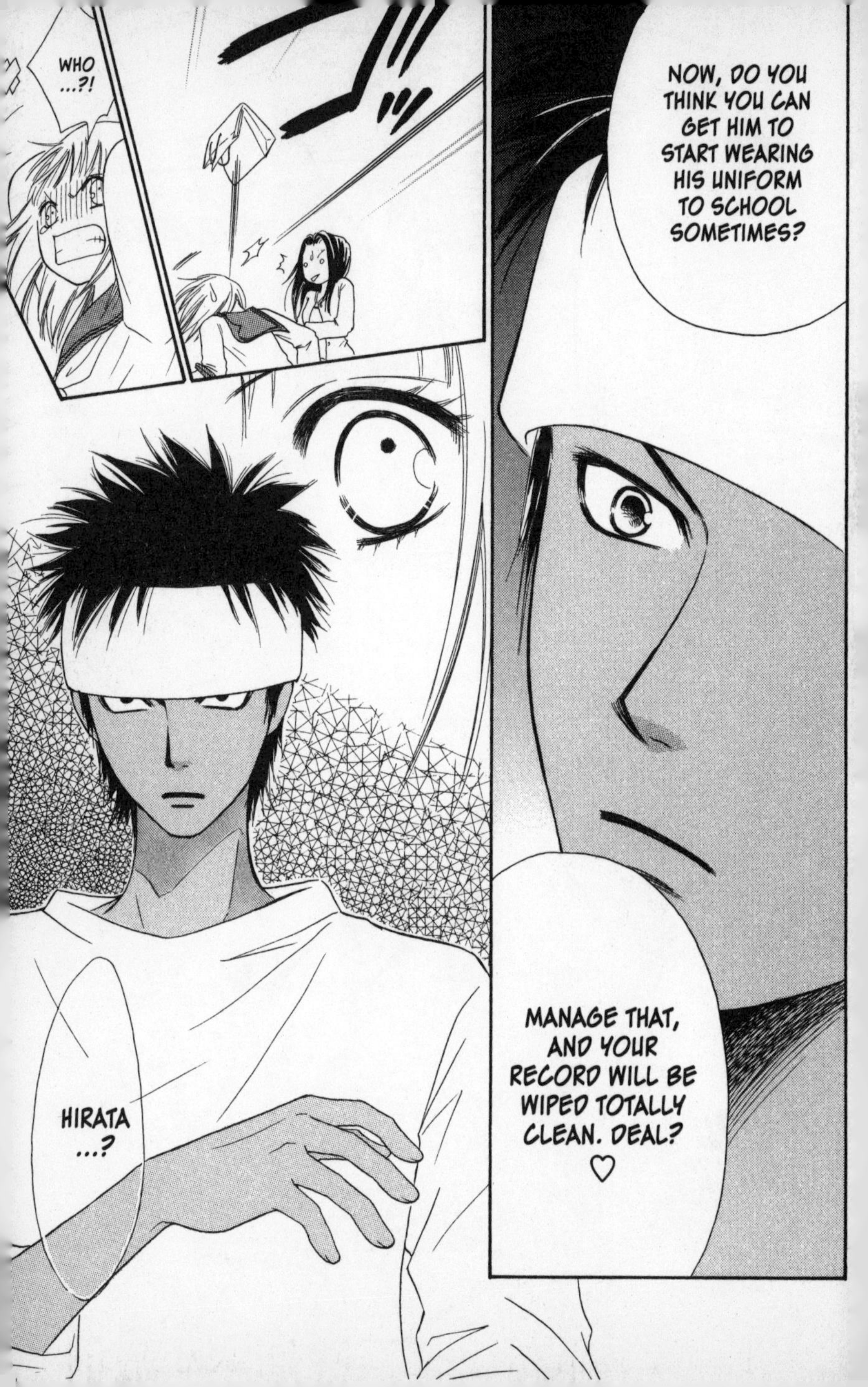
NOW, DO YOU THINK YOU CAN GET HIM TO START WEARING HIS UNIFORM TO SCHOOL SOMETIMES?
MANAGE THAT, AND YOUR RECORD WILL BE WIPED TOTALLY CLEAN. DEAL? ♡
WHO ...?!
HIRATA ...?

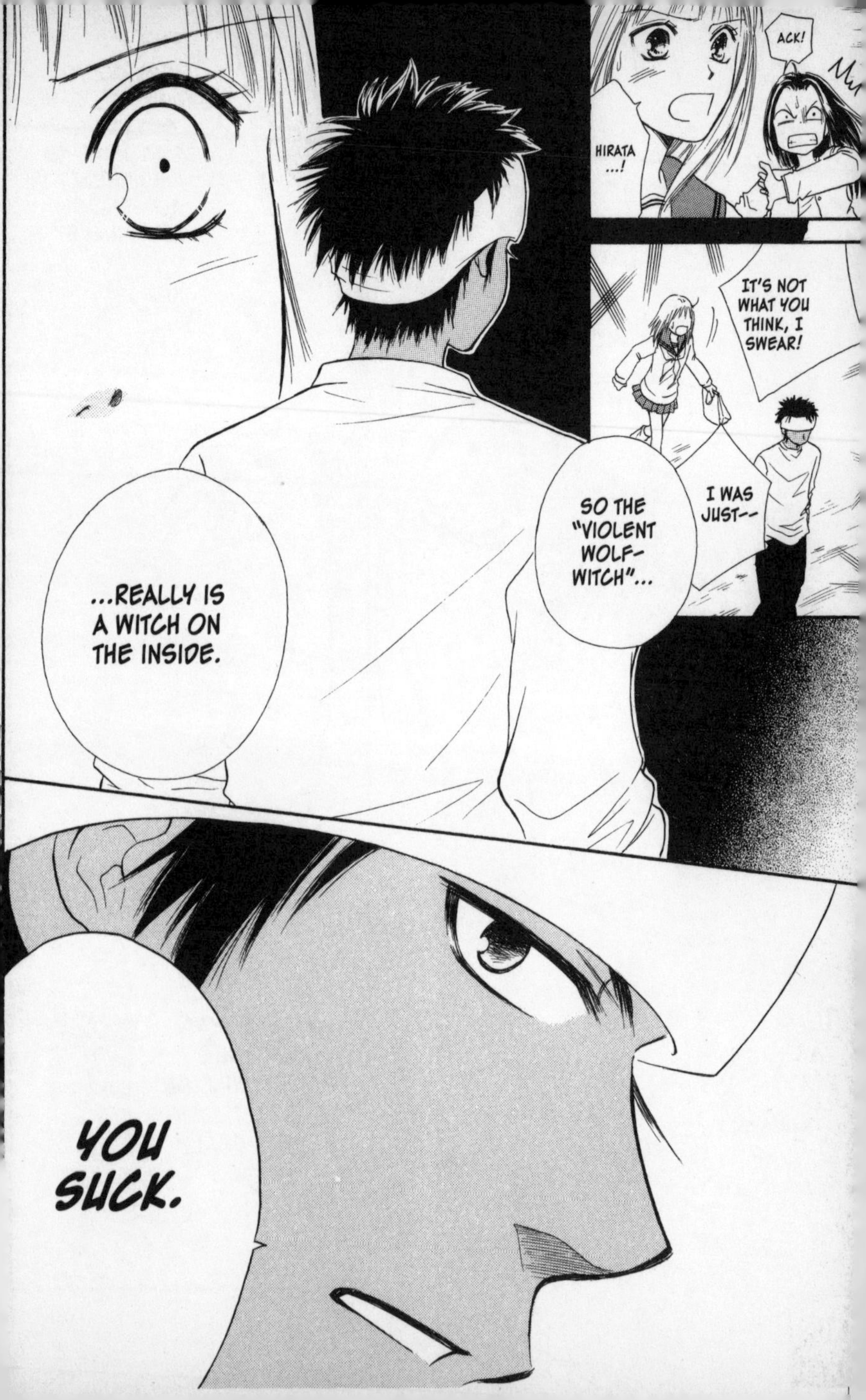
ACK!
HIRATA ...!
IT'S NOT WHAT YOU THINK, I SWEAR!
I WAS JUST--
SO THE "VIOLENT WOLF-WITCH"...
...REALLY IS A WITCH ON THE INSIDE.
YOU SUCK.

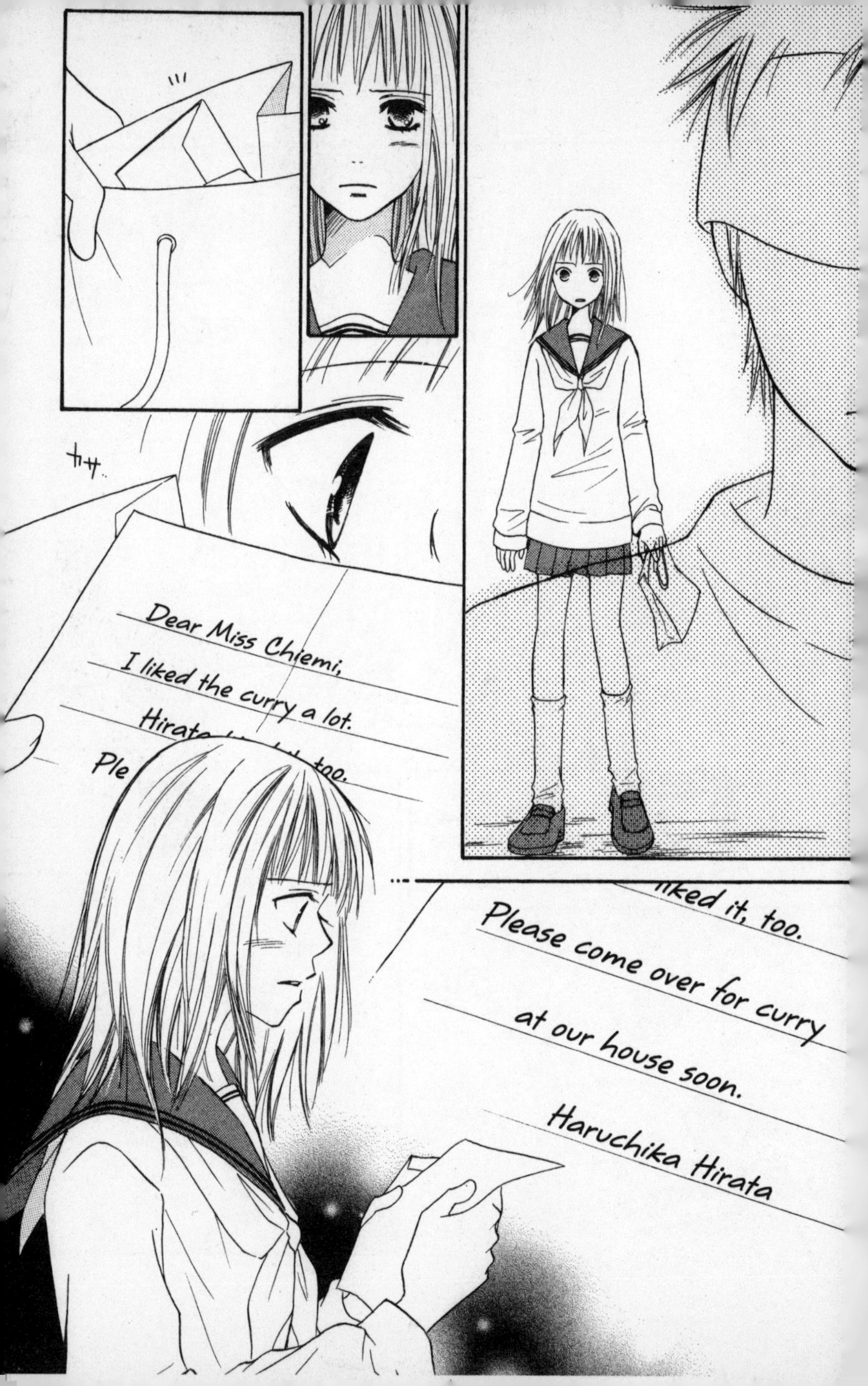

カサ..
Dear Miss Chiemi,
I liked the curry a lot.
Hirata
Ple
iked it, too.
Please come over for curry
at our house soon.
Haruchika Hirata

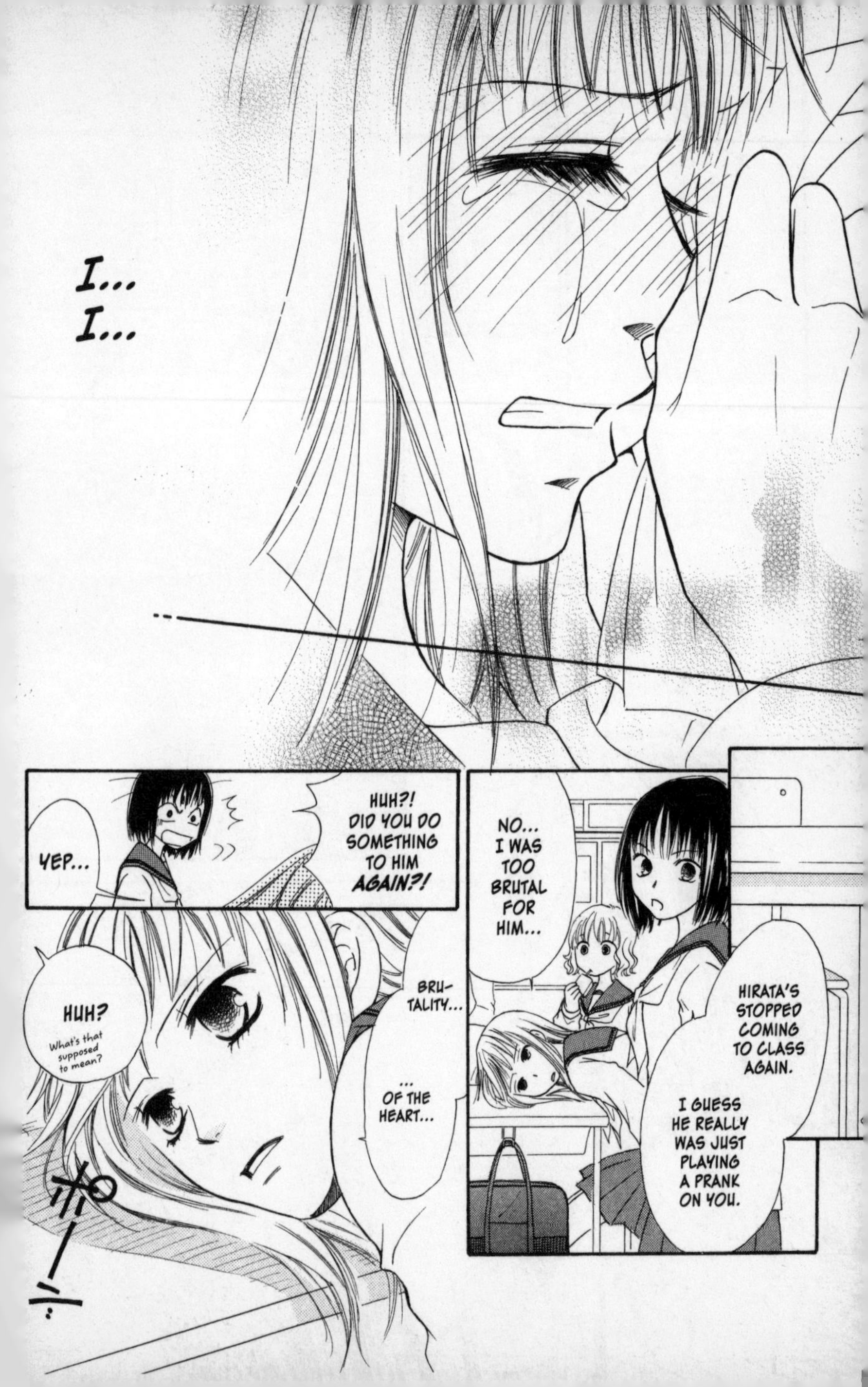
I...
I...
...
HIRATA'S STOPPED COMING TO CLASS AGAIN.
I GUESS HE REALLY WAS JUST PLAYING A PRANK ON YOU.
NO... I WAS TOO BRUTAL FOR HIM...
HUH?! DID YOU DO SOMETHING TO HIM AGAIN?!
YEP...
BRU-TALITY...
... OF THE HEART...
HUH? What's that supposed to mean?

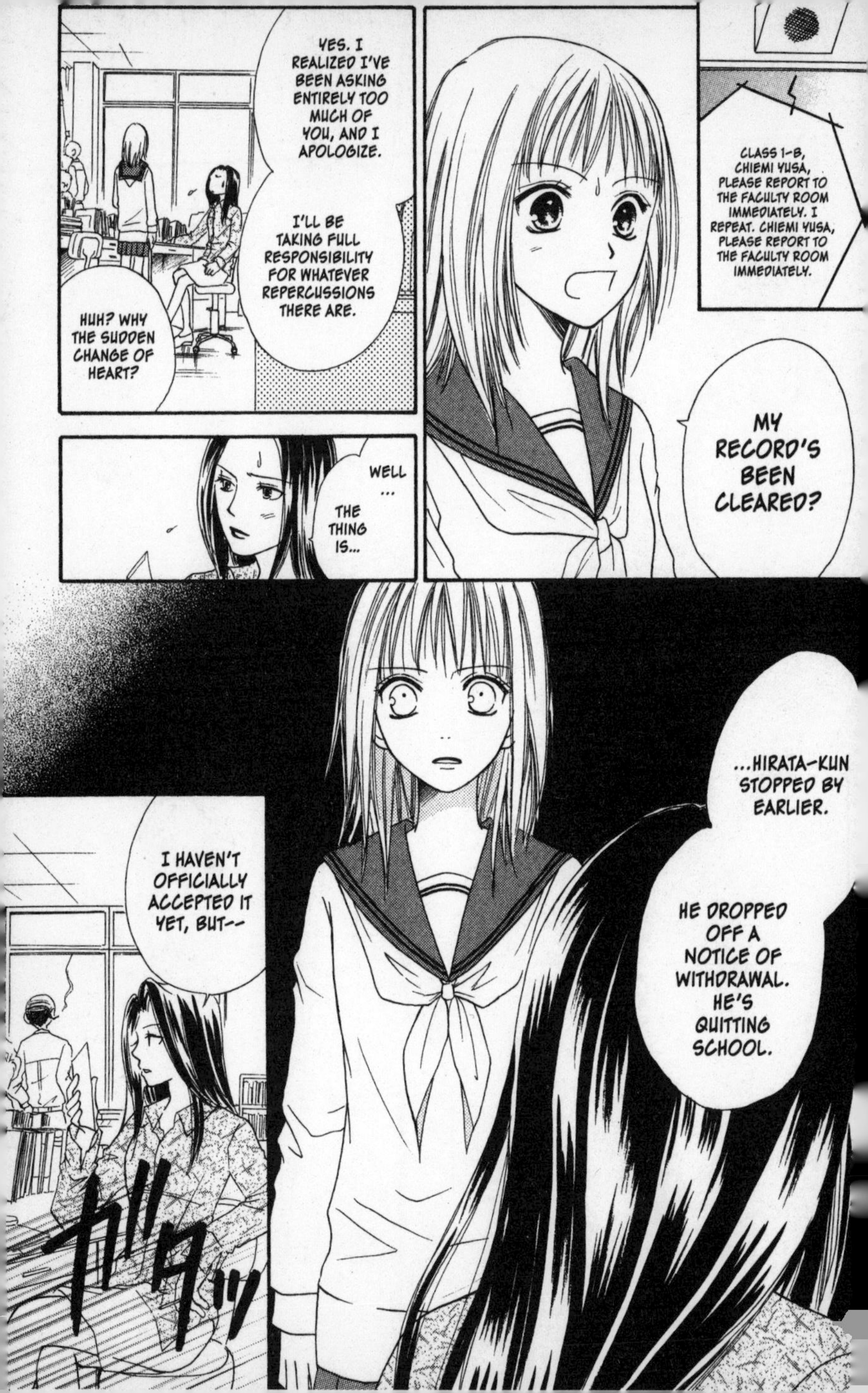
CLASS 1-B, CHIEMI YUSA, PLEASE REPORT TO THE FACULTY ROOM IMMEDIATELY. I REPEAT. CHIEMI YUSA, PLEASE REPORT TO THE FACULTY ROOM IMMEDIATELY.
MY RECORD'S BEEN CLEARED?
YES. I REALIZED I'VE BEEN ASKING ENTIRELY TOO MUCH OF YOU, AND I APOLOGIZE.
I'LL BE TAKING FULL RESPONSIBILITY FOR WHATEVER REPERCUSSIONS THERE ARE.
HUH? WHY THE SUDDEN CHANGE OF HEART?
WELL ...
THE THING IS...
...HIRATA-KUN STOPPED BY EARLIER.
HE DROPPED OFF A NOTICE OF WITHDRAWAL. HE'S QUITTING SCHOOL.
I HAVEN'T OFFICIALLY ACCEPTED IT YET, BUT--
ガタッ

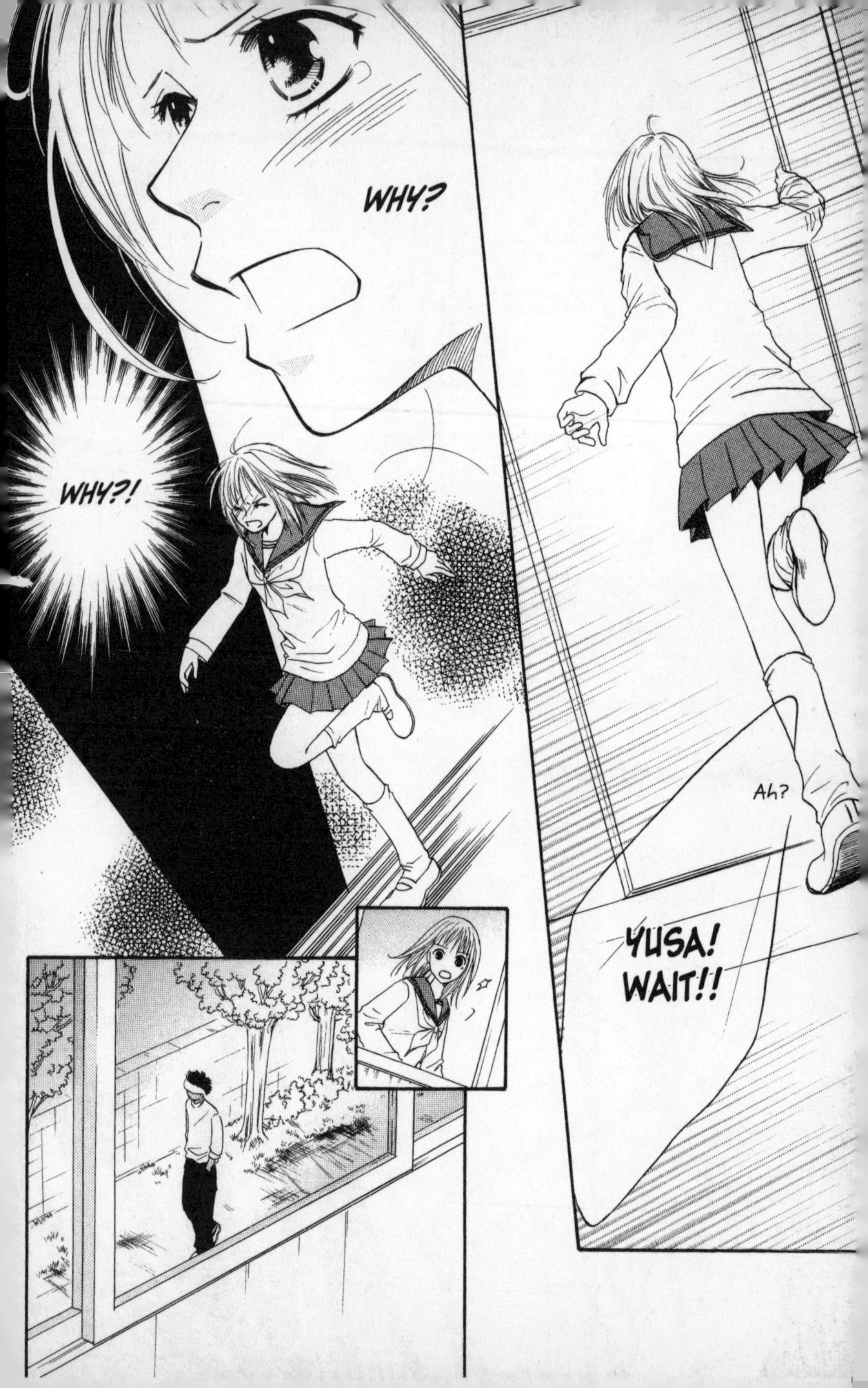

Ah?
YUSA! WAIT!!
WHY?
WHY?!

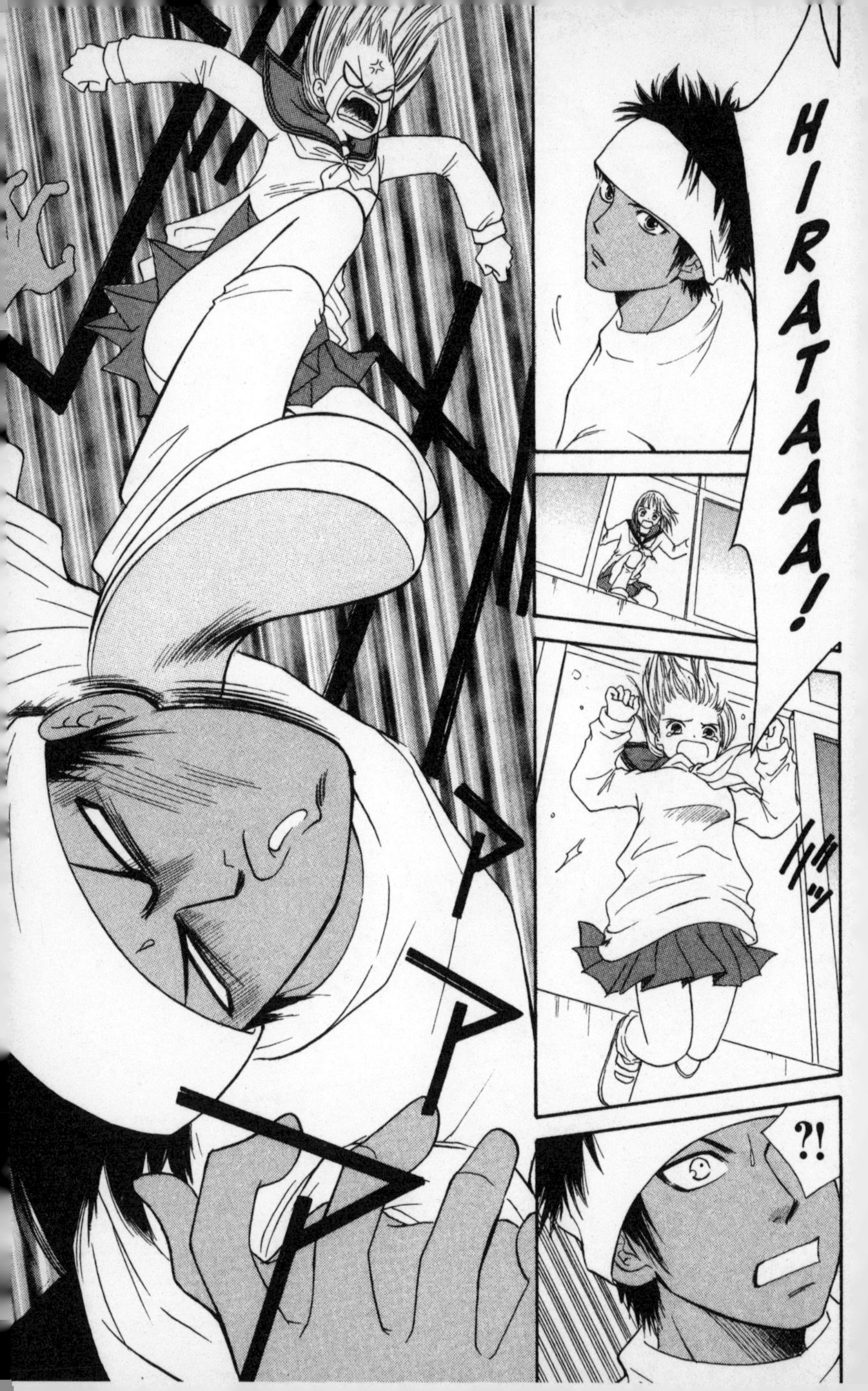
HIRATAAAA!
?!

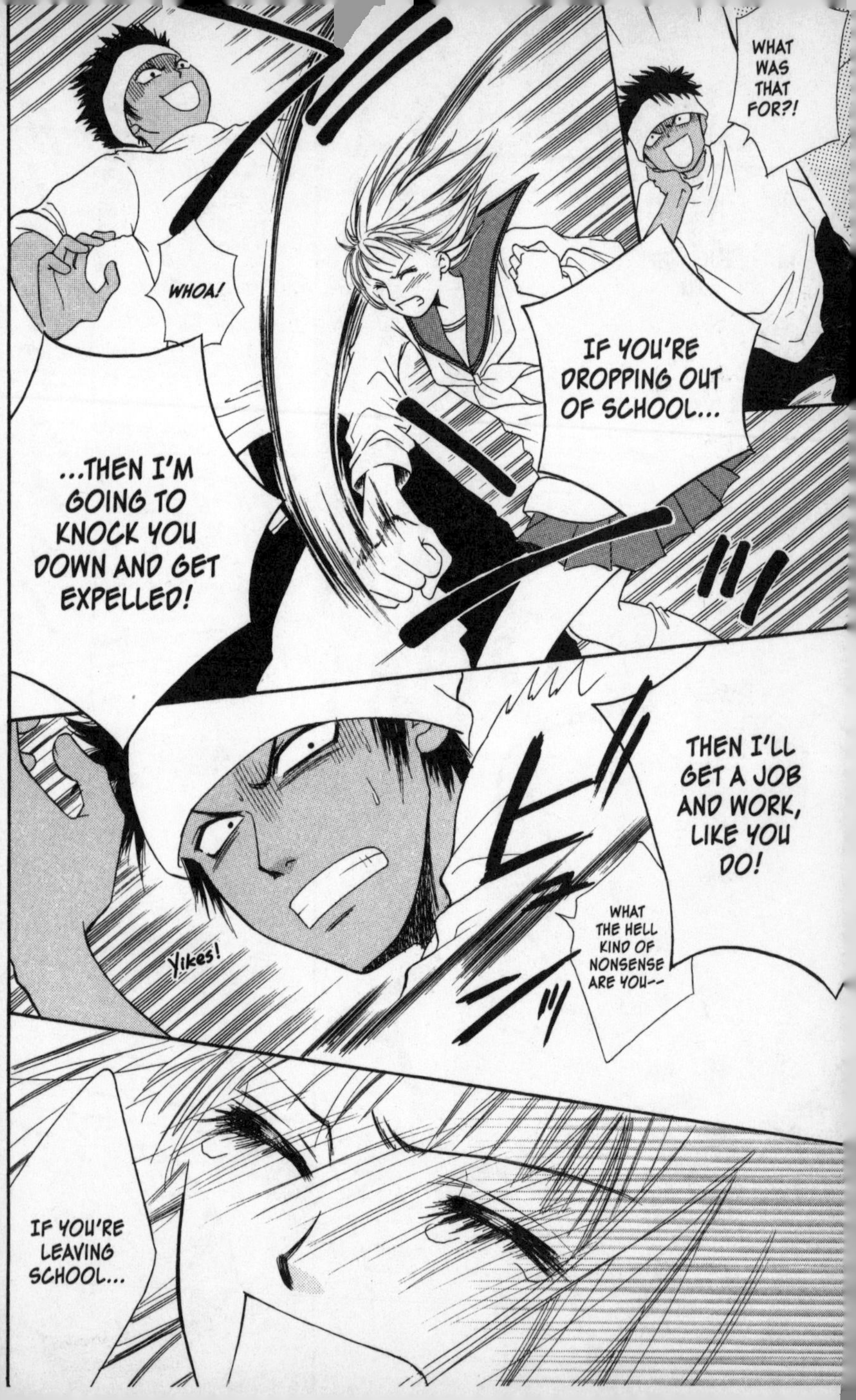
WHAT WAS THAT FOR?!
WHOA!
IF YOU'RE DROPPING OUT OF SCHOOL...
...THEN I'M GOING TO KNOCK YOU DOWN AND GET EXPELLED!
THEN I'LL GET A JOB AND WORK, LIKE YOU DO!
WHAT THE HELL KIND OF NONSENSE ARE YOU--
Yikes!
IF YOU'RE LEAVING SCHOOL...

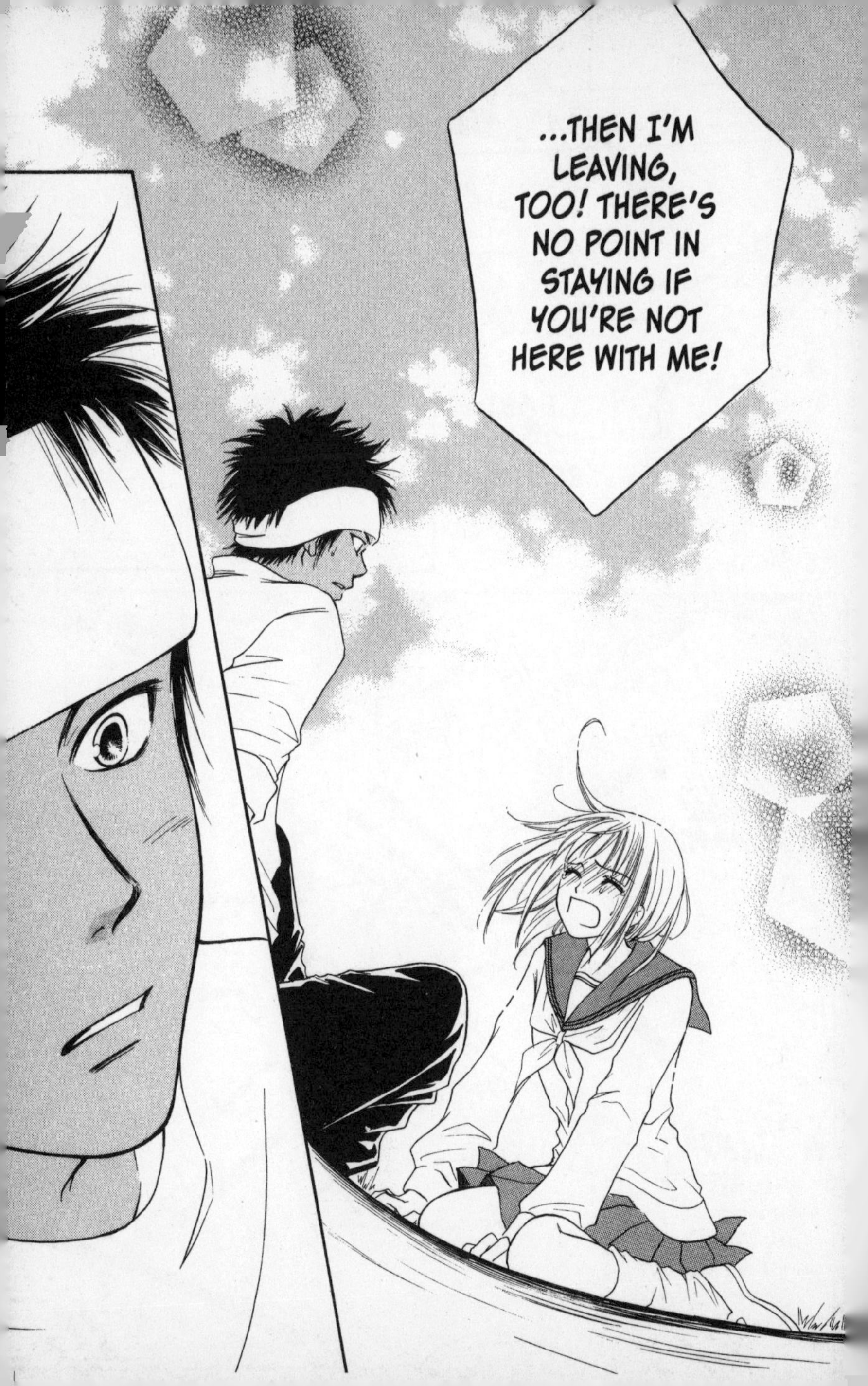
...THEN I'M LEAVING, TOO! THERE'S NO POINT IN STAYING IF YOU'RE NOT HERE WITH ME!

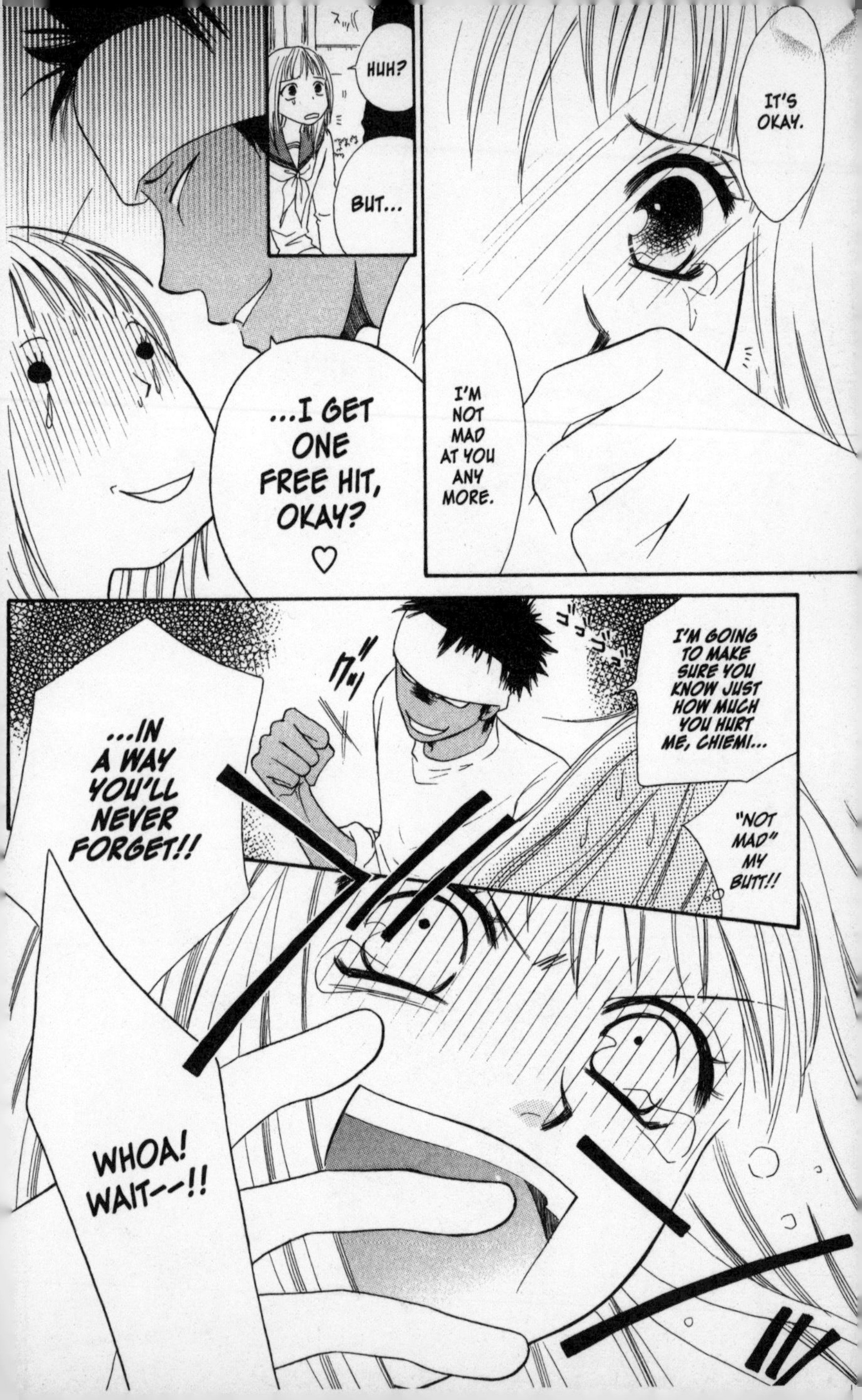
IT'S OKAY.
I'M NOT MAD AT YOU ANY MORE.
HUH?
BUT...
...I GET ONE FREE HIT, OKAY? ♡
I'M GOING TO MAKE SURE YOU KNOW JUST HOW MUCH YOU HURT ME, CHIEMI...
...IN A WAY YOU'LL NEVER FORGET!!
"NOT MAD" MY BUTT!!
WHOA! WAIT--!!

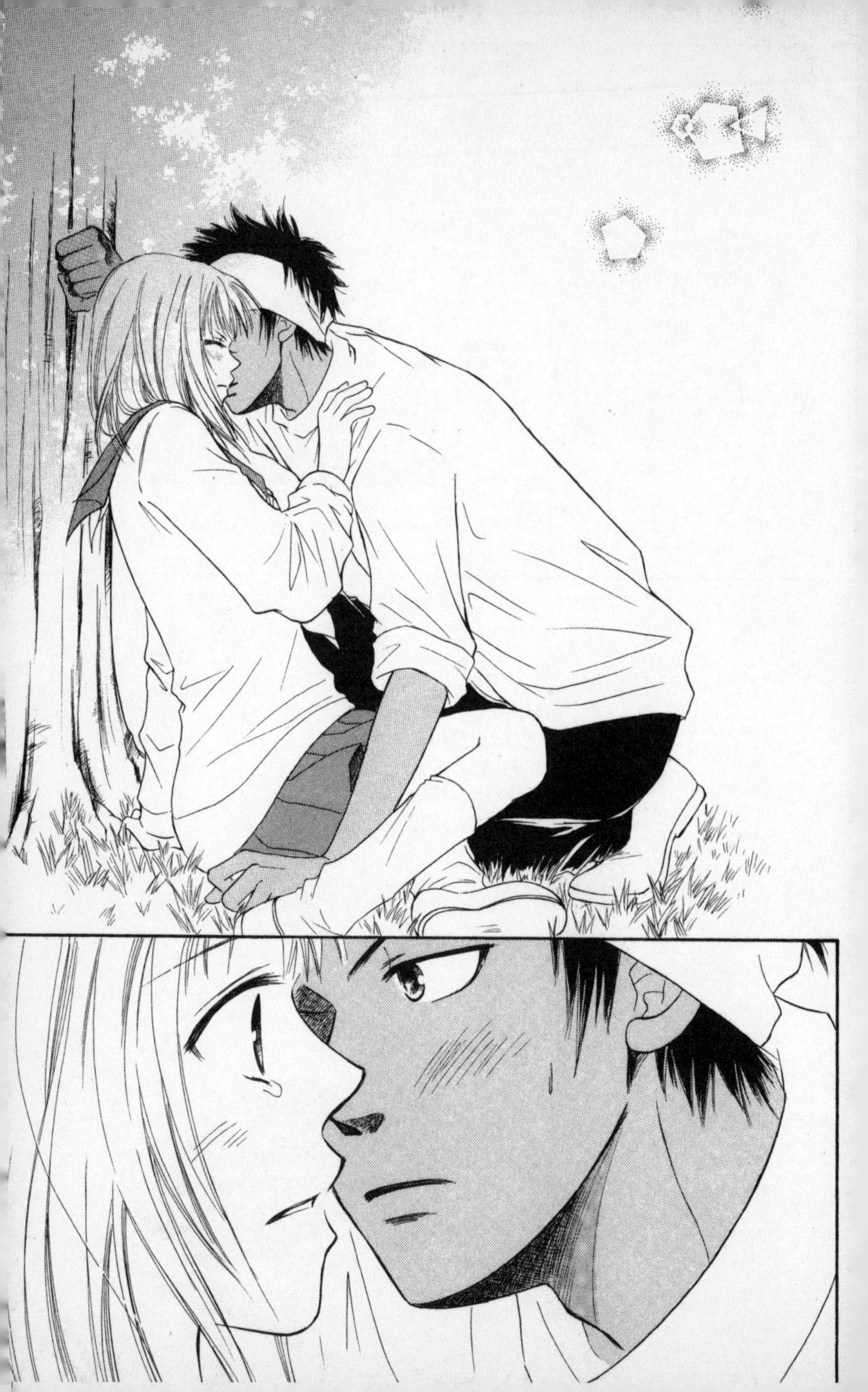

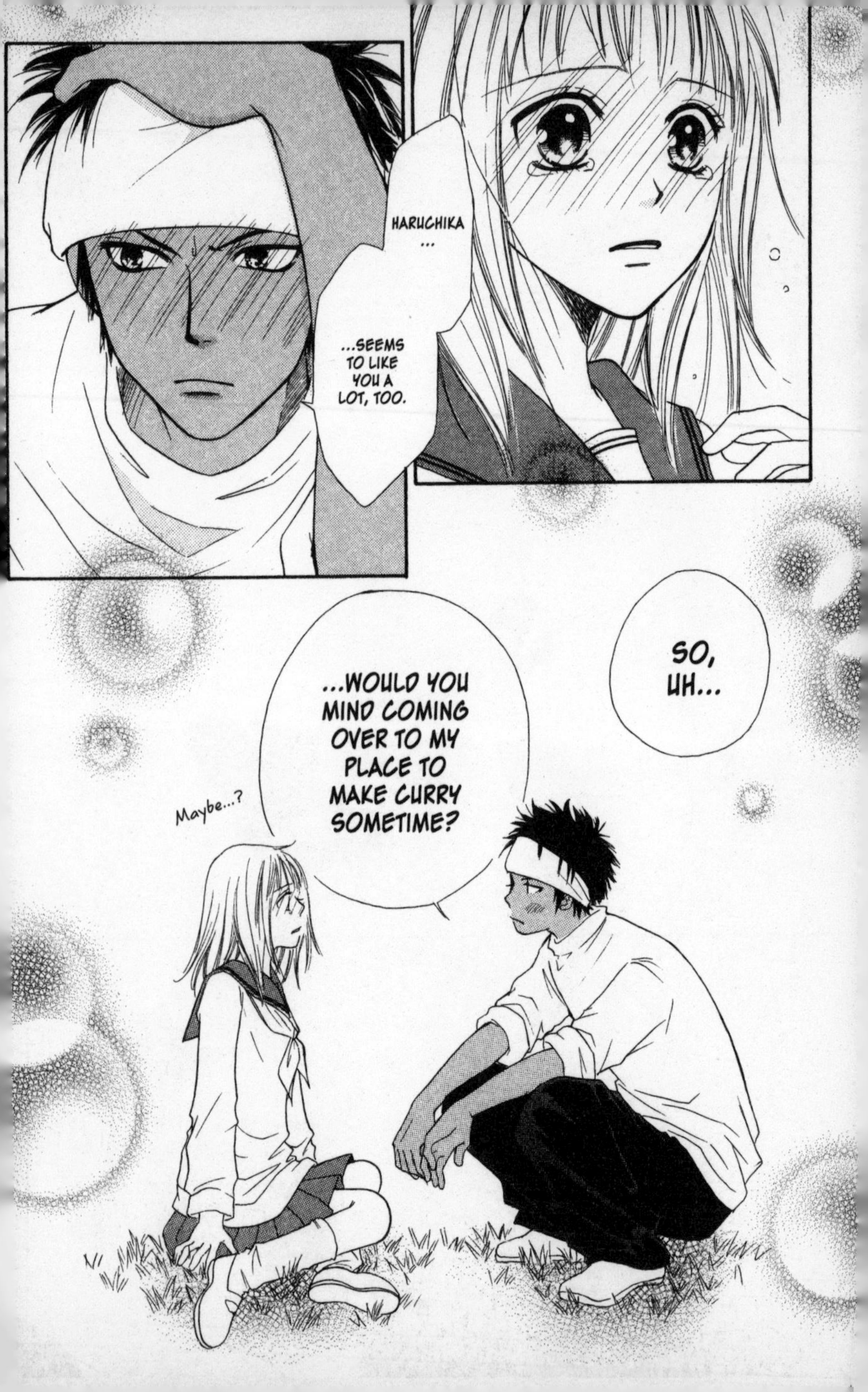
HARUCHIKA ...
...SEEMS TO LIKE YOU A LOT, TOO.
SO, UH...
...WOULD YOU MIND COMING OVER TO MY PLACE TO MAKE CURRY SOMETIME?
Maybe...?

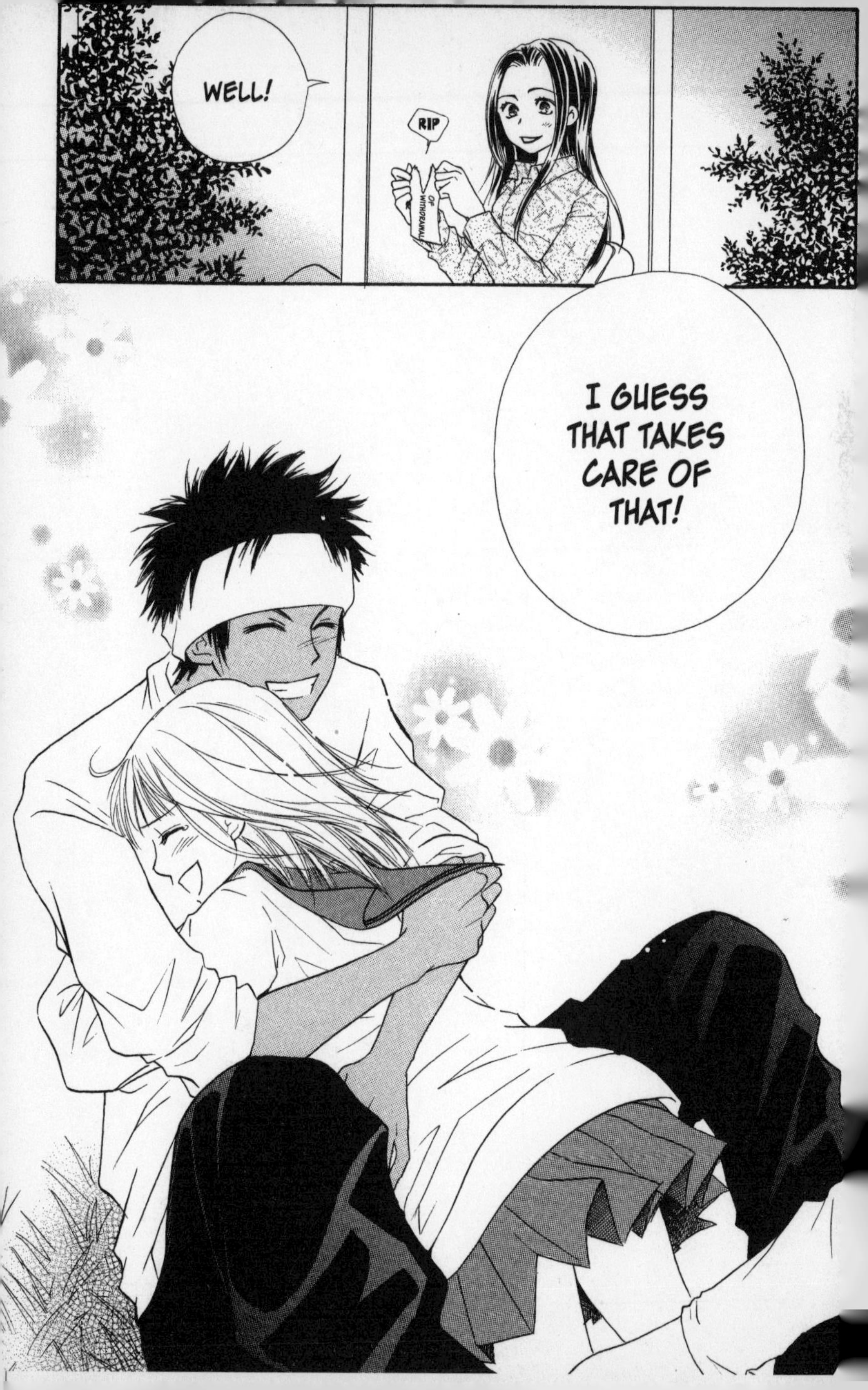
RIP
OF WITHDRAWAL
WELL!
I GUESS THAT TAKES CARE OF THAT!

Ch 2 A Love-filled First Battle...er...Date

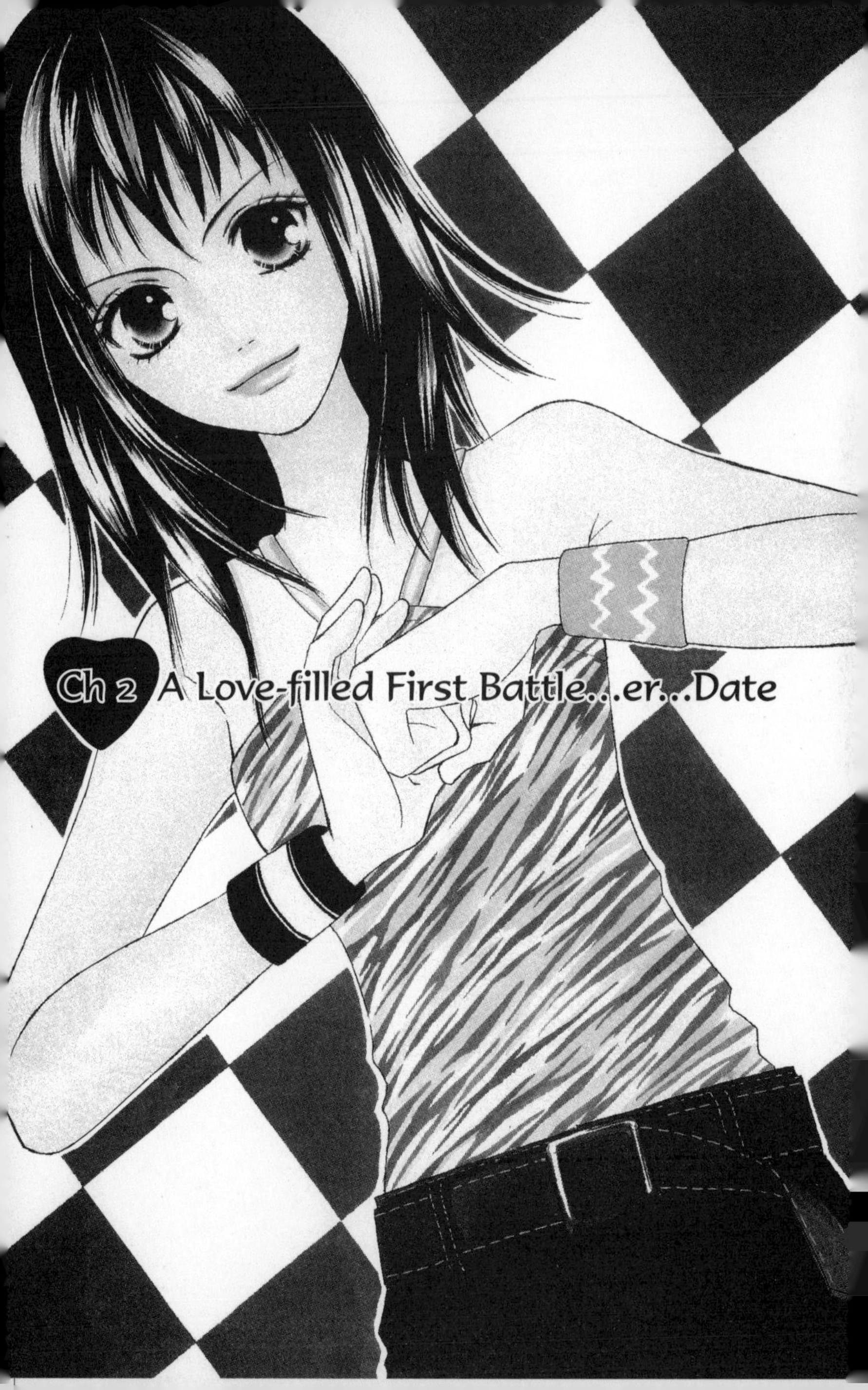

LOVE ATTACK™

JUNAI TOKKO TAICHO!

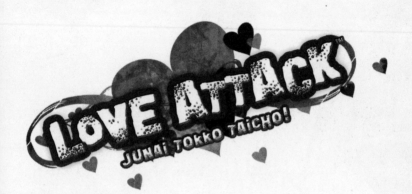

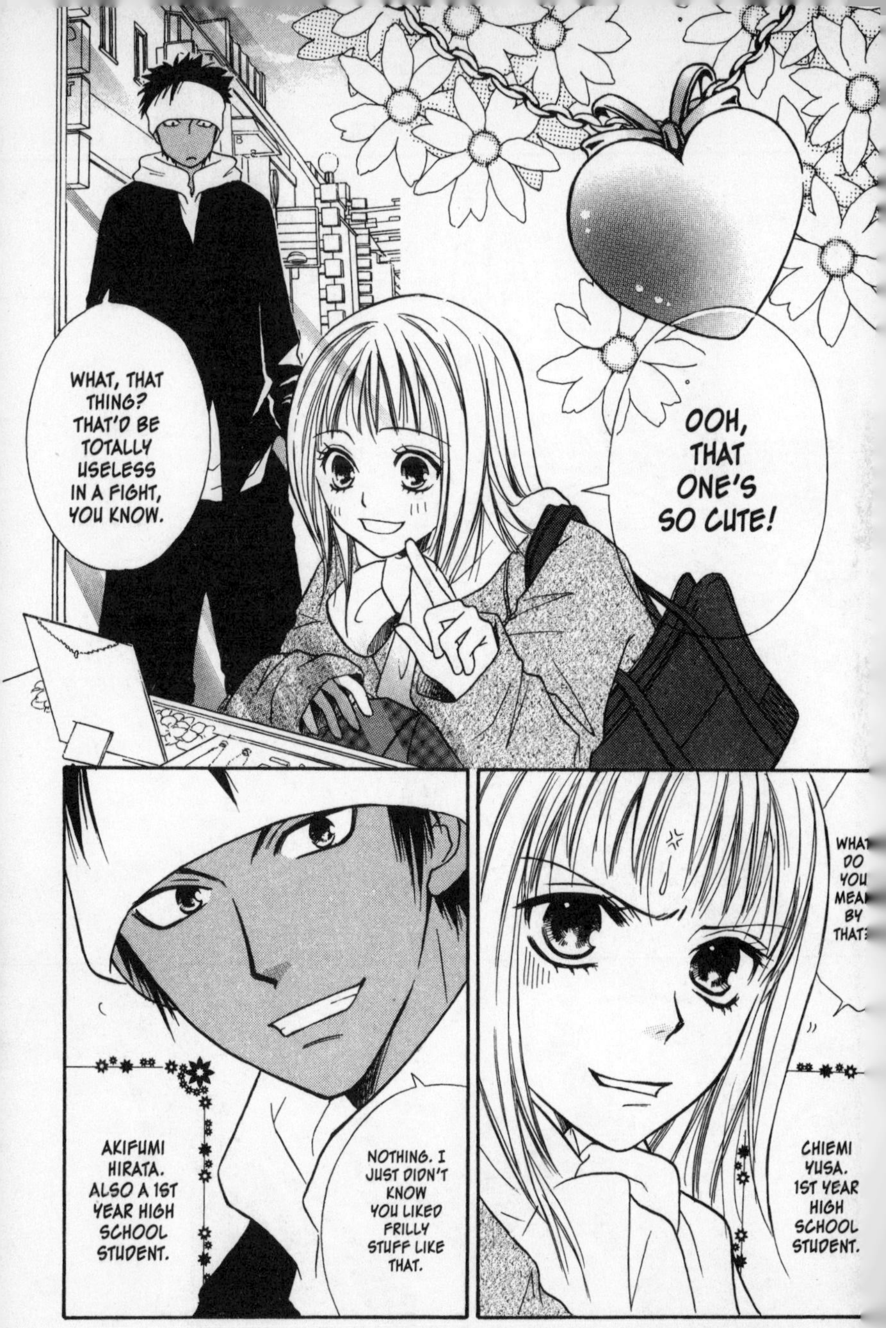
OOH, THAT ONE'S SO CUTE!
WHAT, THAT THING? THAT'D BE TOTALLY USELESS IN A FIGHT, YOU KNOW.
WHAT DO YOU MEA BY THAT
CHIEMI YUSA. 1ST YEAR HIGH SCHOOL STUDENT.
NOTHING. I JUST DIDN'T KNOW YOU LIKED FRILLY STUFF LIKE THAT.
AKIFUMI HIRATA. ALSO A 1ST YEAR HIGH SCHOOL STUDENT.

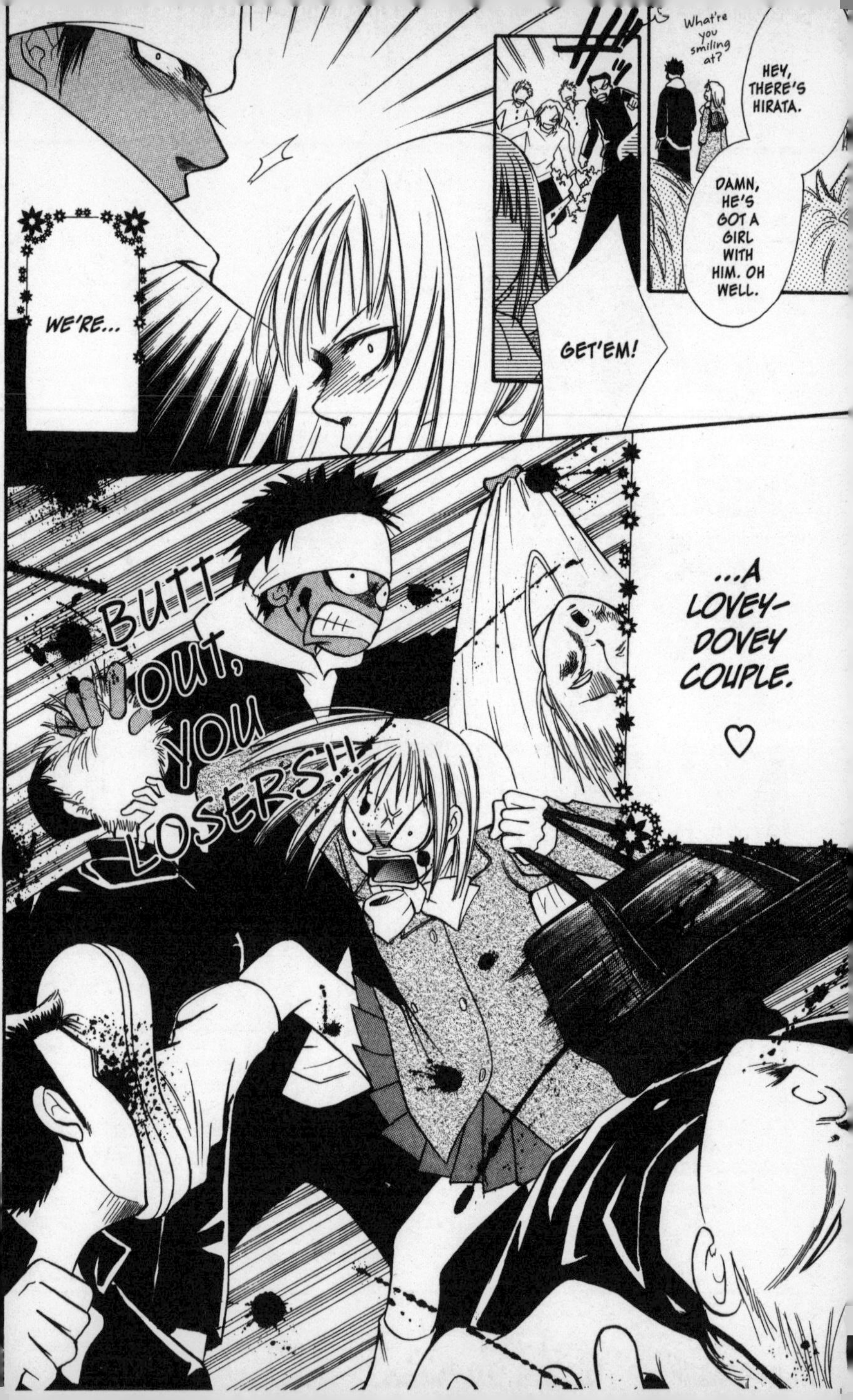
HEY, THERE'S HIRATA.
DAMN, HE'S GOT A GIRL WITH HIM. OH WELL.
What're you smiling at?
GET'EM!
WE'RE...
...A LOVEY-DOVEY COUPLE. ♡
BUTT OUT, YOU LOSERS!!

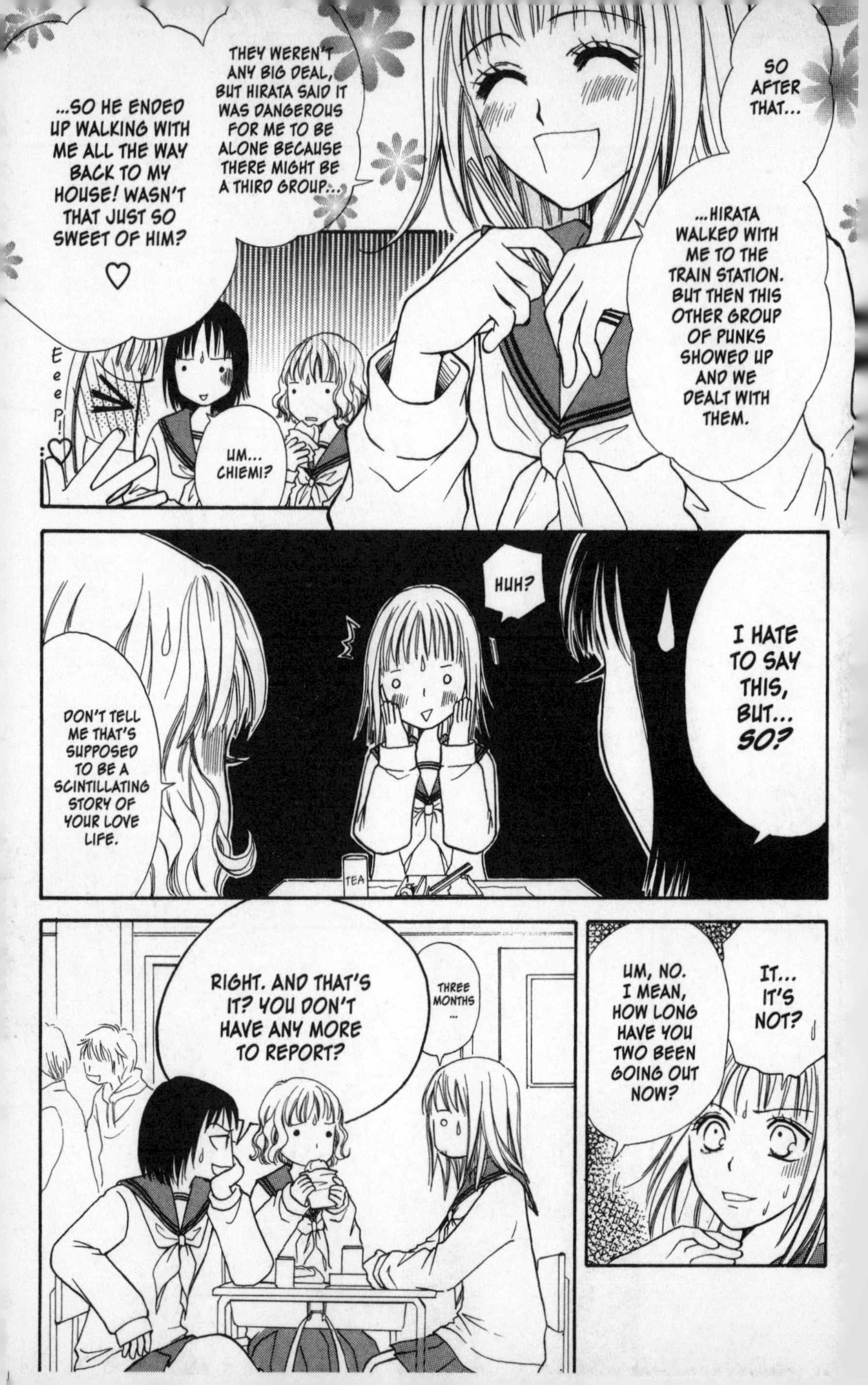
SO AFTER THAT...
...HIRATA WALKED WITH ME TO THE TRAIN STATION. BUT THEN THIS OTHER GROUP OF PUNKS SHOWED UP AND WE DEALT WITH THEM.
THEY WEREN'T ANY BIG DEAL, BUT HIRATA SAID IT WAS DANGEROUS FOR ME TO BE ALONE BECAUSE THERE MIGHT BE A THIRD GROUP...
...SO HE ENDED UP WALKING WITH ME ALL THE WAY BACK TO MY HOUSE! WASN'T THAT JUST SO SWEET OF HIM? ♡
Eeep! ♡
UM... CHIEMI?
I HATE TO SAY THIS, BUT... SO?
HUH?
DON'T TELL ME THAT'S SUPPOSED TO BE A SCINTILLATING STORY OF YOUR LOVE LIFE.
TEA
IT... IT'S NOT?
UM, NO. I MEAN, HOW LONG HAVE YOU TWO BEEN GOING OUT NOW?
THREE MONTHS ...
RIGHT. AND THAT'S IT? YOU DON'T HAVE ANY MORE TO REPORT?

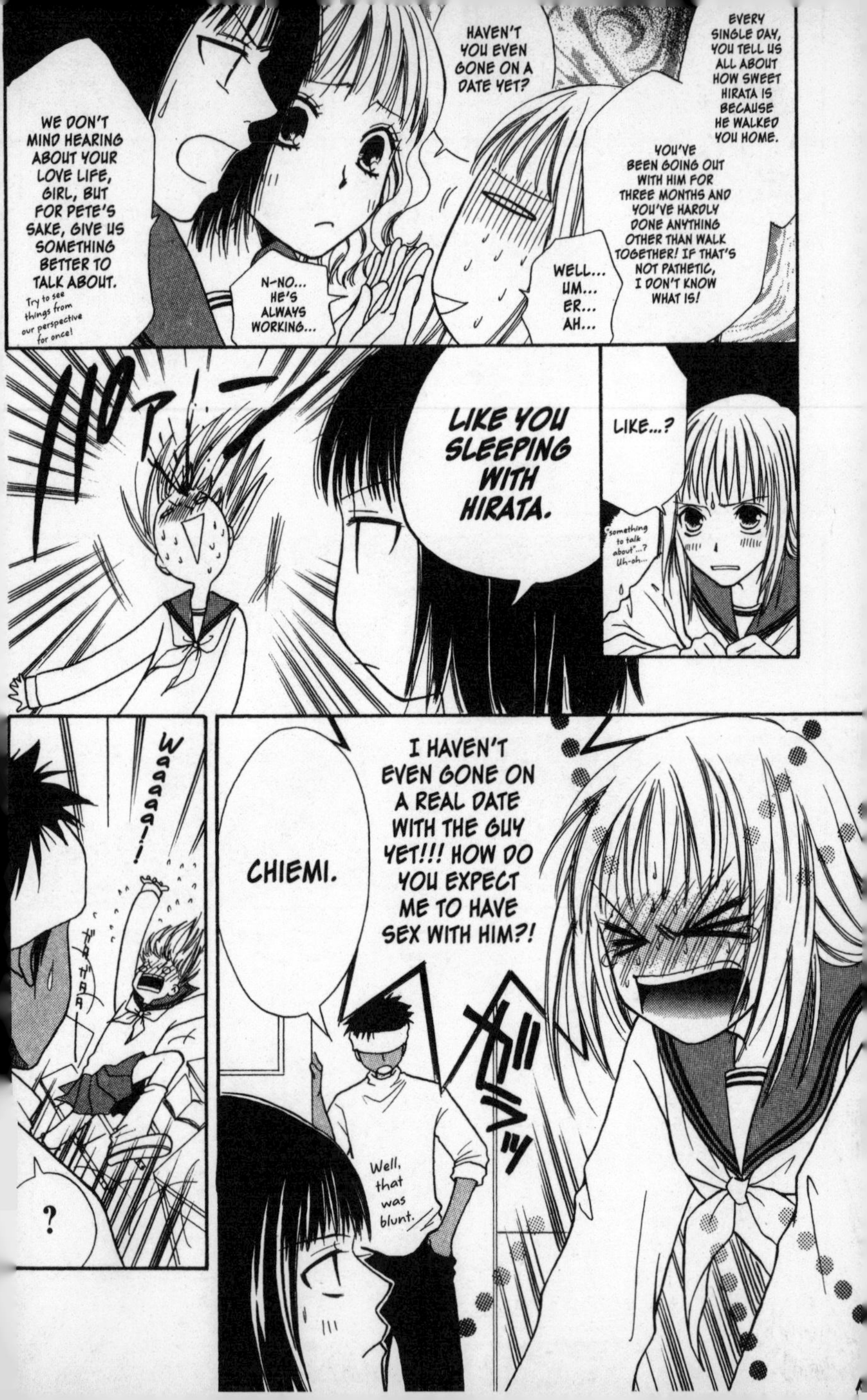
EVERY SINGLE DAY, YOU TELL US ALL ABOUT HOW SWEET HIRATA IS BECAUSE HE WALKED YOU HOME.
YOU'VE BEEN GOING OUT WITH HIM FOR THREE MONTHS AND YOU'VE HARDLY DONE ANYTHING OTHER THAN WALK TOGETHER! IF THAT'S NOT PATHETIC, I DON'T KNOW WHAT IS!
HAVEN'T YOU EVEN GONE ON A DATE YET?
WELL... UM... ER... AH...
N-NO... HE'S ALWAYS WORKING...
WE DON'T MIND HEARING ABOUT YOUR LOVE LIFE, GIRL, BUT FOR PETE'S SAKE, GIVE US SOMETHING BETTER TO TALK ABOUT.
Try to see things from our perspective for once!
LIKE...?
"something to talk about"...? Uh-oh...
LIKE YOU SLEEPING WITH HIRATA.
I HAVEN'T EVEN GONE ON A REAL DATE WITH THE GUY YET!!! HOW DO YOU EXPECT ME TO HAVE SEX WITH HIM?!
CHIEMI.
Well, that was blunt.
Waaaaa!!
?

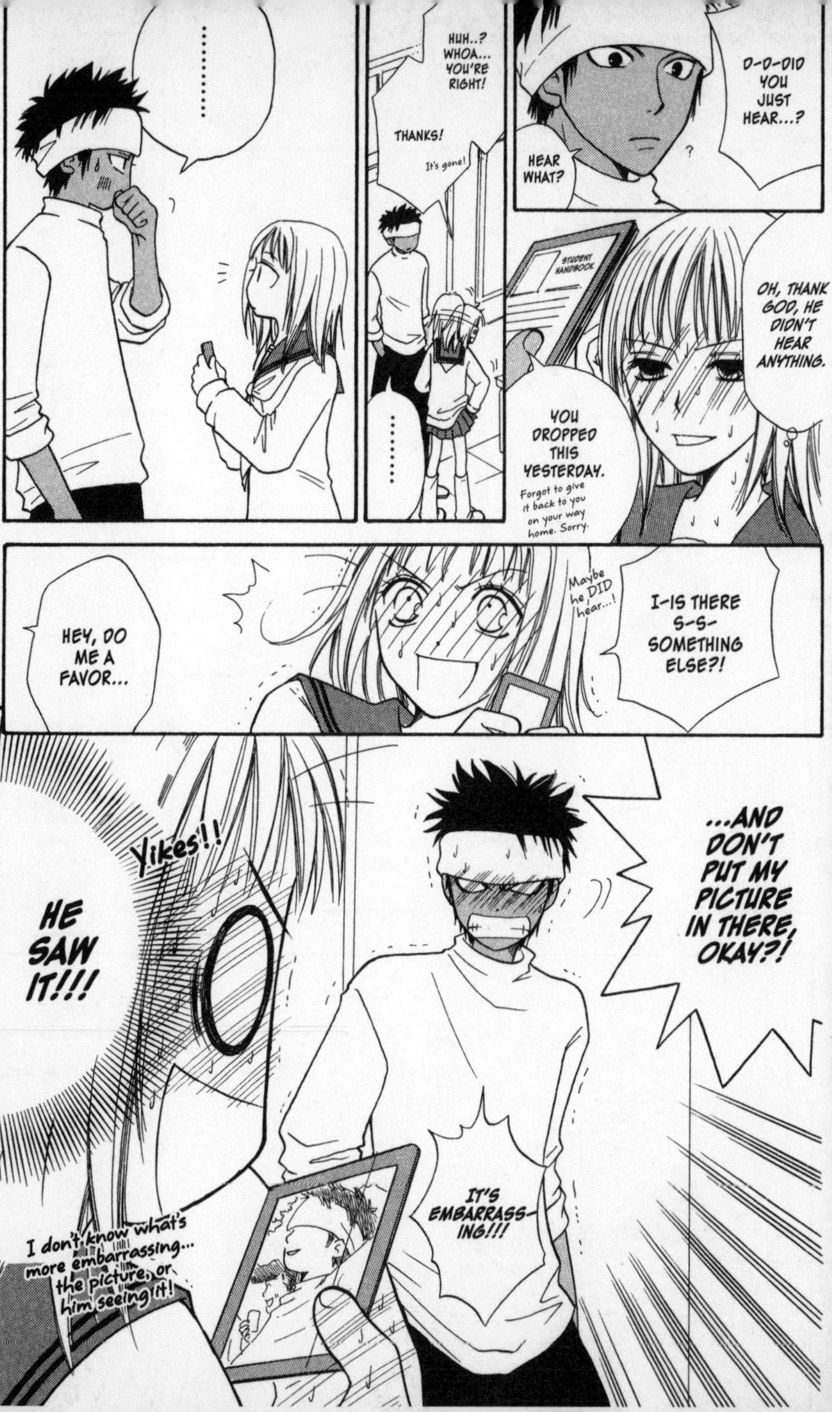
D-D-DID YOU JUST HEAR...?
HEAR WHAT?
OH, THANK GOD, HE DIDN'T HEAR ANYTHING.
STUDENT HANDBOOK
YOU DROPPED THIS YESTERDAY.
Forgot to give it back to you on your way home. Sorry.
HUH..? WHOA... YOU'RE RIGHT!
THANKS!
It's gone!
......
......
I-IS THERE S-S-SOMETHING ELSE?!
Maybe he DID hear...!
HEY, DO ME A FAVOR...
...AND DON'T PUT MY PICTURE IN THERE, OKAY?!
IT'S EMBARRASS-ING!!!
Yikes!!
HE SAW IT!!!
I don't know what's more embarrassing... the picture, or him seeing it!

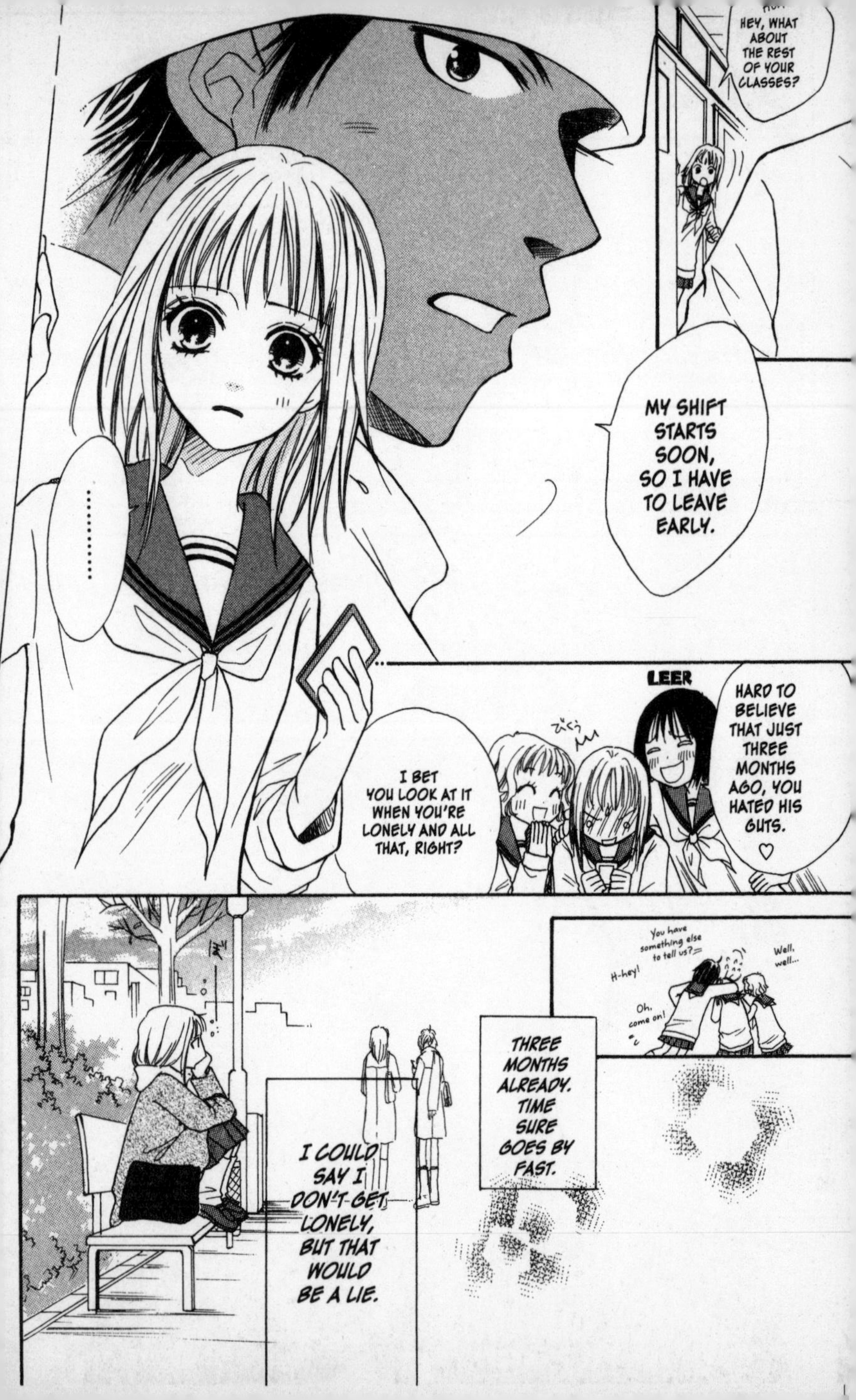
HEY, WHAT ABOUT THE REST OF YOUR CLASSES?
MY SHIFT STARTS SOON, SO I HAVE TO LEAVE EARLY.
......
LEER
HARD TO BELIEVE THAT JUST THREE MONTHS AGO, YOU HATED HIS GUTS. ♡
I BET YOU LOOK AT IT WHEN YOU'RE LONELY AND ALL THAT, RIGHT?
Well, well...
You have something else to tell us?
H-hey!
Oh, come on!
THREE MONTHS ALREADY. TIME SURE GOES BY FAST.
I COULD SAY I DON'T GET LONELY, BUT THAT WOULD BE A LIE.

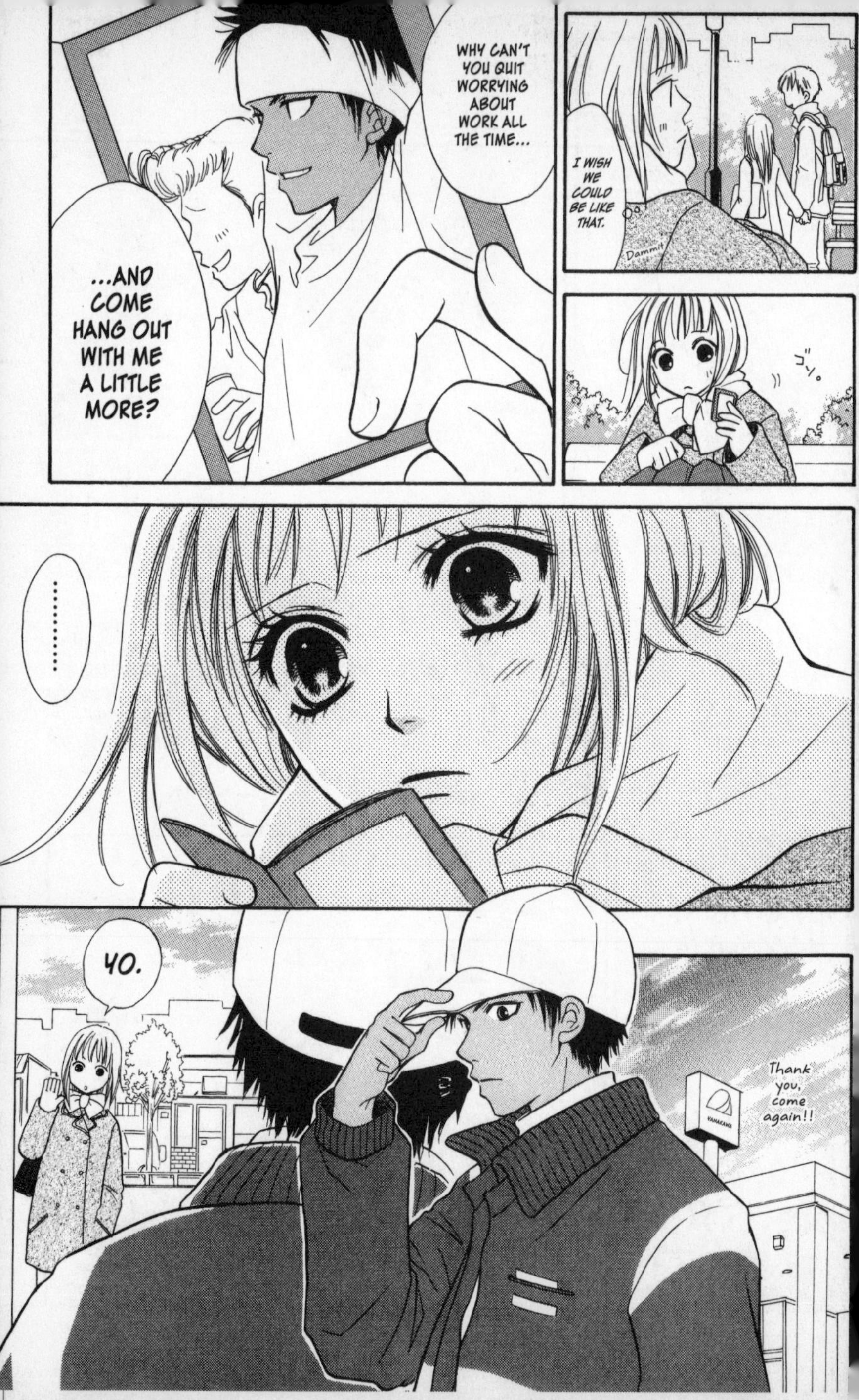
I WISH WE COULD BE LIKE THAT.
Dammit
ゴソ。
WHY CAN'T YOU QUIT WORRYING ABOUT WORK ALL THE TIME...
...AND COME HANG OUT WITH ME A LITTLE MORE?
......
YO.
Thank you, come again!!

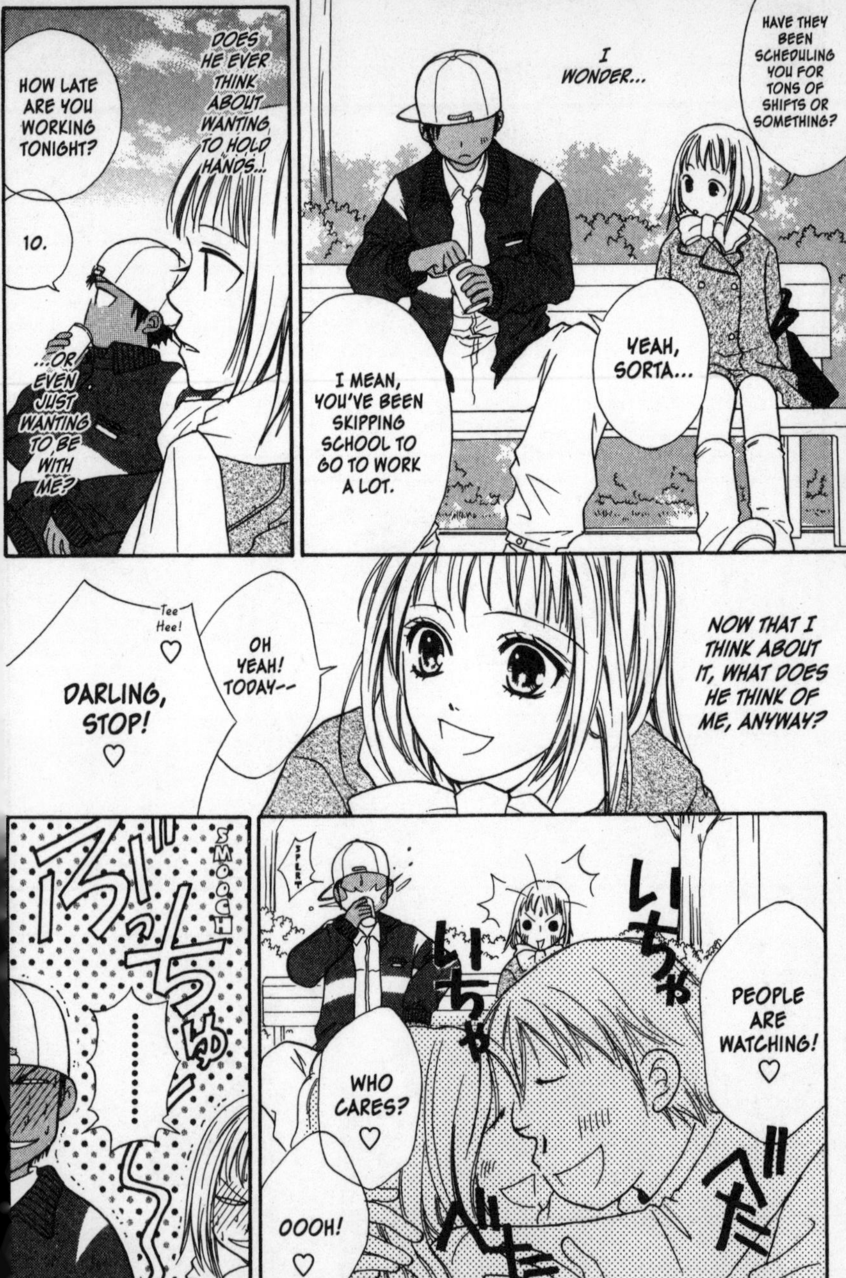
HAVE THEY BEEN SCHEDULING YOU FOR TONS OF SHIFTS OR SOMETHING?
I WONDER...
YEAH, SORTA...
I MEAN, YOU'VE BEEN SKIPPING SCHOOL TO GO TO WORK A LOT.
DOES HE EVER THINK ABOUT WANTING TO HOLD HANDS...
HOW LATE ARE YOU WORKING TONIGHT?
10.
...OR EVEN JUST WANTING TO BE WITH ME?
NOW THAT I THINK ABOUT IT, WHAT DOES HE THINK OF ME, ANYWAY?
OH YEAH! TODAY--
Tee Hee!
DARLING, STOP!
PEOPLE ARE WATCHING!
SPLRT
WHO CARES?
OOOH!
SMOOCH
......

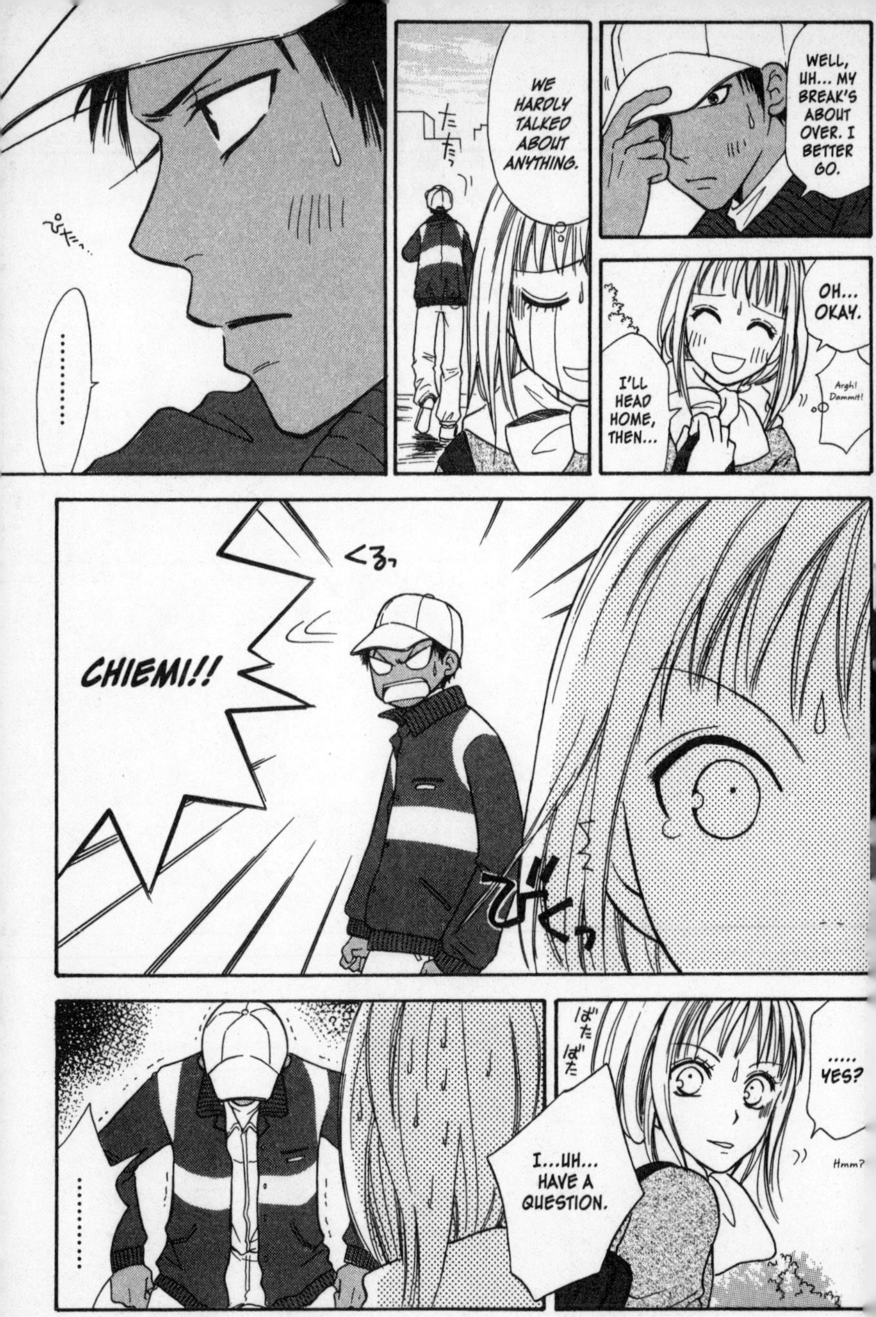
WELL, UH... MY BREAK'S ABOUT OVER. I BETTER GO.
OH... OKAY.
Argh! Dammit!
I'LL HEAD HOME, THEN...
WE HARDLY TALKED ABOUT ANYTHING.
....
くるっ
CHIEMI!!
.....YES?
Hmm?
ばたばた
I...UH... HAVE A QUESTION.
....

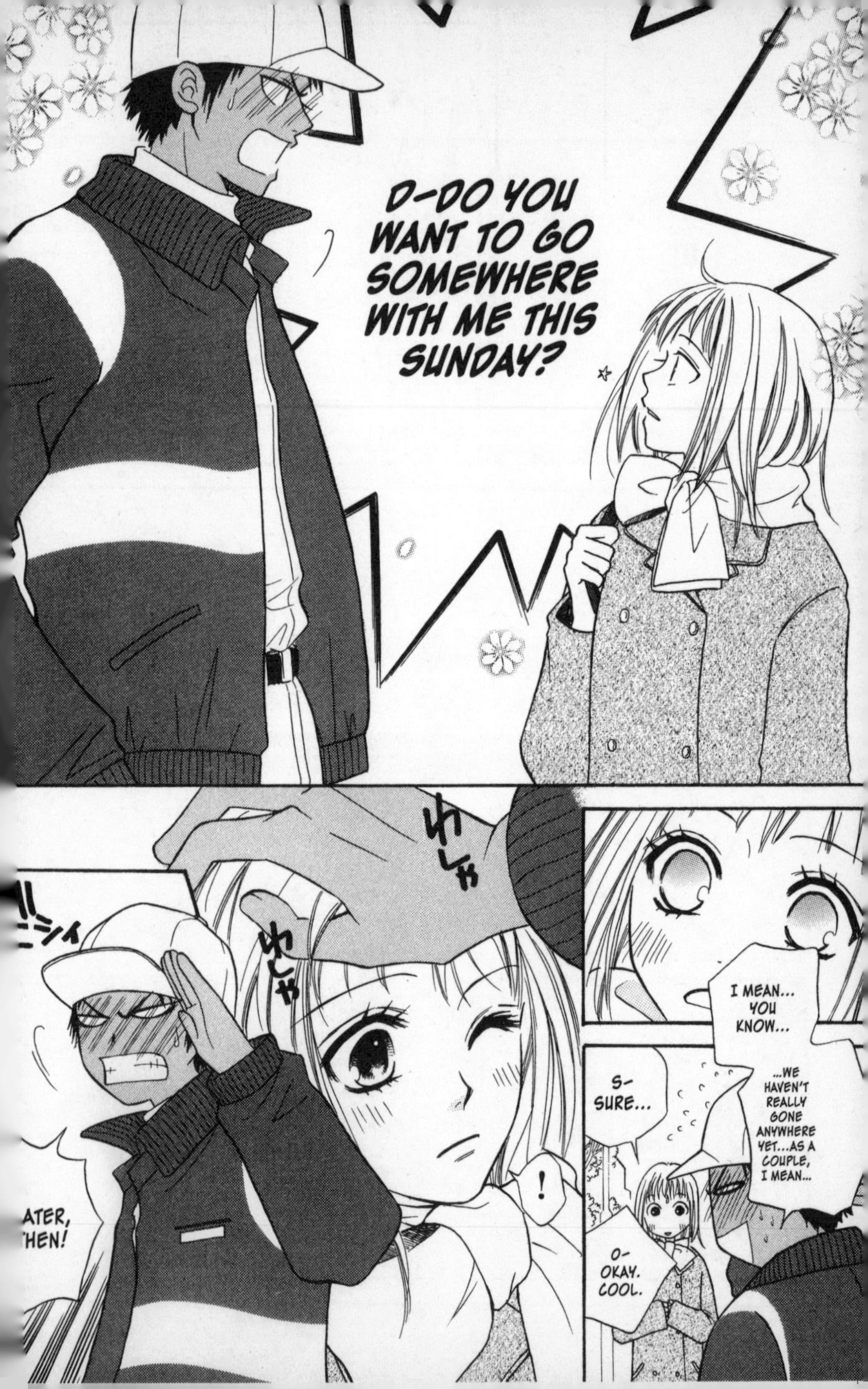
D-DO YOU WANT TO GO SOMEWHERE WITH ME THIS SUNDAY?
I MEAN... YOU KNOW...
...WE HAVEN'T REALLY GONE ANYWHERE YET...AS A COUPLE, I MEAN...
S-SURE...
O-OKAY. COOL.
わしゃ
わしゃ
!
ATER, THEN!

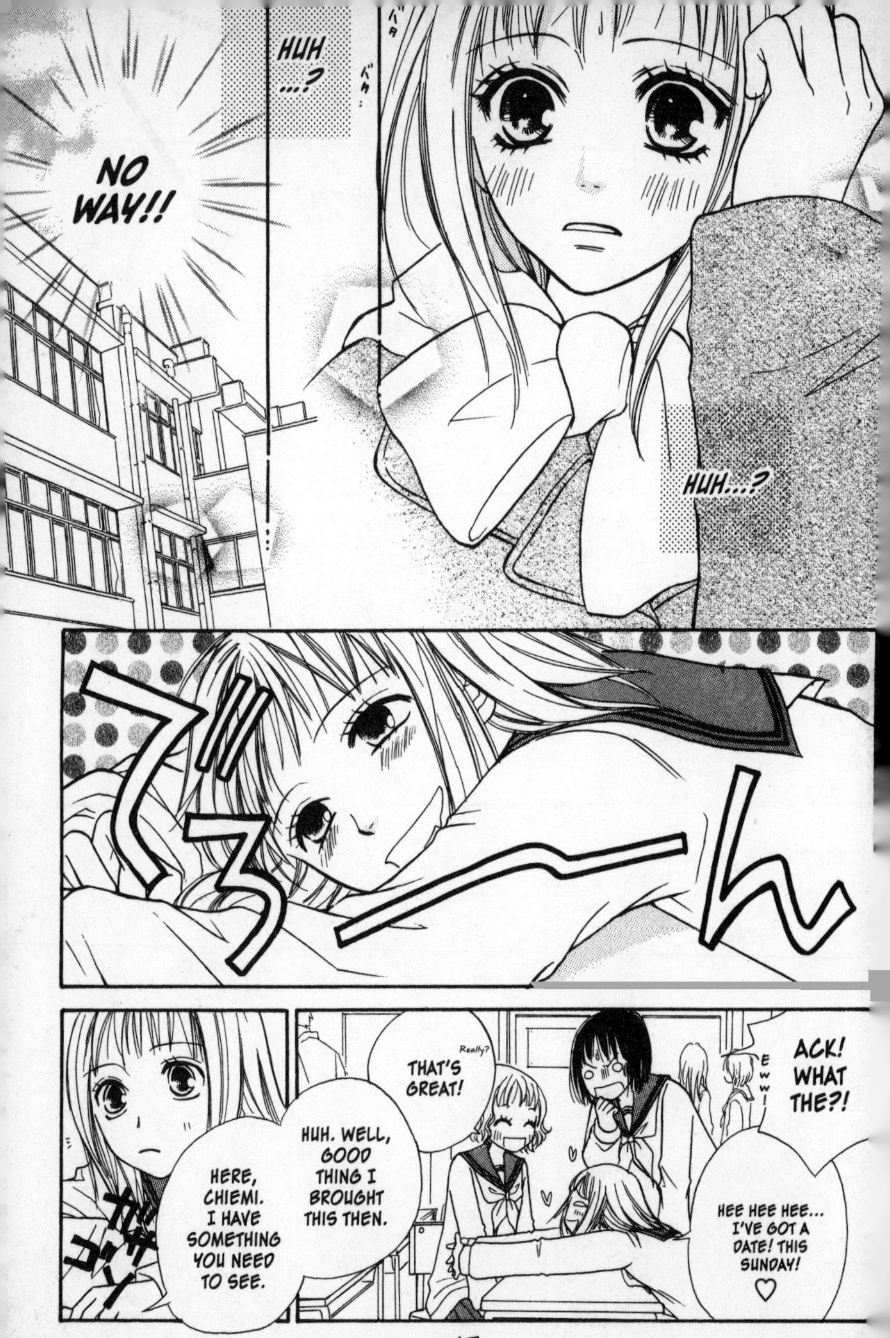
HUH...?
HUH ...?
NO WAY!!
でろ〜ん
ACK! WHAT THE?!
Eww!
HEE HEE HEE... I'VE GOT A DATE! THIS SUNDAY! ♡
Really?
THAT'S GREAT!
HUH. WELL, GOOD THING I BROUGHT THIS THEN.
HERE, CHIEMI. I HAVE SOMETHING YOU NEED TO SEE.

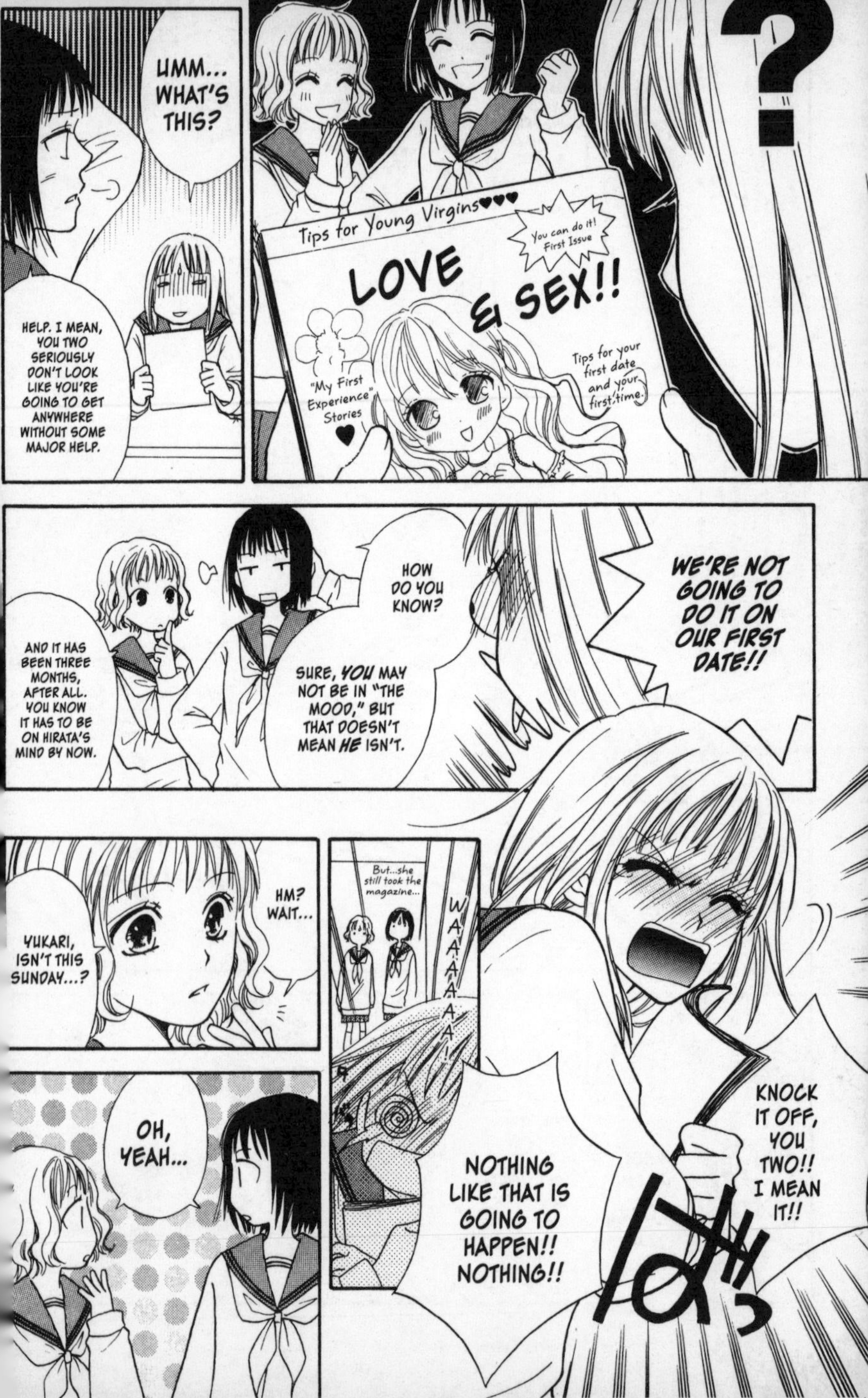
?
Tips for Young Virgins♥♥♥
You can do it! First Issue
LOVE & SEX!!
Tips for your first date and your first time.
"My First Experience" Stories
UMM... WHAT'S THIS?
HELP. I MEAN, YOU TWO SERIOUSLY DON'T LOOK LIKE YOU'RE GOING TO GET ANYWHERE WITHOUT SOME MAJOR HELP.
WE'RE NOT GOING TO DO IT ON OUR FIRST DATE!!
HOW DO YOU KNOW?
SURE, YOU MAY NOT BE IN "THE MOOD," BUT THAT DOESN'T MEAN HE ISN'T.
AND IT HAS BEEN THREE MONTHS, AFTER ALL. YOU KNOW IT HAS TO BE ON HIRATA'S MIND BY NOW.
KNOCK IT OFF, YOU TWO!! I MEAN IT!!
NOTHING LIKE THAT IS GOING TO HAPPEN!! NOTHING!!
But...she still took the magazine...
WAAAAAAA!
HM? WAIT...
YUKARI, ISN'T THIS SUNDAY...?
OH, YEAH...

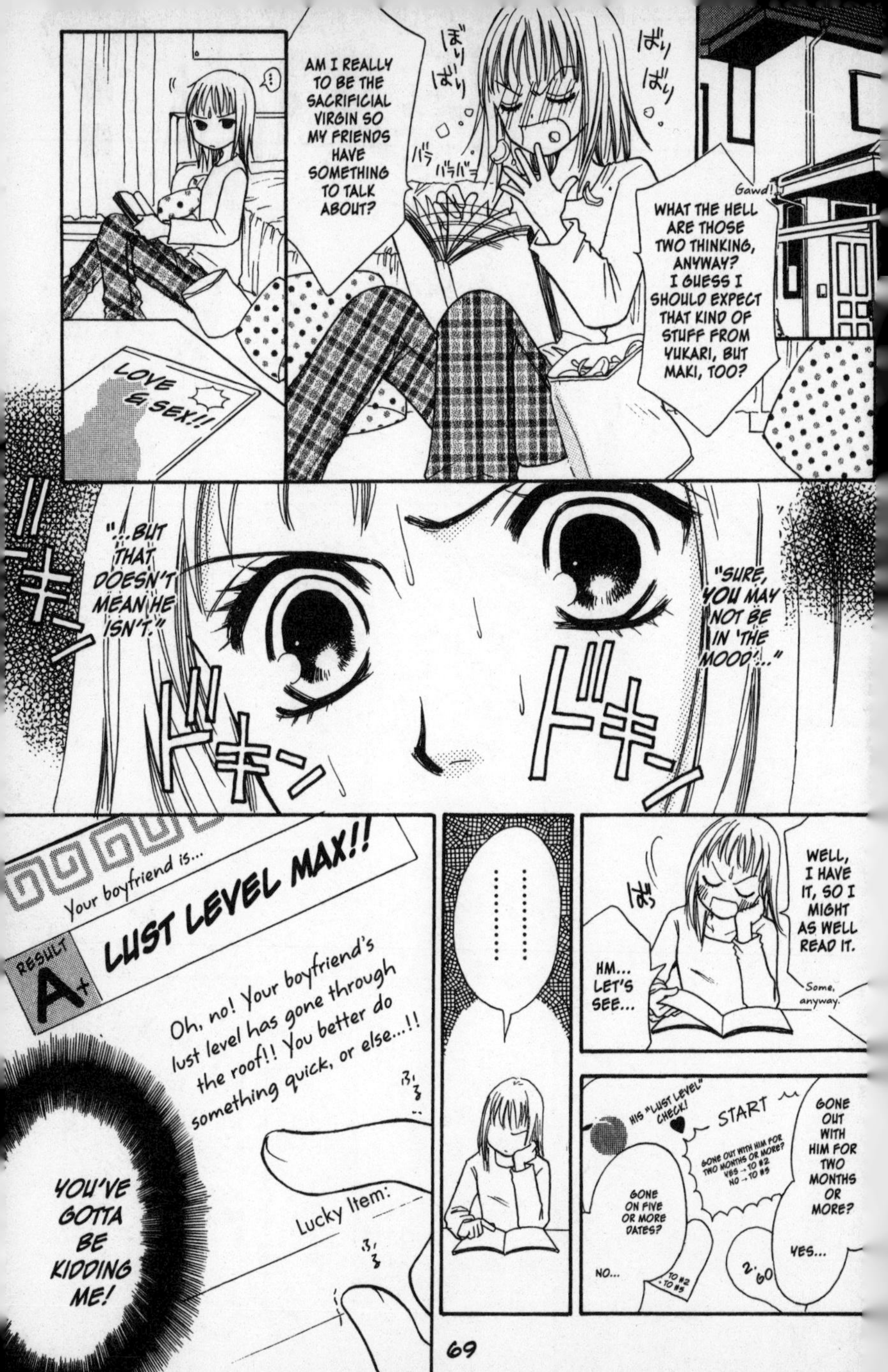
Gawd!
WHAT THE HELL ARE THOSE TWO THINKING, ANYWAY? I GUESS I SHOULD EXPECT THAT KIND OF STUFF FROM YUKARI, BUT MAKI, TOO?
ばりばり
ばりばり
バラバラバ
AM I REALLY TO BE THE SACRIFICIAL VIRGIN SO MY FRIENDS HAVE SOMETHING TO TALK ABOUT?
...
LOVE & SEX!!
"SURE, YOU MAY NOT BE IN 'THE MOOD'..."
ドキーン
"...BUT THAT DOESN'T MEAN HE ISN'T."
ドキーン
WELL, I HAVE IT, SO I MIGHT AS WELL READ IT.
Some, anyway.
ぱっ
HM... LET'S SEE...
GONE OUT WITH HIM FOR TWO MONTHS OR MORE?
YES...
2. GO
HIS "LUST LEVEL" CHECK!
START
GONE OUT WITH HIM FOR TWO MONTHS OR MORE? YES → TO #2 NO → TO #5
GONE ON FIVE OR MORE DATES?
NO...
......
Your boyfriend is...
LUST LEVEL MAX!!
RESULT A+
Oh, no! Your boyfriend's lust level has gone through the roof!! You better do something quick, or else...!!
Lucky Item:
YOU'VE GOTTA BE KIDDING ME!

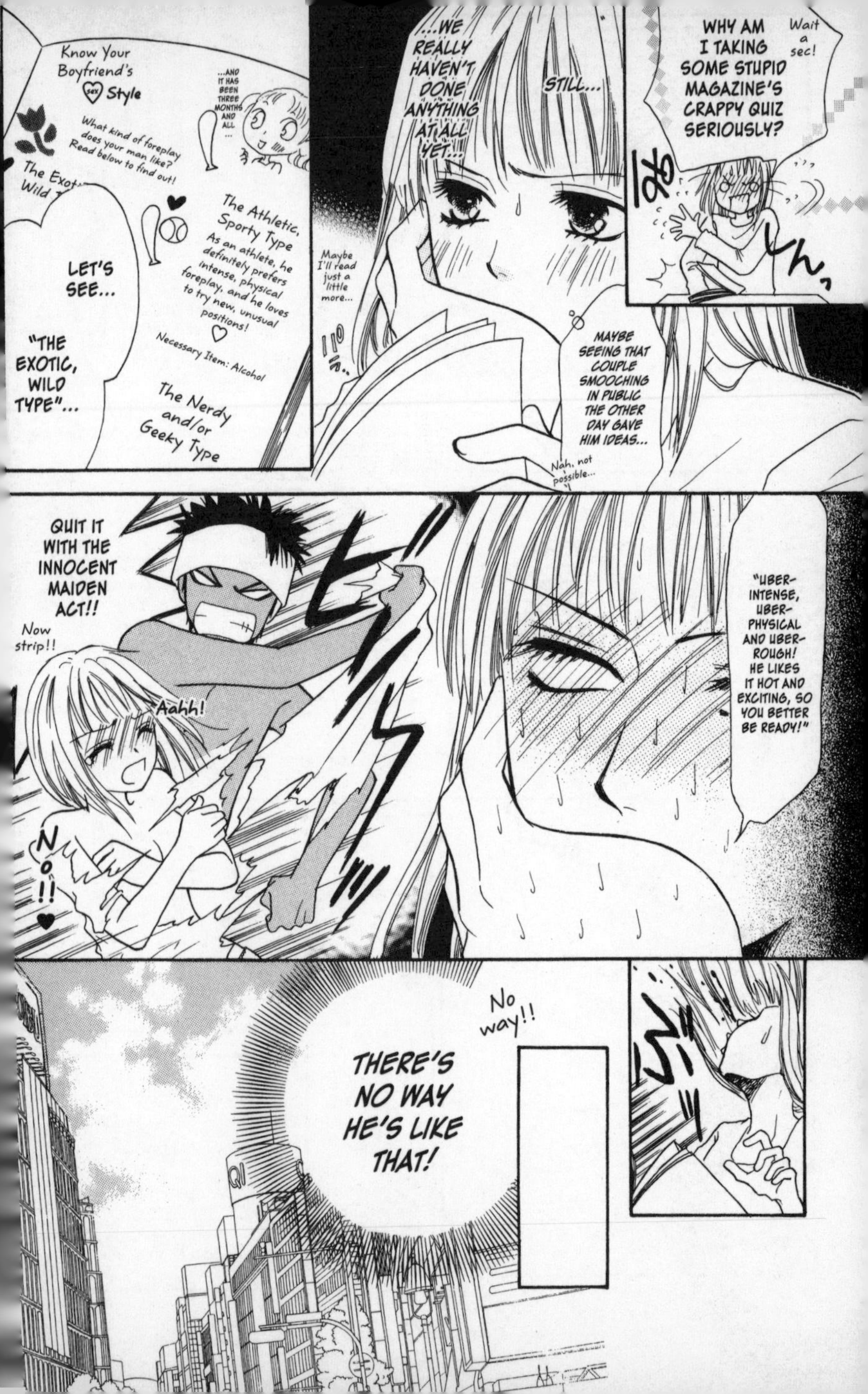

WHY AM I TAKING SOME STUPID MAGAZINE'S CRAPPY QUIZ SERIOUSLY?
Wait a sec!
STILL...
...WE REALLY HAVEN'T DONE ANYTHING AT ALL YET...
MAYBE SEEING THAT COUPLE SMOOCHING IN PUBLIC THE OTHER DAY GAVE HIM IDEAS...
Nah, not possible...
Maybe I'll read just a little more...
Know Your Boyfriend's sex Style
...AND IT HAS BEEN THREE MONTHS AND ALL...
What kind of foreplay does your man like? Read below to find out!
The Athletic, Sporty Type
As an athlete, he definitely prefers intense, physical foreplay, and he loves to try new, unusual positions!
Necessary Item: Alcohol
The Nerdy and/or Geeky Type
LET'S SEE...
"THE EXOTIC, WILD TYPE"...
"UBER-INTENSE, UBER-PHYSICAL AND UBER-ROUGH! HE LIKES IT HOT AND EXCITING, SO YOU BETTER BE READY!"
QUIT IT WITH THE INNOCENT MAIDEN ACT!!
Now strip!!
Aahh!
No!!
No way!!
THERE'S NO WAY HE'S LIKE THAT!

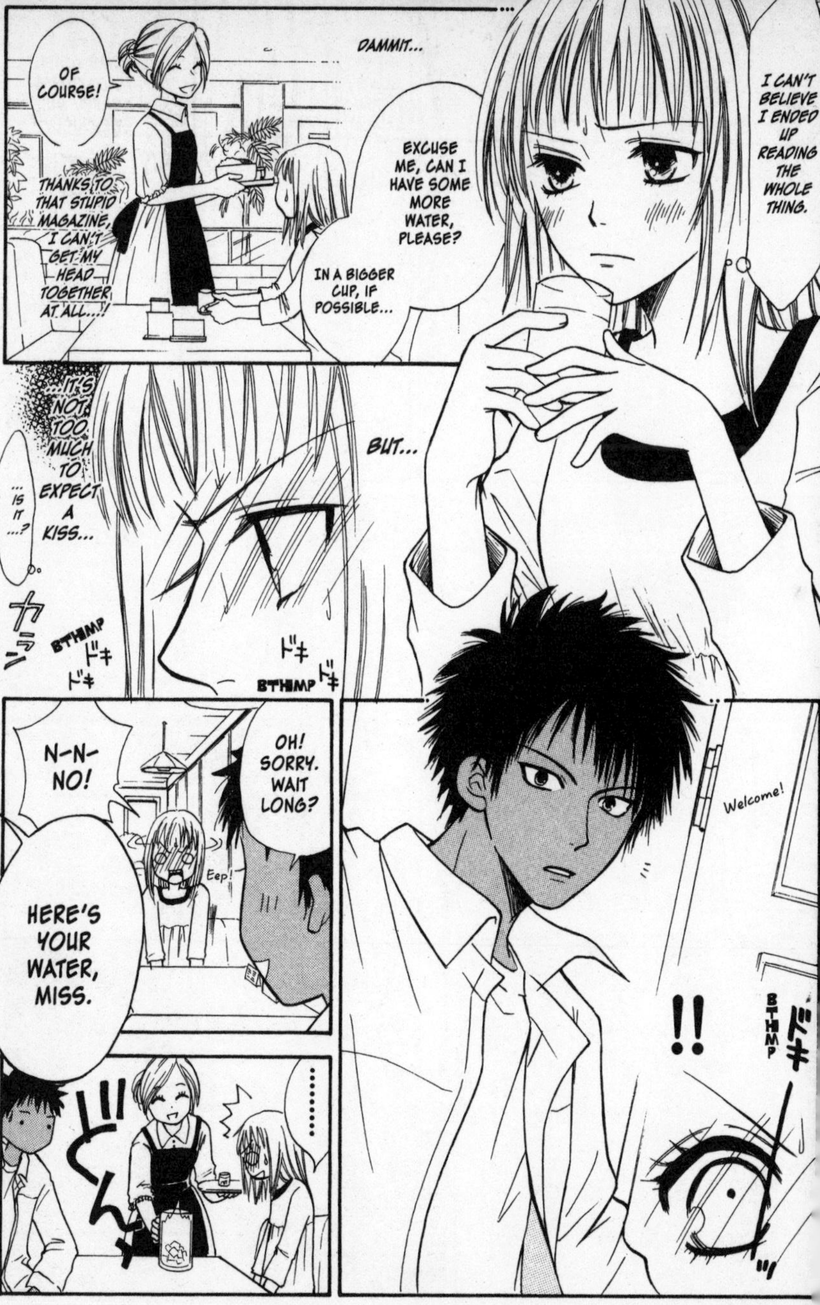
I CAN'T BELIEVE I ENDED UP READING THE WHOLE THING.
DAMMIT...
EXCUSE ME, CAN I HAVE SOME MORE WATER, PLEASE?
IN A BIGGER CUP, IF POSSIBLE...
OF COURSE!
THANKS TO THAT STUPID MAGAZINE, I CAN'T GET MY HEAD TOGETHER AT ALL...!
BUT...
...IT'S NOT TOO MUCH TO EXPECT A KISS...
...IS IT...?
BTHMP ドキ
ドキ
ドキ
BTHMP ドキ
カラン
カラン
Welcome!
!!
BTHMP ドキ
OH! SORRY. WAIT LONG?
N-N-NO!
Eep!
HERE'S YOUR WATER, MISS.
....

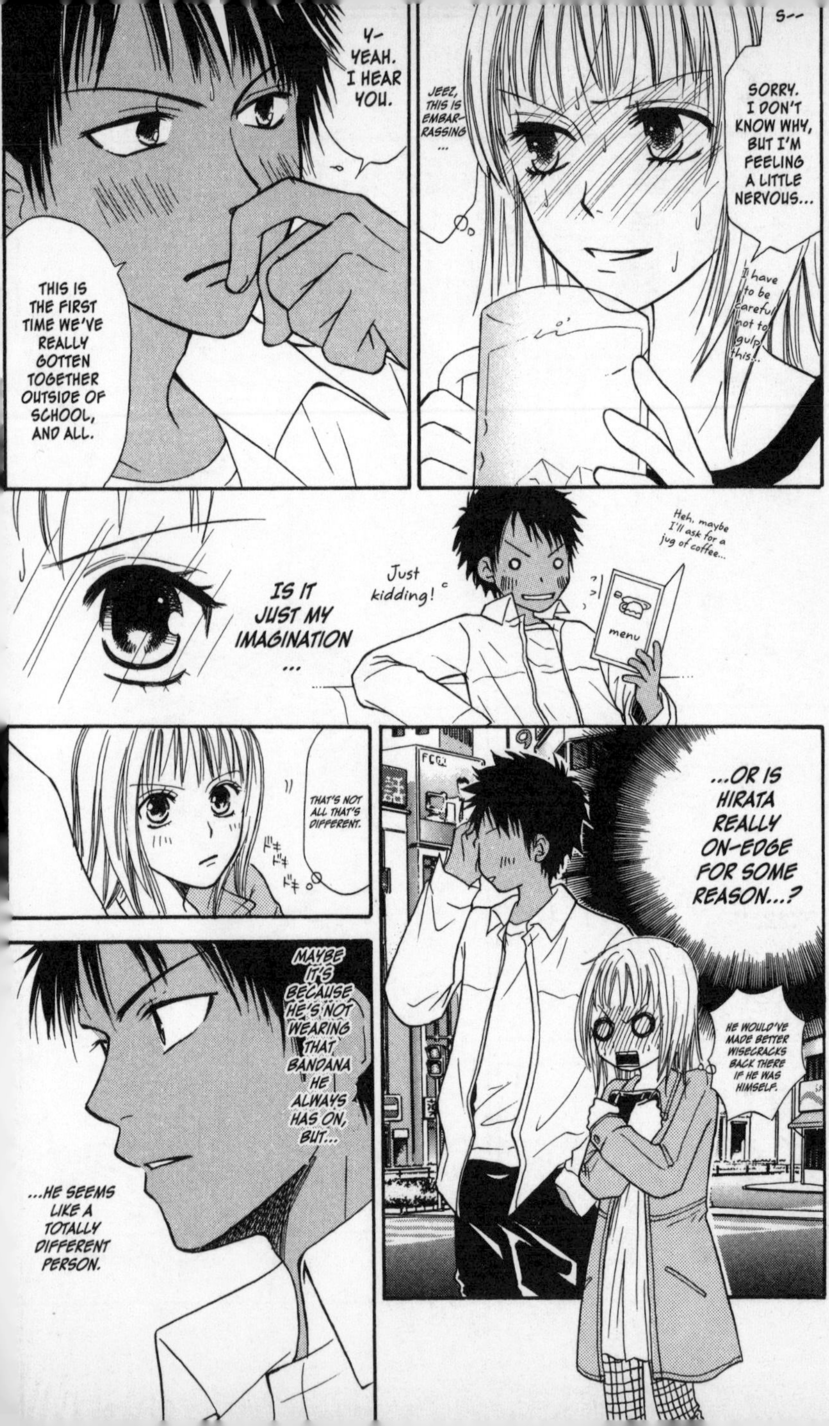
S--
SORRY. I DON'T KNOW WHY, BUT I'M FEELING A LITTLE NERVOUS...
JEEZ, THIS IS EMBARRASSING...
I have to be careful not to gulp this...
Y-YEAH. I HEAR YOU.
THIS IS THE FIRST TIME WE'VE REALLY GOTTEN TOGETHER OUTSIDE OF SCHOOL, AND ALL.
Heh, maybe I'll ask for a jug of coffee...
Just kidding!
menu
IS IT JUST MY IMAGINATION...
...OR IS HIRATA REALLY ON-EDGE FOR SOME REASON...?
HE WOULD'VE MADE BETTER WISECRACKS BACK THERE IF HE WAS HIMSELF.
THAT'S NOT ALL THAT'S DIFFERENT.
ドキドキドキ
MAYBE IT'S BECAUSE HE'S NOT WEARING THAT BANDANA HE ALWAYS HAS ON, BUT...
...HE SEEMS LIKE A TOTALLY DIFFERENT PERSON.

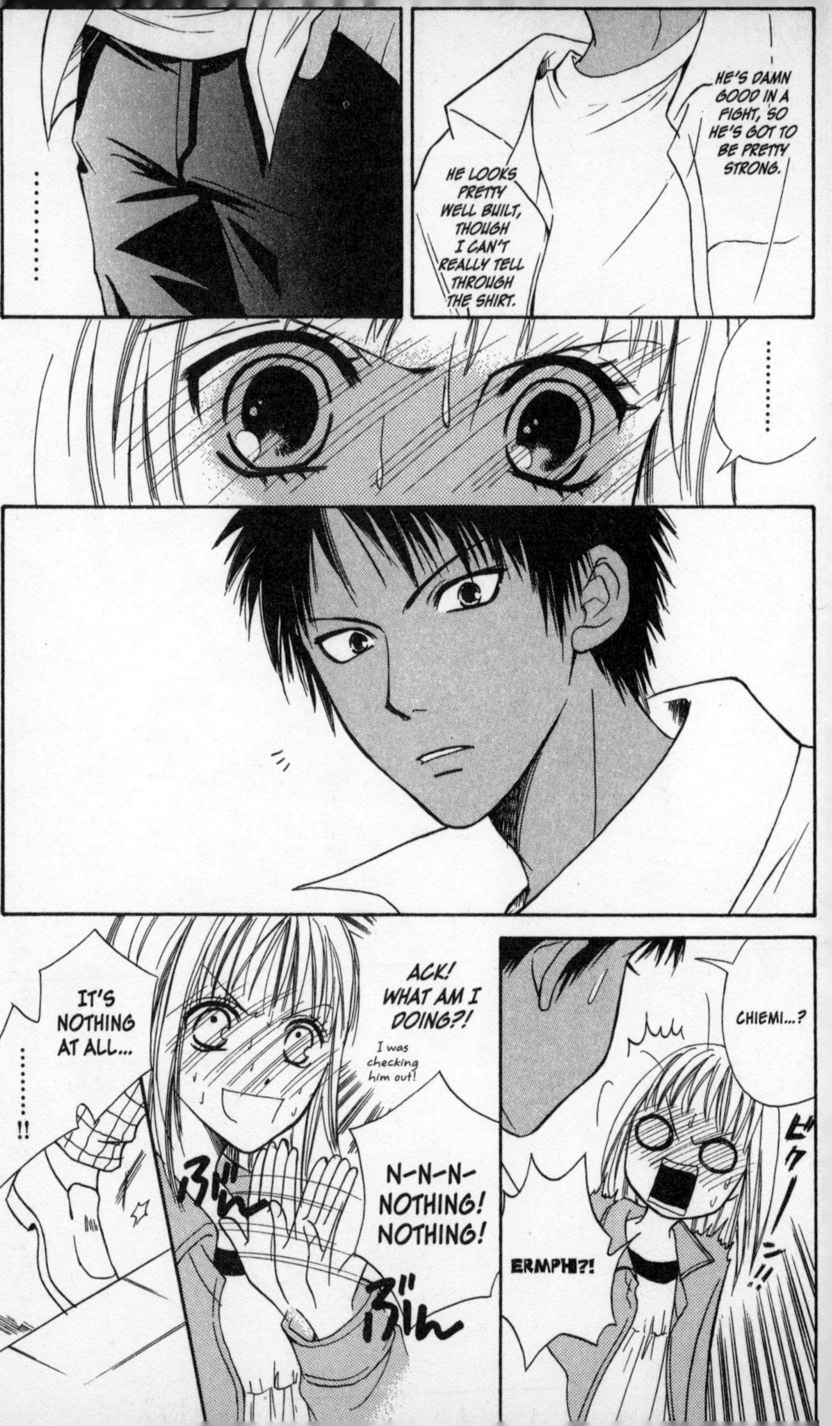
HE'S DAMN GOOD IN A FIGHT, SO HE'S GOT TO BE PRETTY STRONG.
HE LOOKS PRETTY WELL BUILT, THOUGH I CAN'T REALLY TELL THROUGH THE SHIRT.
......
......
CHIEMI...?
ERMPH?!
ACK! WHAT AM I DOING?!
I was checking him out!
N-N-N-NOTHING! NOTHING!
ぶん
ぶん
IT'S NOTHING AT ALL...
......!!

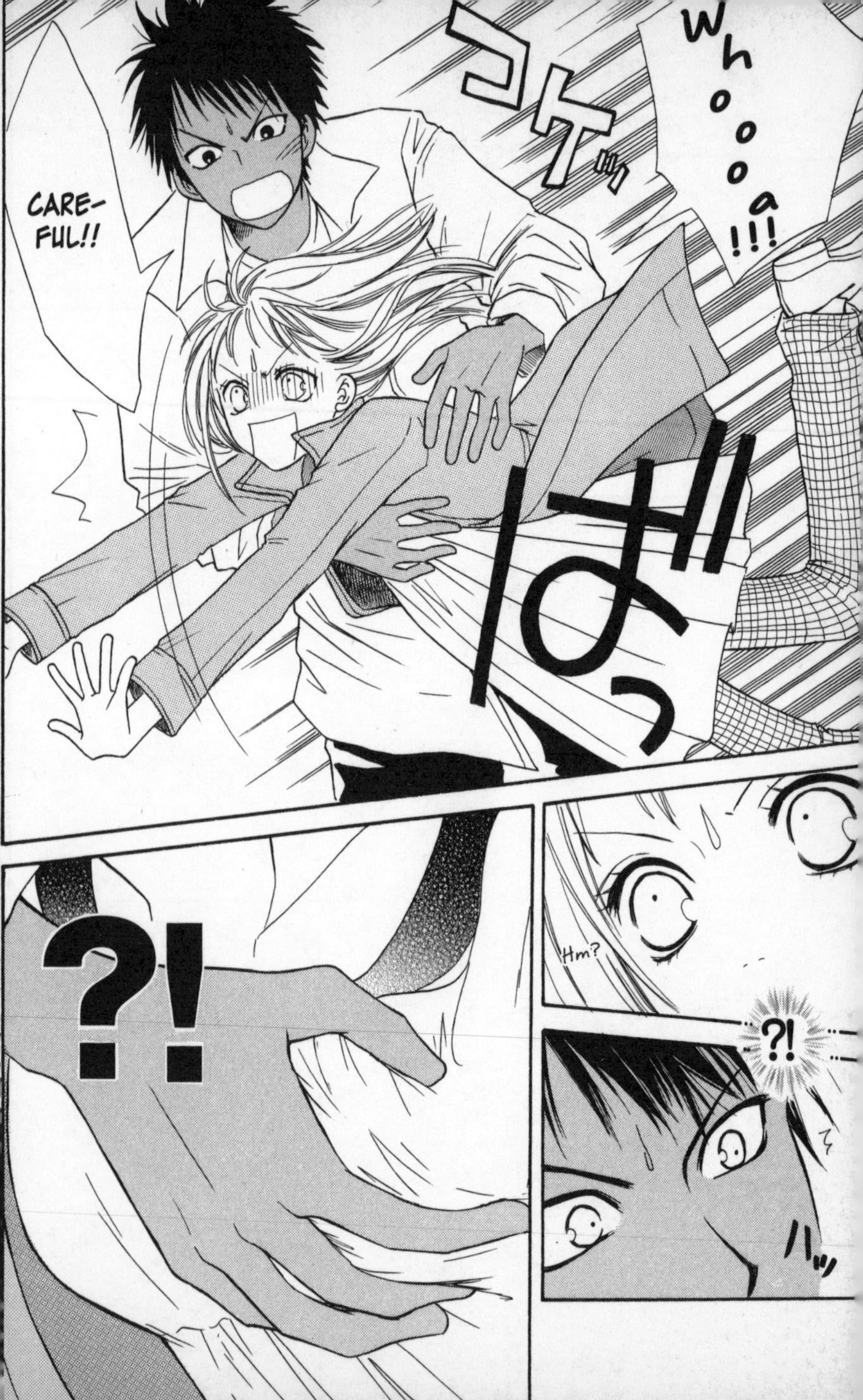
Whoooa!!!
コケッ
CARE-FUL!!
ばっ
Hm?
?!
ハッ
?!

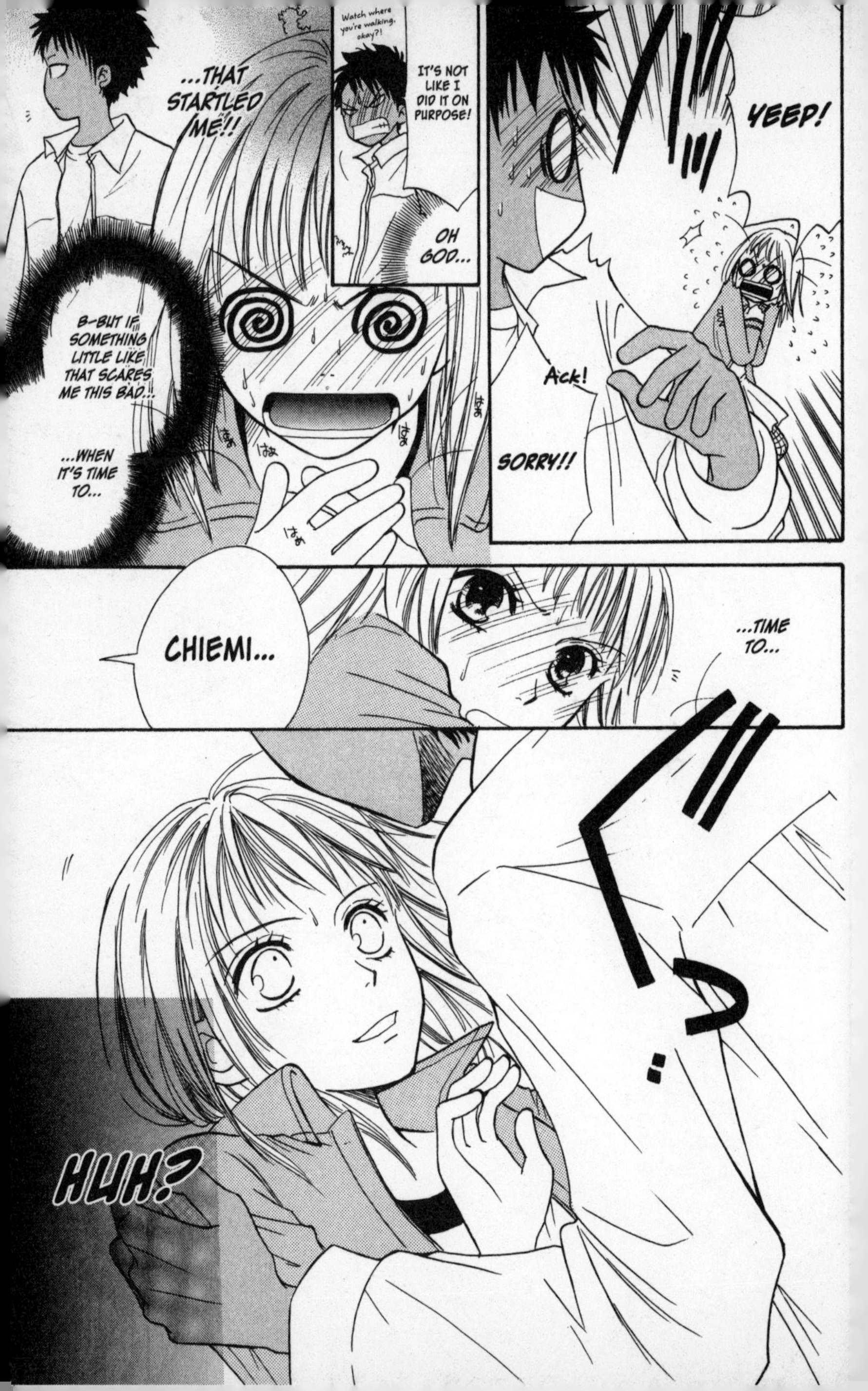
YEEP!
Ack!
SORRY!!
Watch where you're walking, okay?!
IT'S NOT LIKE I DID IT ON PURPOSE!
OH GOD...
...THAT STARTLED ME!!
B-BUT IF SOMETHING LITTLE LIKE THAT SCARES ME THIS BAD...
...WHEN IT'S TIME TO...
...TIME TO...
CHIEMI...
HUH?

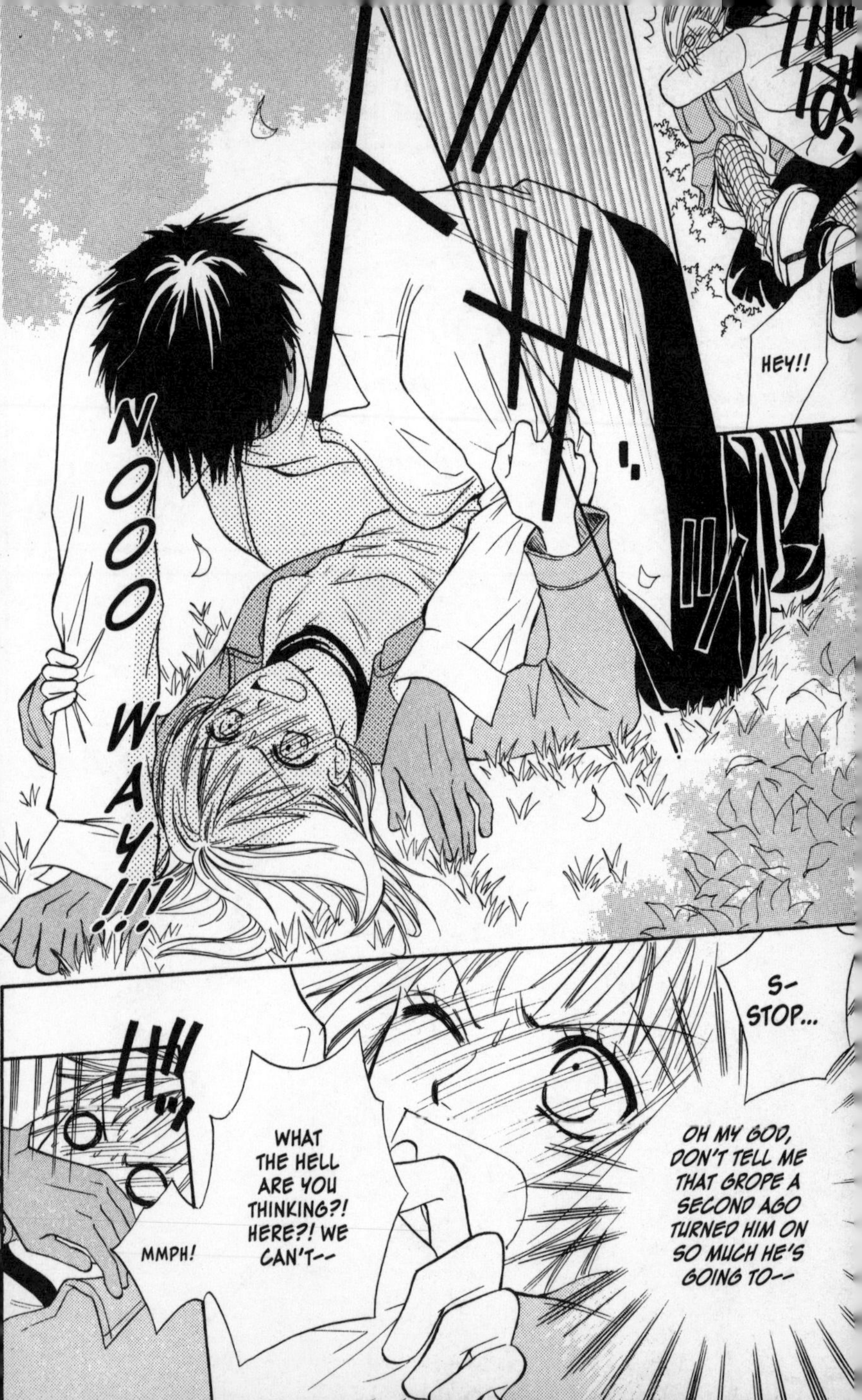
HEY!!
NOOOO WAY!!!
S-STOP...
OH MY GOD, DON'T TELL ME THAT GROPE A SECOND AGO TURNED HIM ON SO MUCH HE'S GOING TO--
WHAT THE HELL ARE YOU THINKING?! HERE?! WE CAN'T--
MMPH!

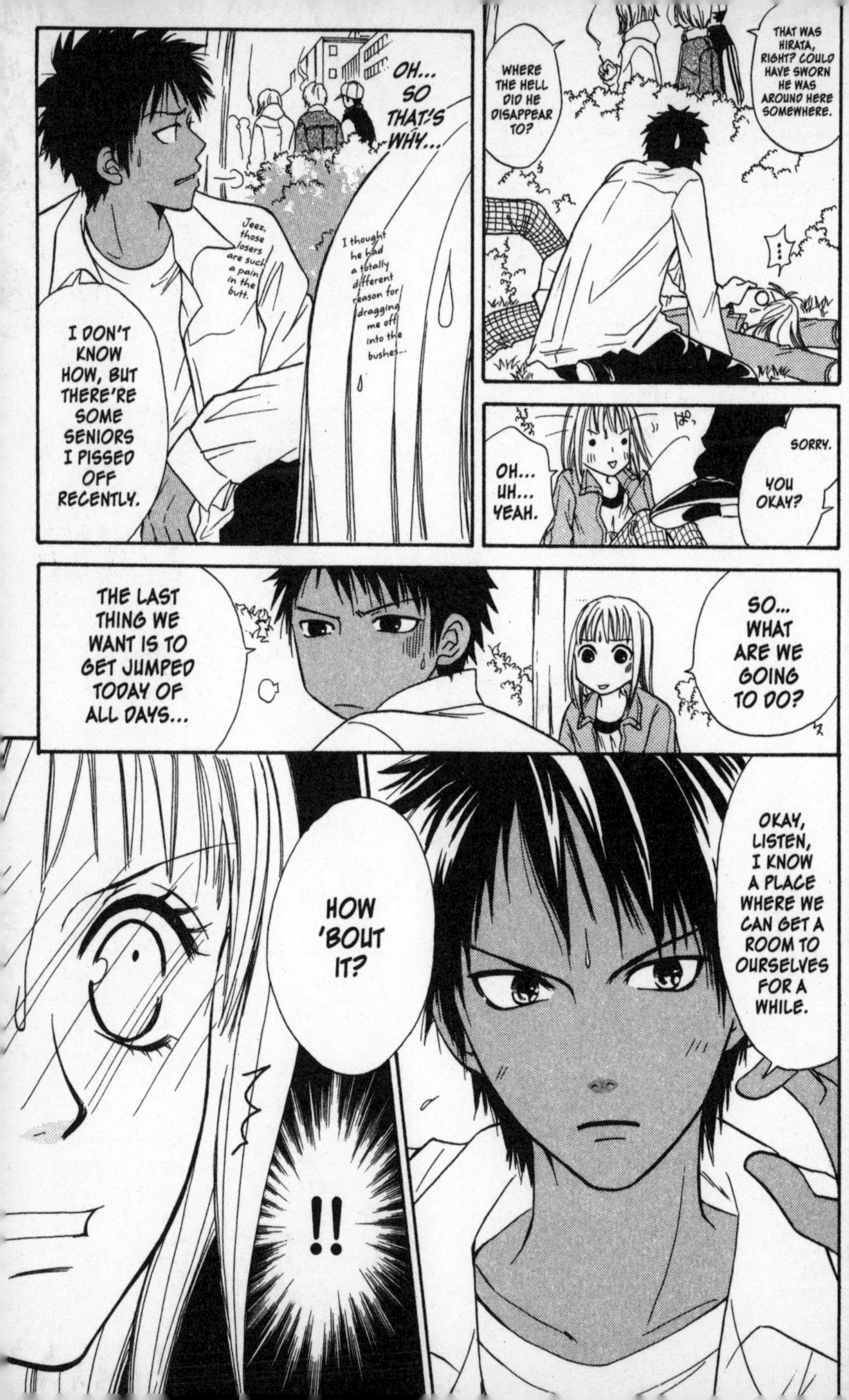
THAT WAS HIRATA, RIGHT? COULD HAVE SWORN HE WAS AROUND HERE SOMEWHERE.
WHERE THE HELL DID HE DISAPPEAR TO?
...
SORRY.
YOU OKAY?
OH... UH... YEAH.
OH... SO THAT'S WHY...
I thought he had a totally different reason for dragging me off into the bushes...
Jeez, those losers are such a pain in the butt.
I DON'T KNOW HOW, BUT THERE'RE SOME SENIORS I PISSED OFF RECENTLY.
SO... WHAT ARE WE GOING TO DO?
THE LAST THING WE WANT IS TO GET JUMPED TODAY OF ALL DAYS...
OKAY, LISTEN, I KNOW A PLACE WHERE WE CAN GET A ROOM TO OURSELVES FOR A WHILE.
HOW 'BOUT IT?
!!

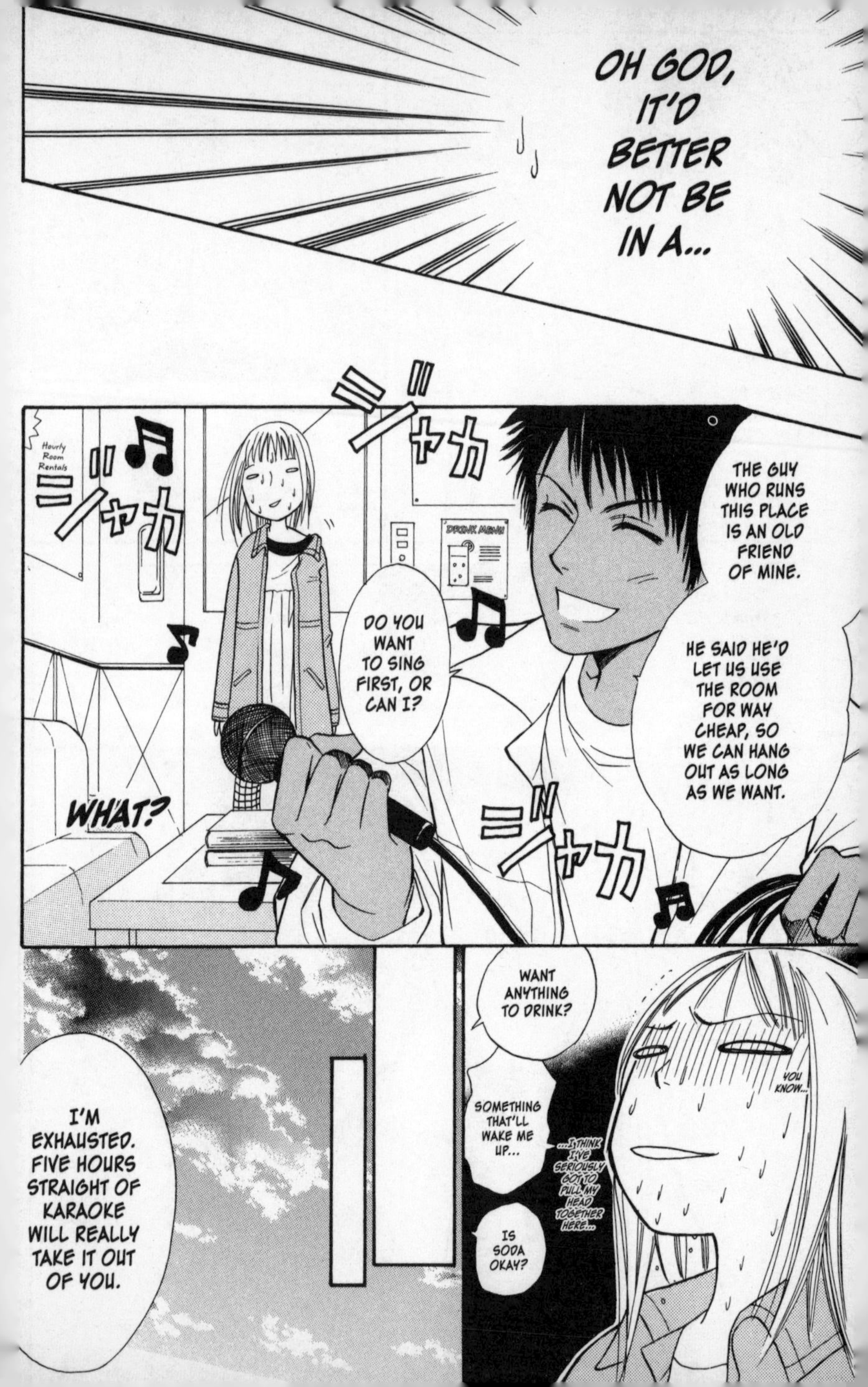
OH GOD, IT'D BETTER NOT BE IN A...
THE GUY WHO RUNS THIS PLACE IS AN OLD FRIEND OF MINE.
HE SAID HE'D LET US USE THE ROOM FOR WAY CHEAP, SO WE CAN HANG OUT AS LONG AS WE WANT.
ジャカ
ジャカ
DRINK MENU
DO YOU WANT TO SING FIRST, OR CAN I?
Hourly Room Rentals
ジャカ
WHAT?
YOU KNOW...
WANT ANYTHING TO DRINK?
SOMETHING THAT'LL WAKE ME UP...
...I THINK I'VE SERIOUSLY GOT TO PULL MY HEAD TOGETHER HERE...
IS SODA OKAY?
I'M EXHAUSTED. FIVE HOURS STRAIGHT OF KARAOKE WILL REALLY TAKE IT OUT OF YOU.

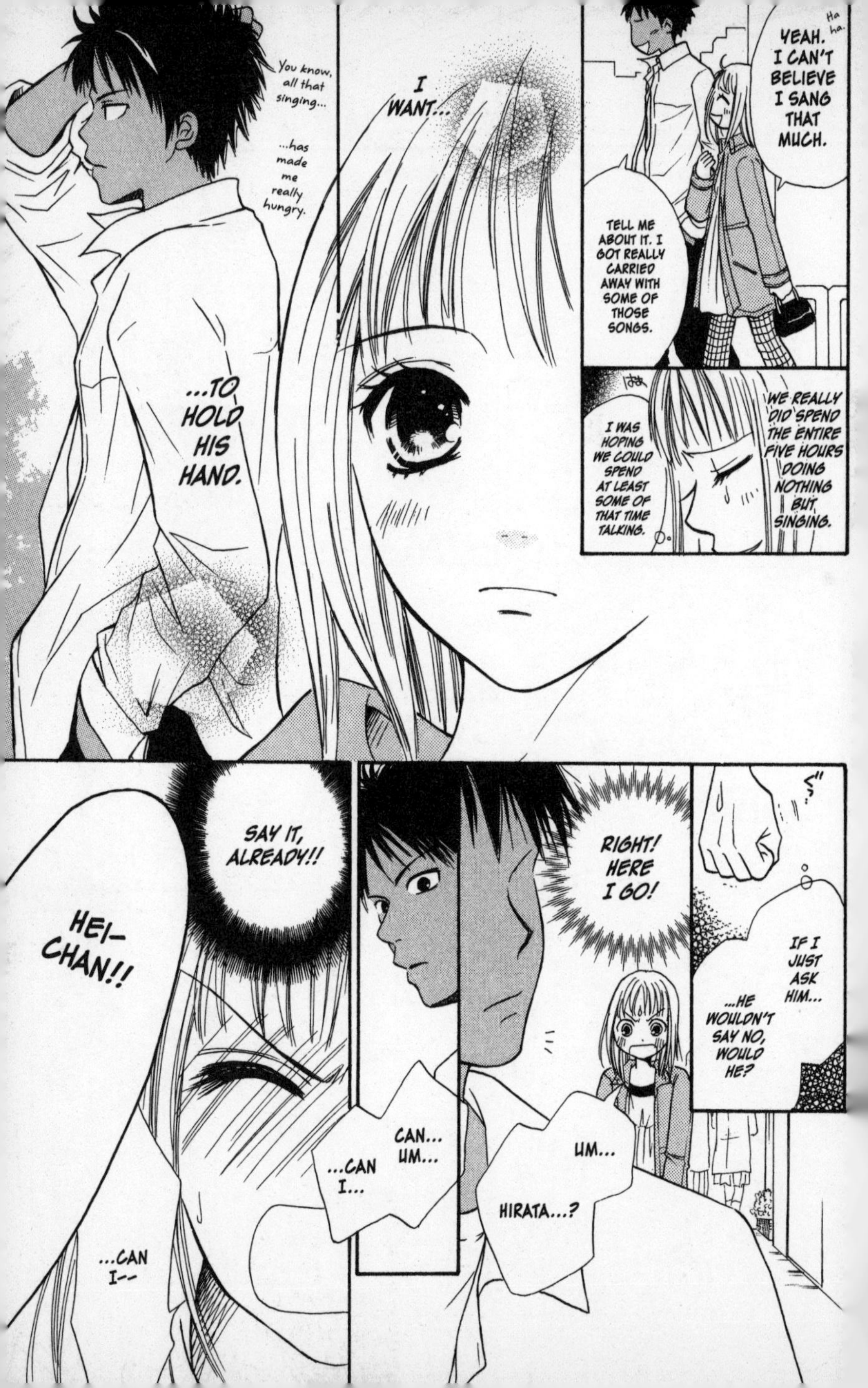
YEAH. I CAN'T BELIEVE I SANG THAT MUCH.
Ha ha.
TELL ME ABOUT IT. I GOT REALLY CARRIED AWAY WITH SOME OF THOSE SONGS.
はぁ
WE REALLY DID SPEND THE ENTIRE FIVE HOURS DOING NOTHING BUT SINGING.
I WAS HOPING WE COULD SPEND AT LEAST SOME OF THAT TIME TALKING.
I WANT...
...TO HOLD HIS HAND.
You know, all that singing...
...has made me really hungry.
IF I JUST ASK HIM...
...HE WOULDN'T SAY NO, WOULD HE?
RIGHT! HERE I GO!
UM...
HIRATA...?
CAN... UM...
...CAN I...
SAY IT, ALREADY!!
HEI-CHAN!!
...CAN I--

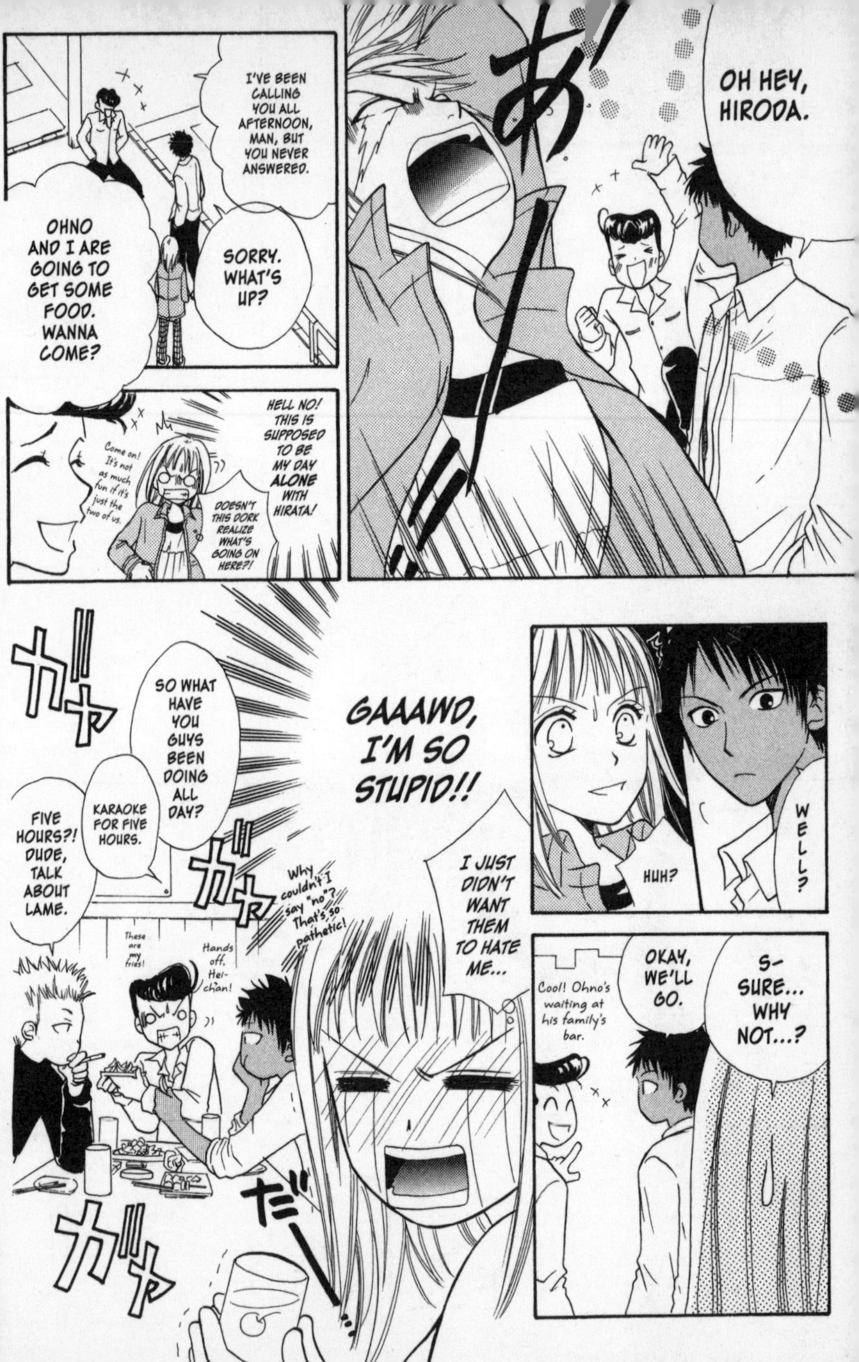
あ!
OH HEY, HIRODA.
I'VE BEEN CALLING YOU ALL AFTERNOON, MAN, BUT YOU NEVER ANSWERED.
SORRY. WHAT'S UP?
OHNO AND I ARE GOING TO GET SOME FOOD. WANNA COME?
HELL NO! THIS IS SUPPOSED TO BE MY DAY ALONE WITH HIRATA!
DOESN'T THIS DORK REALIZE WHAT'S GOING ON HERE?!
Come on! It's not as much fun if it's just the two of us.
WELL?
HUH?
S-SURE... WHY NOT...?
OKAY, WE'LL GO.
Cool! Ohno's waiting at his family's bar.
GAAAWD, I'M SO STUPID!!
I JUST DIDN'T WANT THEM TO HATE ME...
SO WHAT HAVE YOU GUYS BEEN DOING ALL DAY?
KARAOKE FOR FIVE HOURS.
FIVE HOURS?! DUDE, TALK ABOUT LAME.
Why couldn't I say "no"? That's so pathetic!
Hands off, Hei-chan!
These are my fries!
ガヤ
ガヤ
ガヤ
だー

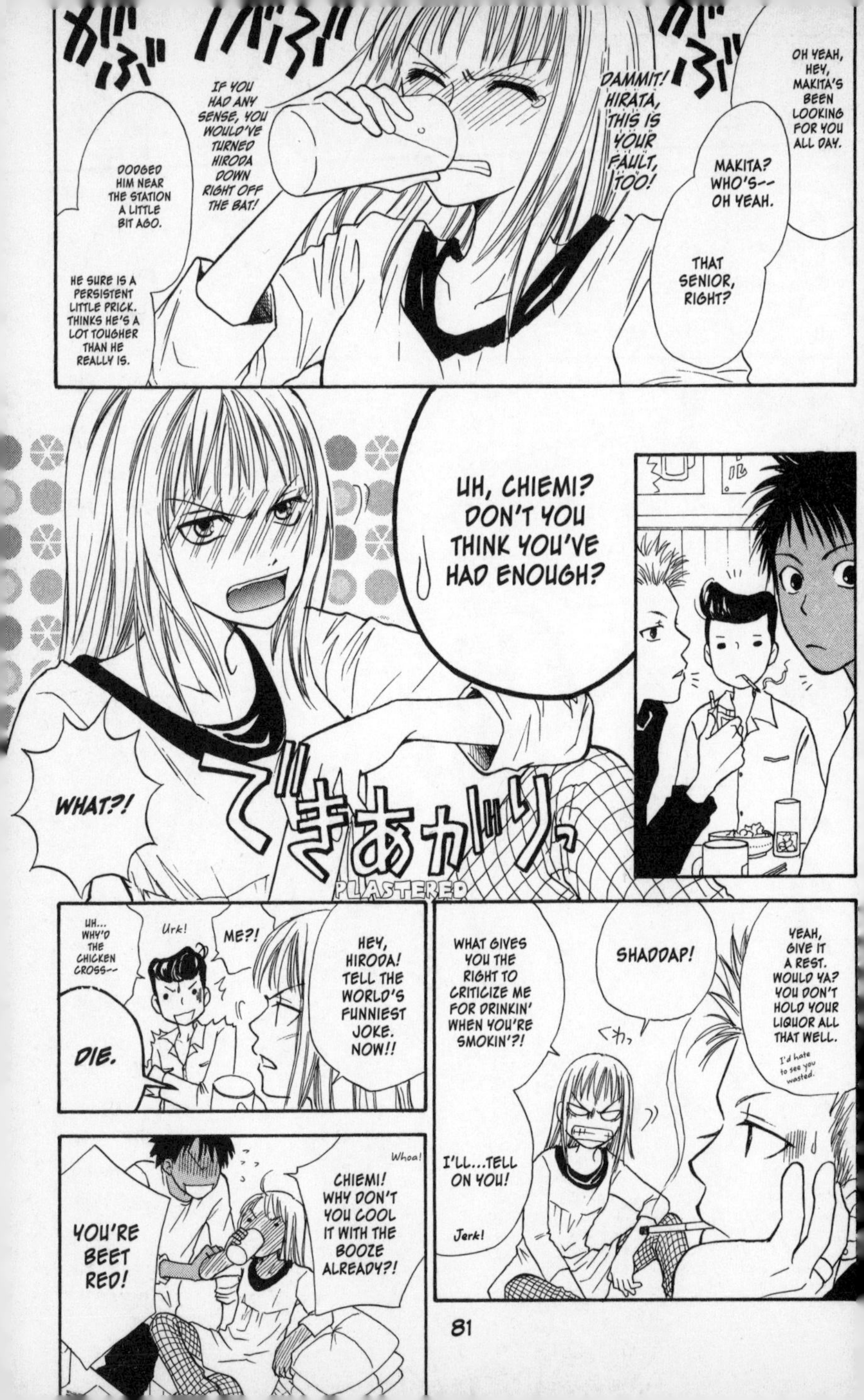
OH YEAH, HEY, MAKITA'S BEEN LOOKING FOR YOU ALL DAY.
MAKITA? WHO'S-- OH YEAH.
THAT SENIOR, RIGHT?
DAMMIT! HIRATA, THIS IS YOUR FAULT, TOO!
IF YOU HAD ANY SENSE, YOU WOULD'VE TURNED HIRODA DOWN RIGHT OFF THE BAT!
DODGED HIM NEAR THE STATION A LITTLE BIT AGO.
HE SURE IS A PERSISTENT LITTLE PRICK. THINKS HE'S A LOT TOUGHER THAN HE REALLY IS.
UH, CHIEMI? DON'T YOU THINK YOU'VE HAD ENOUGH?
WHAT?!
PLASTERED
YEAH, GIVE IT A REST. WOULD YA? YOU DON'T HOLD YOUR LIQUOR ALL THAT WELL.
I'd hate to see you wasted.
SHADDAP!
WHAT GIVES YOU THE RIGHT TO CRITICIZE ME FOR DRINKIN' WHEN YOU'RE SMOKIN'?!
I'LL...TELL ON YOU!
Jerk!
HEY, HIRODA! TELL THE WORLD'S FUNNIEST JOKE. NOW!!
ME?!
Urk!
UH... WHY'D THE CHICKEN CROSS--
DIE.
Whoa!
CHIEMI! WHY DON'T YOU COOL IT WITH THE BOOZE ALREADY?!
YOU'RE BEET RED!

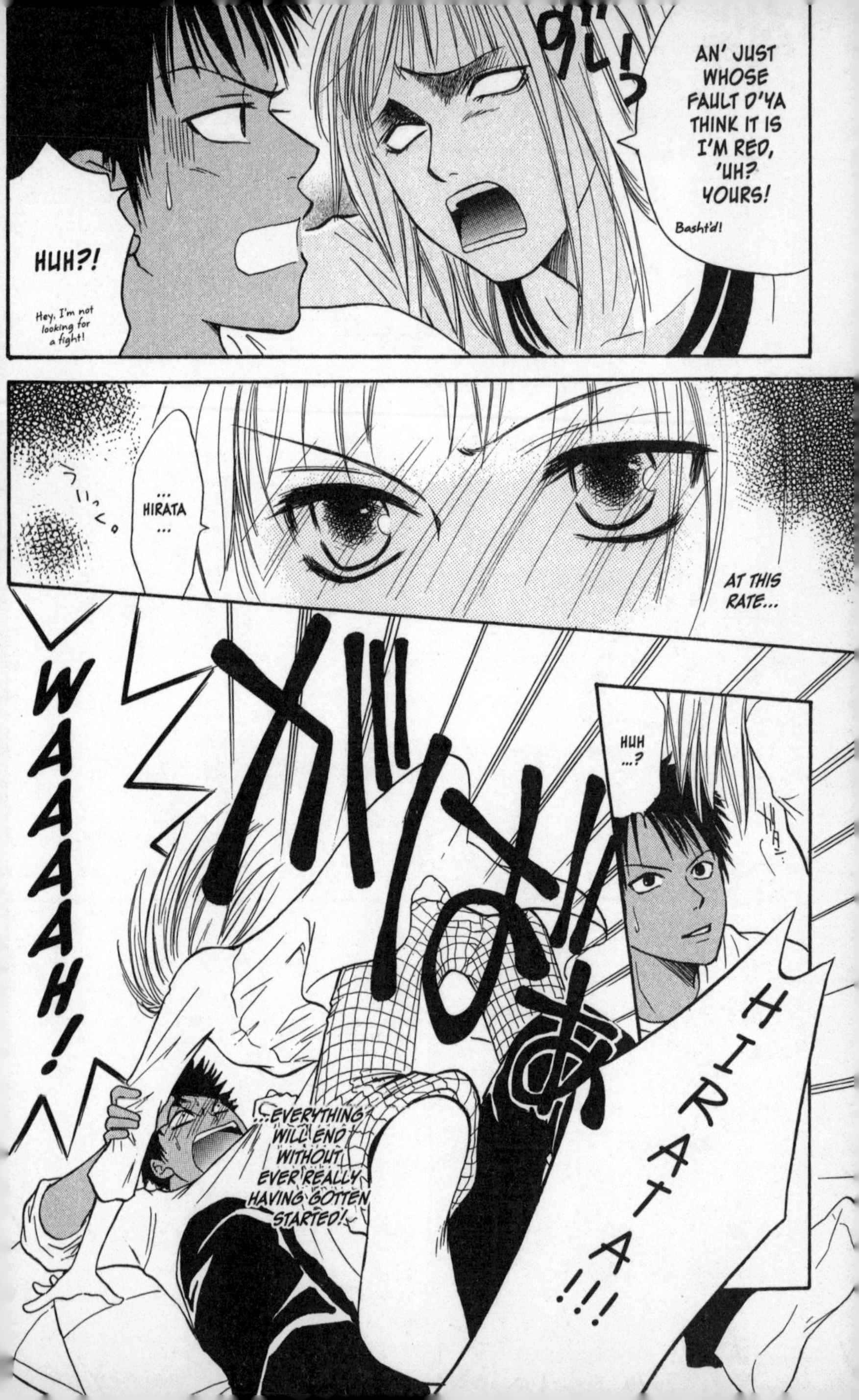
AN' JUST WHOSE FAULT D'YA THINK IT IS I'M RED, 'UH? YOURS!
Basht'd!
HUH?!
Hey, I'm not looking for a fight!
...HIRATA...
AT THIS RATE...
HUH...?
HIRATAAA!!!
...EVERYTHING WILL END WITHOUT EVER REALLY HAVING GOTTEN STARTED!
WAAAAAH!

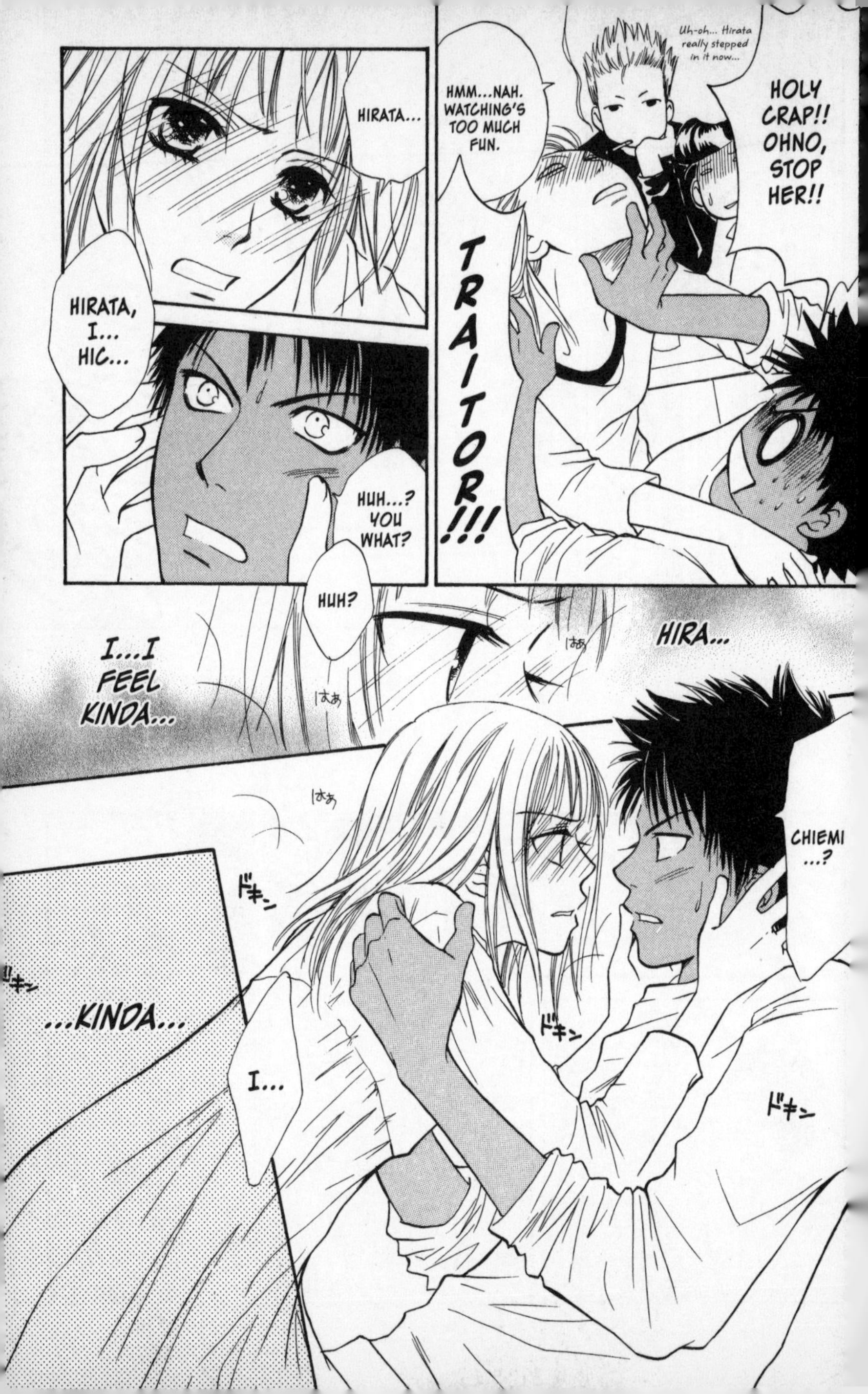
Uh-oh... Hirata really stepped in it now...
HOLY CRAP!! OHNO, STOP HER!!
HMM...NAH. WATCHING'S TOO MUCH FUN.
TRAITOR!!!
HIRATA...
HIRATA, I... HIC...
HUH...? YOU WHAT?
HIRA...
はあ
HUH?
はあ
I...I FEEL KINDA...
CHIEMI ...?
ドキン
ドキン
はあ
ドキン
I...
...KINDA...

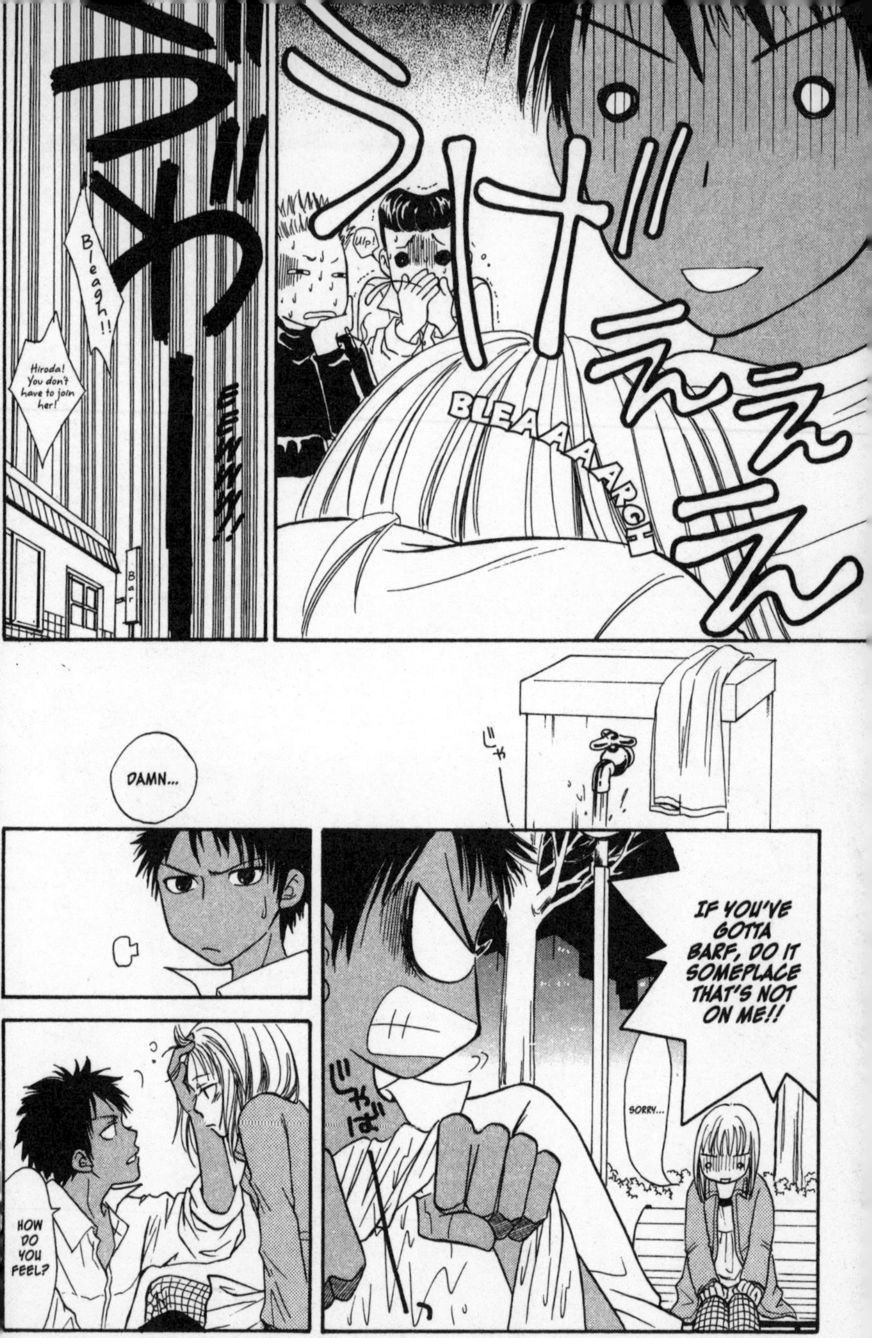
Ulp!
BLEAAAAARGH
Bleagh!!
Hiroda! You don't have to join her!
EEWWW!!
Bar
じゃー
DAMN...
IF YOU'VE GOTTA BARF, DO IT SOMEPLACE THAT'S NOT ON ME!!
SORRY...
HOW DO YOU FEEL?

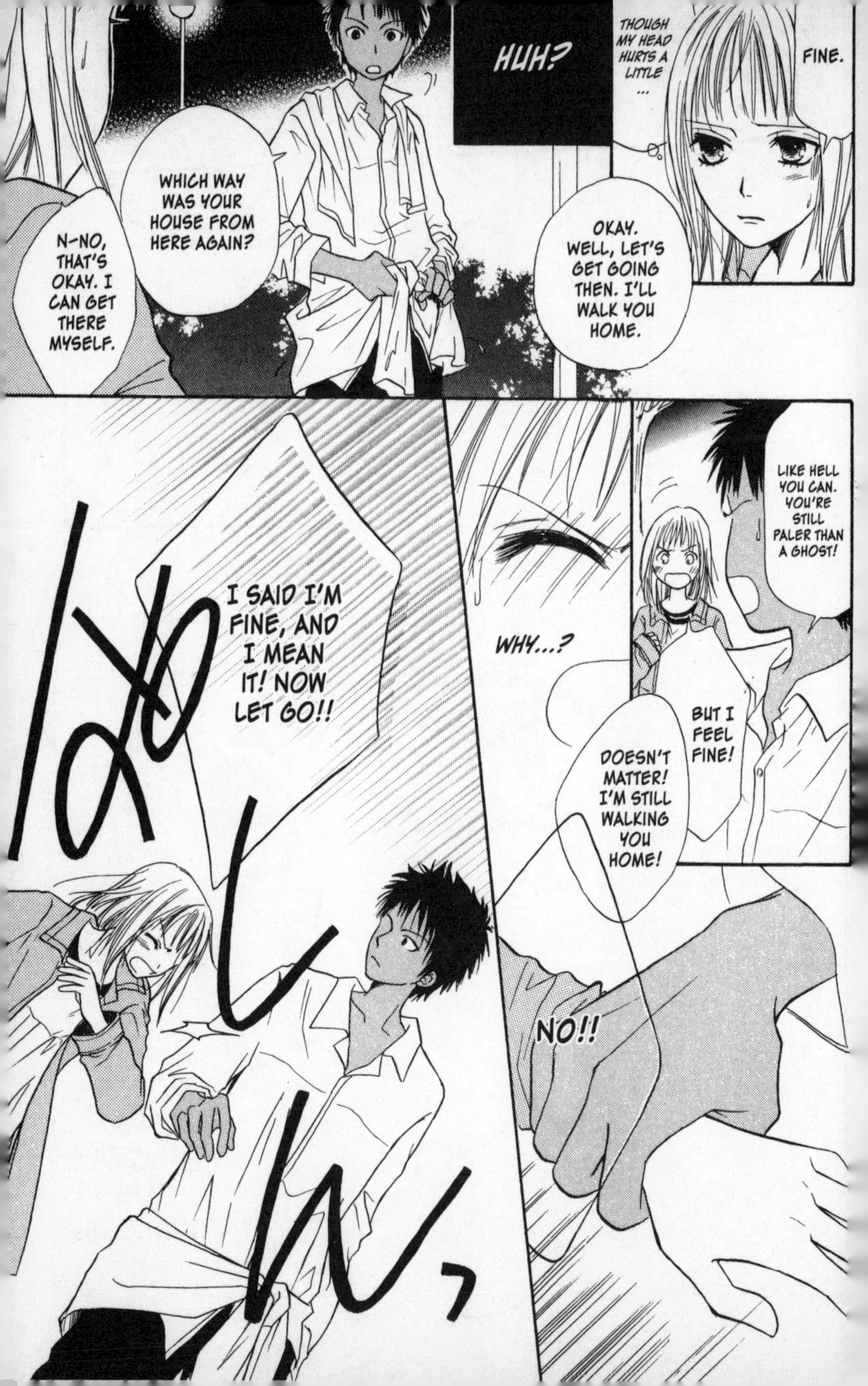
FINE.
THOUGH MY HEAD HURTS A LITTLE ...
OKAY. WELL, LET'S GET GOING THEN. I'LL WALK YOU HOME.
HUH?
WHICH WAY WAS YOUR HOUSE FROM HERE AGAIN?
N-NO, THAT'S OKAY. I CAN GET THERE MYSELF.
LIKE HELL YOU CAN. YOU'RE STILL PALER THAN A GHOST!
BUT I FEEL FINE!
DOESN'T MATTER! I'M STILL WALKING YOU HOME!
WHY...?
NO!!
I SAID I'M FINE, AND I MEAN IT! NOW LET GO!!

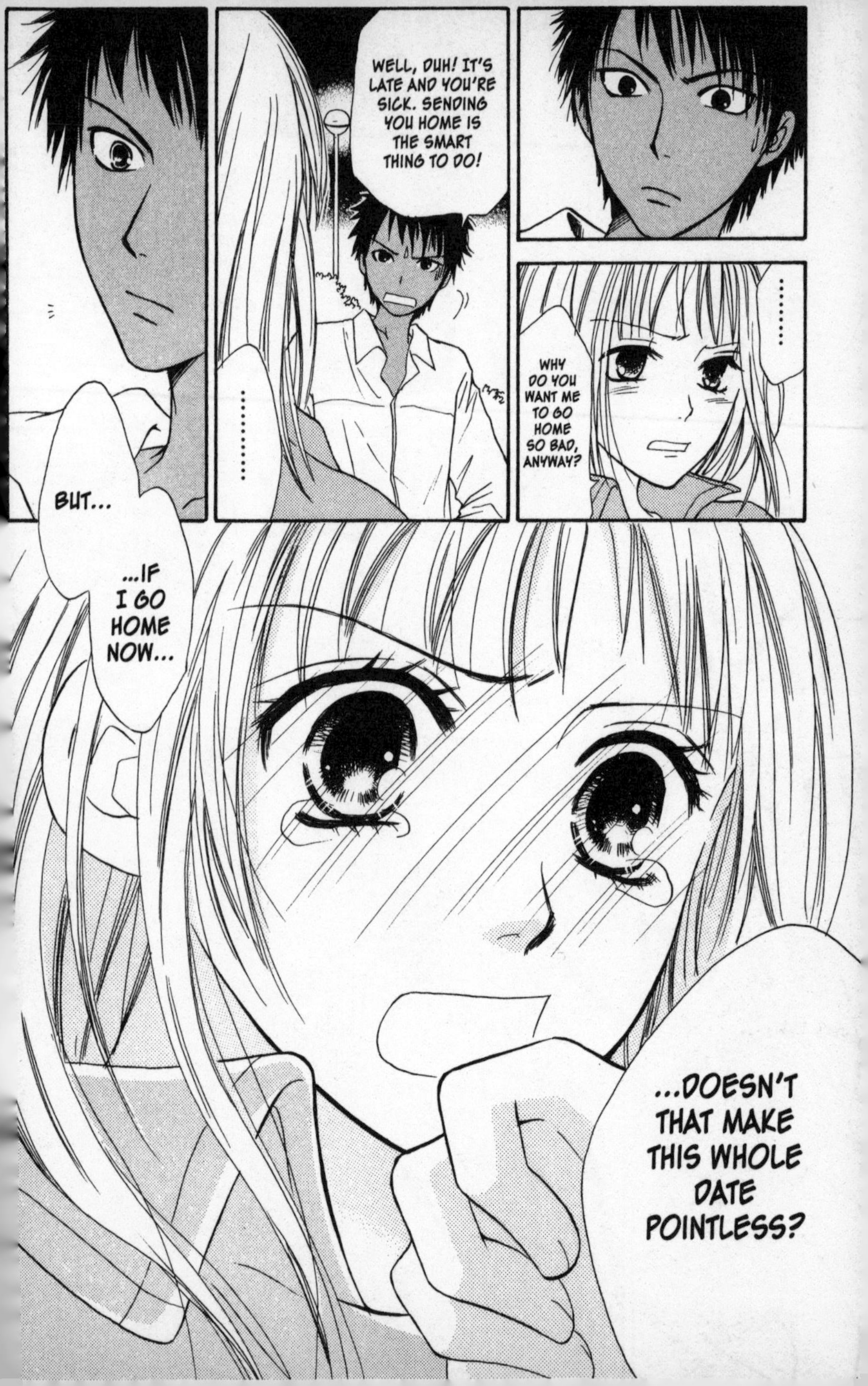
......
WHY DO YOU WANT ME TO GO HOME SO BAD, ANYWAY?
WELL, DUH! IT'S LATE AND YOU'RE SICK. SENDING YOU HOME IS THE SMART THING TO DO!
....
BUT...
...IF I GO HOME NOW...
...DOESN'T THAT MAKE THIS WHOLE DATE POINTLESS?

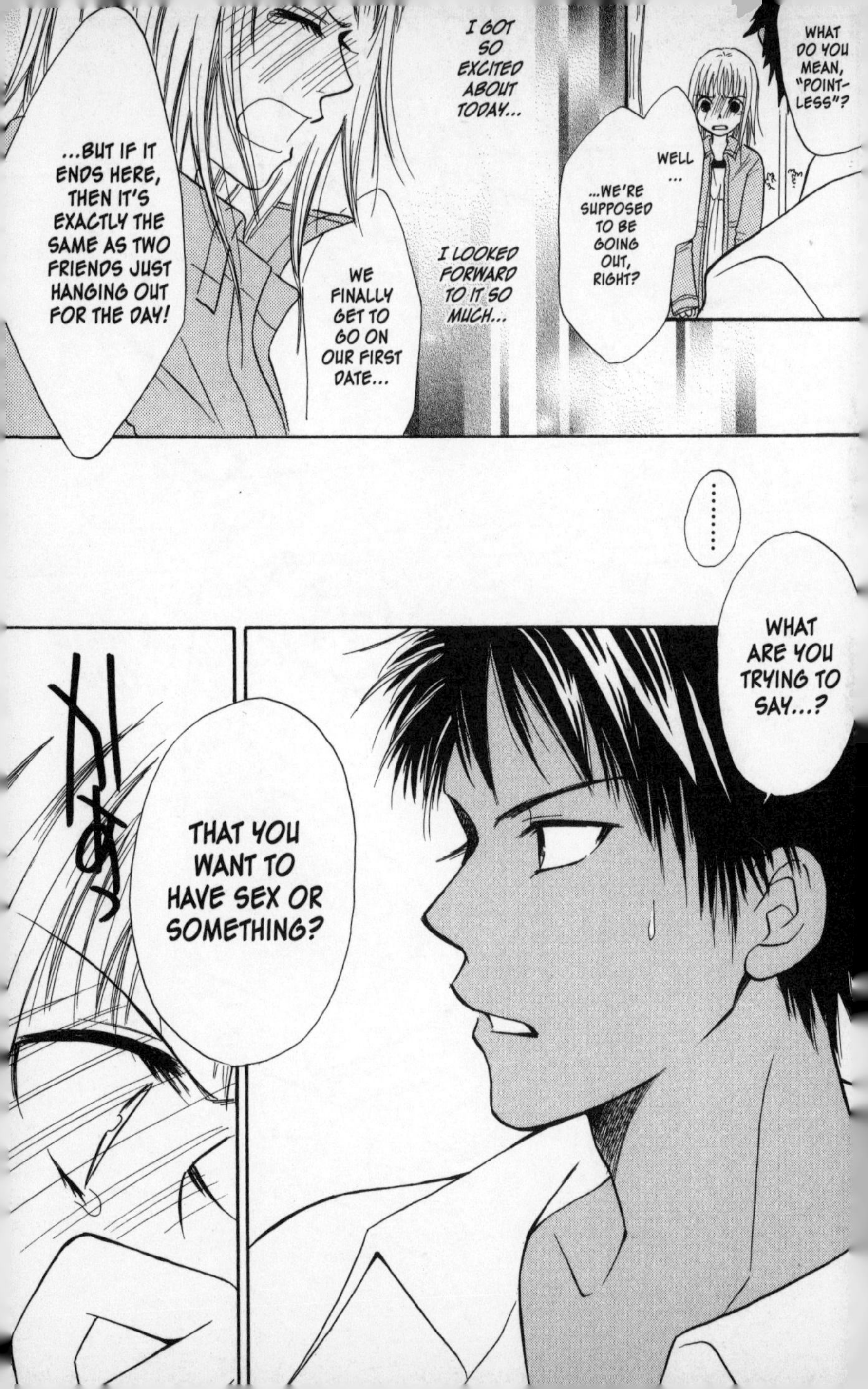
WHAT DO YOU MEAN, "POINTLESS"?
WELL...
...WE'RE SUPPOSED TO BE GOING OUT, RIGHT?
I GOT SO EXCITED ABOUT TODAY...
I LOOKED FORWARD TO IT SO MUCH...
WE FINALLY GET TO GO ON OUR FIRST DATE...
...BUT IF IT ENDS HERE, THEN IT'S EXACTLY THE SAME AS TWO FRIENDS JUST HANGING OUT FOR THE DAY!
......
WHAT ARE YOU TRYING TO SAY...?
THAT YOU WANT TO HAVE SEX OR SOMETHING?

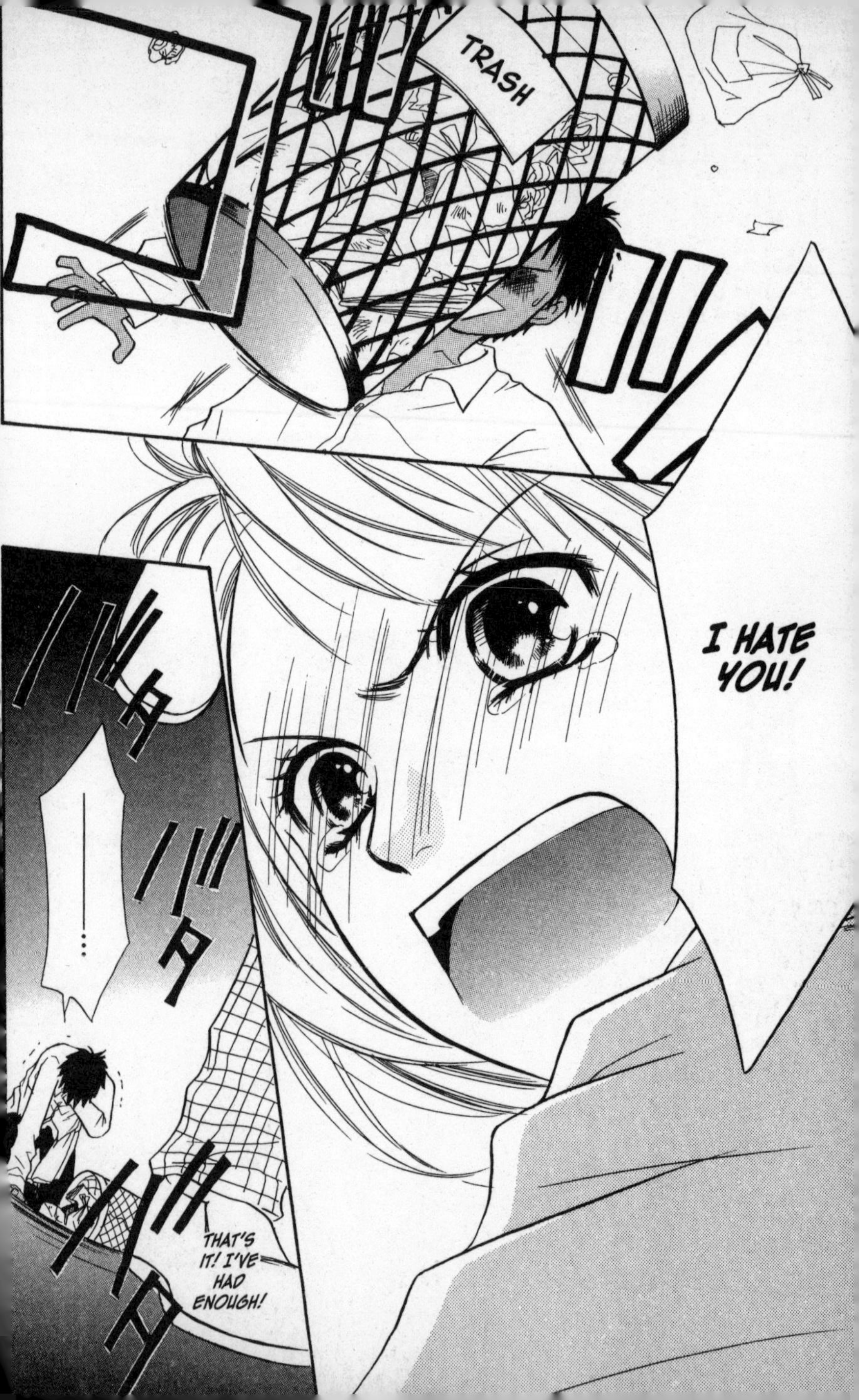
TRASH
I HATE YOU!
...
THAT'S IT! I'VE HAD ENOUGH!

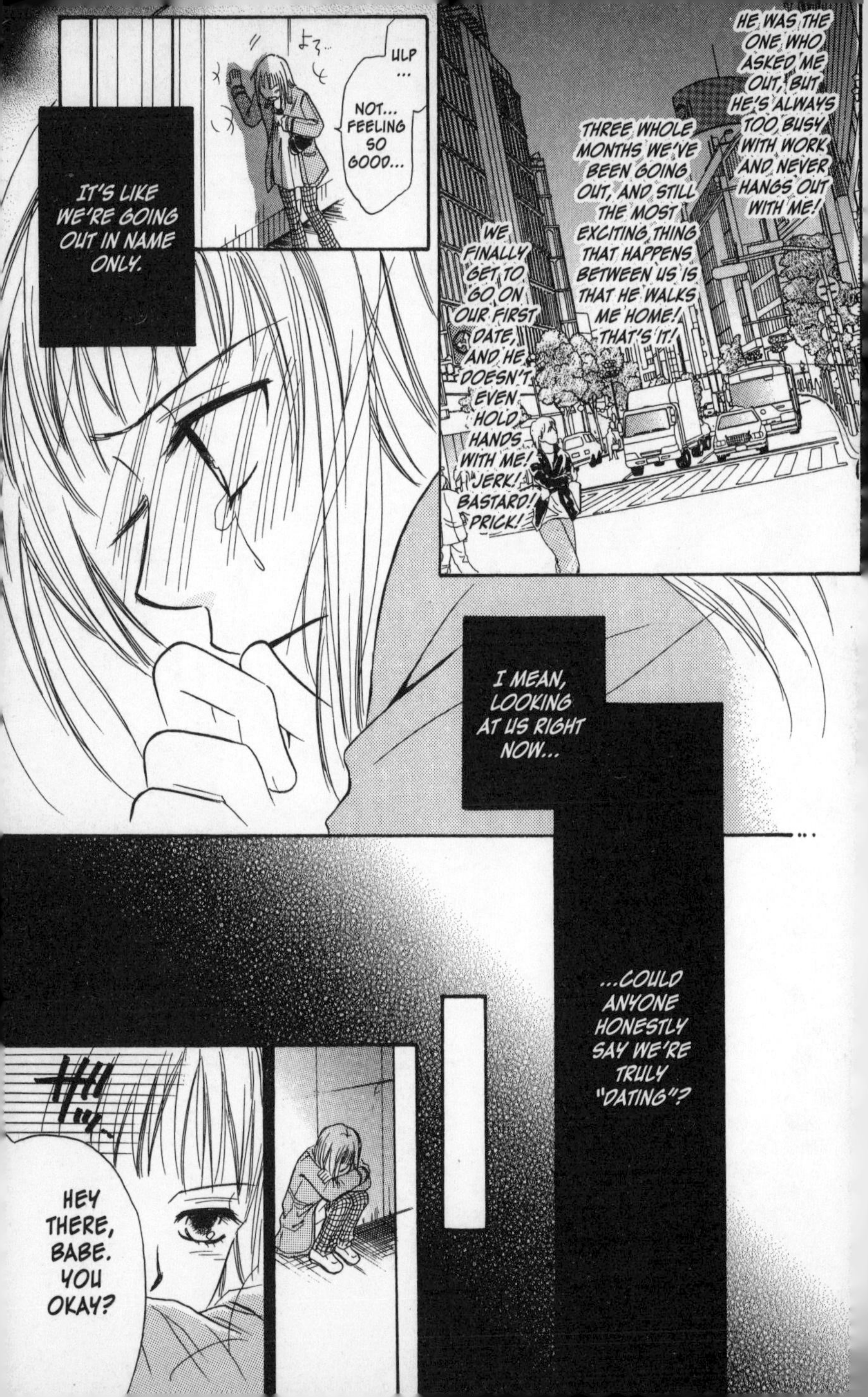
HE WAS THE ONE WHO ASKED ME OUT, BUT HE'S ALWAYS TOO BUSY WITH WORK AND NEVER HANGS OUT WITH ME!
THREE WHOLE MONTHS WE'VE BEEN GOING OUT, AND STILL THE MOST EXCITING THING THAT HAPPENS BETWEEN US IS THAT HE WALKS ME HOME! THAT'S IT!
WE FINALLY GET TO GO ON OUR FIRST DATE, AND HE DOESN'T EVEN HOLD HANDS WITH ME! JERK! BASTARD! PRICK!
ULP ...
NOT... FEELING SO GOOD...
IT'S LIKE WE'RE GOING OUT IN NAME ONLY.
I MEAN, LOOKING AT US RIGHT NOW...
...COULD ANYONE HONESTLY SAY WE'RE TRULY "DATING"?
HEY THERE, BABE. YOU OKAY?

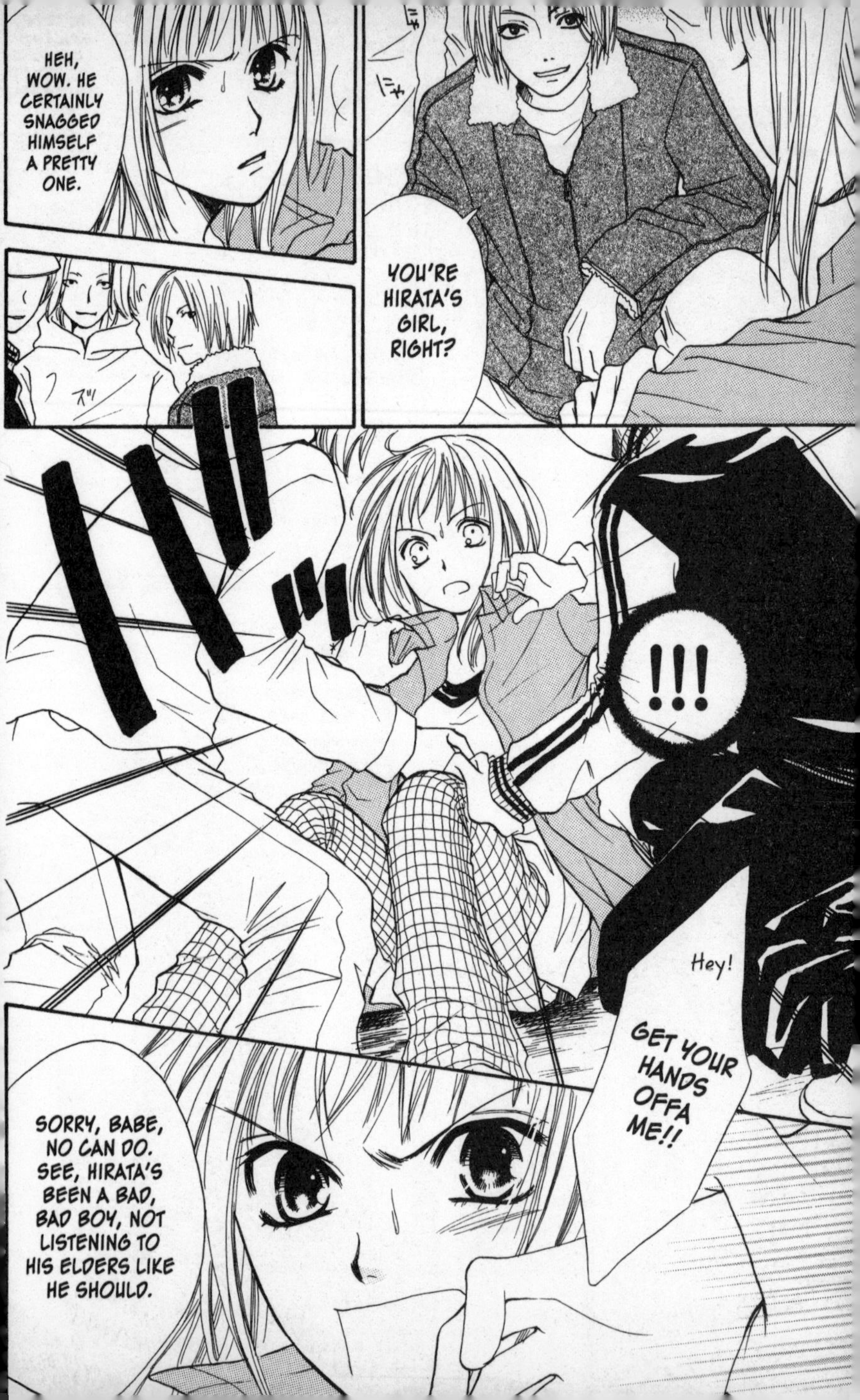
YOU'RE HIRATA'S GIRL, RIGHT?
HEH, WOW. HE CERTAINLY SNAGGED HIMSELF A PRETTY ONE.
!!!
Hey!
GET YOUR HANDS OFFA ME!!
SORRY, BABE, NO CAN DO. SEE, HIRATA'S BEEN A BAD, BAD BOY, NOT LISTENING TO HIS ELDERS LIKE HE SHOULD.

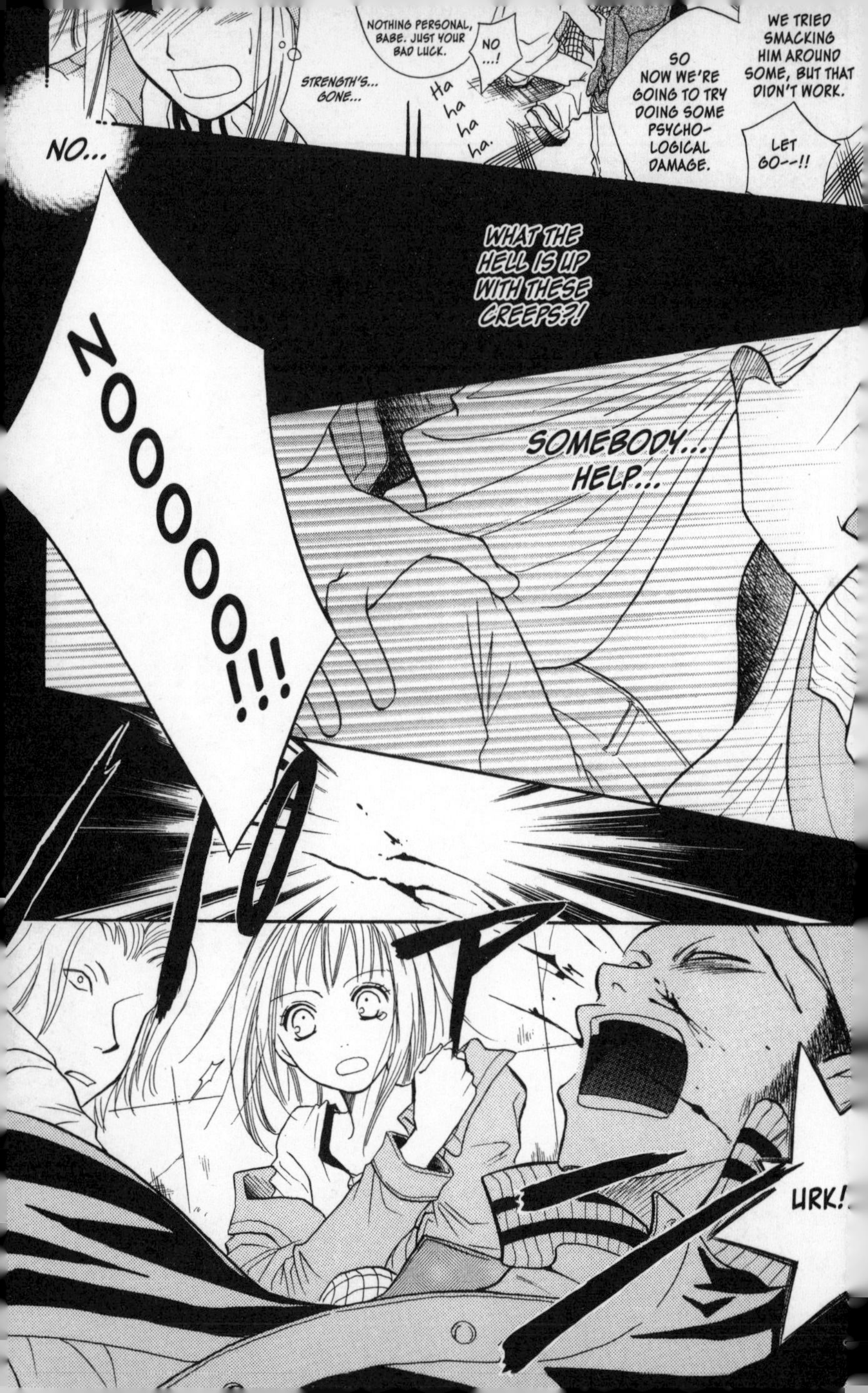
WE TRIED SMACKING HIM AROUND SOME, BUT THAT DIDN'T WORK.
SO NOW WE'RE GOING TO TRY DOING SOME PSYCHOLOGICAL DAMAGE.
LET GO--!!
NO ...!
Ha ha ha ha.
NOTHING PERSONAL, BABE. JUST YOUR BAD LUCK.
STRENGTH'S... GONE...
NO...
WHAT THE HELL IS UP WITH THESE CREEPS?!
SOMEBODY... HELP...
ZOOOOOO!!!
URK!

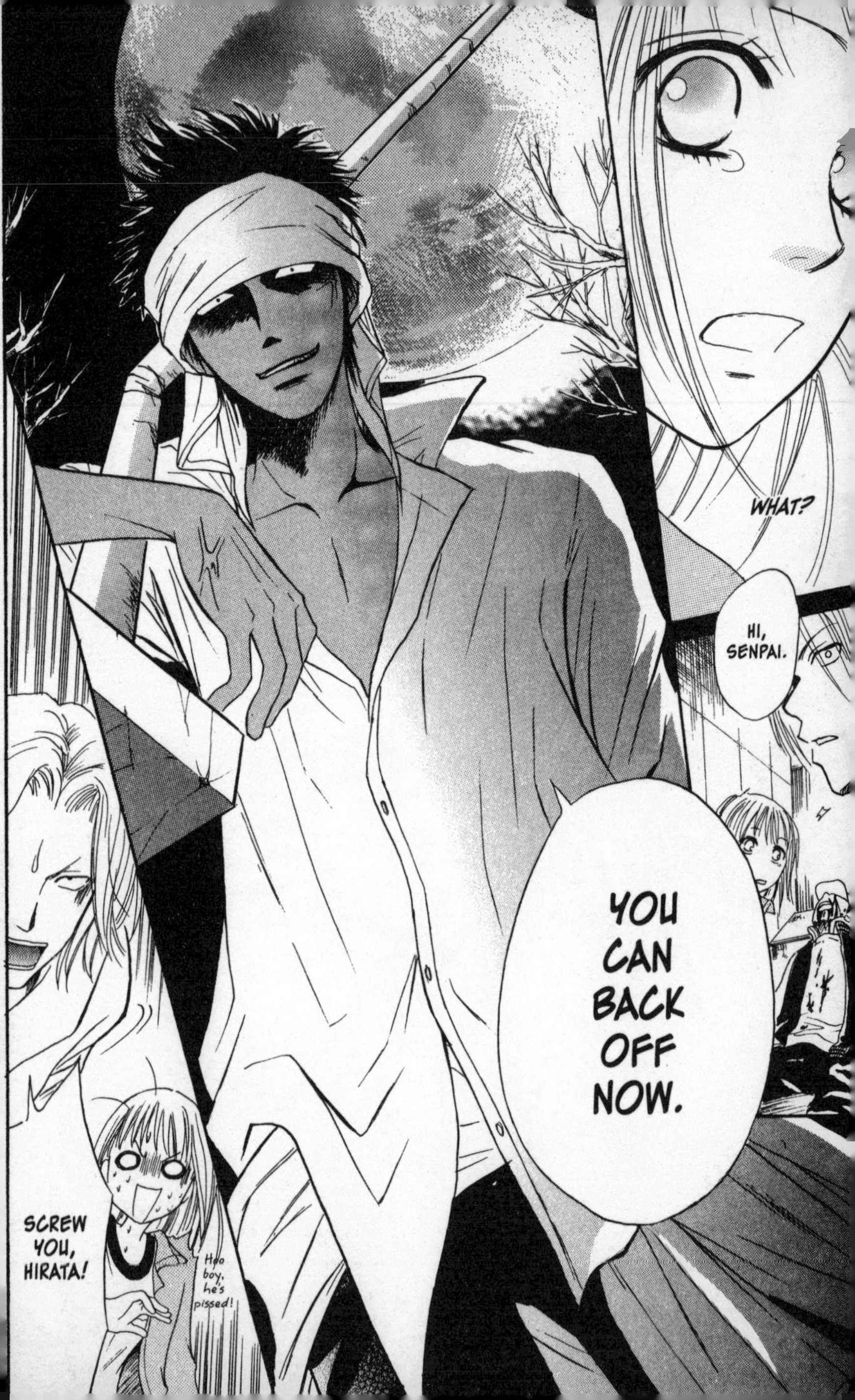
WHAT?
HI, SENPAI.
YOU CAN BACK OFF NOW.
Hoo boy, he's pissed!
SCREW YOU, HIRATA!

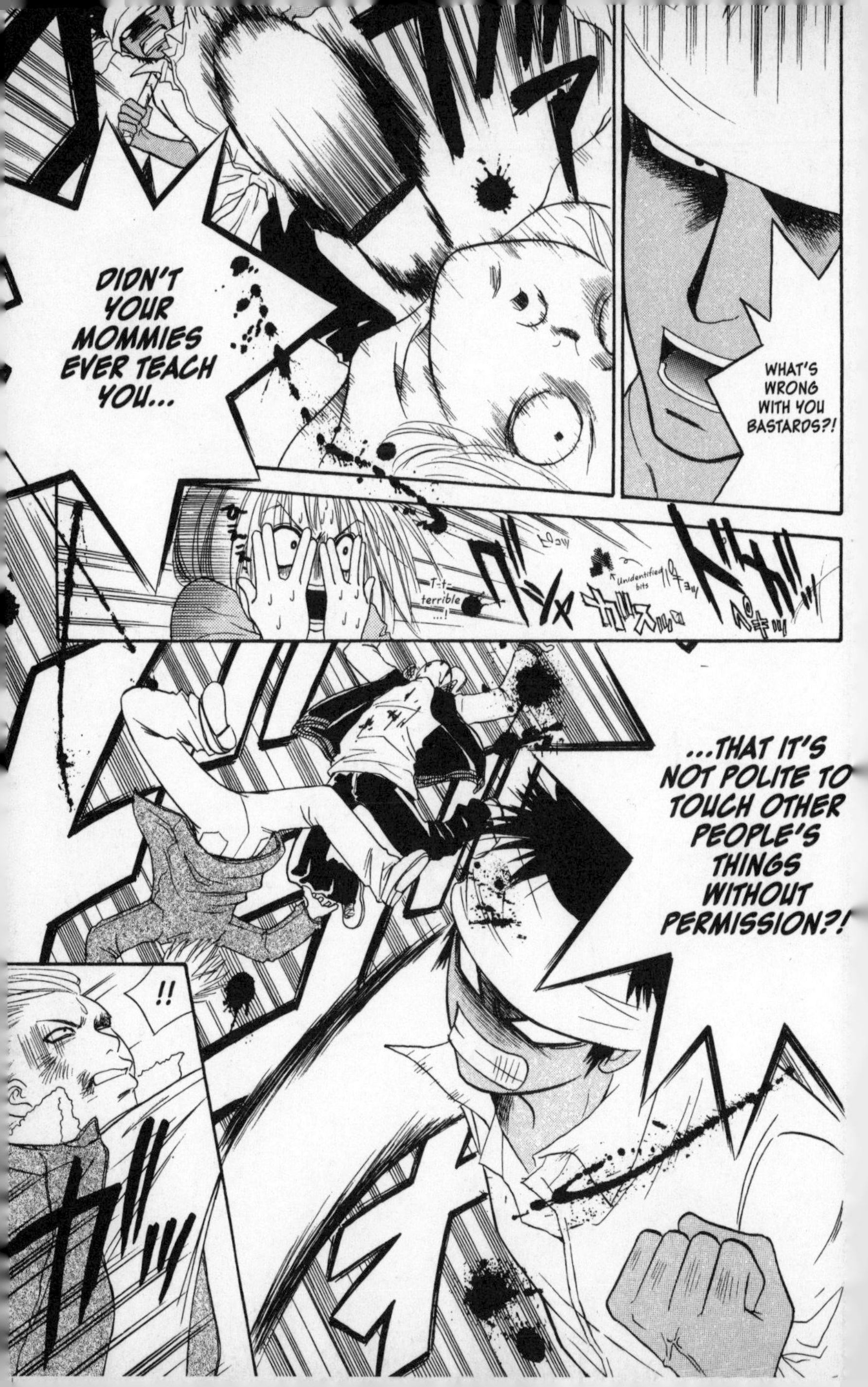
WHAT'S WRONG WITH YOU BASTARDS?!
DIDN'T YOUR MOMMIES EVER TEACH YOU...
Unidentified bits
T-t-terrible...!
...THAT IT'S NOT POLITE TO TOUCH OTHER PEOPLE'S THINGS WITHOUT PERMISSION?!
!!

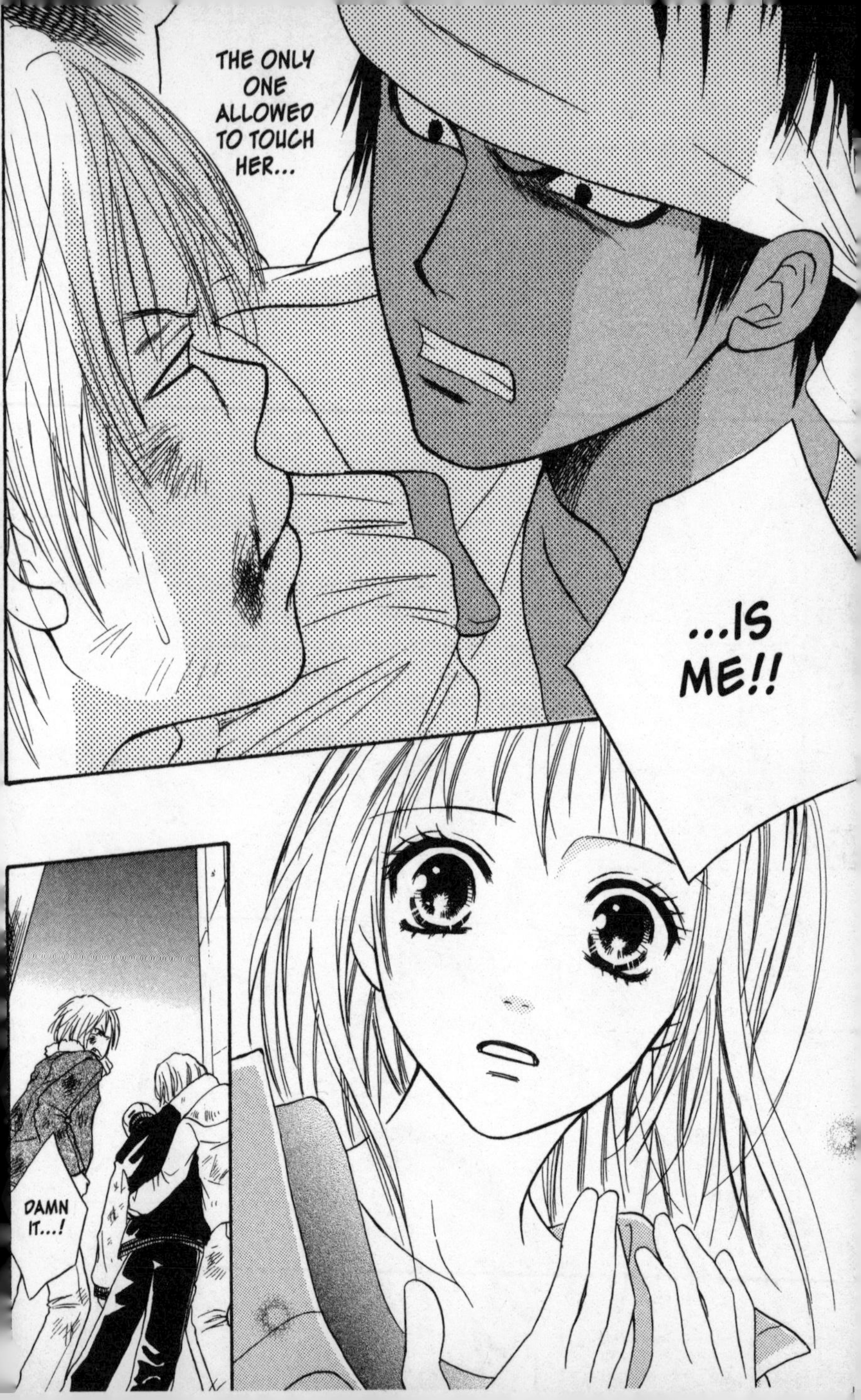
THE ONLY ONE ALLOWED TO TOUCH HER...
...IS ME!!
DAMN IT...!

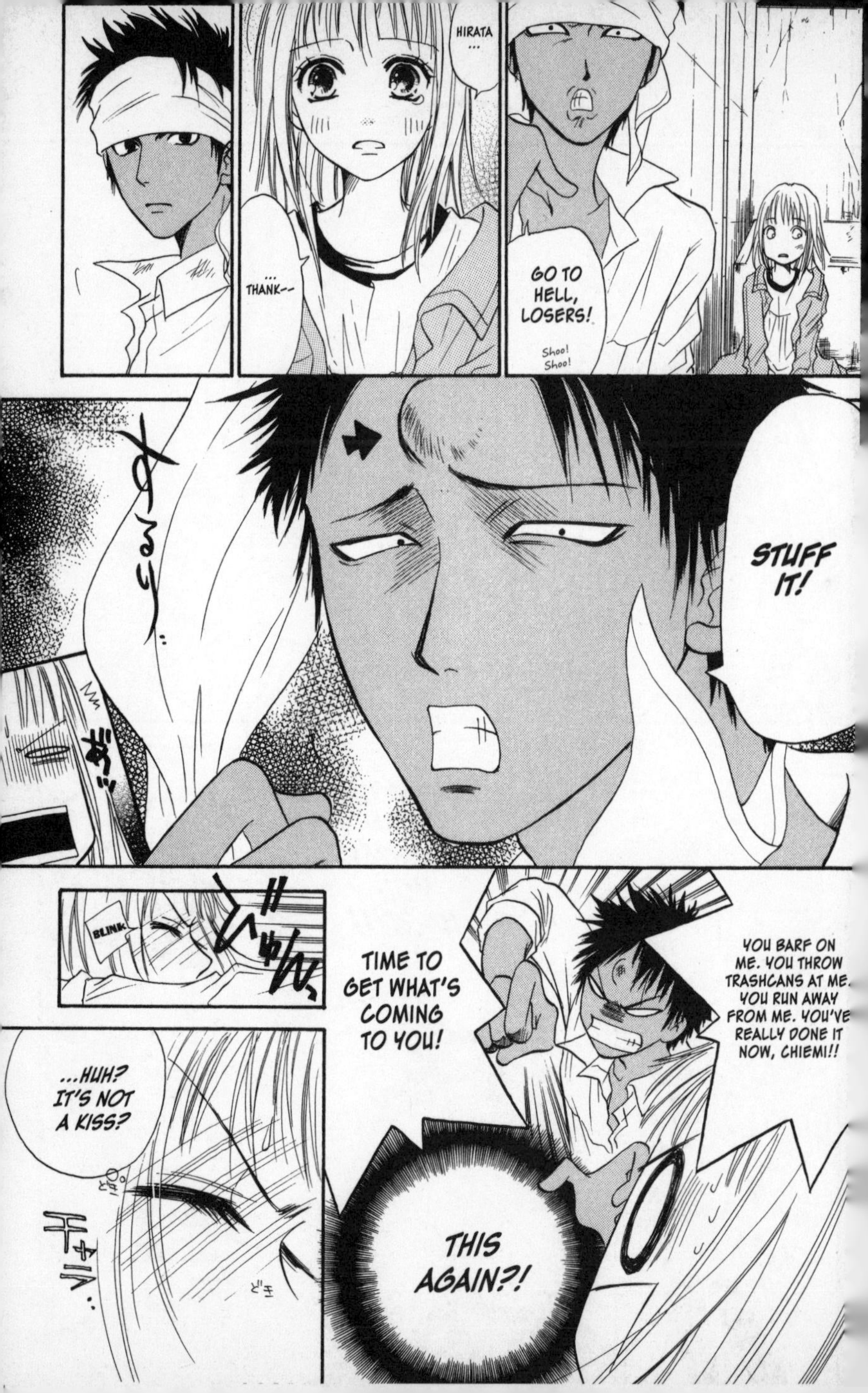
GO TO HELL, LOSERS!
Shoo! Shoo!
HIRATA ...
... THANK--
STUFF IT!
YOU BARF ON ME. YOU THROW TRASHCANS AT ME. YOU RUN AWAY FROM ME. YOU'VE REALLY DONE IT NOW, CHIEMI!!
TIME TO GET WHAT'S COMING TO YOU!
BLINK
THIS AGAIN?!
...HUH? IT'S NOT A KISS?

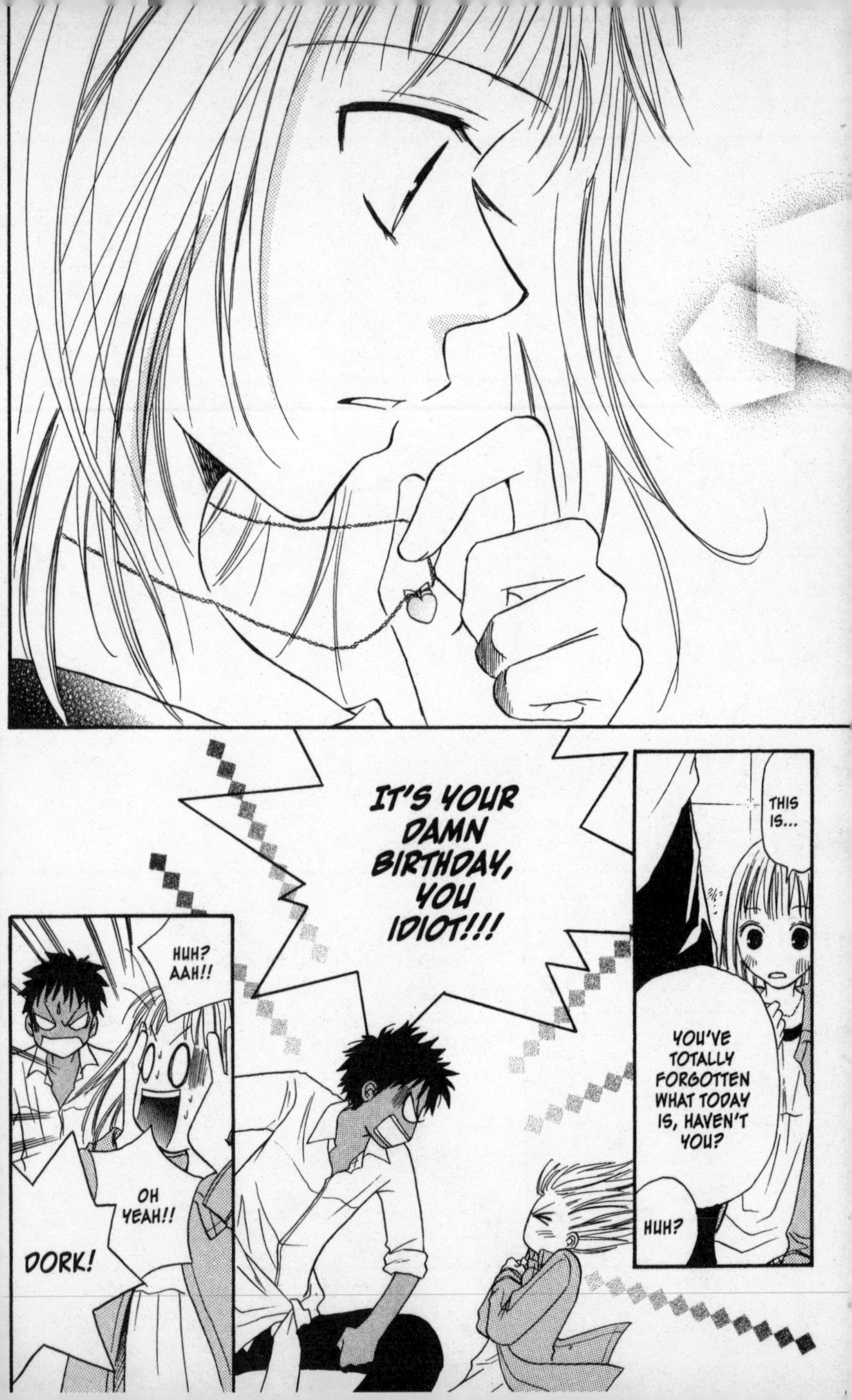
THIS IS...
YOU'VE TOTALLY FORGOTTEN WHAT TODAY IS, HAVEN'T YOU?
HUH?
IT'S YOUR DAMN BIRTHDAY, YOU IDIOT!!!
HUH? AAH!!
OH YEAH!!
DORK!

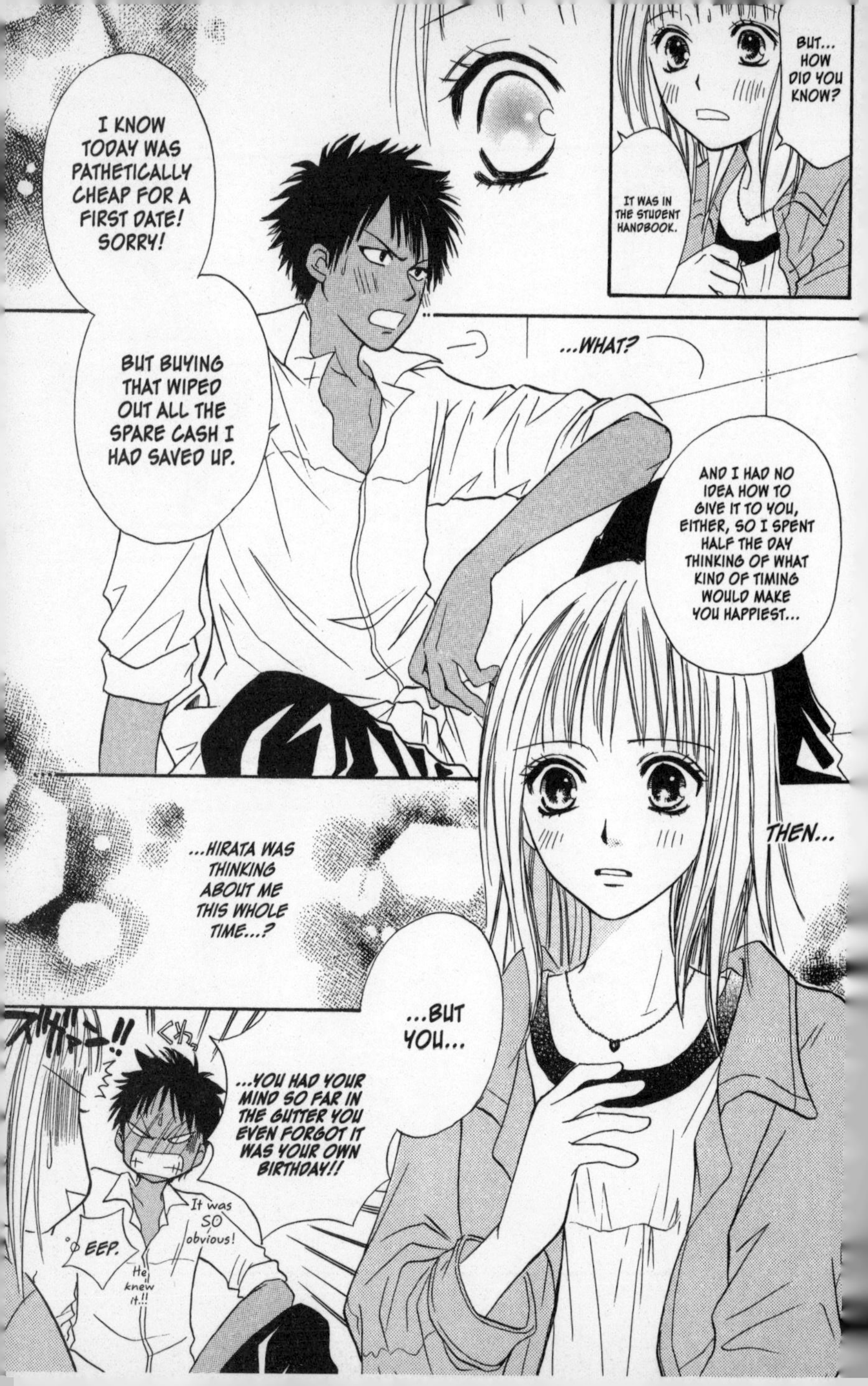
BUT... HOW DID YOU KNOW?
IT WAS IN THE STUDENT HANDBOOK.
I KNOW TODAY WAS PATHETICALLY CHEAP FOR A FIRST DATE! SORRY!
...WHAT?
BUT BUYING THAT WIPED OUT ALL THE SPARE CASH I HAD SAVED UP.
AND I HAD NO IDEA HOW TO GIVE IT TO YOU, EITHER, SO I SPENT HALF THE DAY THINKING OF WHAT KIND OF TIMING WOULD MAKE YOU HAPPIEST...
THEN...
...HIRATA WAS THINKING ABOUT ME THIS WHOLE TIME...?
...BUT YOU...
...YOU HAD YOUR MIND SO FAR IN THE GUTTER YOU EVEN FORGOT IT WAS YOUR OWN BIRTHDAY!!
It was SO obvious!
EEP.
He knew it!!

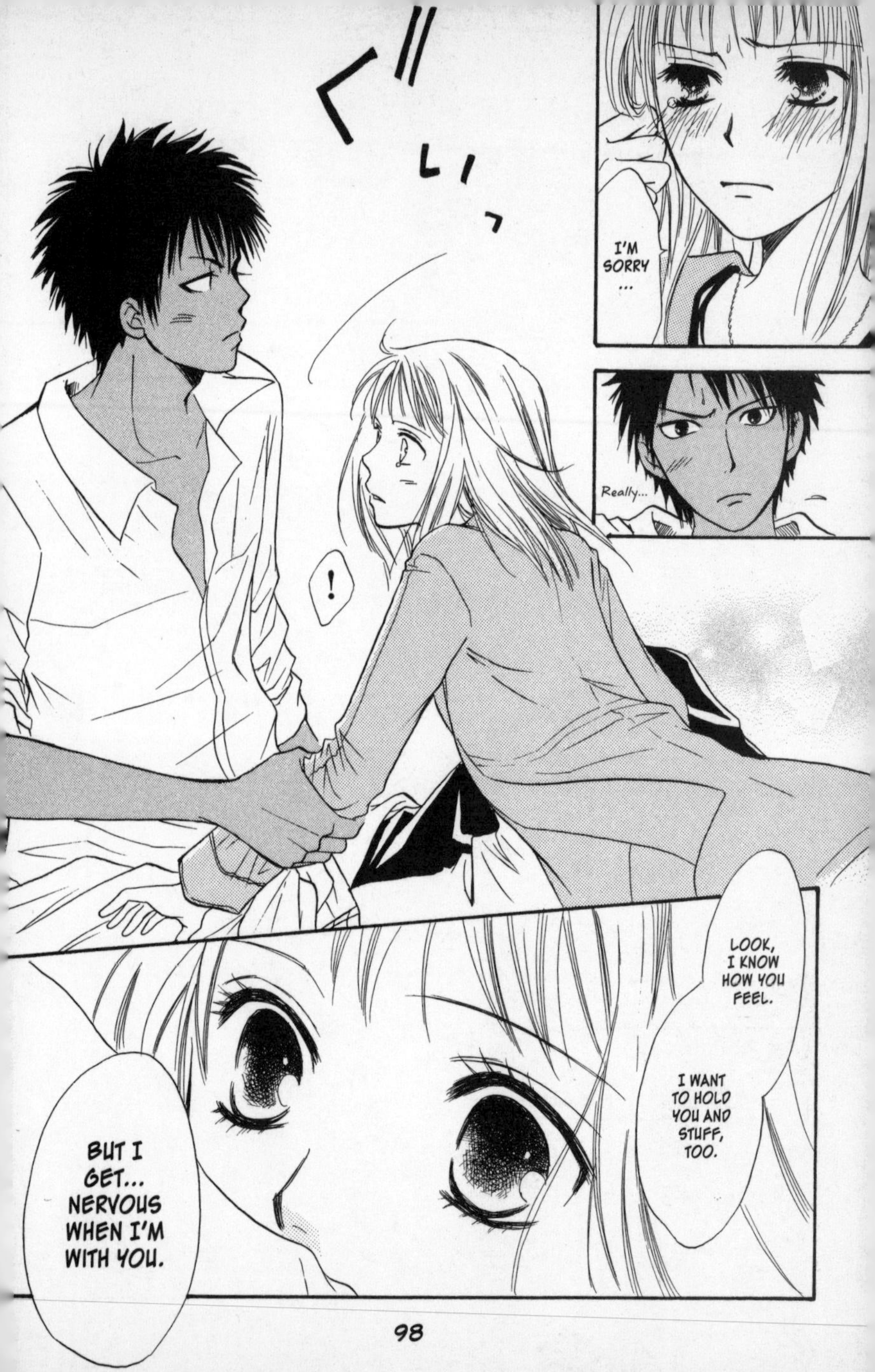

I'M SORRY ...
Really...
!
LOOK, I KNOW HOW YOU FEEL.
I WANT TO HOLD YOU AND STUFF, TOO.
BUT I GET... NERVOUS WHEN I'M WITH YOU.

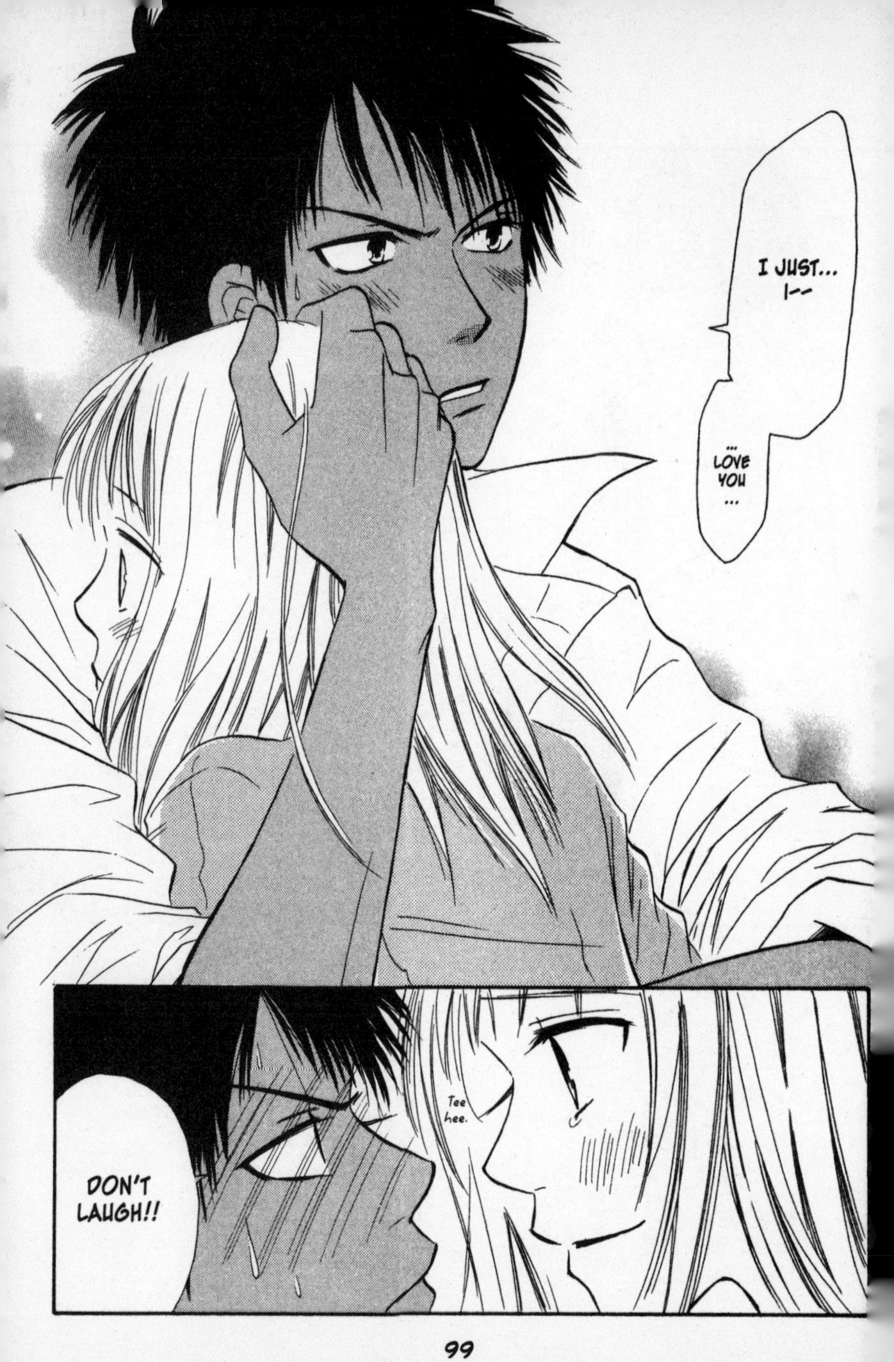
I JUST... I--
... LOVE YOU ...
Tee hee.
DON'T LAUGH!!

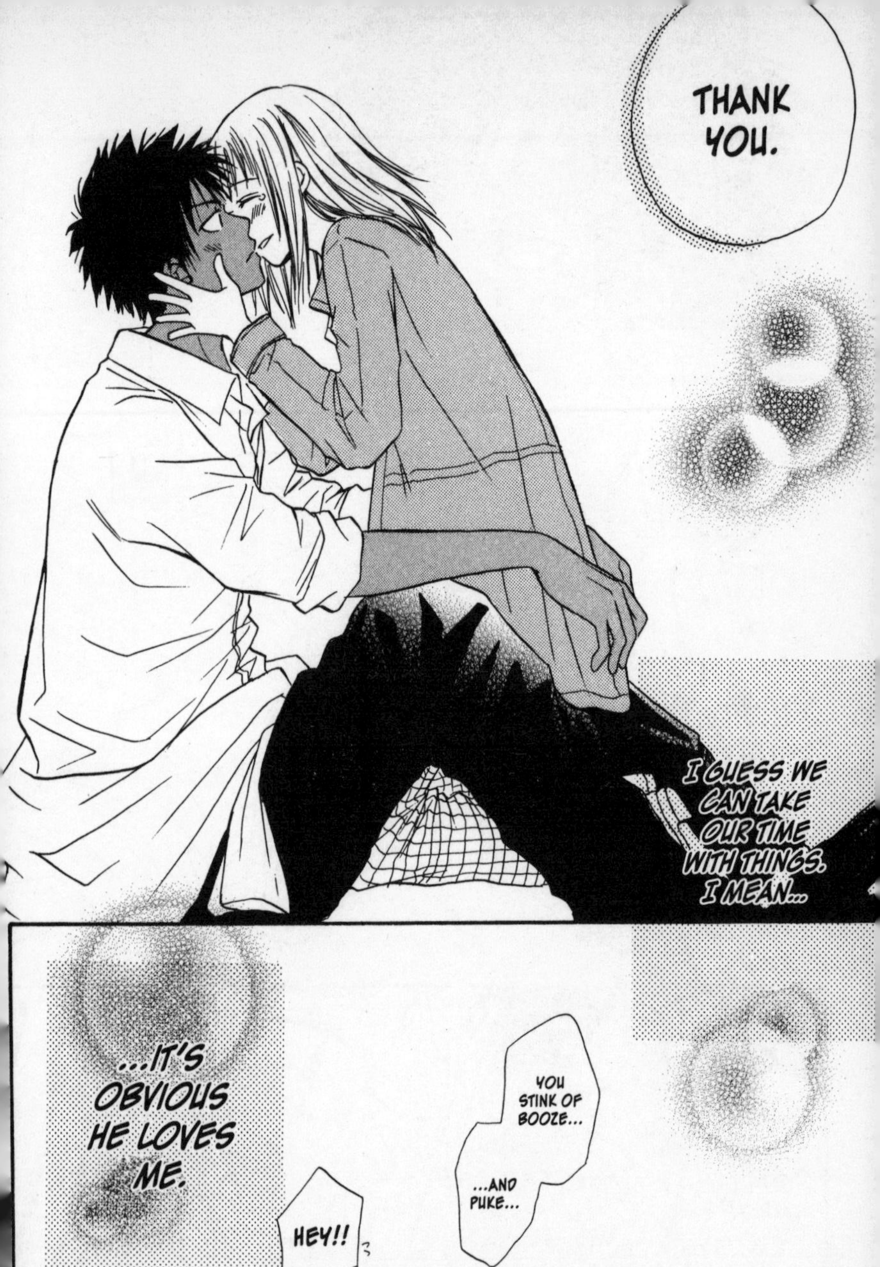
THANK YOU.
I GUESS WE CAN TAKE OUR TIME WITH THINGS. I MEAN...
YOU STINK OF BOOZE...
...AND PUKE...
HEY!!
...IT'S OBVIOUS HE LOVES ME.

LOVE ATTACK™
JUNAI TOKKO TAICHO!

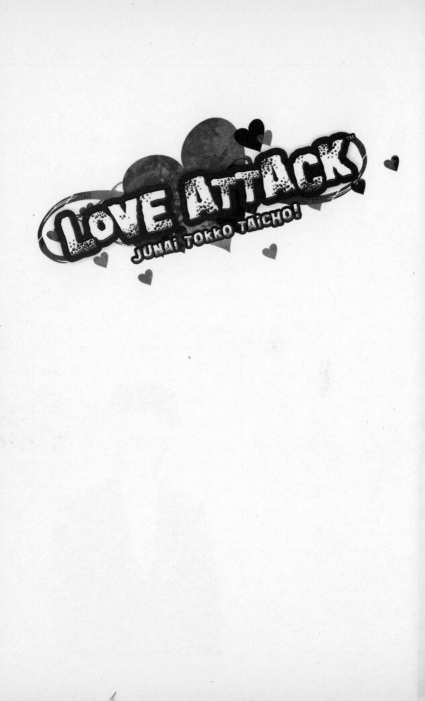

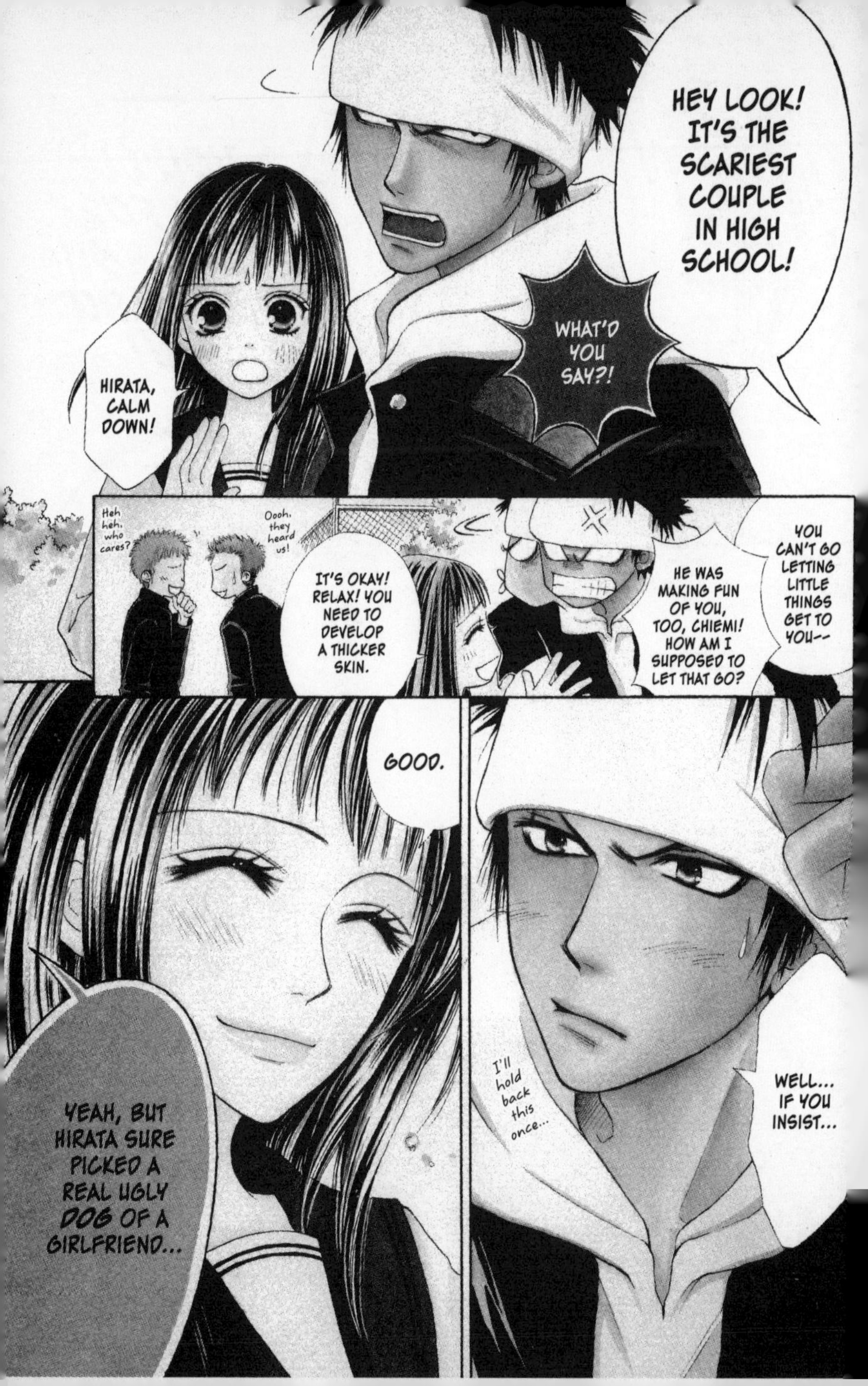
HEY LOOK! IT'S THE SCARIEST COUPLE IN HIGH SCHOOL!
WHAT'D YOU SAY?!
HIRATA, CALM DOWN!
YOU CAN'T GO LETTING LITTLE THINGS GET TO YOU--
HE WAS MAKING FUN OF YOU, TOO, CHIEMI! HOW AM I SUPPOSED TO LET THAT GO?
IT'S OKAY! RELAX! YOU NEED TO DEVELOP A THICKER SKIN.
Oooh, they heard us!
Heh heh, who cares?
WELL... IF YOU INSIST...
I'll hold back this once...
GOOD.
YEAH, BUT HIRATA SURE PICKED A REAL UGLY DOG OF A GIRLFRIEND...

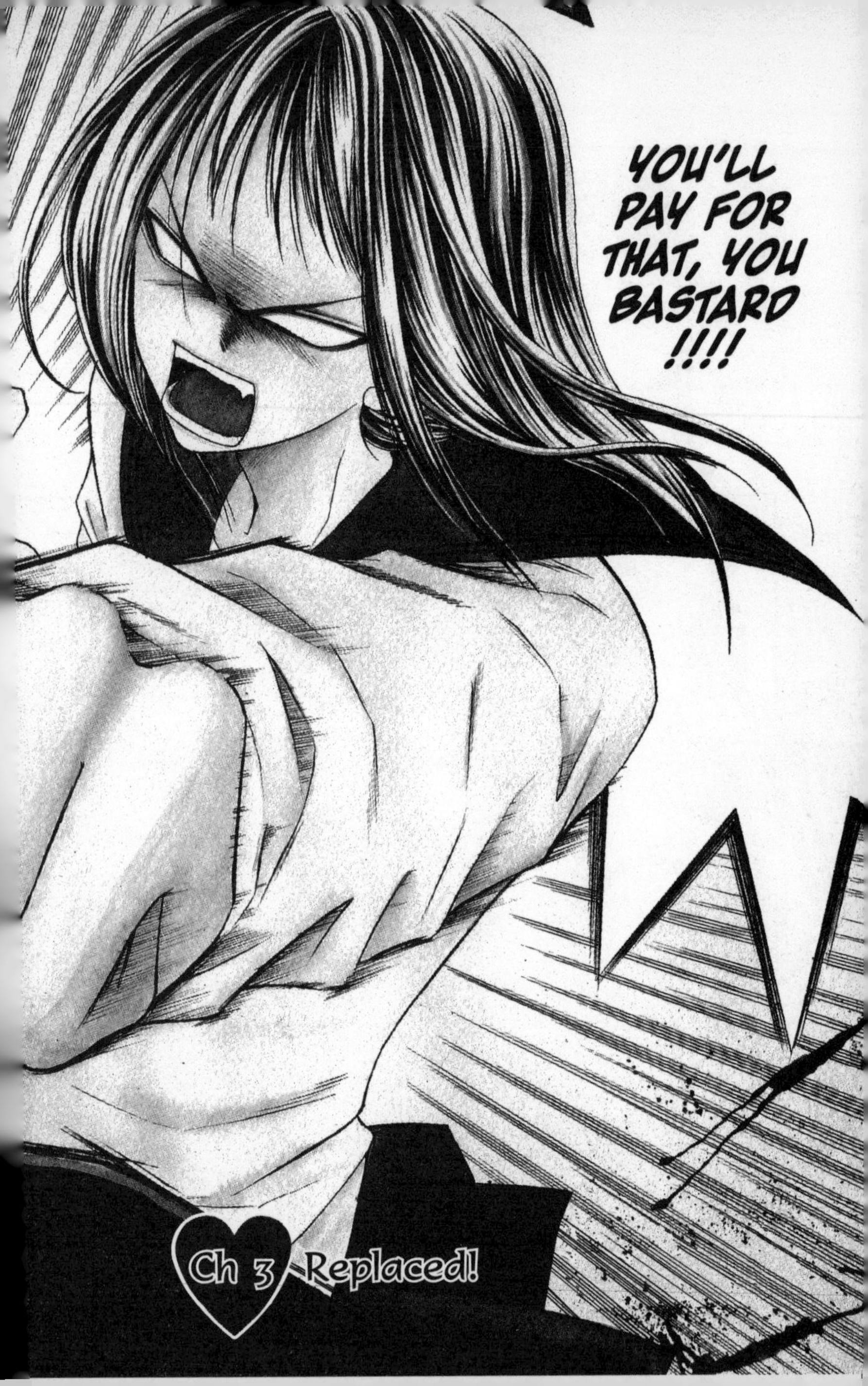
YOU'LL PAY FOR THAT, YOU BASTARD !!!!
Ch 3 Replaced!

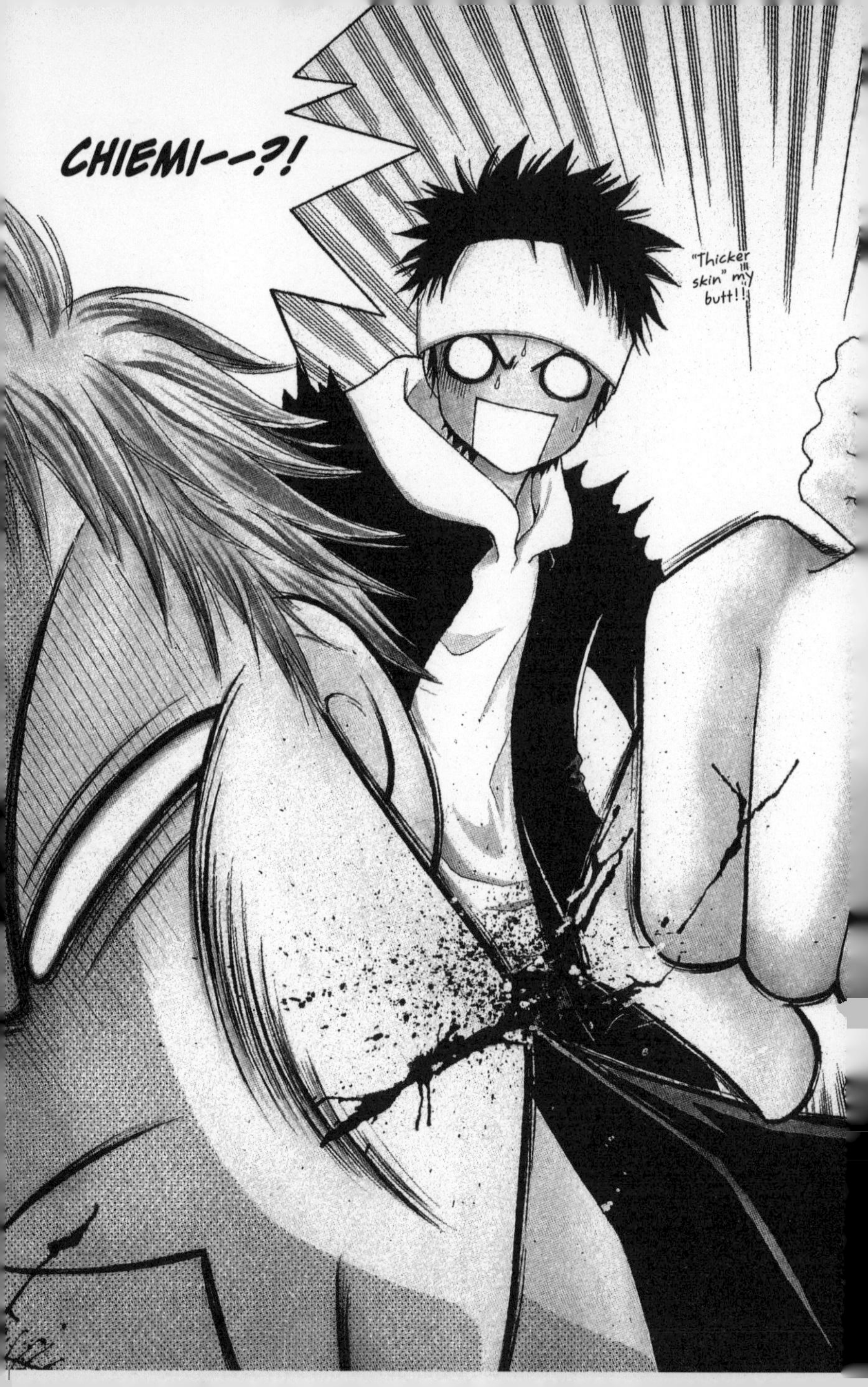
"Thicker skin" my butt!!
CHIEMI--?!

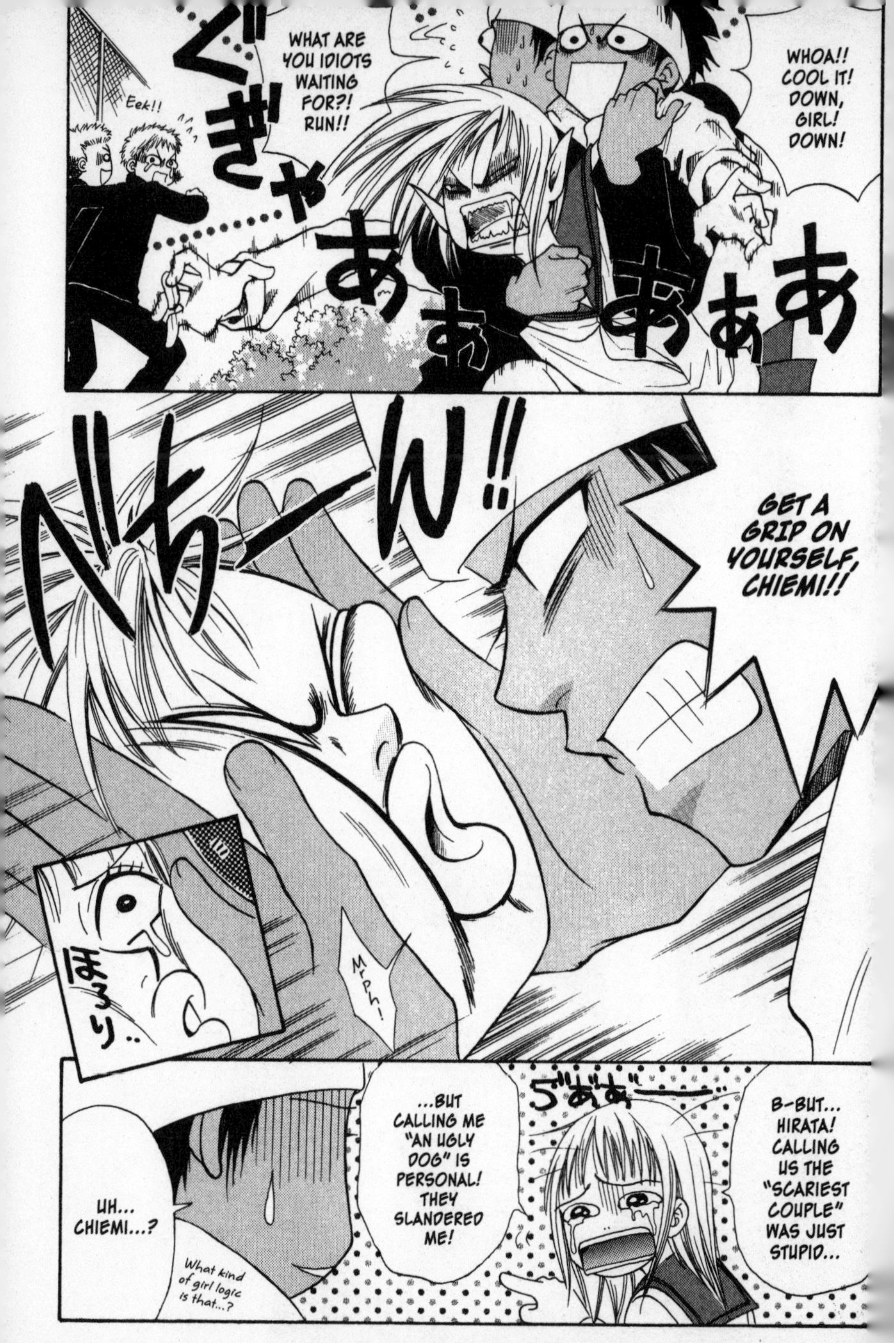
WHOA!! COOL IT! DOWN, GIRL! DOWN!
WHAT ARE YOU IDIOTS WAITING FOR?! RUN!!
Eek!!
ぐぎゃあぁあ
あぁあ
べちーん!!
GET A GRIP ON YOURSELF, CHIEMI!!
Mrph!
ぽろり..
ぢあぁーー
B-BUT... HIRATA! CALLING US THE "SCARIEST COUPLE" WAS JUST STUPID...
...BUT CALLING ME "AN UGLY DOG" IS PERSONAL! THEY SLANDERED ME!
UH... CHIEMI...?
What kind of girl logic is that...?

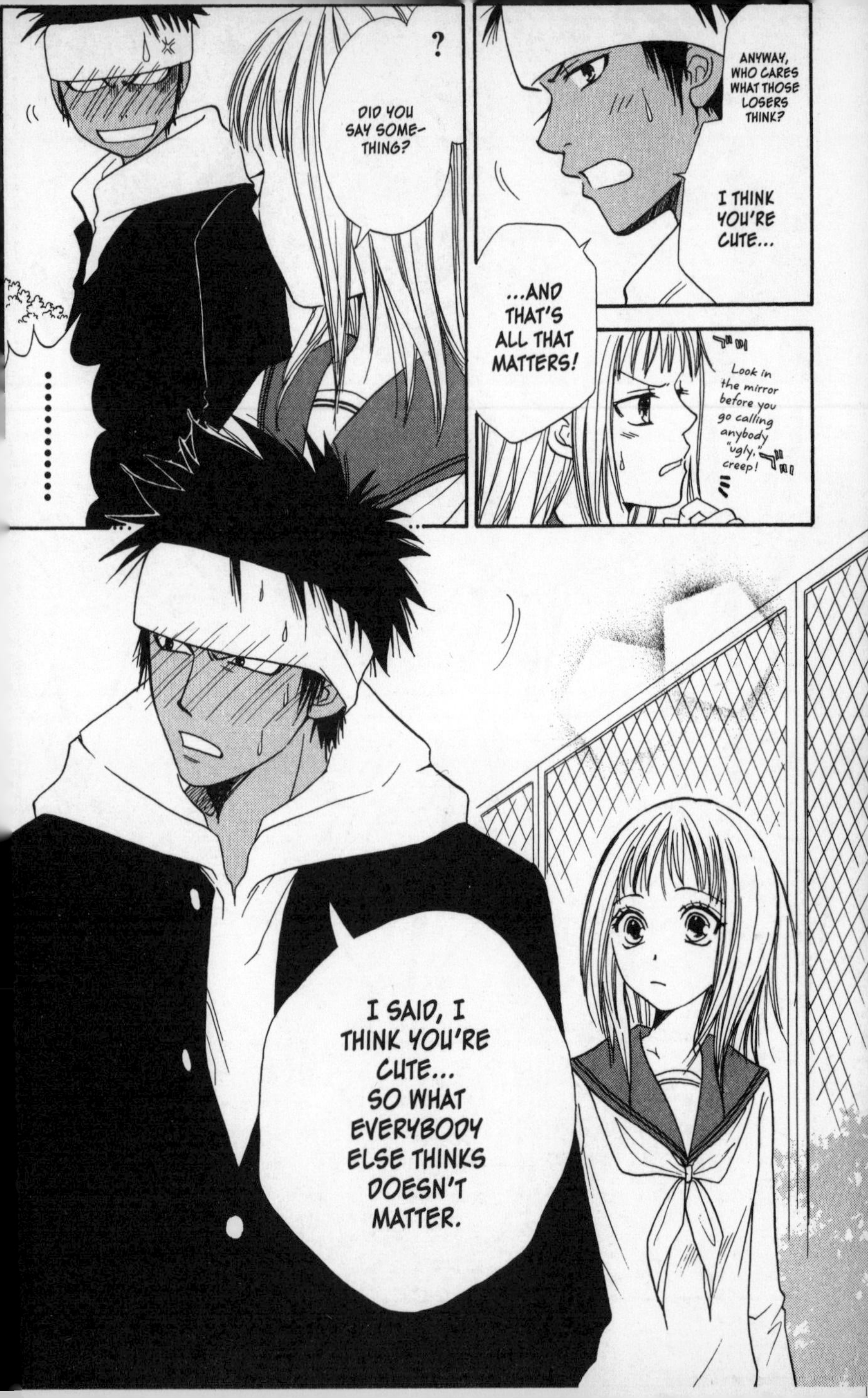
ANYWAY, WHO CARES WHAT THOSE LOSERS THINK?
I THINK YOU'RE CUTE...
...AND THAT'S ALL THAT MATTERS!
Look in the mirror before you go calling anybody "ugly," creep!
?
DID YOU SAY SOME-THING?
....
I SAID, I THINK YOU'RE CUTE... SO WHAT EVERYBODY ELSE THINKS DOESN'T MATTER.

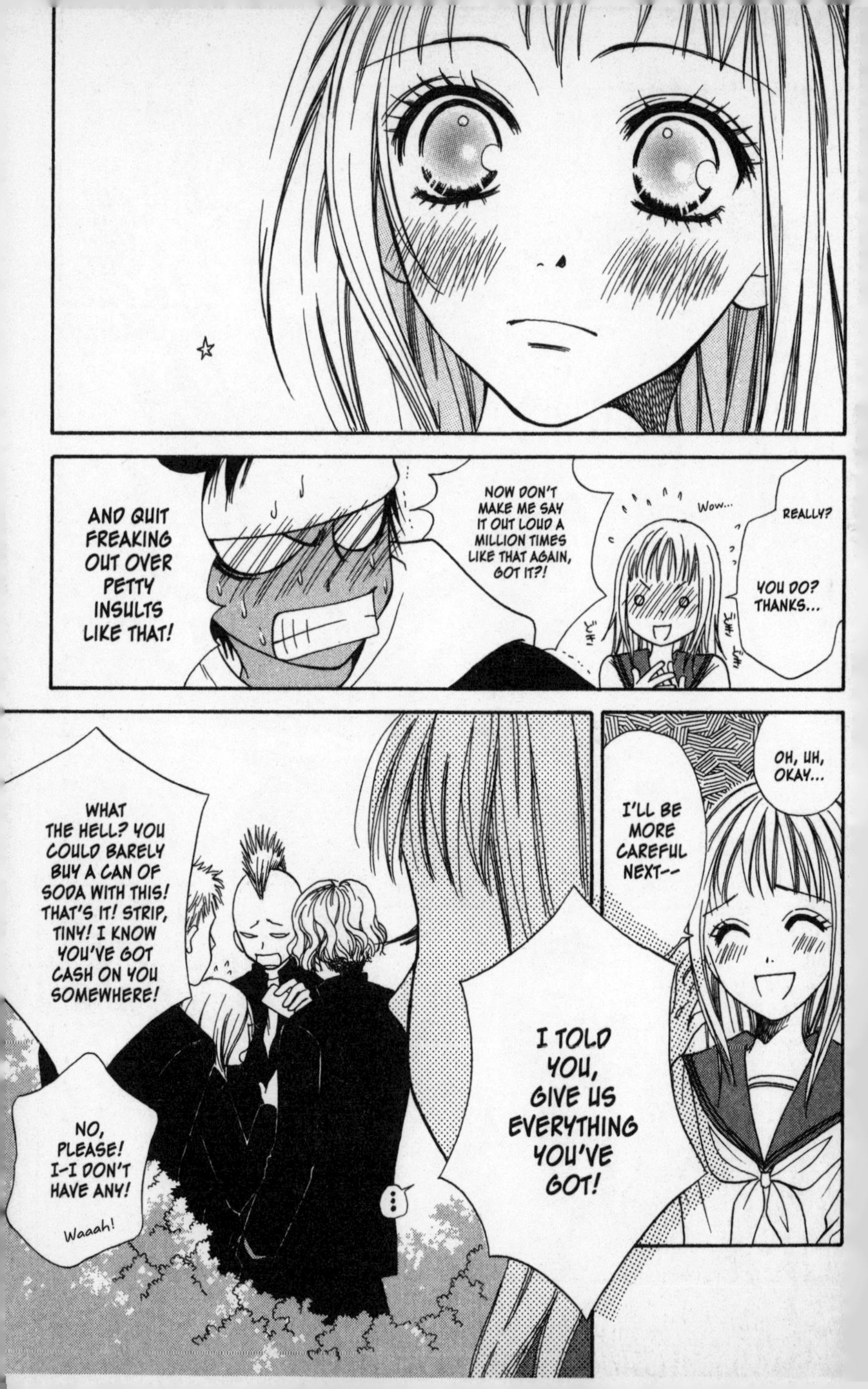
REALLY?
YOU DO? THANKS...
Wow...
NOW DON'T MAKE ME SAY IT OUT LOUD A MILLION TIMES LIKE THAT AGAIN, GOT IT?!
AND QUIT FREAKING OUT OVER PETTY INSULTS LIKE THAT!
OH, UH, OKAY...
I'LL BE MORE CAREFUL NEXT--
I TOLD YOU, GIVE US EVERYTHING YOU'VE GOT!
WHAT THE HELL? YOU COULD BARELY BUY A CAN OF SODA WITH THIS! THAT'S IT! STRIP, TINY! I KNOW YOU'VE GOT CASH ON YOU SOMEWHERE!
NO, PLEASE! I-I DON'T HAVE ANY!
Waaah!
...

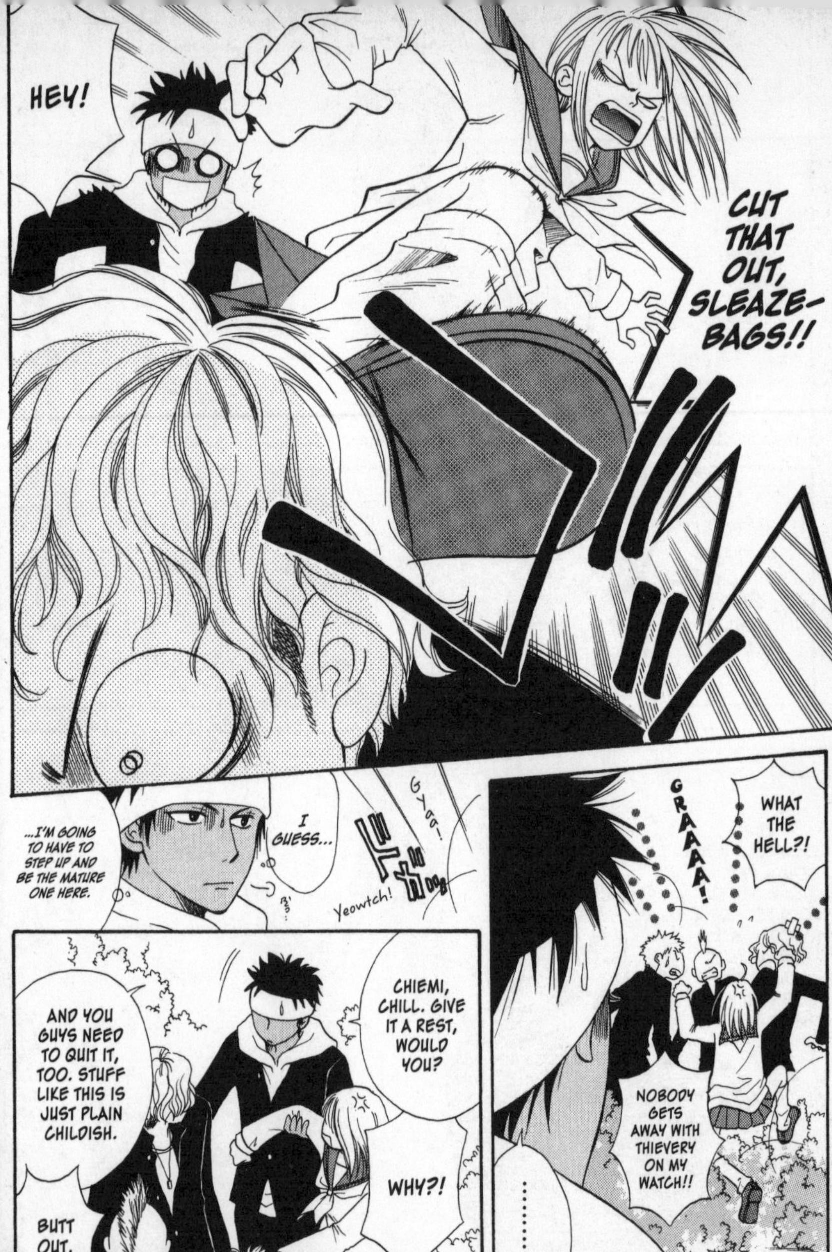
CUT THAT OUT, SLEAZE-BAGS!!
HEY!
WHAT THE HELL?!
GRAAAA!
NOBODY GETS AWAY WITH THIEVERY ON MY WATCH!!
......
I GUESS...
...I'M GOING TO HAVE TO STEP UP AND BE THE MATURE ONE HERE.
Gyaa!
Yeowtch!
CHIEMI, CHILL. GIVE IT A REST, WOULD YOU?
WHY?!
AND YOU GUYS NEED TO QUIT IT, TOO. STUFF LIKE THIS IS JUST PLAIN CHILDISH.
BUTT OUT, DUDE!!

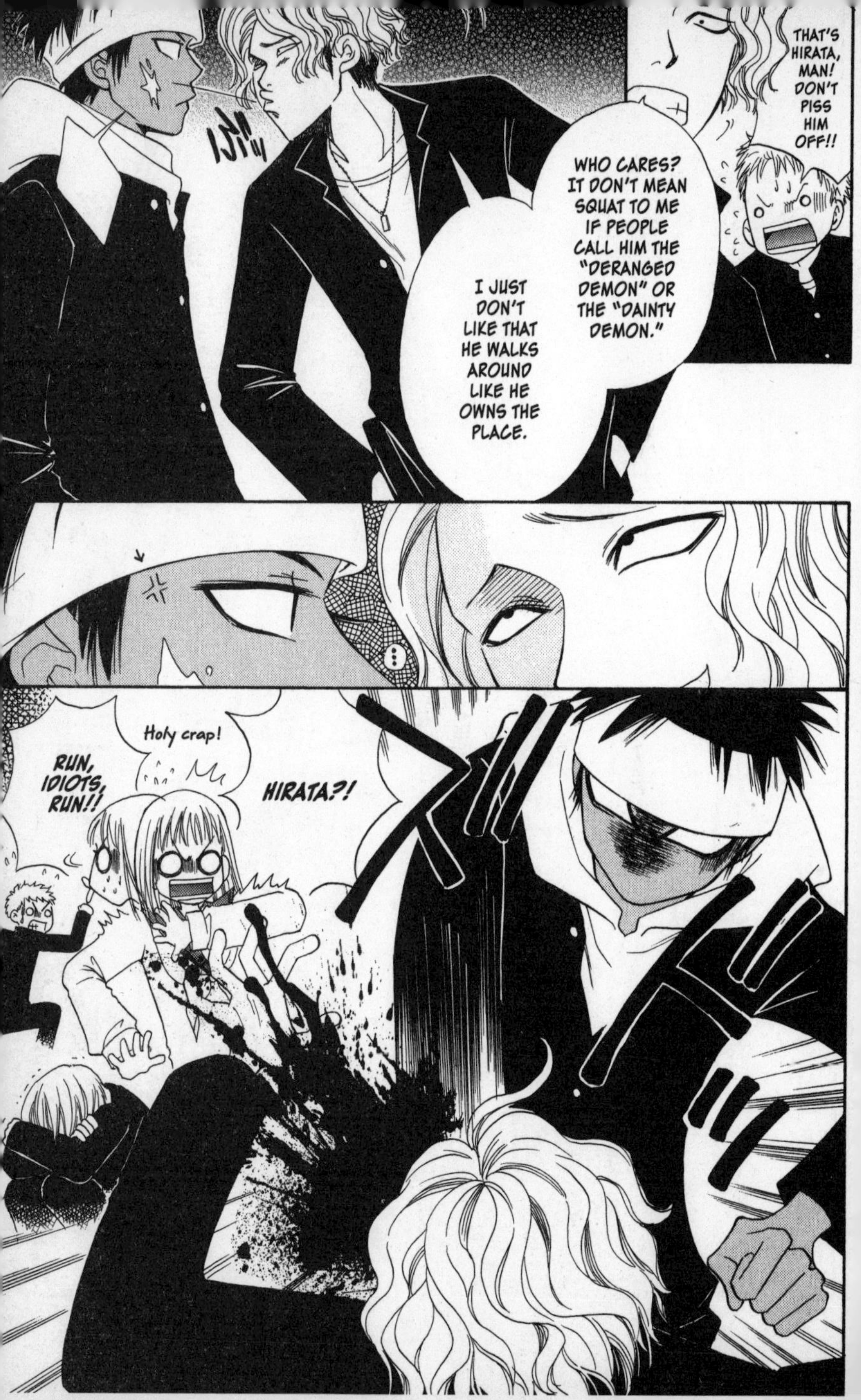
THAT'S HIRATA, MAN! DON'T PISS HIM OFF!!
WHO CARES? IT DON'T MEAN SQUAT TO ME IF PEOPLE CALL HIM THE "DERANGED DEMON" OR THE "DAINTY DEMON."
I JUST DON'T LIKE THAT HE WALKS AROUND LIKE HE OWNS THE PLACE.
HIRATA?!
Holy crap!
RUN, IDIOTS, RUN!!

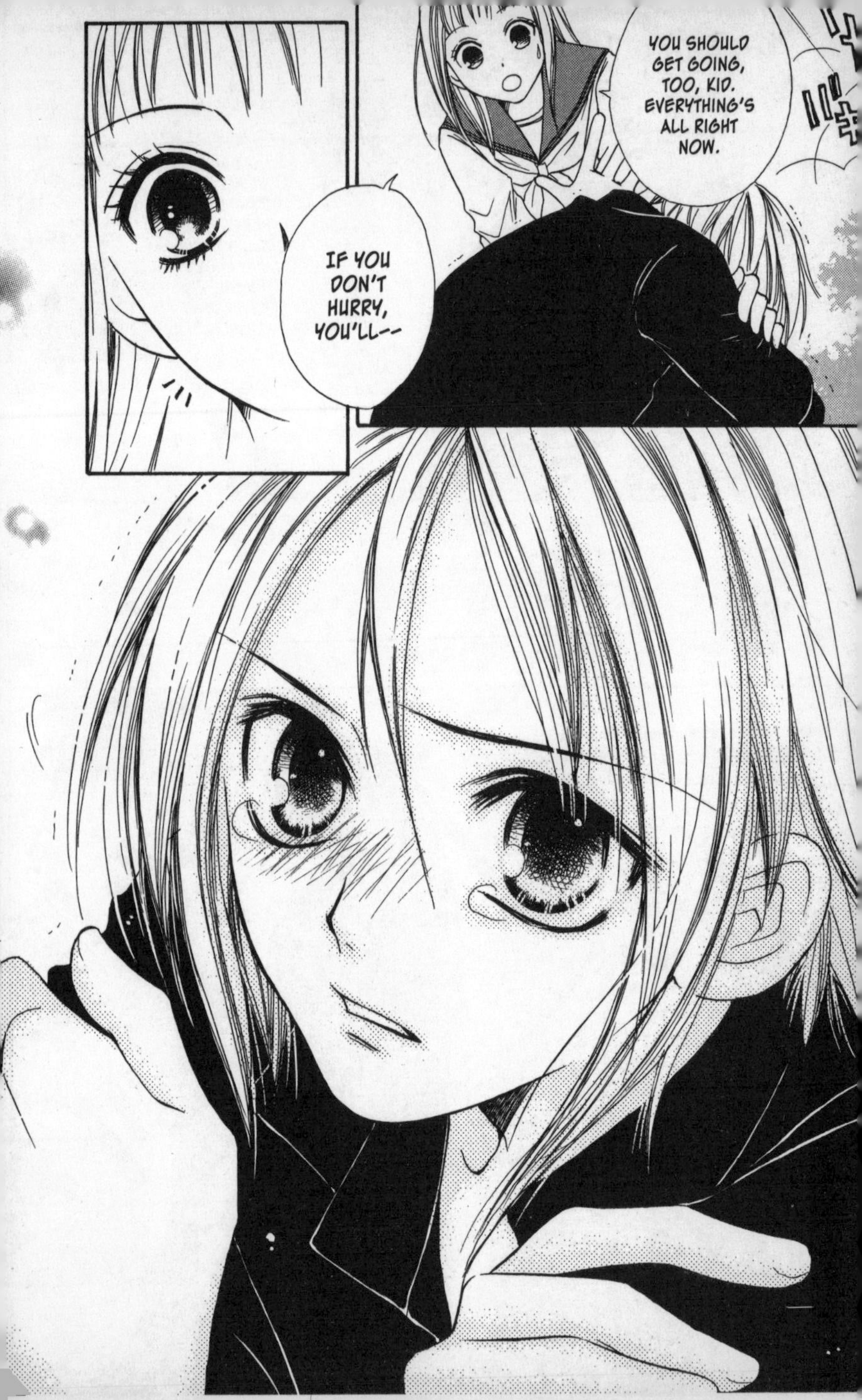
YOU SHOULD GET GOING, TOO, KID. EVERYTHING'S ALL RIGHT NOW.
IF YOU DON'T HURRY, YOU'LL--

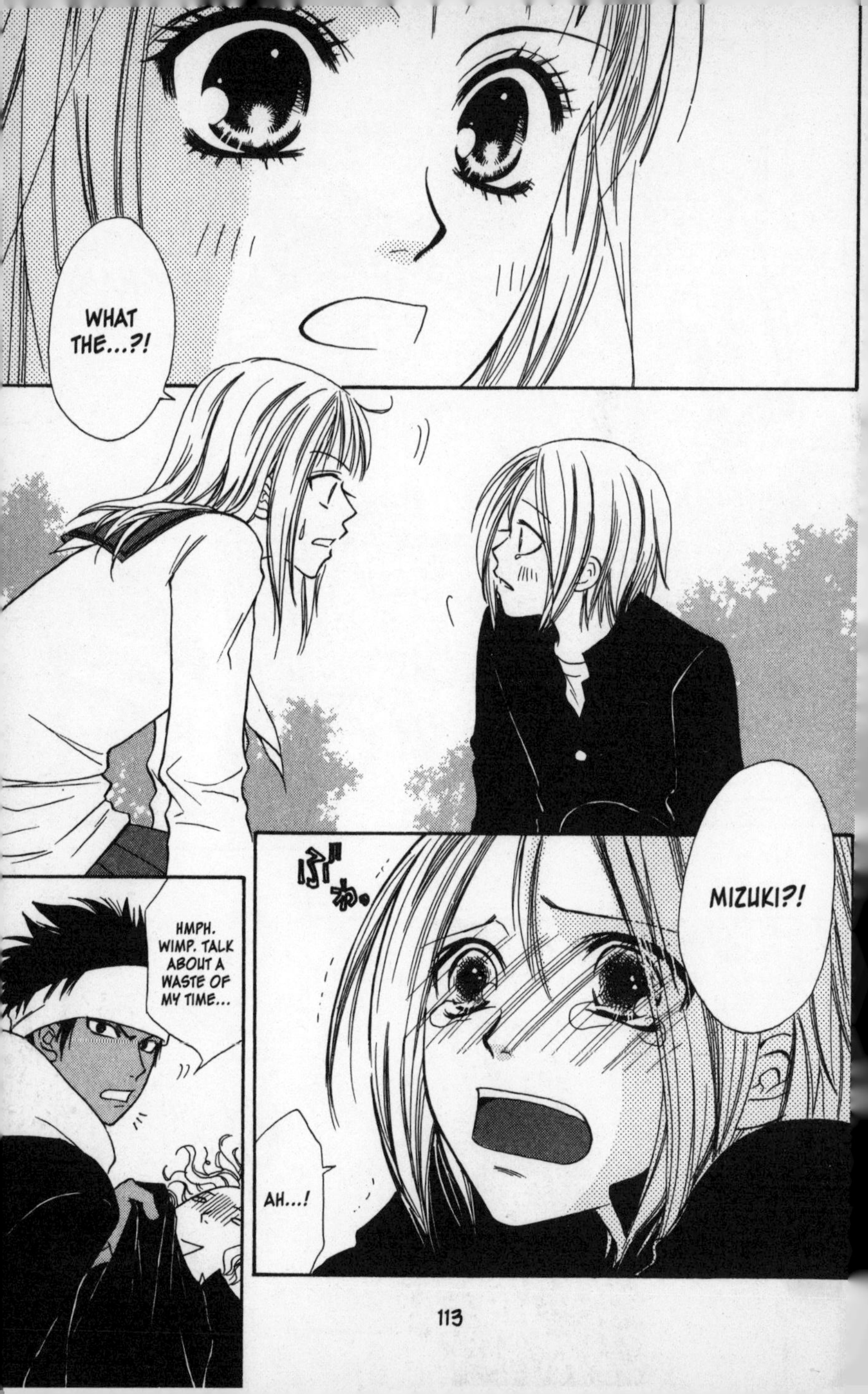
WHAT THE...?!
MIZUKI?!
ぶわ
AH...!
HMPH. WIMP. TALK ABOUT A WASTE OF MY TIME...

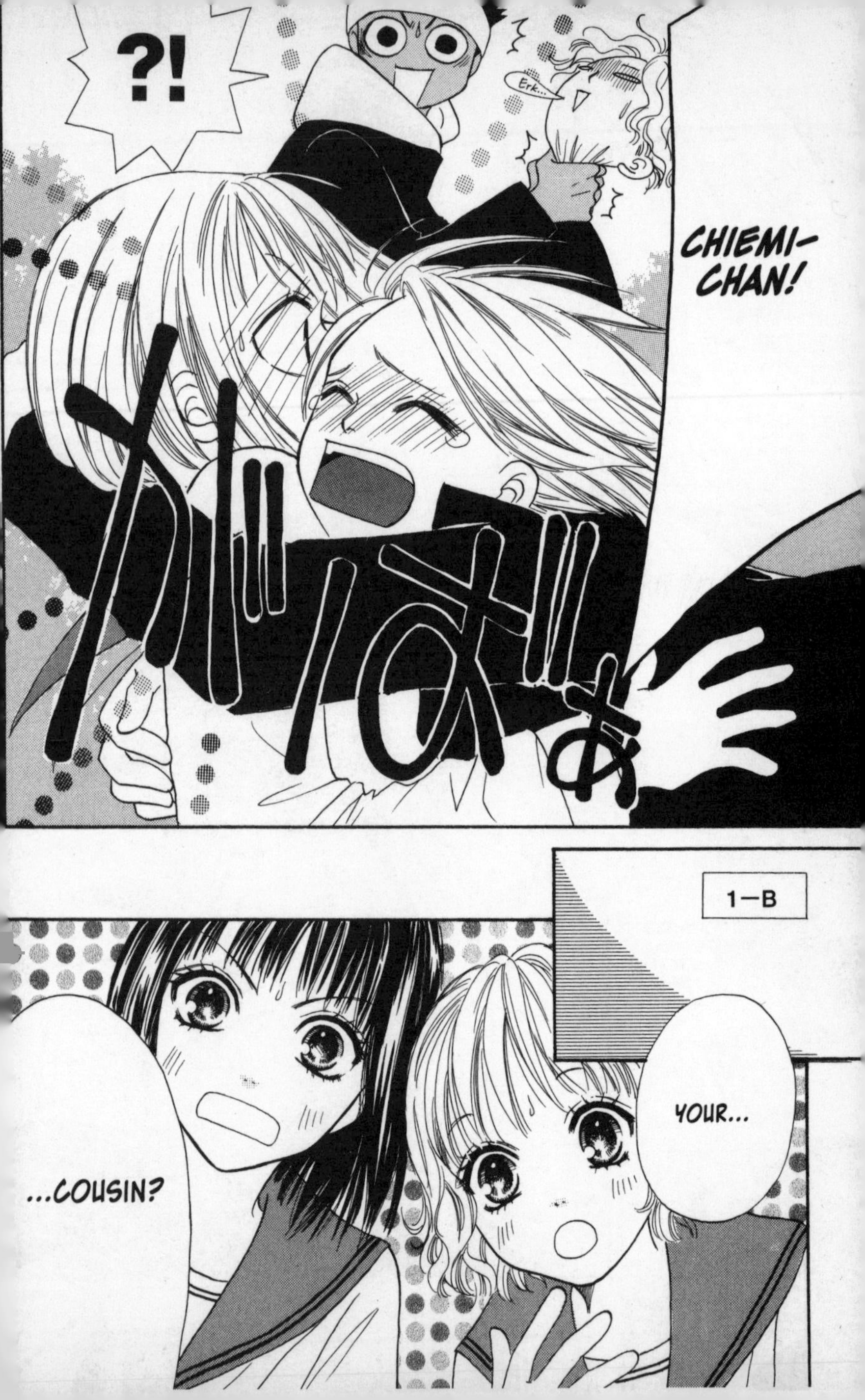
CHIEMI-CHAN!
Erk...
?!
1—B
YOUR...
...COUSIN?

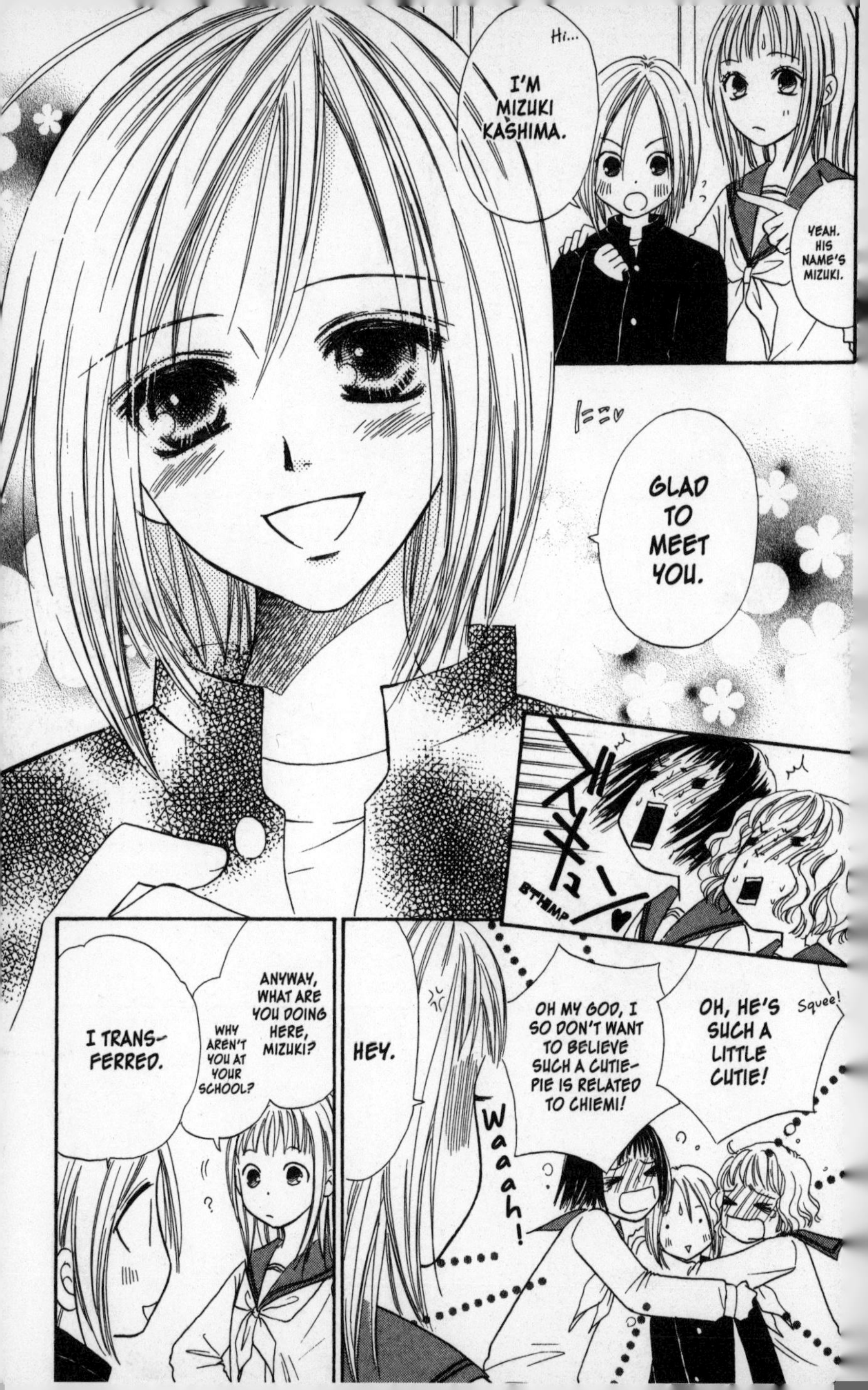
Hi...
I'M MIZUKI KASHIMA.
YEAH. HIS NAME'S MIZUKI.
GLAD TO MEET YOU.
STHUMP
Squee!
OH, HE'S SUCH A LITTLE CUTIE!
OH MY GOD, I SO DON'T WANT TO BELIEVE SUCH A CUTIE-PIE IS RELATED TO CHIEMI!
Waaah!
HEY.
ANYWAY, WHAT ARE YOU DOING HERE, MIZUKI?
WHY AREN'T YOU AT YOUR SCHOOL?
I TRANS-FERRED.

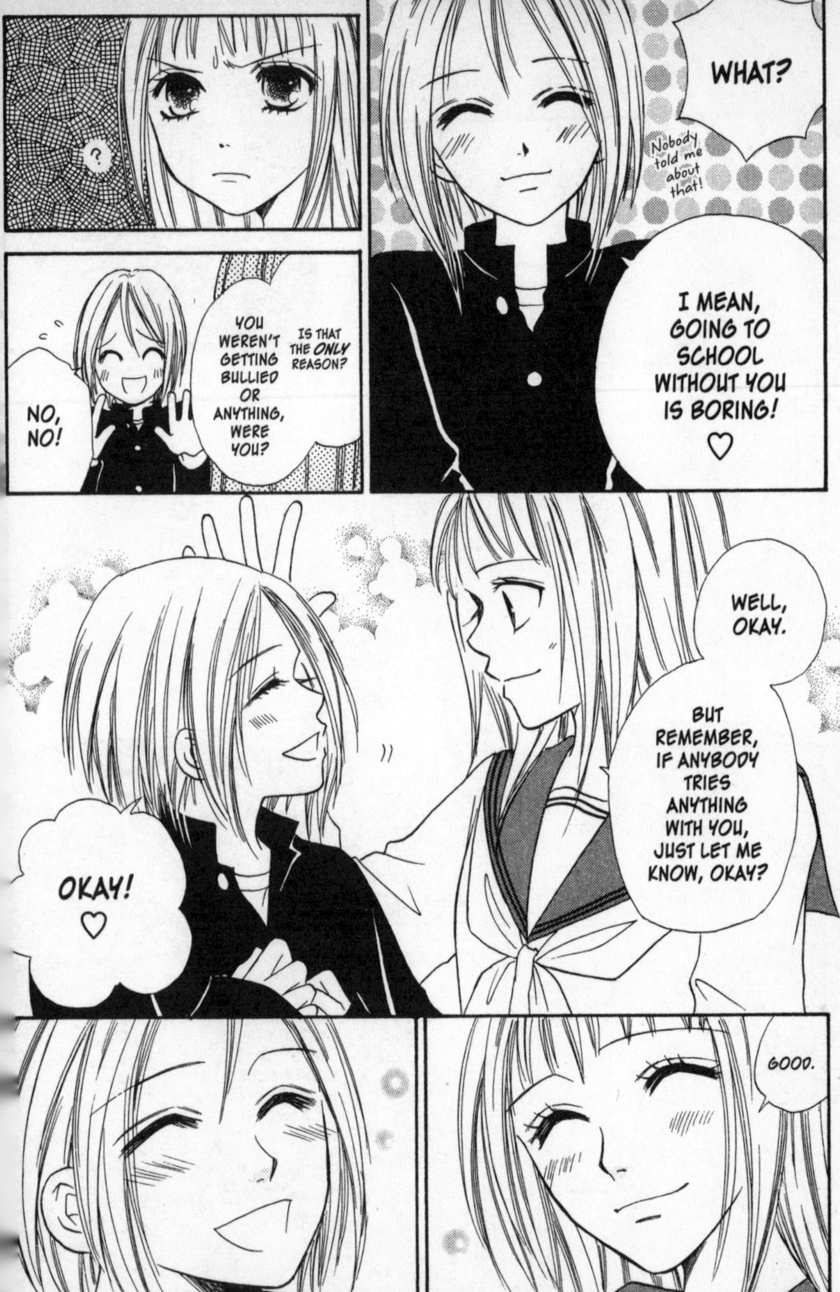
WHAT?
Nobody told me about that!
I MEAN, GOING TO SCHOOL WITHOUT YOU IS BORING! ♡
?
IS THAT THE *ONLY* REASON?
YOU WEREN'T GETTING BULLIED OR ANYTHING, WERE YOU?
NO, NO!
WELL, OKAY.
BUT REMEMBER, IF ANYBODY TRIES ANYTHING WITH YOU, JUST LET ME KNOW, OKAY?
OKAY! ♡
GOOD.

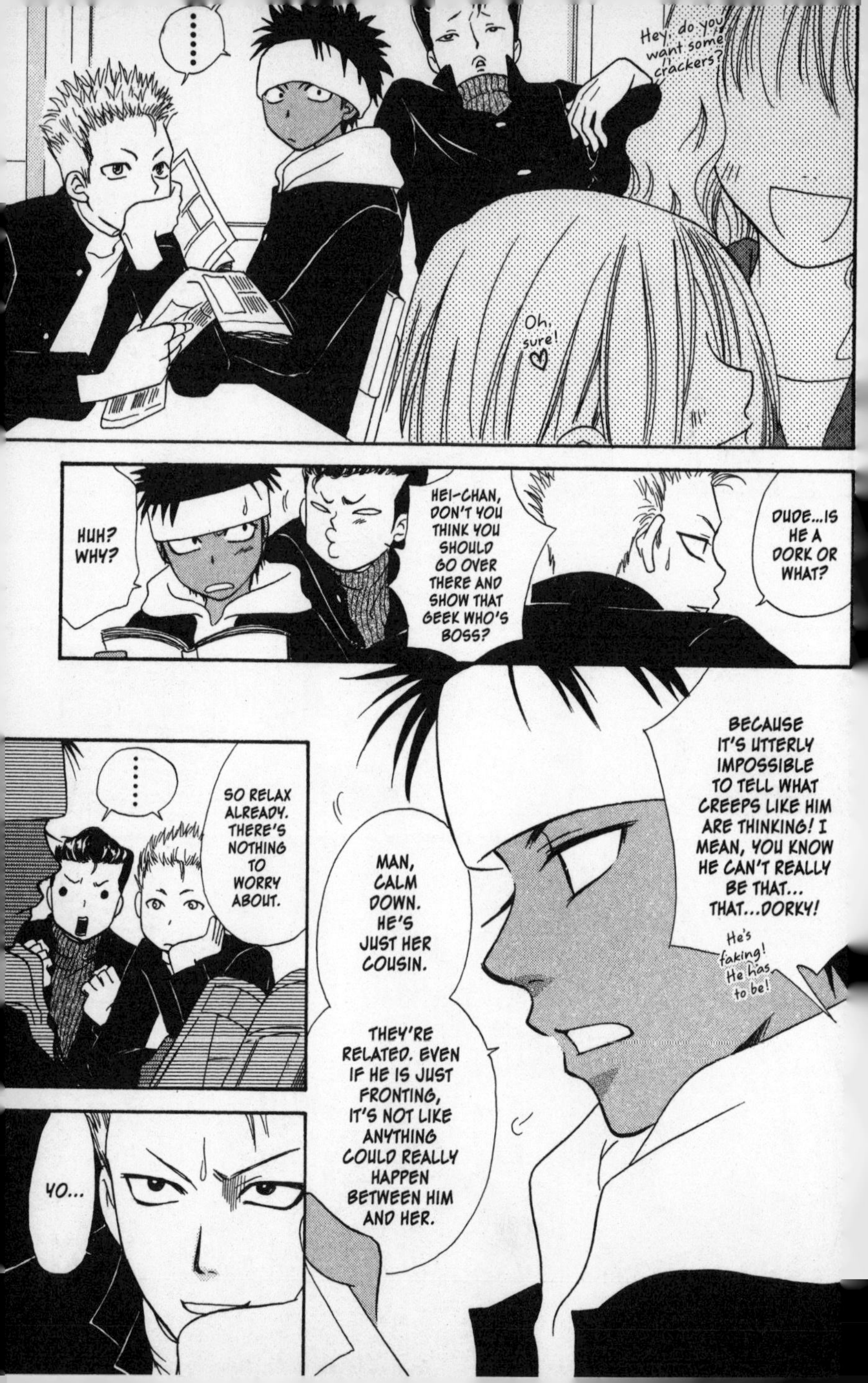
Hey, do you want some crackers?
Oh, sure! ♥
......
DUDE...IS HE A DORK OR WHAT?
HEI-CHAN, DON'T YOU THINK YOU SHOULD GO OVER THERE AND SHOW THAT GEEK WHO'S BOSS?
HUH? WHY?
BECAUSE IT'S UTTERLY IMPOSSIBLE TO TELL WHAT CREEPS LIKE HIM ARE THINKING! I MEAN, YOU KNOW HE CAN'T REALLY BE THAT... THAT...DORKY!
He's faking! He has to be!
MAN, CALM DOWN. HE'S JUST HER COUSIN.
THEY'RE RELATED. EVEN IF HE IS JUST FRONTING, IT'S NOT LIKE ANYTHING COULD REALLY HAPPEN BETWEEN HIM AND HER.
SO RELAX ALREADY. THERE'S NOTHING TO WORRY ABOUT.
......
YO...

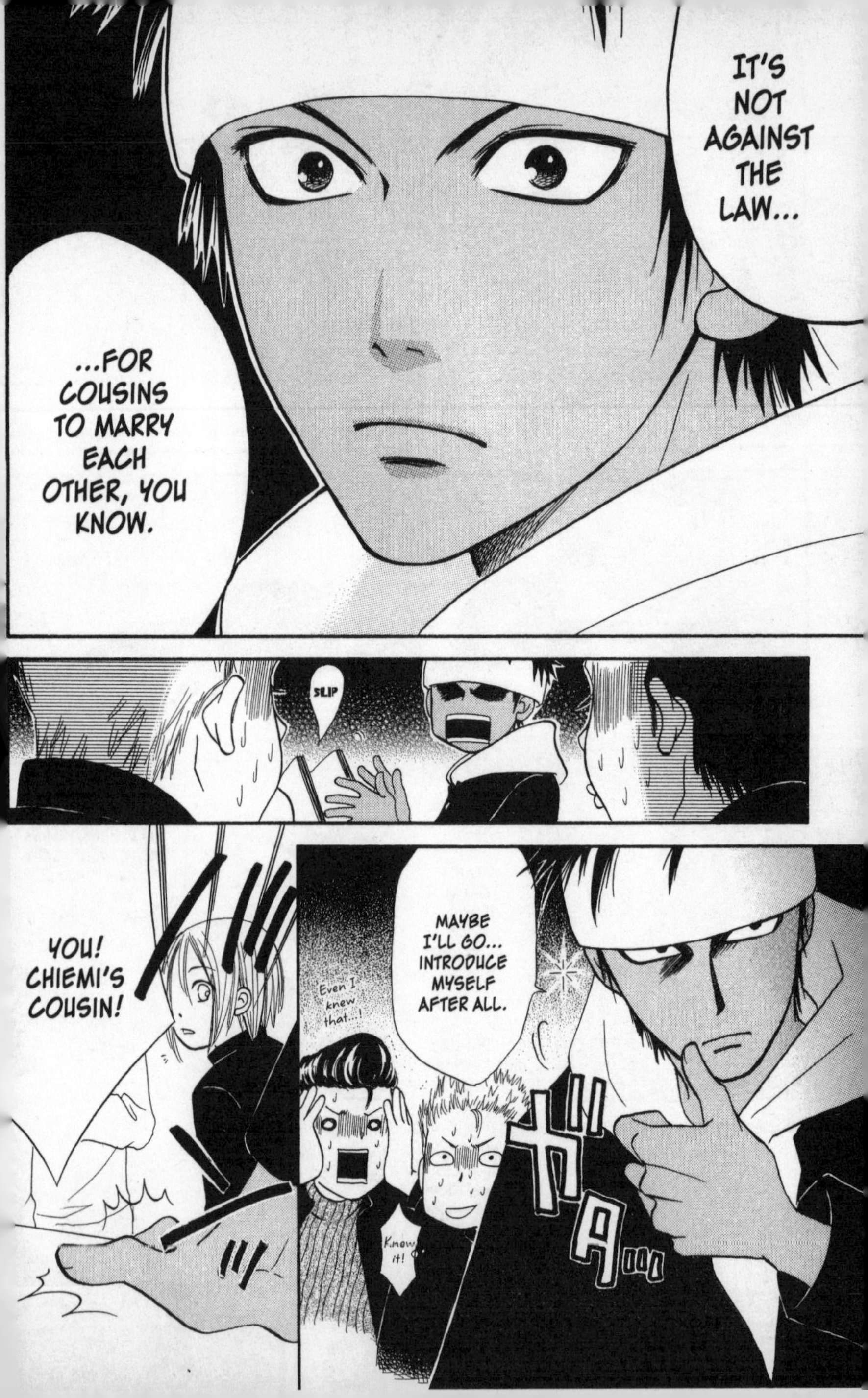
IT'S NOT AGAINST THE LAW...
...FOR COUSINS TO MARRY EACH OTHER, YOU KNOW.
SLIP
MAYBE I'LL GO... INTRODUCE MYSELF AFTER ALL.
Even I knew that...!
Knew it!
YOU! CHIEMI'S COUSIN!

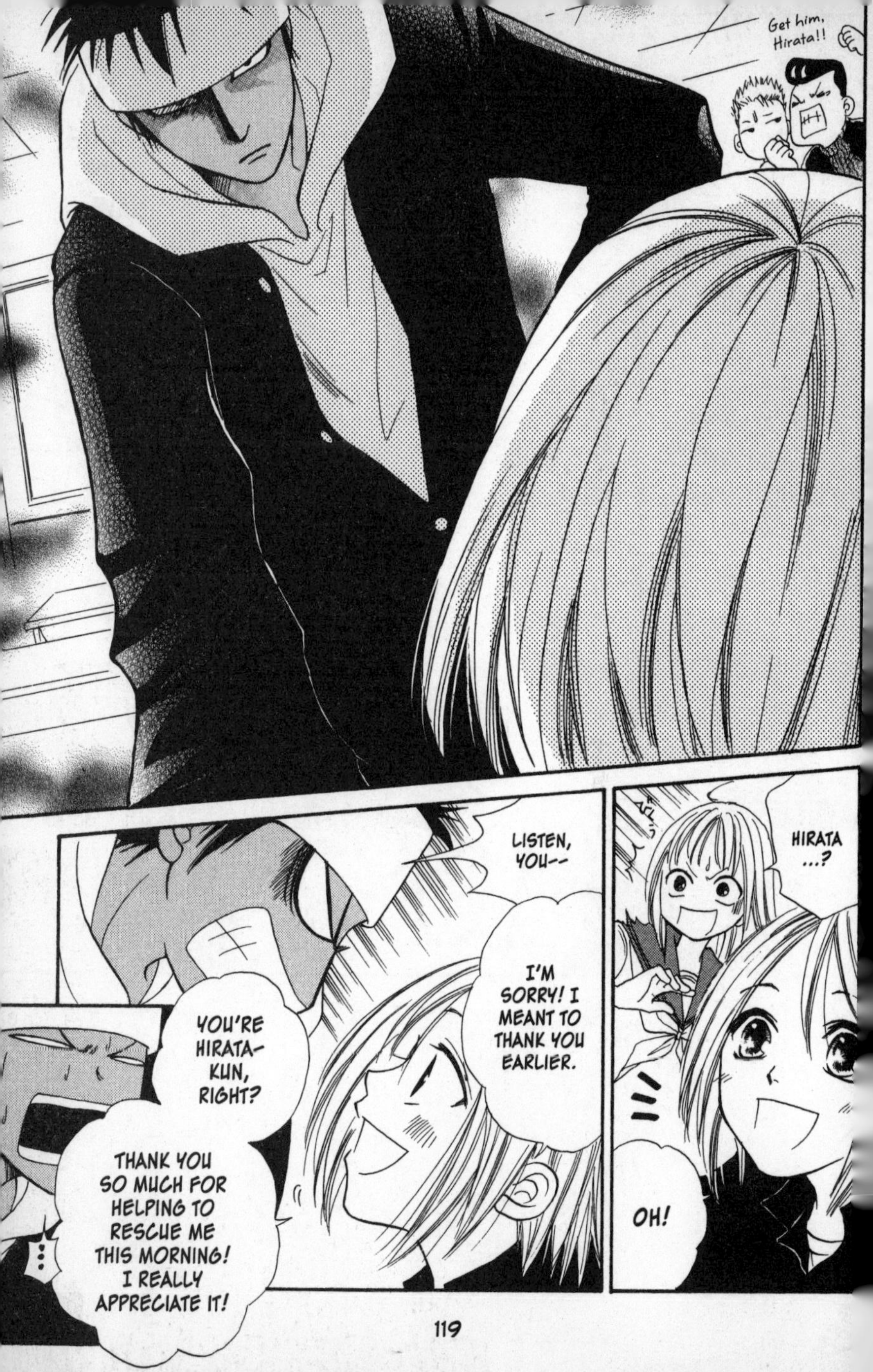
Get him, Hirata!!
HIRATA ...?
OH!
LISTEN, YOU--
I'M SORRY! I MEANT TO THANK YOU EARLIER.
YOU'RE HIRATA-KUN, RIGHT?
THANK YOU SO MUCH FOR HELPING TO RESCUE ME THIS MORNING! I REALLY APPRECIATE IT!
...

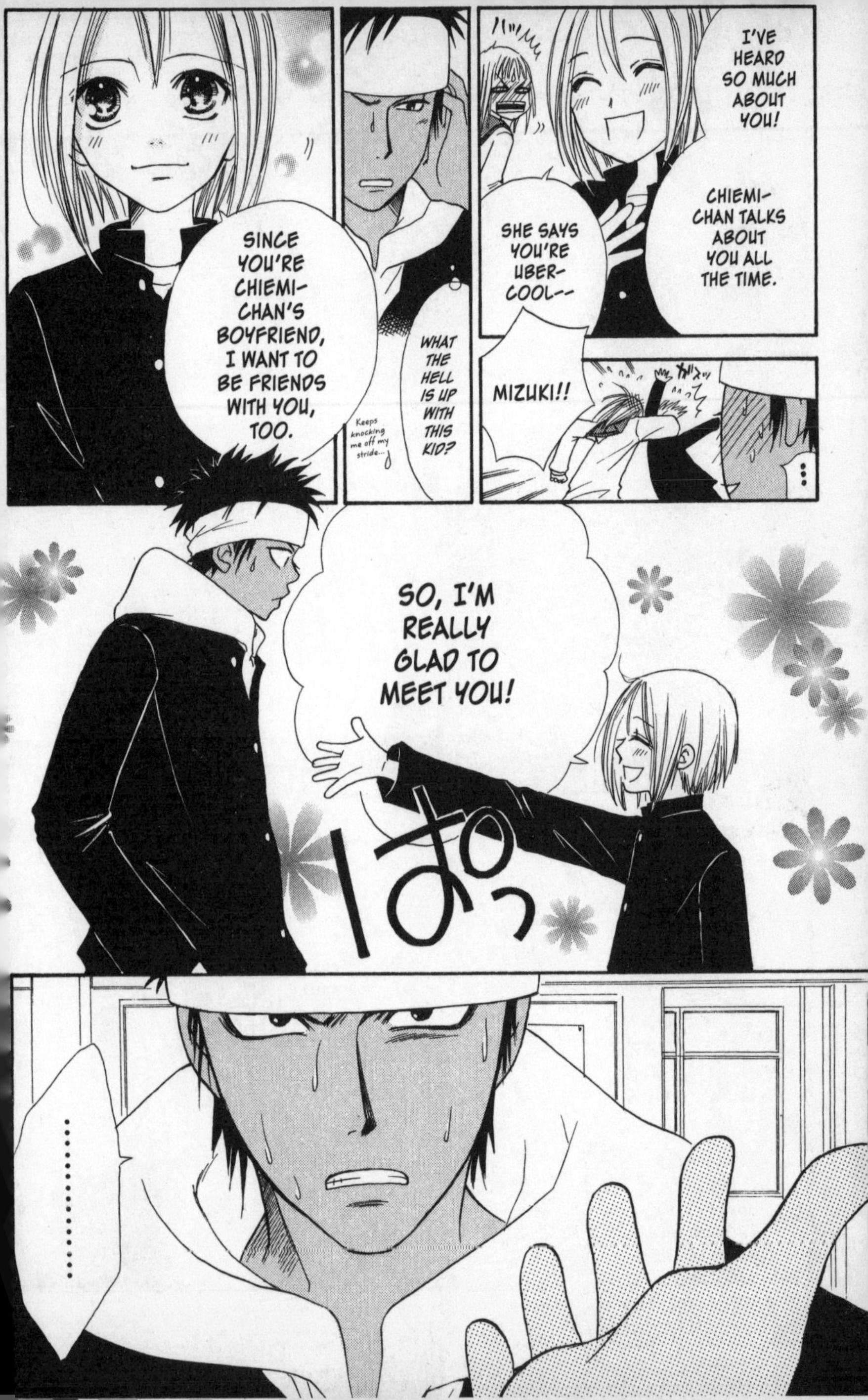

I'VE HEARD SO MUCH ABOUT YOU!
CHIEMI-CHAN TALKS ABOUT YOU ALL THE TIME.
SHE SAYS YOU'RE UBER-COOL--
MIZUKI!!
...
WHAT THE HELL IS UP WITH THIS KID?
Keeps knocking me off my stride...
SINCE YOU'RE CHIEMI-CHAN'S BOYFRIEND, I WANT TO BE FRIENDS WITH YOU, TOO.
SO, I'M REALLY GLAD TO MEET YOU!
ぱっ
....

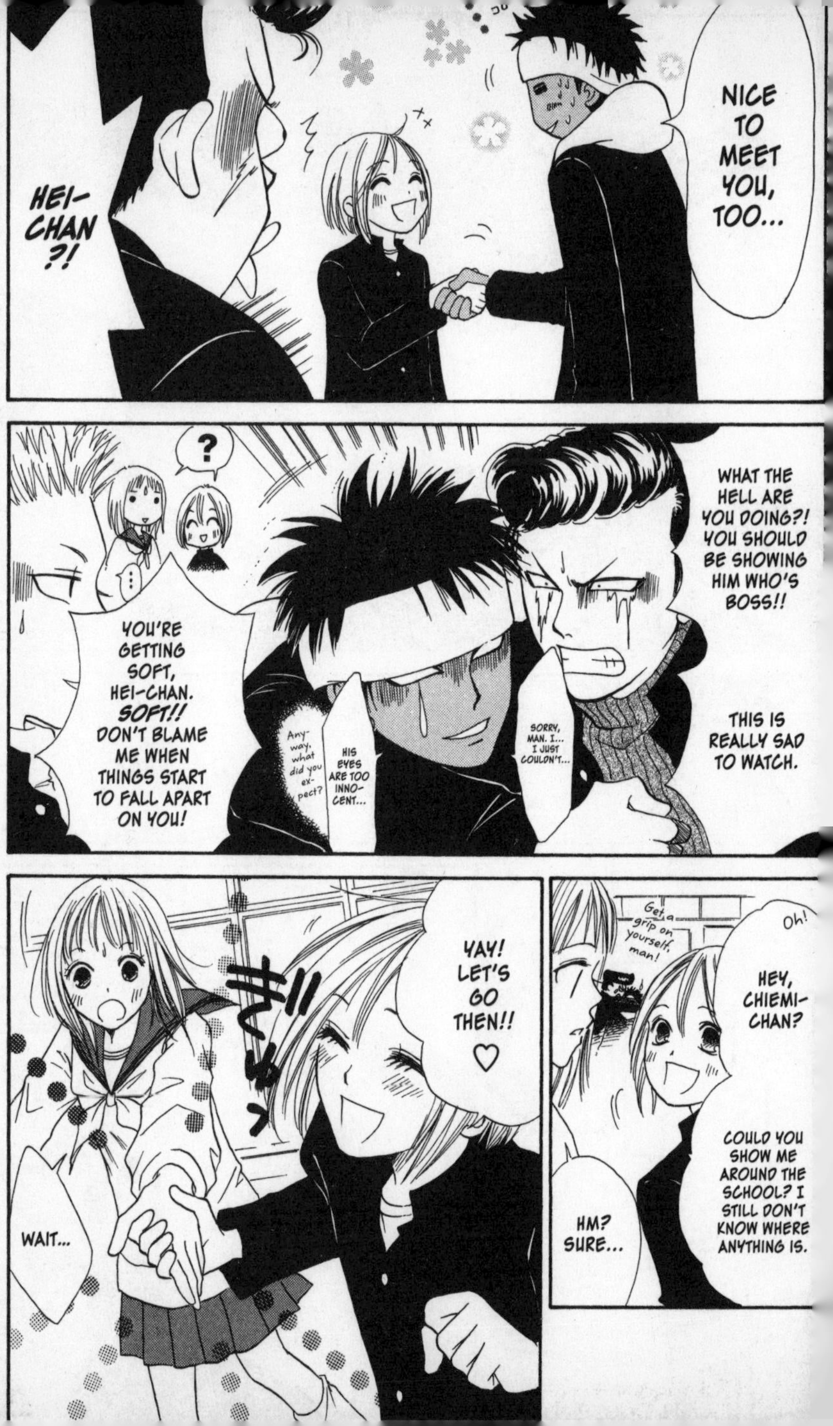
NICE TO MEET YOU, TOO...
HEI-CHAN?!
WHAT THE HELL ARE YOU DOING?! YOU SHOULD BE SHOWING HIM WHO'S BOSS!!
THIS IS REALLY SAD TO WATCH.
SORRY, MAN. I... I JUST COULDN'T...
HIS EYES ARE TOO INNO-CENT...
Any-way, what did you ex-pect?
?
YOU'RE GETTING SOFT, HEI-CHAN. SOFT!! DON'T BLAME ME WHEN THINGS START TO FALL APART ON YOU!
Oh!
HEY, CHIEMI-CHAN?
Get a grip on yourself, man!
COULD YOU SHOW ME AROUND THE SCHOOL? I STILL DON'T KNOW WHERE ANYTHING IS.
HM? SURE...
YAY! LET'S GO THEN!! ♡
ぎゅっ
WAIT...

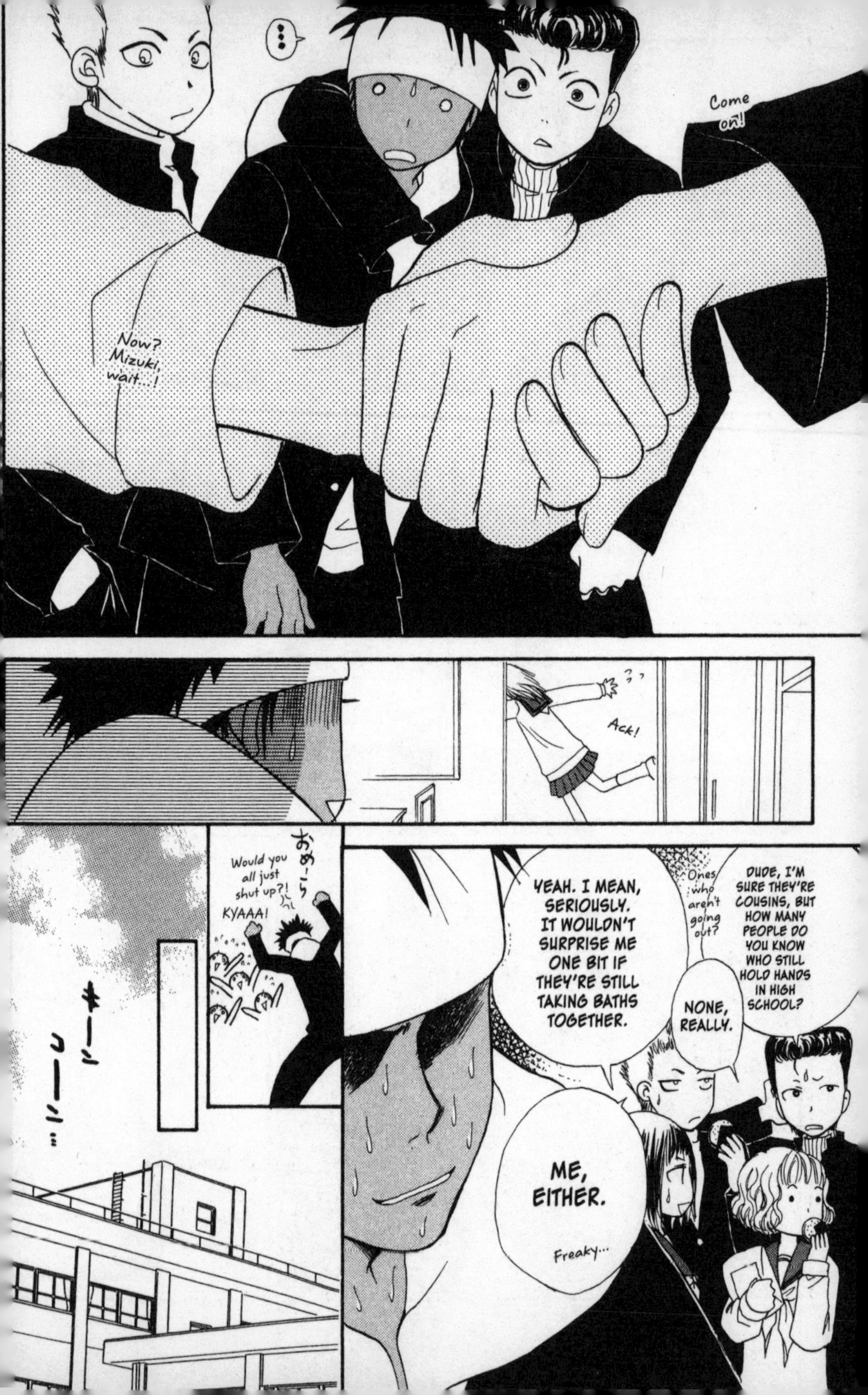

Come on!
...
Now? Mizuki, wait...!
Ack!
DUDE, I'M SURE THEY'RE COUSINS, BUT HOW MANY PEOPLE DO YOU KNOW WHO STILL HOLD HANDS IN HIGH SCHOOL?
Ones who aren't going out?
YEAH. I MEAN, SERIOUSLY. IT WOULDN'T SURPRISE ME ONE BIT IF THEY'RE STILL TAKING BATHS TOGETHER.
NONE, REALLY.
ME, EITHER.
Freaky...
おめーら
Would you all just shut up?!
KYAAA!
キーン
コーン…

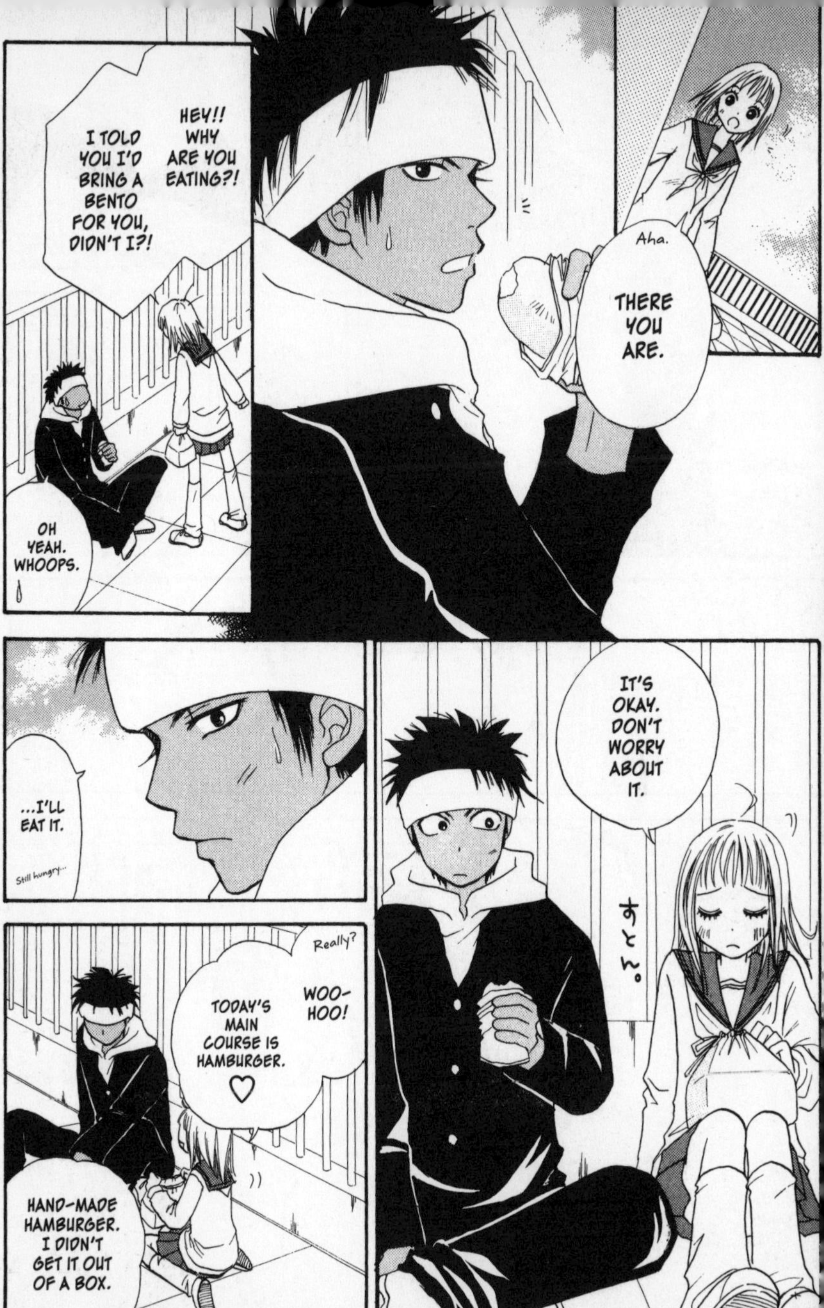
Aha.
THERE YOU ARE.
HEY!! WHY ARE YOU EATING?!
I TOLD YOU I'D BRING A BENTO FOR YOU, DIDN'T I?!
OH YEAH. WHOOPS.
IT'S OKAY. DON'T WORRY ABOUT IT.
すとん。
...I'LL EAT IT.
Still hungry...
Really?
WOO-HOO!
TODAY'S MAIN COURSE IS HAMBURGER. ♡
HAND-MADE HAMBURGER. I DIDN'T GET IT OUT OF A BOX.

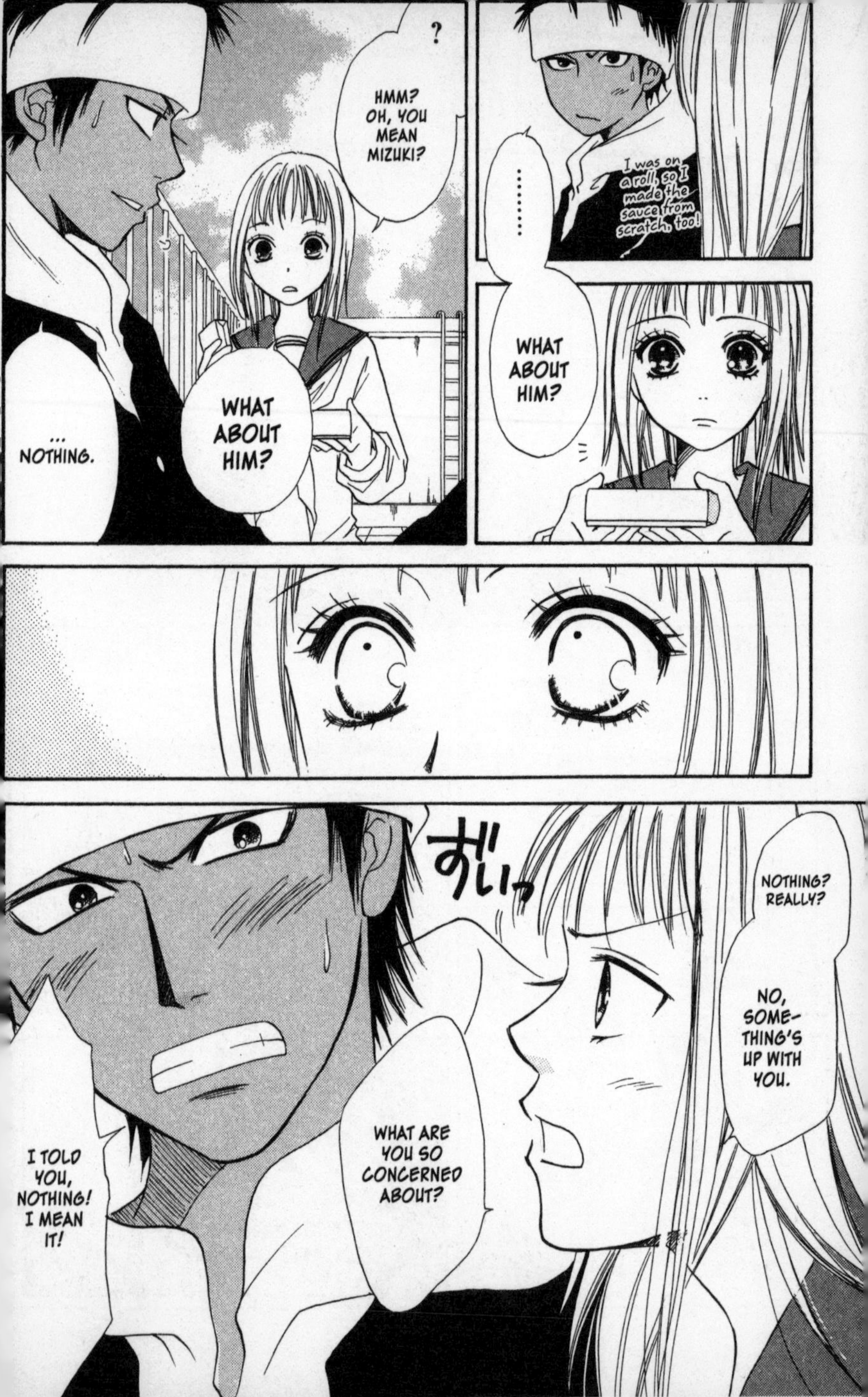
I was on a roll, so I made the sauce from scratch, too!
......
WHAT ABOUT HIM?
?
HMM? OH, YOU MEAN MIZUKI?
WHAT ABOUT HIM?
... NOTHING.
NOTHING? REALLY?
NO, SOME-THING'S UP WITH YOU.
ずいっ
WHAT ARE YOU SO CONCERNED ABOUT?
I TOLD YOU, NOTHING! I MEAN IT!

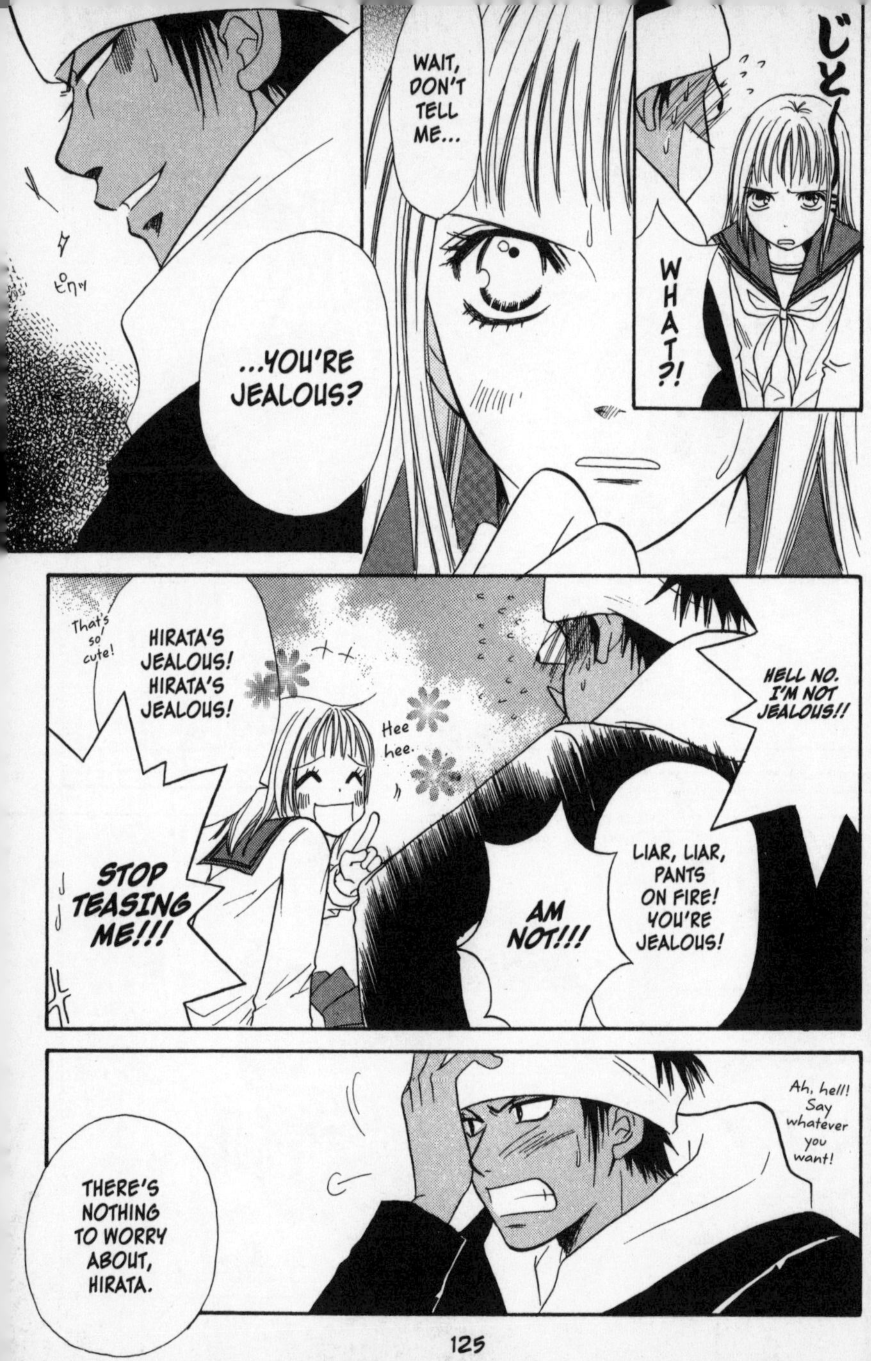
じとー
WHAT?!
WAIT, DON'T TELL ME...
...YOU'RE JEALOUS?
ピクッ
HELL NO. I'M NOT JEALOUS!!
Hee hee.
HIRATA'S JEALOUS! HIRATA'S JEALOUS!
That's so cute!
LIAR, LIAR, PANTS ON FIRE! YOU'RE JEALOUS!
AM NOT!!!
STOP TEASING ME!!!
Ah, hell! Say whatever you want!
THERE'S NOTHING TO WORRY ABOUT, HIRATA.

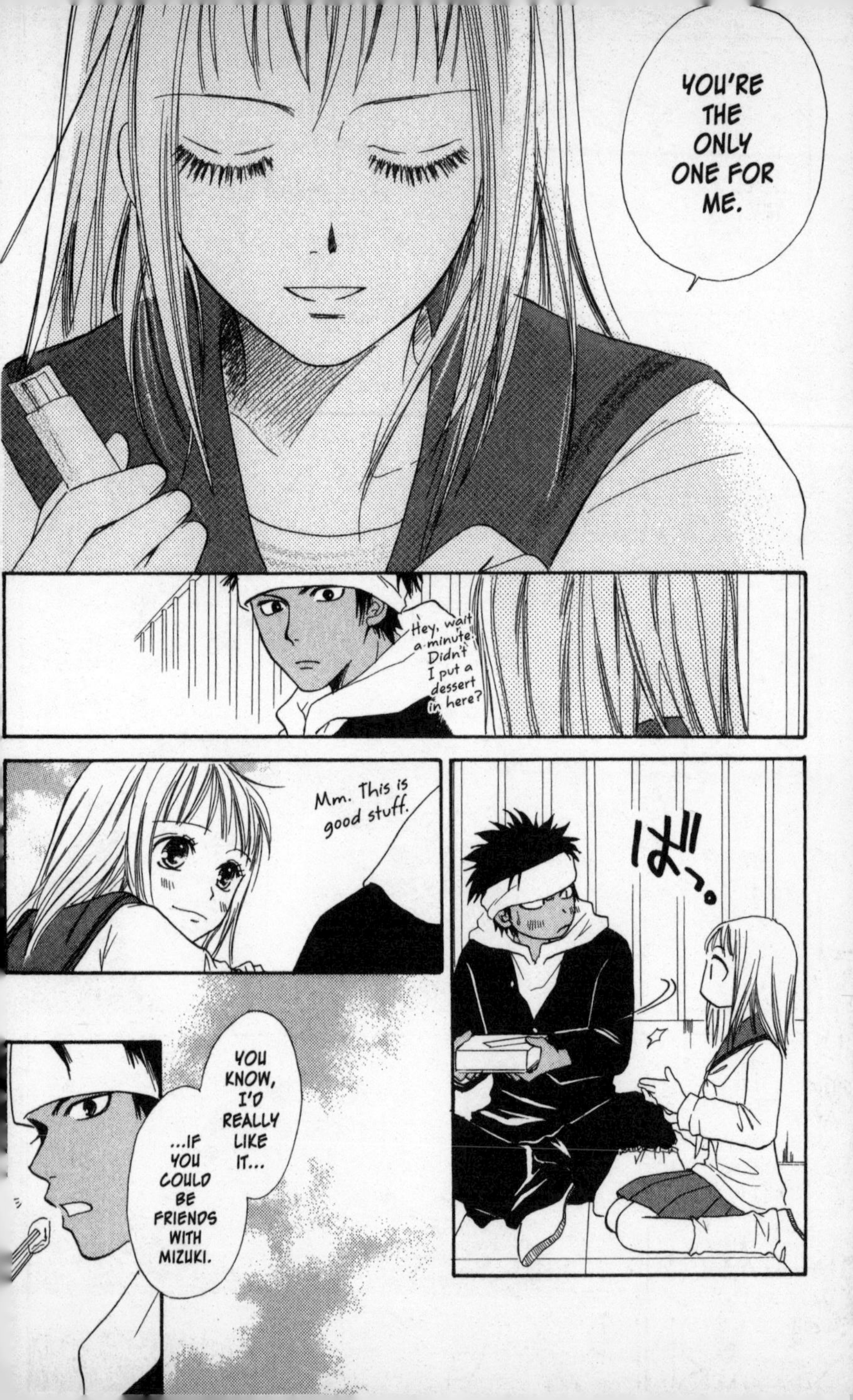
YOU'RE THE ONLY ONE FOR ME.
Hey, wait a minute. Didn't I put a dessert in here?
ぱっ。
Mm. This is good stuff.
YOU KNOW, I'D REALLY LIKE IT...
...IF YOU COULD BE FRIENDS WITH MIZUKI.

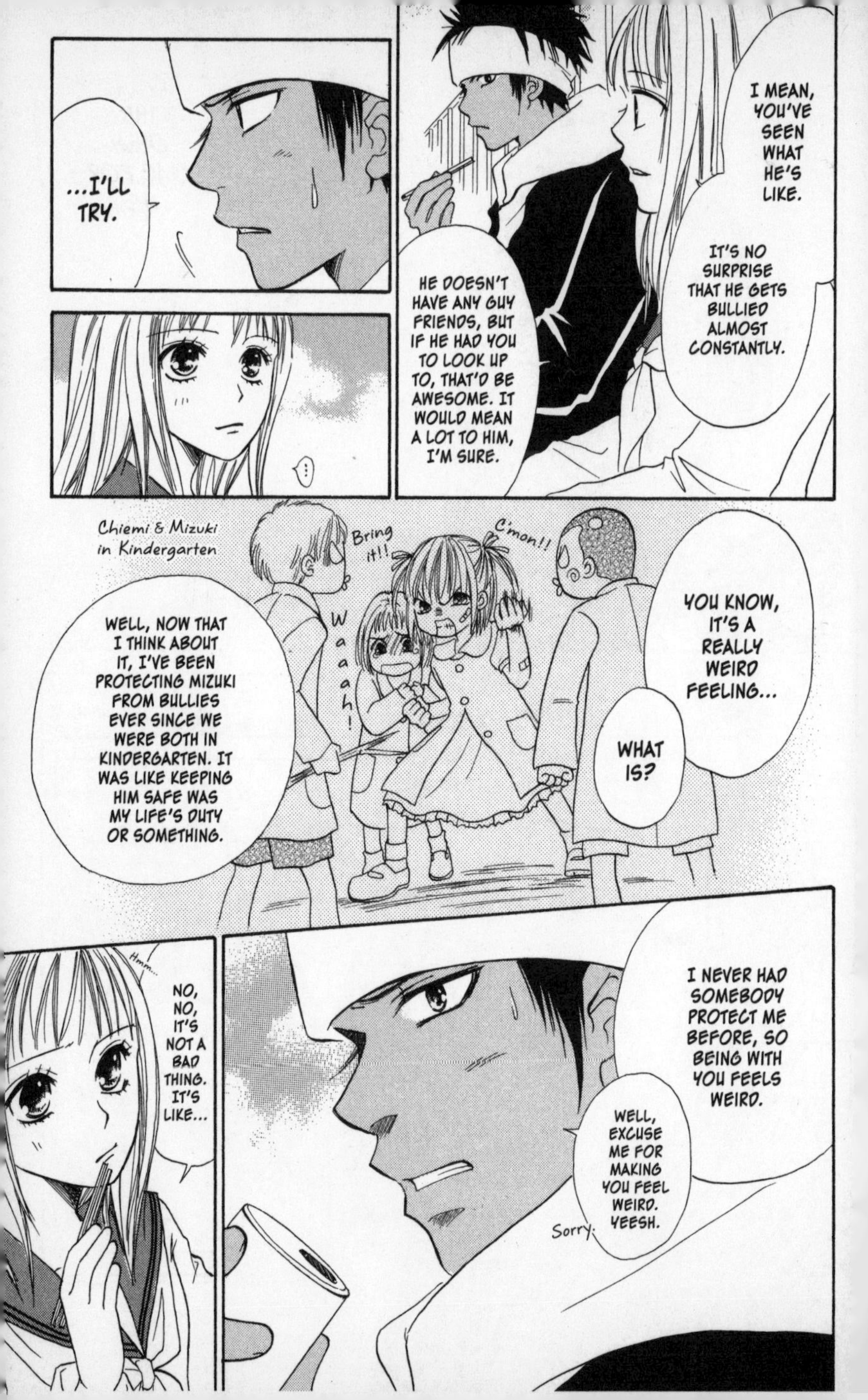
I MEAN, YOU'VE SEEN WHAT HE'S LIKE.
IT'S NO SURPRISE THAT HE GETS BULLIED ALMOST CONSTANTLY.
HE DOESN'T HAVE ANY GUY FRIENDS, BUT IF HE HAD YOU TO LOOK UP TO, THAT'D BE AWESOME. IT WOULD MEAN A LOT TO HIM, I'M SURE.
...I'LL TRY.
...
YOU KNOW, IT'S A REALLY WEIRD FEELING...
WHAT IS?
C'mon!!
Bring it!!
Waaah!
WELL, NOW THAT I THINK ABOUT IT, I'VE BEEN PROTECTING MIZUKI FROM BULLIES EVER SINCE WE WERE BOTH IN KINDERGARTEN. IT WAS LIKE KEEPING HIM SAFE WAS MY LIFE'S DUTY OR SOMETHING.
Chiemi & Mizuki in Kindergarten
I NEVER HAD SOMEBODY PROTECT ME BEFORE, SO BEING WITH YOU FEELS WEIRD.
WELL, EXCUSE ME FOR MAKING YOU FEEL WEIRD. YEESH.
Sorry.
Hmm...
NO, NO, IT'S NOT A BAD THING. IT'S LIKE...

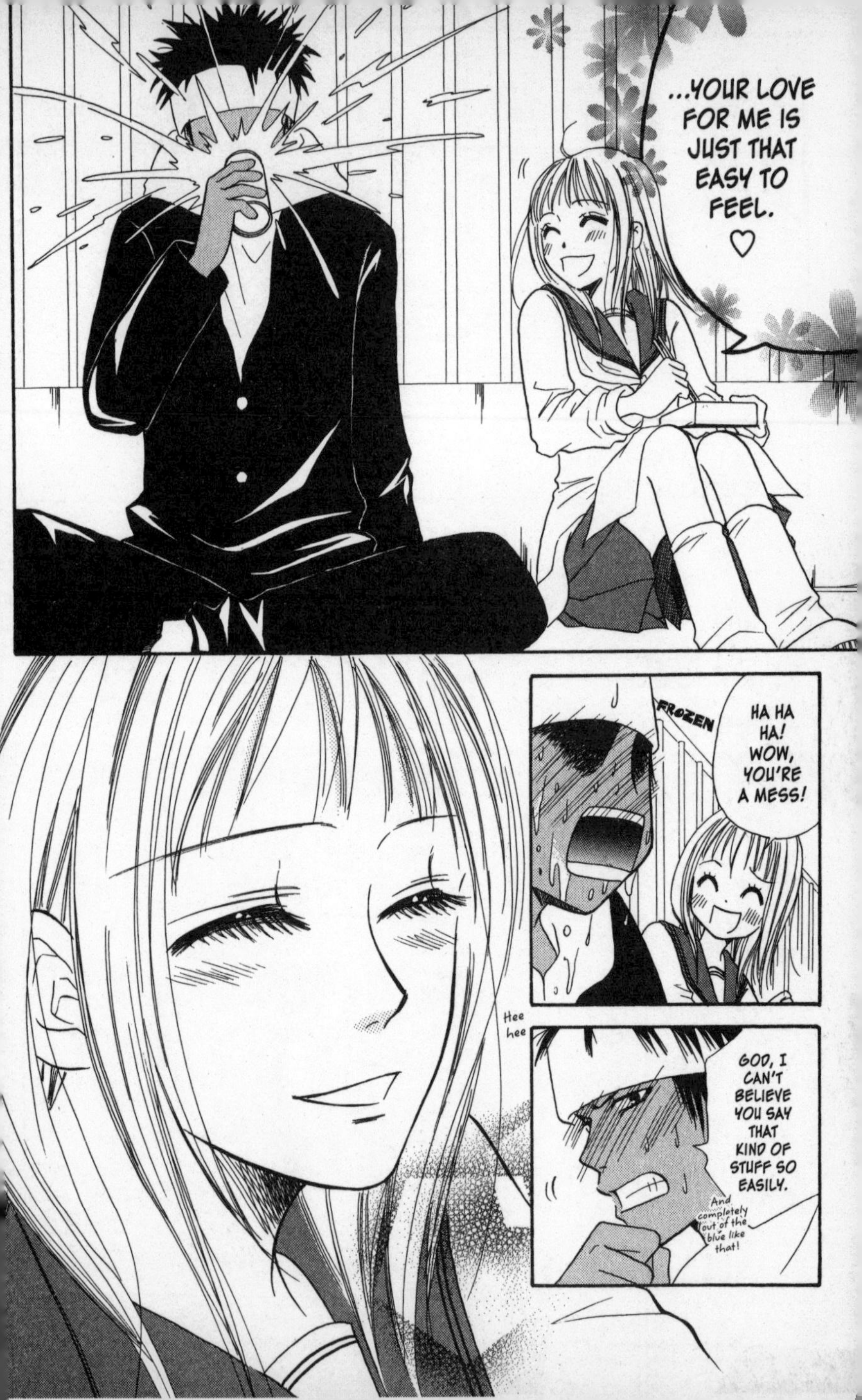
...YOUR LOVE FOR ME IS JUST THAT EASY TO FEEL. ♡
FROZEN
HA HA HA! WOW, YOU'RE A MESS!
Hee hee
GOD, I CAN'T BELIEVE YOU SAY THAT KIND OF STUFF SO EASILY.
And completely out of the blue like that!

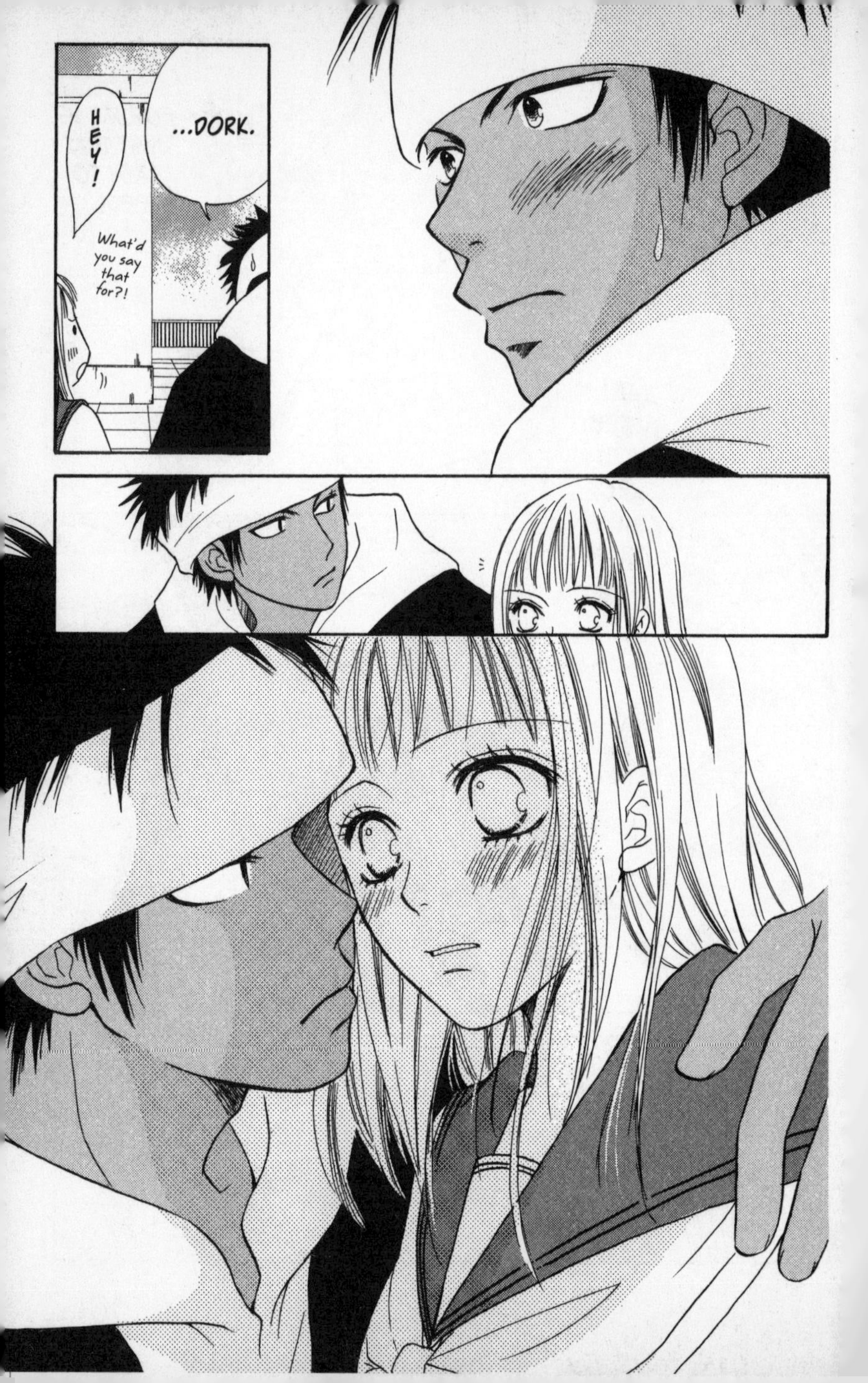
...DORK.
HEY!
What'd you say that for?!

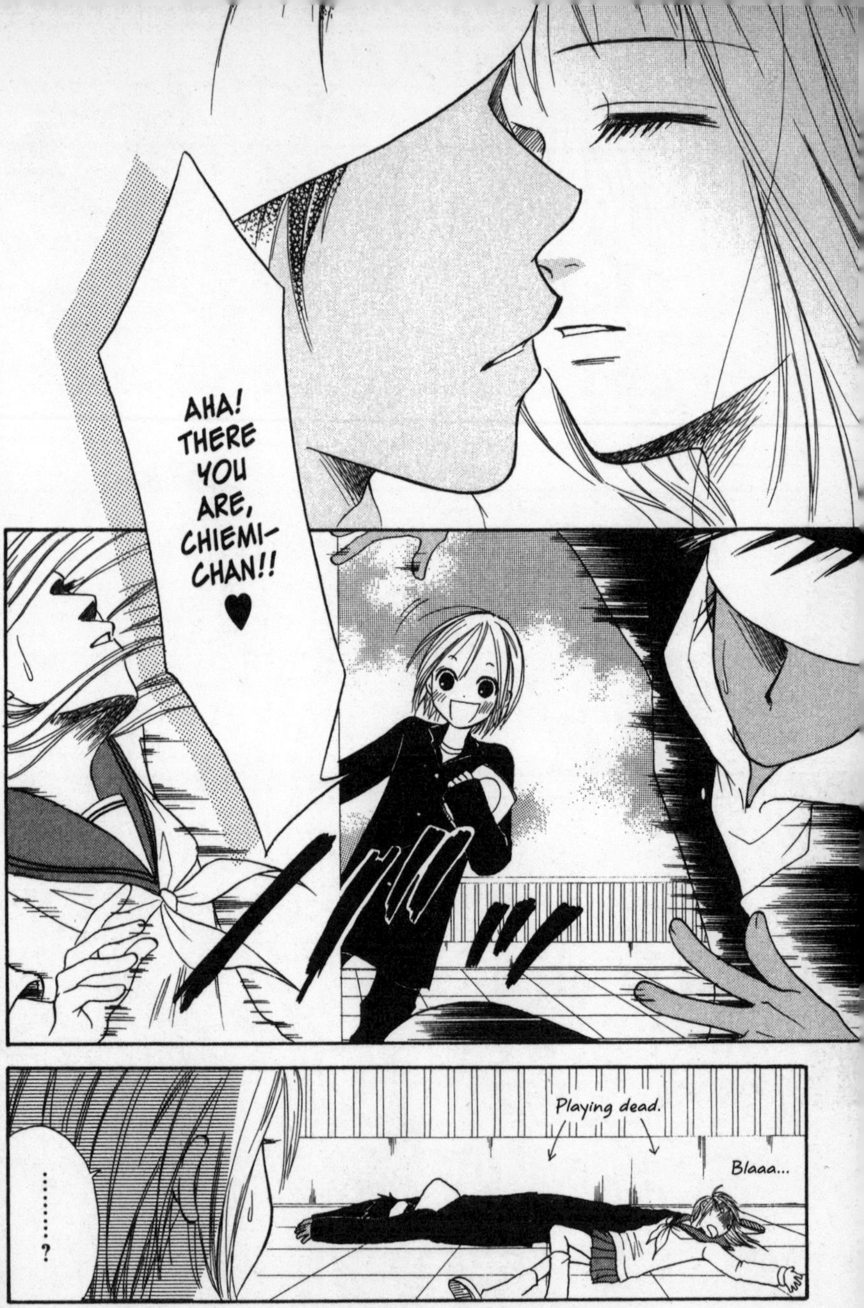
AHA! THERE YOU ARE, CHIEMI-CHAN!! ♥
Playing dead.
Blaaa...
.........?

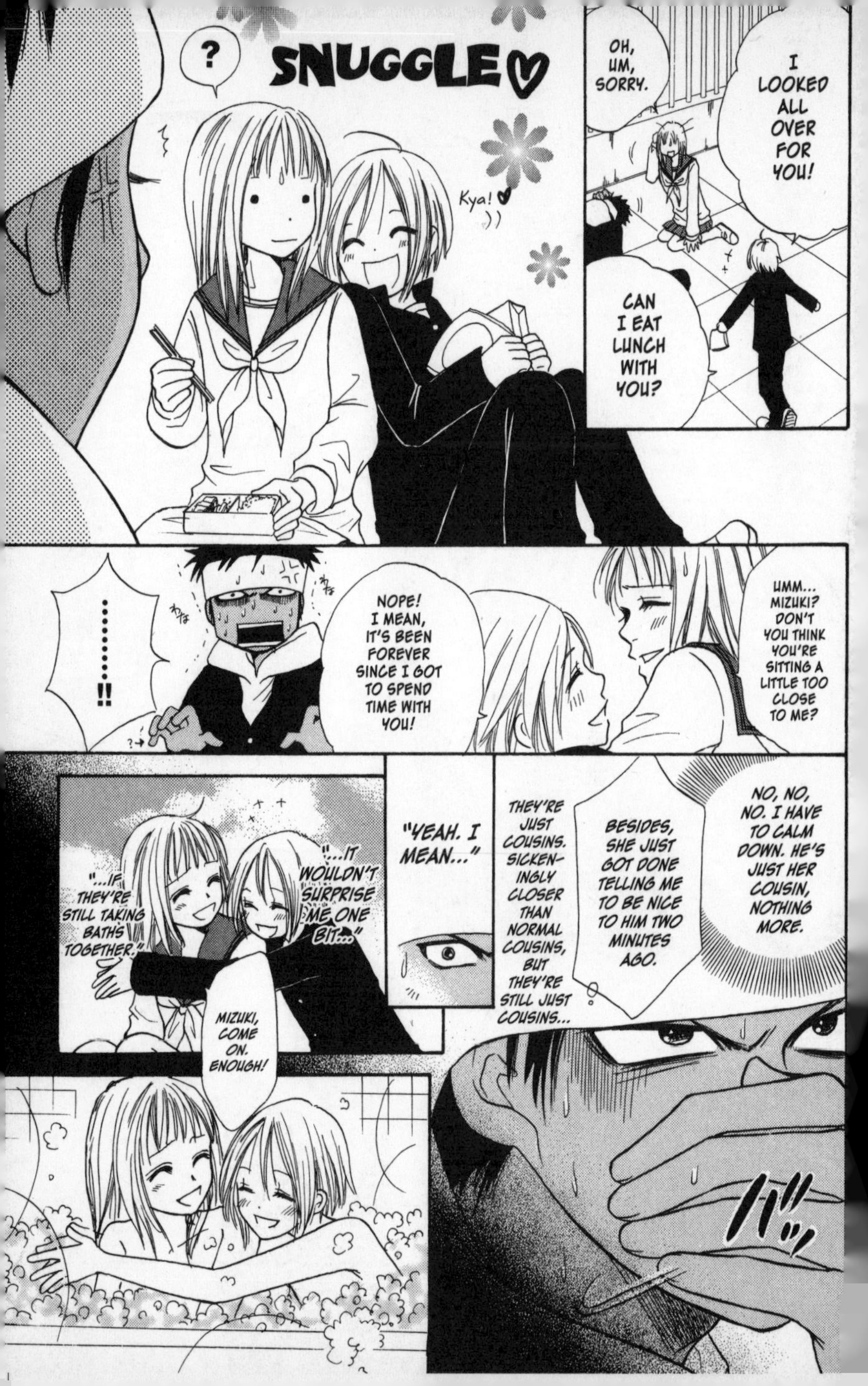
I LOOKED ALL OVER FOR YOU!
OH, UM, SORRY.
CAN I EAT LUNCH WITH YOU?
SNUGGLE♥
Kya!
?
UMM... MIZUKI? DON'T YOU THINK YOU'RE SITTING A LITTLE TOO CLOSE TO ME?
NOPE! I MEAN, IT'S BEEN FOREVER SINCE I GOT TO SPEND TIME WITH YOU!
.......!!
NO, NO, NO. I HAVE TO CALM DOWN. HE'S JUST HER COUSIN, NOTHING MORE.
BESIDES, SHE JUST GOT DONE TELLING ME TO BE NICE TO HIM TWO MINUTES AGO.
THEY'RE JUST COUSINS. SICKEN-INGLY CLOSER THAN NORMAL COUSINS, BUT THEY'RE STILL JUST COUSINS...
"YEAH. I MEAN..."
"...IT WOULDN'T SURPRISE ME ONE BIT..."
"...IF THEY'RE STILL TAKING BATHS TOGETHER."
MIZUKI, COME ON. ENOUGH!

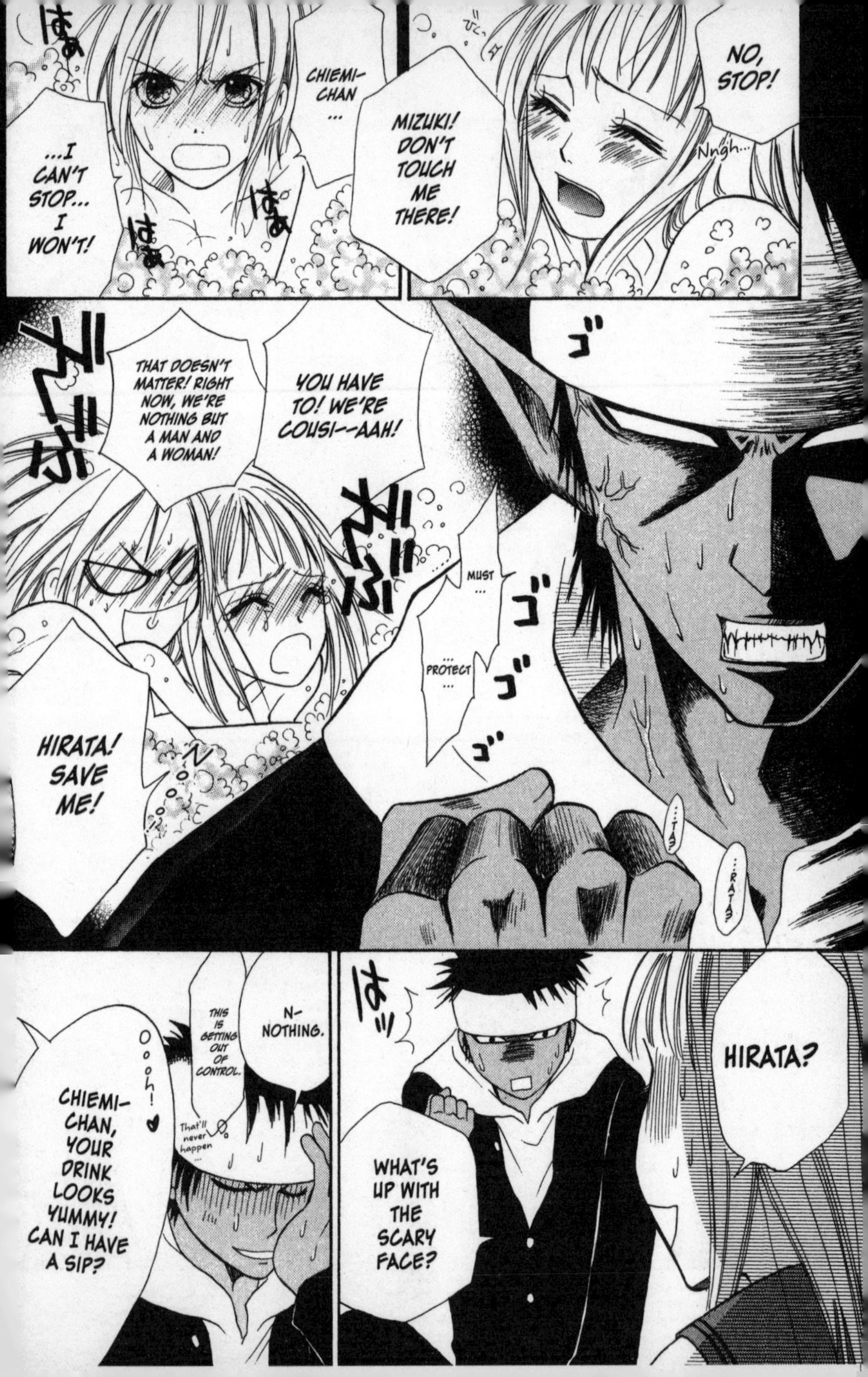
NO, STOP!
Nngh...
MIZUKI! DON'T TOUCH ME THERE!
CHIEMI-CHAN ...
...I CAN'T STOP... I WON'T!
YOU HAVE TO! WE'RE COUSI--AAH!
THAT DOESN'T MATTER! RIGHT NOW, WE'RE NOTHING BUT A MAN AND A WOMAN!
MUST ...
... PROTECT ...
HIRATA! SAVE ME!
...TA♪
...RATA♪
HIRATA?
WHAT'S UP WITH THE SCARY FACE?
N-NOTHING.
THIS IS GETTING OUT OF CONTROL.
Ooooh! ♥
CHIEMI-CHAN, YOUR DRINK LOOKS YUMMY! CAN I HAVE A SIP?
That'll never happen ...

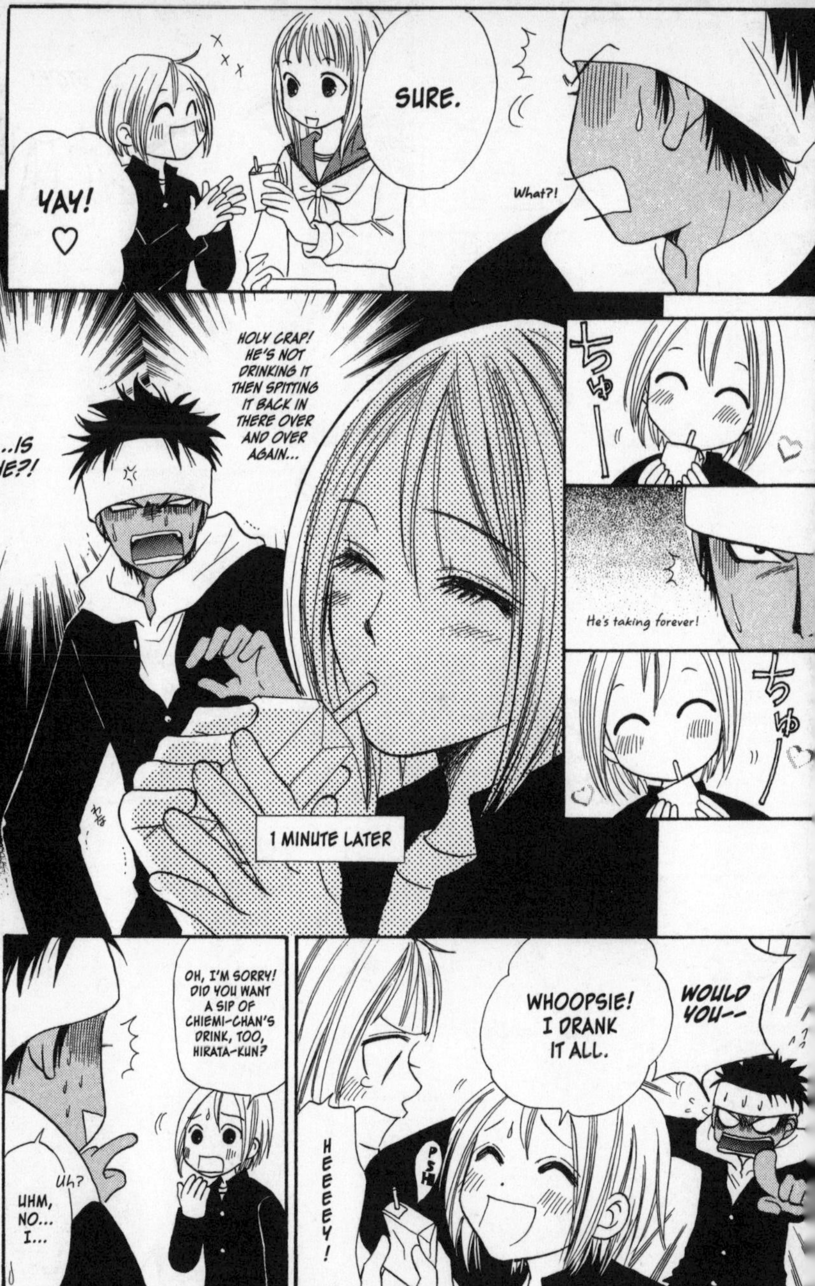
What?!
SURE.
YAY! ♡
ちゅー
He's taking forever!
ちゅー
HOLY CRAP! HE'S NOT DRINKING IT THEN SPITTING IT BACK IN THERE OVER AND OVER AGAIN...
...IS HE?!
1 MINUTE LATER
WOULD YOU--
WHOOPSIE! I DRANK IT ALL.
PSH
HEEEEEY!
OH, I'M SORRY! DID YOU WANT A SIP OF CHIEMI-CHAN'S DRINK, TOO, HIRATA-KUN?
Uh?
UHM, NO... I...

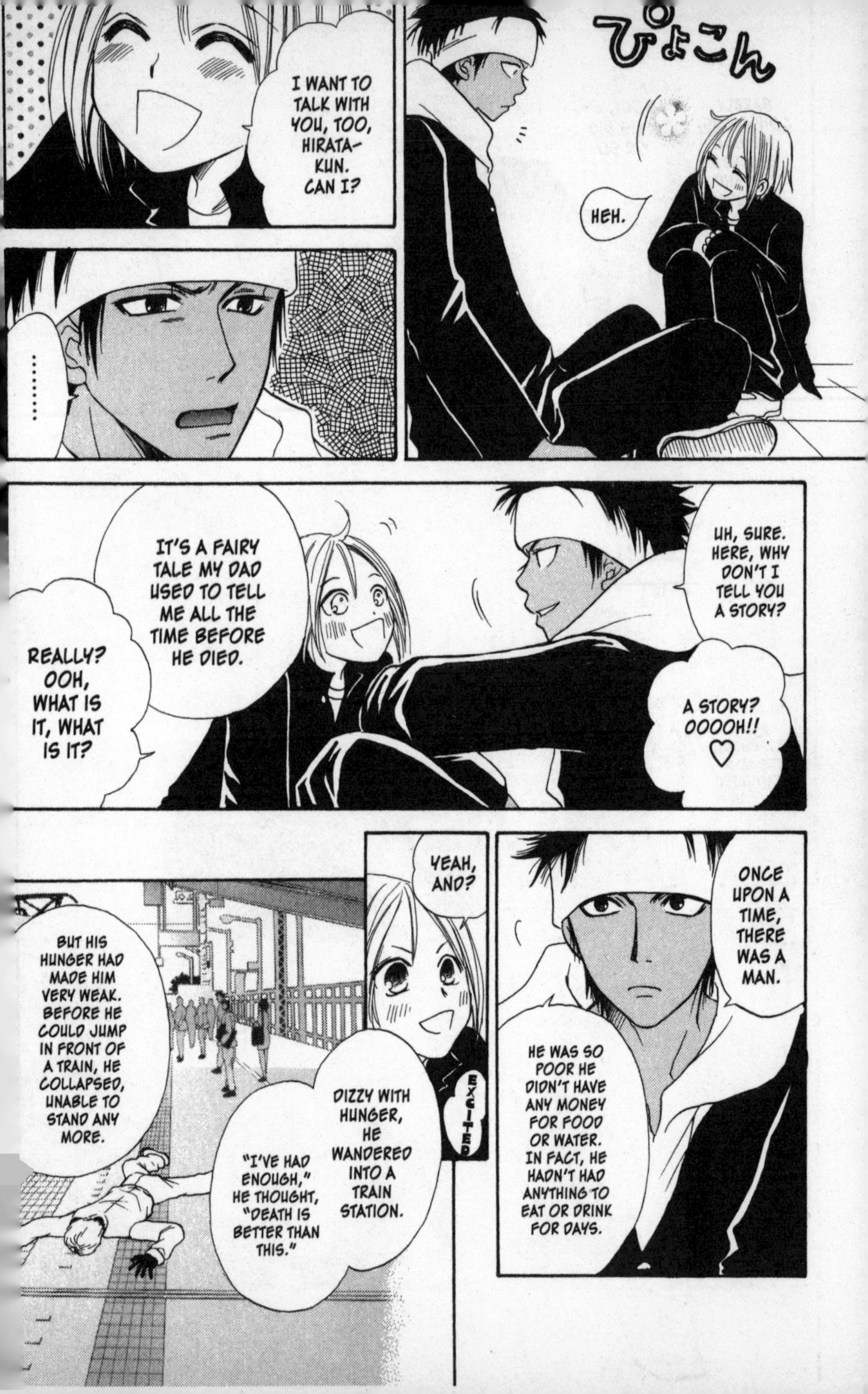
ぴょこん
HEH.
I WANT TO TALK WITH YOU, TOO, HIRATA-KUN. CAN I?
....
UH, SURE. HERE, WHY DON'T I TELL YOU A STORY?
A STORY? OOOOH!! ♡
IT'S A FAIRY TALE MY DAD USED TO TELL ME ALL THE TIME BEFORE HE DIED.
REALLY? OOH, WHAT IS IT, WHAT IS IT?
ONCE UPON A TIME, THERE WAS A MAN.
HE WAS SO POOR HE DIDN'T HAVE ANY MONEY FOR FOOD OR WATER. IN FACT, HE HADN'T HAD ANYTHING TO EAT OR DRINK FOR DAYS.
YEAH, AND?
EXCITED
DIZZY WITH HUNGER, HE WANDERED INTO A TRAIN STATION.
"I'VE HAD ENOUGH," HE THOUGHT, "DEATH IS BETTER THAN THIS."
BUT HIS HUNGER HAD MADE HIM VERY WEAK. BEFORE HE COULD JUMP IN FRONT OF A TRAIN, HE COLLAPSED, UNABLE TO STAND ANY MORE.

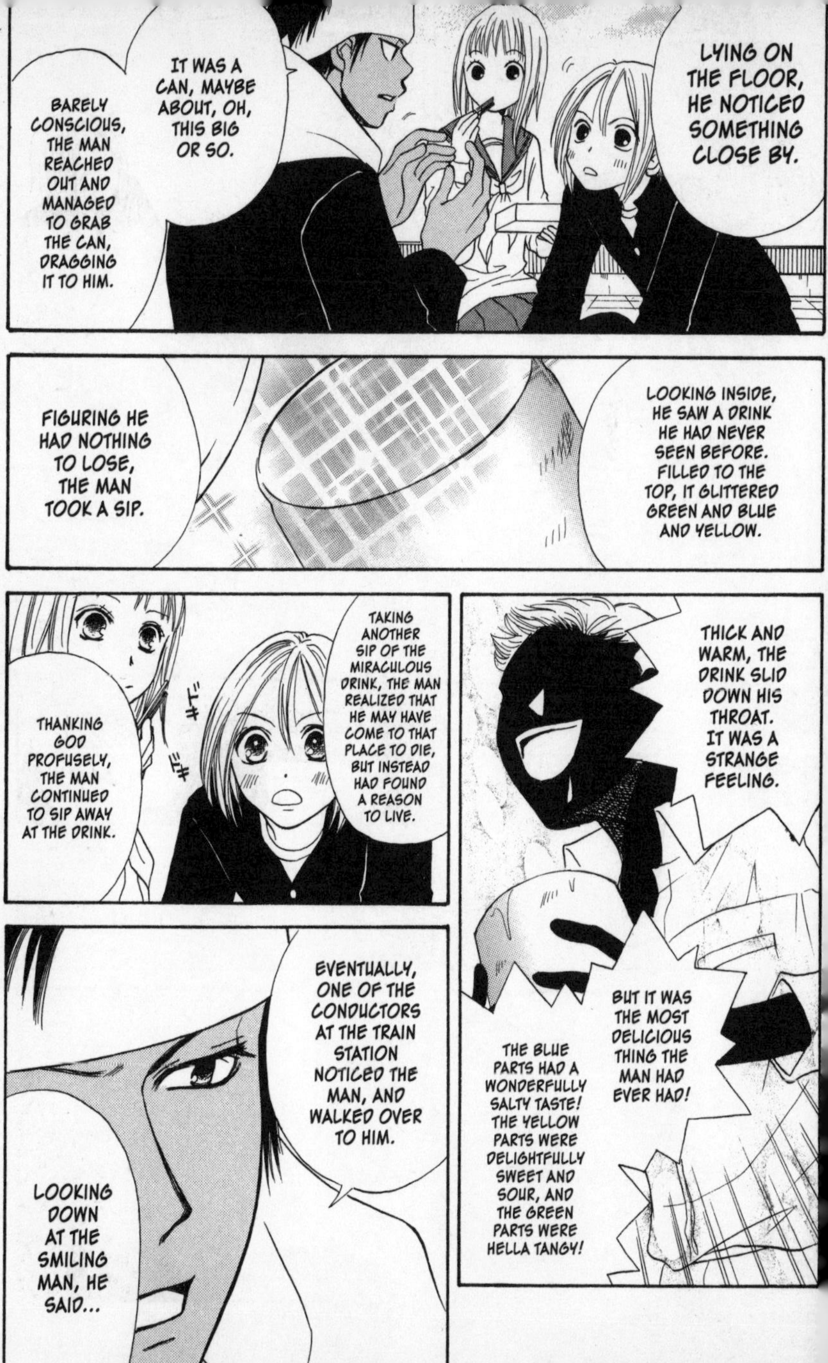
LYING ON THE FLOOR, HE NOTICED SOMETHING CLOSE BY.
IT WAS A CAN, MAYBE ABOUT, OH, THIS BIG OR SO.
BARELY CONSCIOUS, THE MAN REACHED OUT AND MANAGED TO GRAB THE CAN, DRAGGING IT TO HIM.
LOOKING INSIDE, HE SAW A DRINK HE HAD NEVER SEEN BEFORE. FILLED TO THE TOP, IT GLITTERED GREEN AND BLUE AND YELLOW.
FIGURING HE HAD NOTHING TO LOSE, THE MAN TOOK A SIP.
THICK AND WARM, THE DRINK SLID DOWN HIS THROAT. IT WAS A STRANGE FEELING.
BUT IT WAS THE MOST DELICIOUS THING THE MAN HAD EVER HAD!
THE BLUE PARTS HAD A WONDERFULLY SALTY TASTE! THE YELLOW PARTS WERE DELIGHTFULLY SWEET AND SOUR, AND THE GREEN PARTS WERE HELLA TANGY!
TAKING ANOTHER SIP OF THE MIRACULOUS DRINK, THE MAN REALIZED THAT HE MAY HAVE COME TO THAT PLACE TO DIE, BUT INSTEAD HAD FOUND A REASON TO LIVE.
ドキ
ドキ
THANKING GOD PROFUSELY, THE MAN CONTINUED TO SIP AWAY AT THE DRINK.
EVENTUALLY, ONE OF THE CONDUCTORS AT THE TRAIN STATION NOTICED THE MAN, AND WALKED OVER TO HIM.
LOOKING DOWN AT THE SMILING MAN, HE SAID...

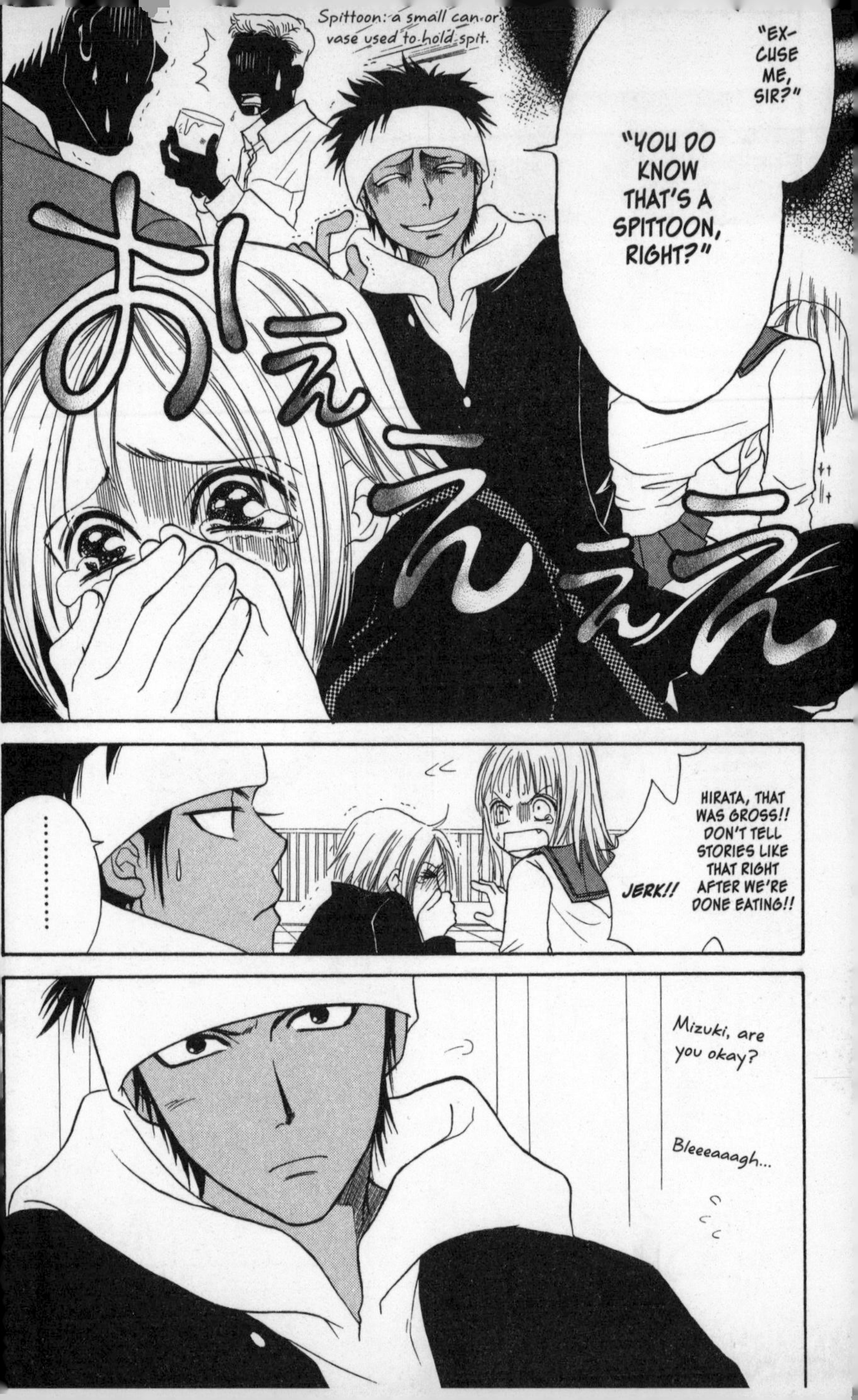
"EX-CUSE ME, SIR?"
"YOU DO KNOW THAT'S A SPITTOON, RIGHT?"
Spittoon: a small can or vase used to hold spit.
HIRATA, THAT WAS GROSS!! DON'T TELL STORIES LIKE THAT RIGHT AFTER WE'RE DONE EATING!!
JERK!!
....
Mizuki, are you okay?
Bleeeaaagh...

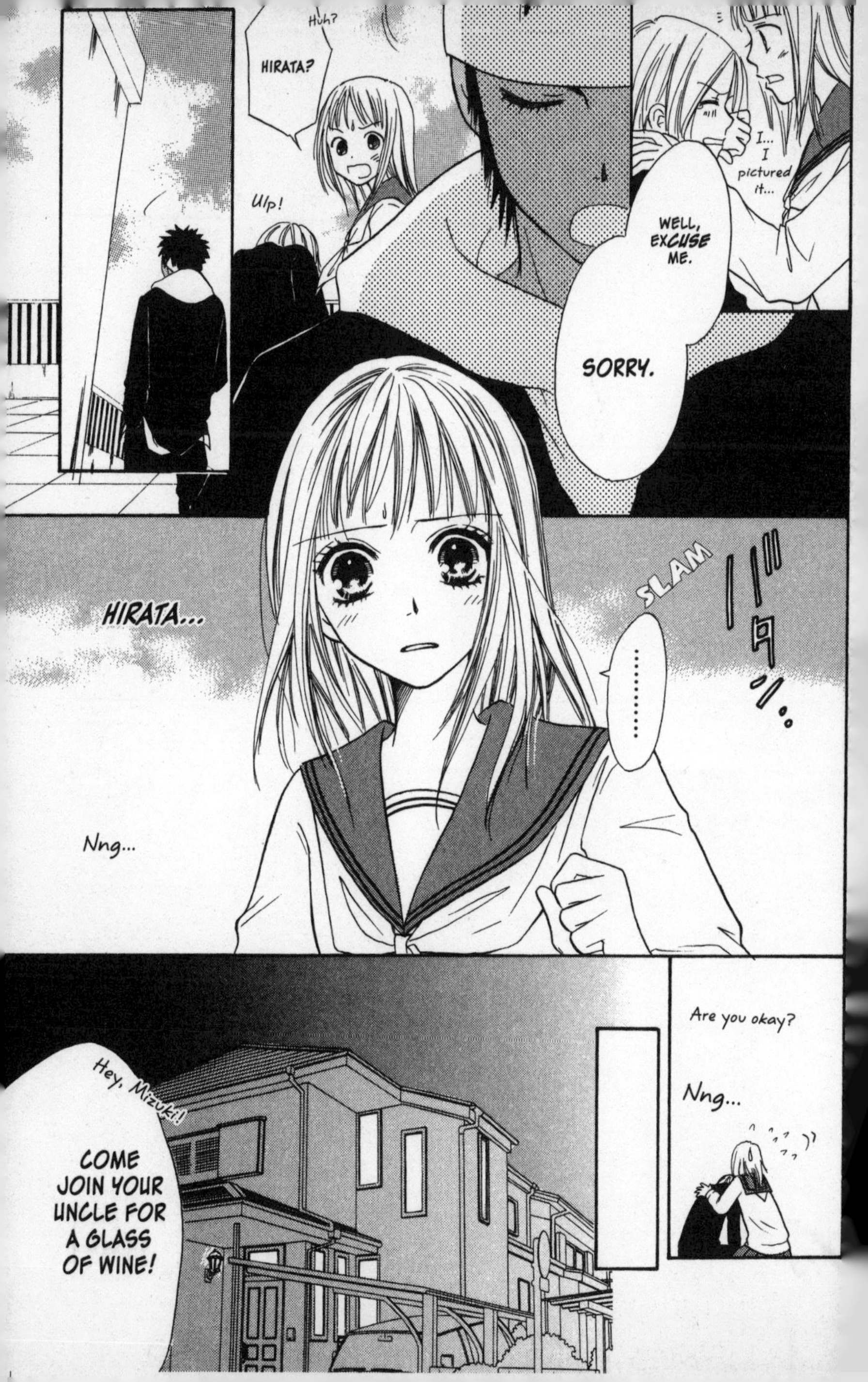
I... I pictured it...
WELL, EXCUSE ME.
SORRY.
Huh?
HIRATA?
Ulp!
SLAM
......
HIRATA...
Nng...
Are you okay?
Nng...
Hey, Mizuki!
COME JOIN YOUR UNCLE FOR A GLASS OF WINE!

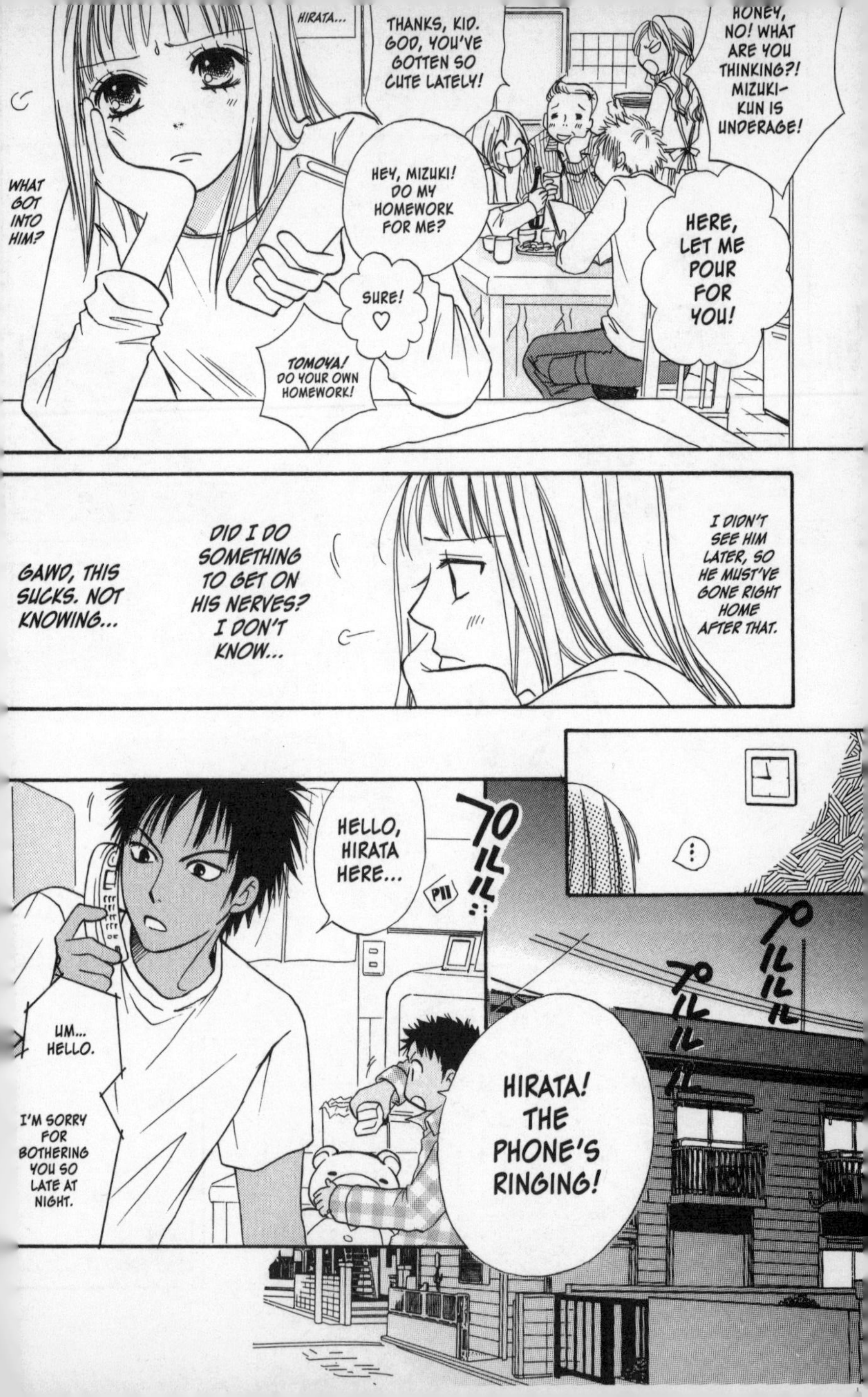
HONEY, NO! WHAT ARE YOU THINKING?! MIZUKI-KUN IS UNDERAGE!
HERE, LET ME POUR FOR YOU!
THANKS, KID. GOD, YOU'VE GOTTEN SO CUTE LATELY!
HIRATA...
HEY, MIZUKI! DO MY HOMEWORK FOR ME?
SURE! ♡
TOMOYA! DO YOUR OWN HOMEWORK!
WHAT GOT INTO HIM?
I DIDN'T SEE HIM LATER, SO HE MUST'VE GONE RIGHT HOME AFTER THAT.
DID I DO SOMETHING TO GET ON HIS NERVES? I DON'T KNOW...
GAWD, THIS SUCKS. NOT KNOWING...
...
プルルル
プルルル
HIRATA! THE PHONE'S RINGING!
プルル
PII
HELLO, HIRATA HERE...
UM... HELLO.
I'M SORRY FOR BOTHERING YOU SO LATE AT NIGHT.

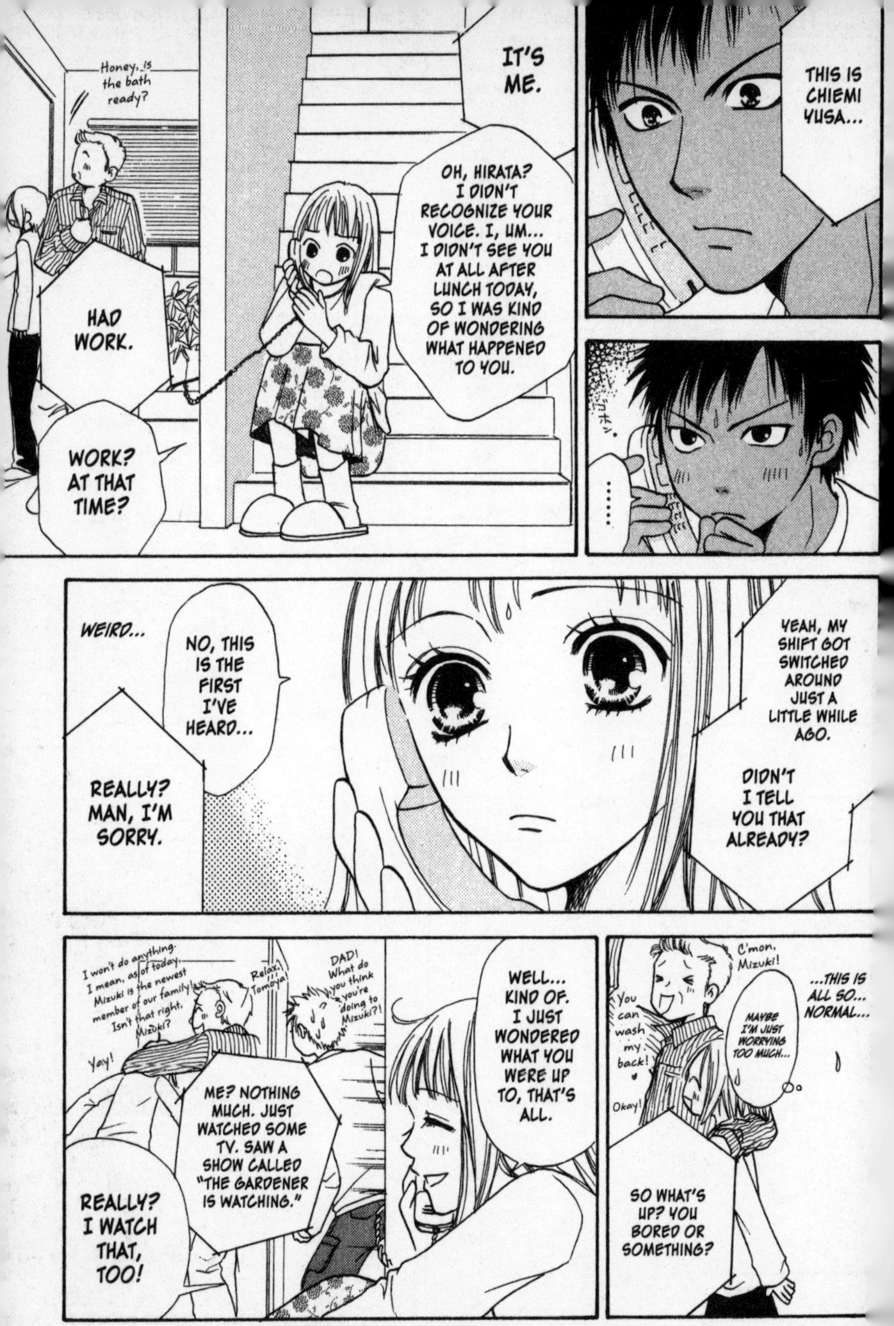
THIS IS CHIEMI YUSA...
ゴホン
....
IT'S ME.
OH, HIRATA? I DIDN'T RECOGNIZE YOUR VOICE. I, UM... I DIDN'T SEE YOU AT ALL AFTER LUNCH TODAY, SO I WAS KIND OF WONDERING WHAT HAPPENED TO YOU.
Honey, is the bath ready?
HAD WORK.
WORK? AT THAT TIME?
YEAH, MY SHIFT GOT SWITCHED AROUND JUST A LITTLE WHILE AGO.
DIDN'T I TELL YOU THAT ALREADY?
NO, THIS IS THE FIRST I'VE HEARD...
WEIRD...
REALLY? MAN, I'M SORRY.
...THIS IS ALL SO... NORMAL...
C'mon, Mizuki!
MAYBE I'M JUST WORRYING TOO MUCH...
You can wash my back!
Okay!
SO WHAT'S UP? YOU BORED OR SOMETHING?
WELL... KIND OF. I JUST WONDERED WHAT YOU WERE UP TO, THAT'S ALL.
DAD! What do you think you're doing to Mizuki?!
Relax, Tomoya!
I won't do anything. I mean, as of today, Mizuki is the newest member of our family! Isn't that right, Mizuki?
Yay!
ME? NOTHING MUCH. JUST WATCHED SOME TV. SAW A SHOW CALLED "THE GARDENER IS WATCHING."
REALLY? I WATCH THAT, TOO!

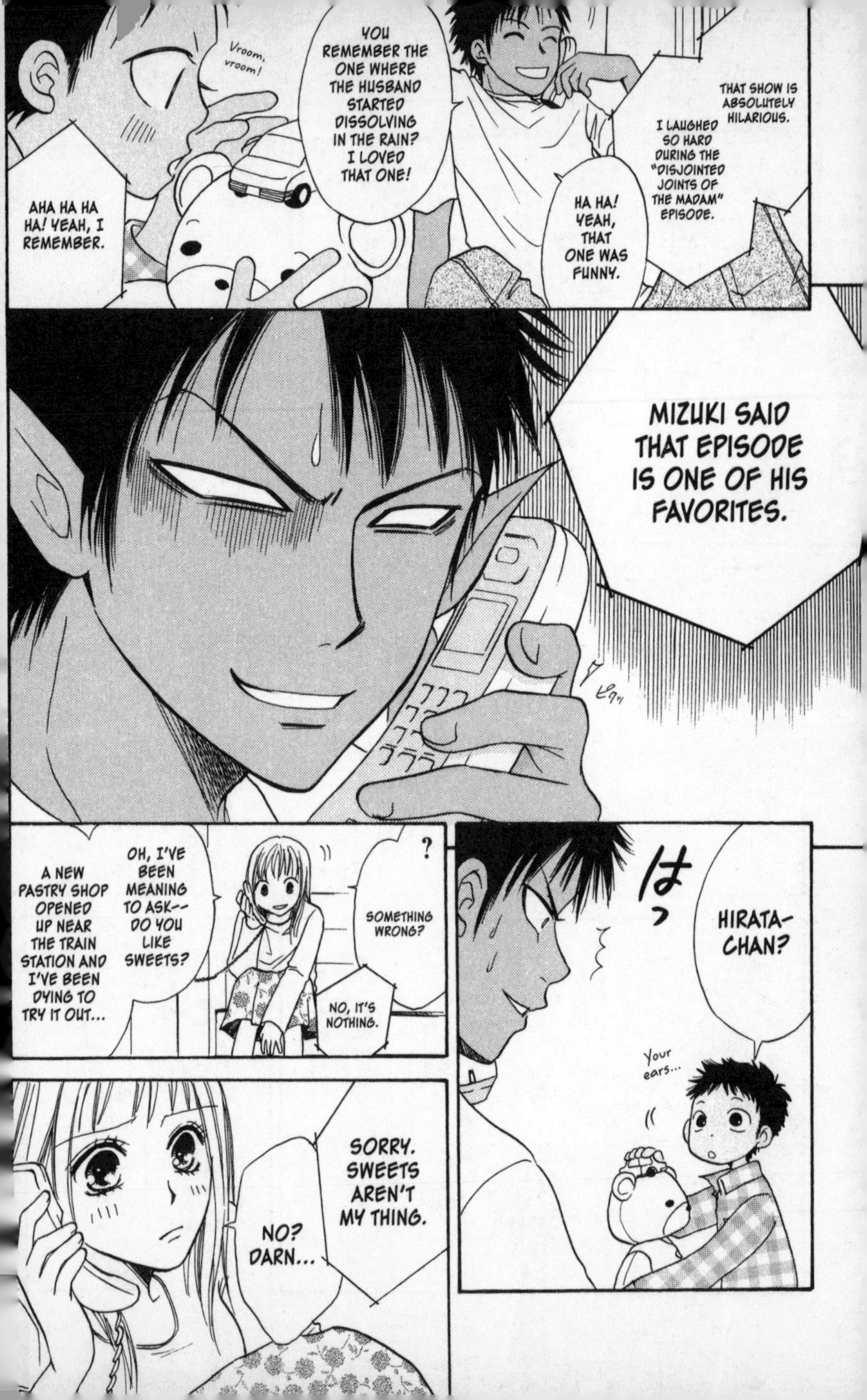
THAT SHOW IS ABSOLUTELY HILARIOUS.
I LAUGHED SO HARD DURING THE "DISJOINTED JOINTS OF THE MADAM" EPISODE.
HA HA! YEAH, THAT ONE WAS FUNNY.
YOU REMEMBER THE ONE WHERE THE HUSBAND STARTED DISSOLVING IN THE RAIN? I LOVED THAT ONE!
Vroom, vroom!
AHA HA HA HA! YEAH, I REMEMBER.
MIZUKI SAID THAT EPISODE IS ONE OF HIS FAVORITES.
ピクッ
HIRATA-CHAN?
はっ
Your ears...
?
SOMETHING WRONG?
NO, IT'S NOTHING.
OH, I'VE BEEN MEANING TO ASK-- DO YOU LIKE SWEETS?
A NEW PASTRY SHOP OPENED UP NEAR THE TRAIN STATION AND I'VE BEEN DYING TO TRY IT OUT...
SORRY. SWEETS AREN'T MY THING.
NO? DARN...

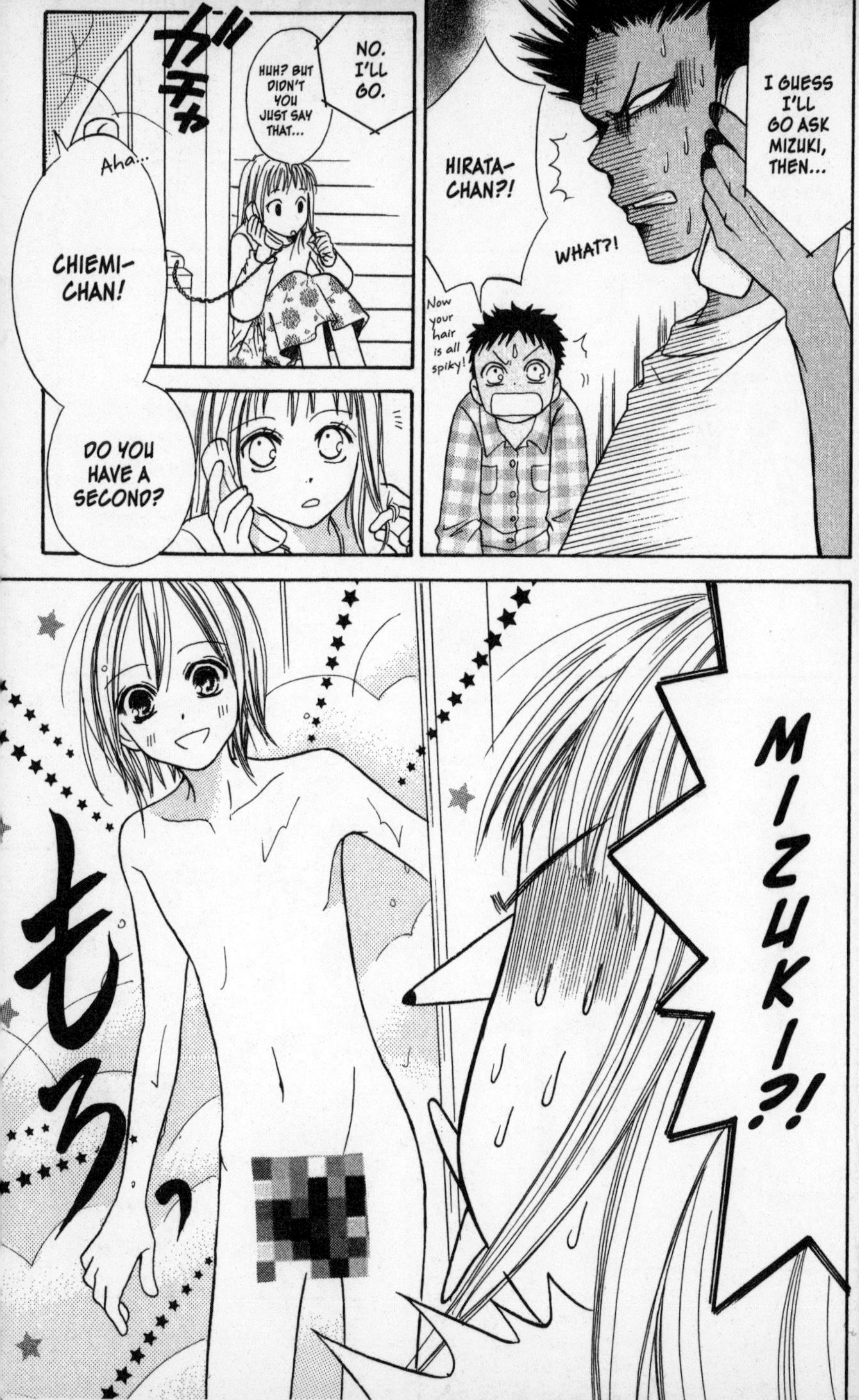
I GUESS I'LL GO ASK MIZUKI, THEN...
HIRATA-CHAN?!
WHAT?!
Now your hair is all spiky!
NO. I'LL GO.
HUH? BUT DIDN'T YOU JUST SAY THAT...
ガチャ
Aha...
CHIEMI-CHAN!
DO YOU HAVE A SECOND?
MIZUKI?!
もろっ

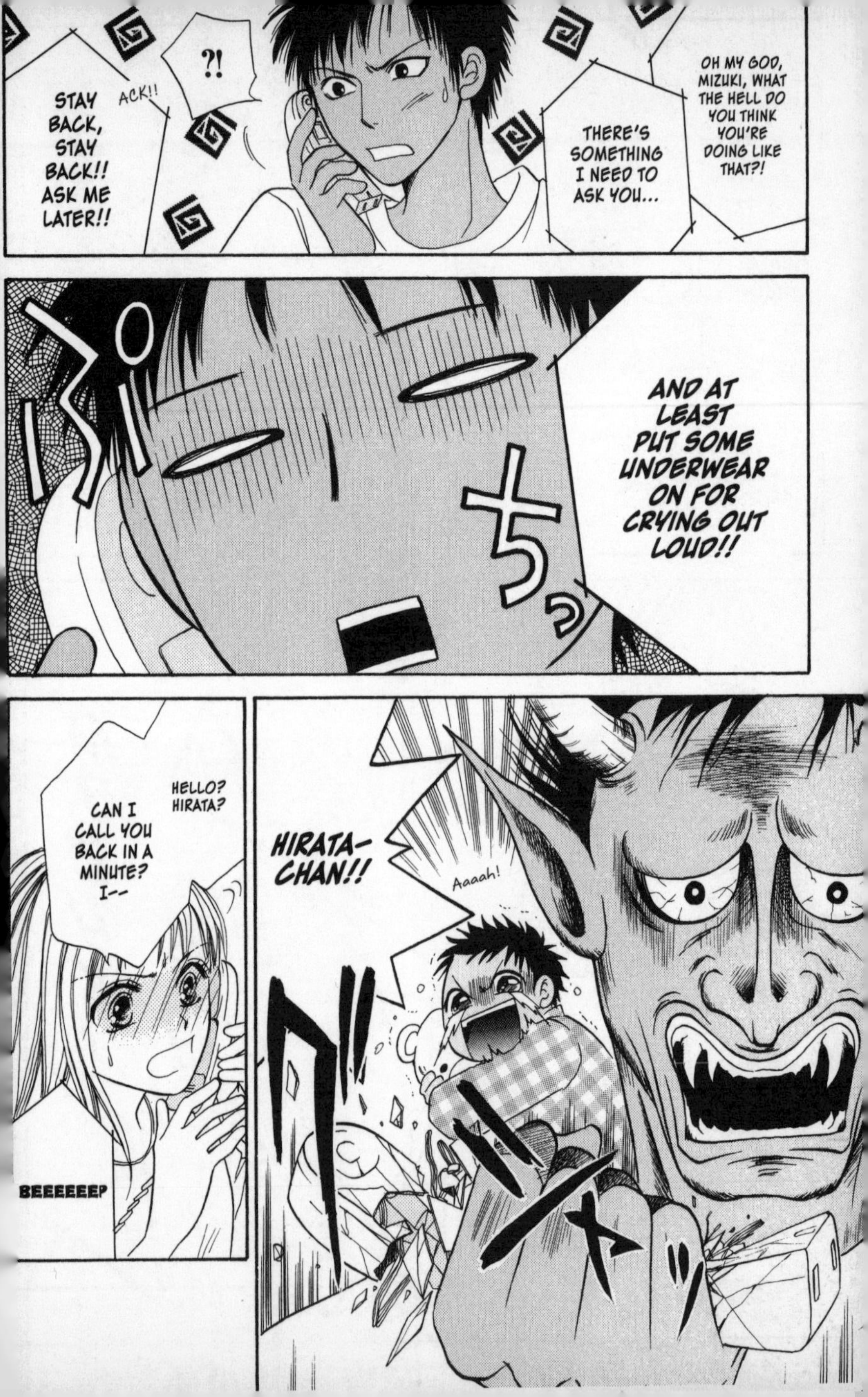
OH MY GOD, MIZUKI, WHAT THE HELL DO YOU THINK YOU'RE DOING LIKE THAT?!
THERE'S SOMETHING I NEED TO ASK YOU...
?!
ACK!!
STAY BACK, STAY BACK!! ASK ME LATER!!
AND AT LEAST PUT SOME UNDERWEAR ON FOR CRYING OUT LOUD!!
HIRATA-CHAN!!
Aaaah!
HELLO? HIRATA?
CAN I CALL YOU BACK IN A MINUTE? I--
BEEEEEEP

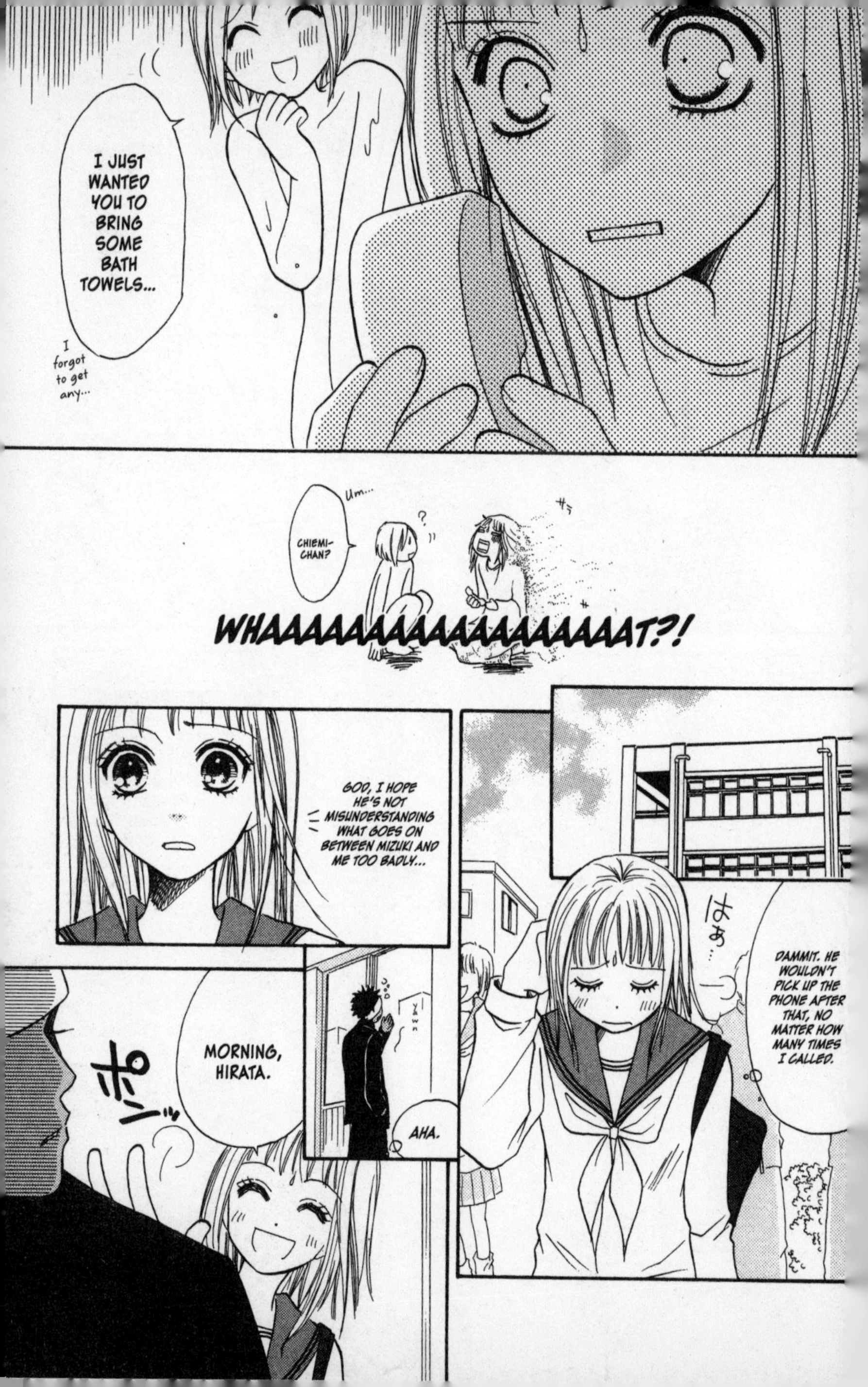
I JUST WANTED YOU TO BRING SOME BATH TOWELS...
I forgot to get any...
Um...
CHIEMI-CHAN?
WHAAAAAAAAAAAAAAAAAT?!
はぁ…
DAMMIT. HE WOULDN'T PICK UP THE PHONE AFTER THAT, NO MATTER HOW MANY TIMES I CALLED.
GOD, I HOPE HE'S NOT MISUNDERSTANDING WHAT GOES ON BETWEEN MIZUKI AND ME TOO BADLY...
AHA.
MORNING, HIRATA.
ポンッ

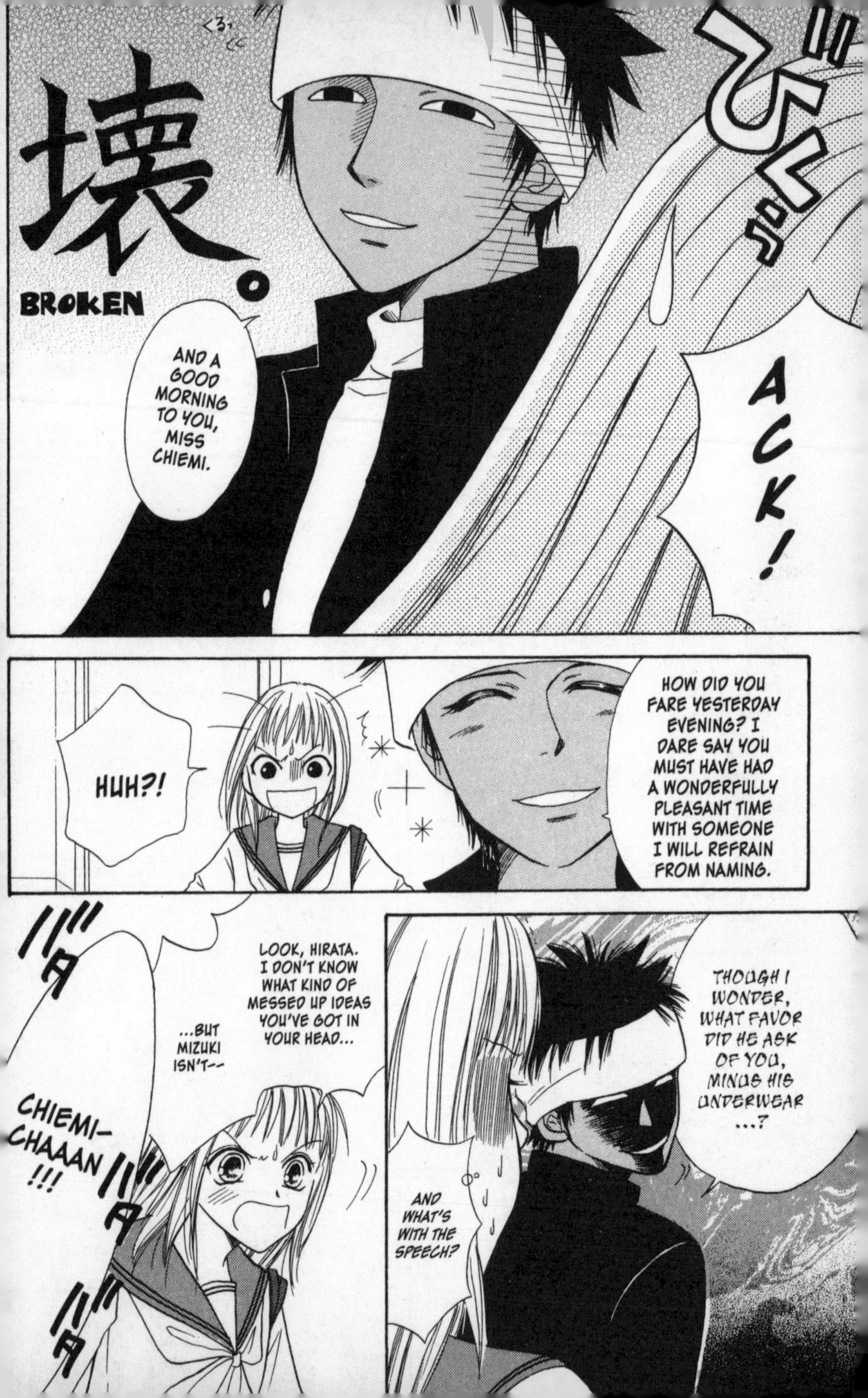

びくっ
ACK!
壊。
BROKEN
AND A GOOD MORNING TO YOU, MISS CHIEMI.
HOW DID YOU FARE YESTERDAY EVENING? I DARE SAY YOU MUST HAVE HAD A WONDERFULLY PLEASANT TIME WITH SOMEONE I WILL REFRAIN FROM NAMING.
HUH?!
THOUGH I WONDER, WHAT FAVOR DID HE ASK OF YOU, MINUS HIS UNDERWEAR ...?
AND WHAT'S WITH THE SPEECH?
LOOK, HIRATA. I DON'T KNOW WHAT KIND OF MESSED UP IDEAS YOU'VE GOT IN YOUR HEAD...
...BUT MIZUKI ISN'T--
バタ
CHIEMI-CHAAAN!!!
バタ
バタ

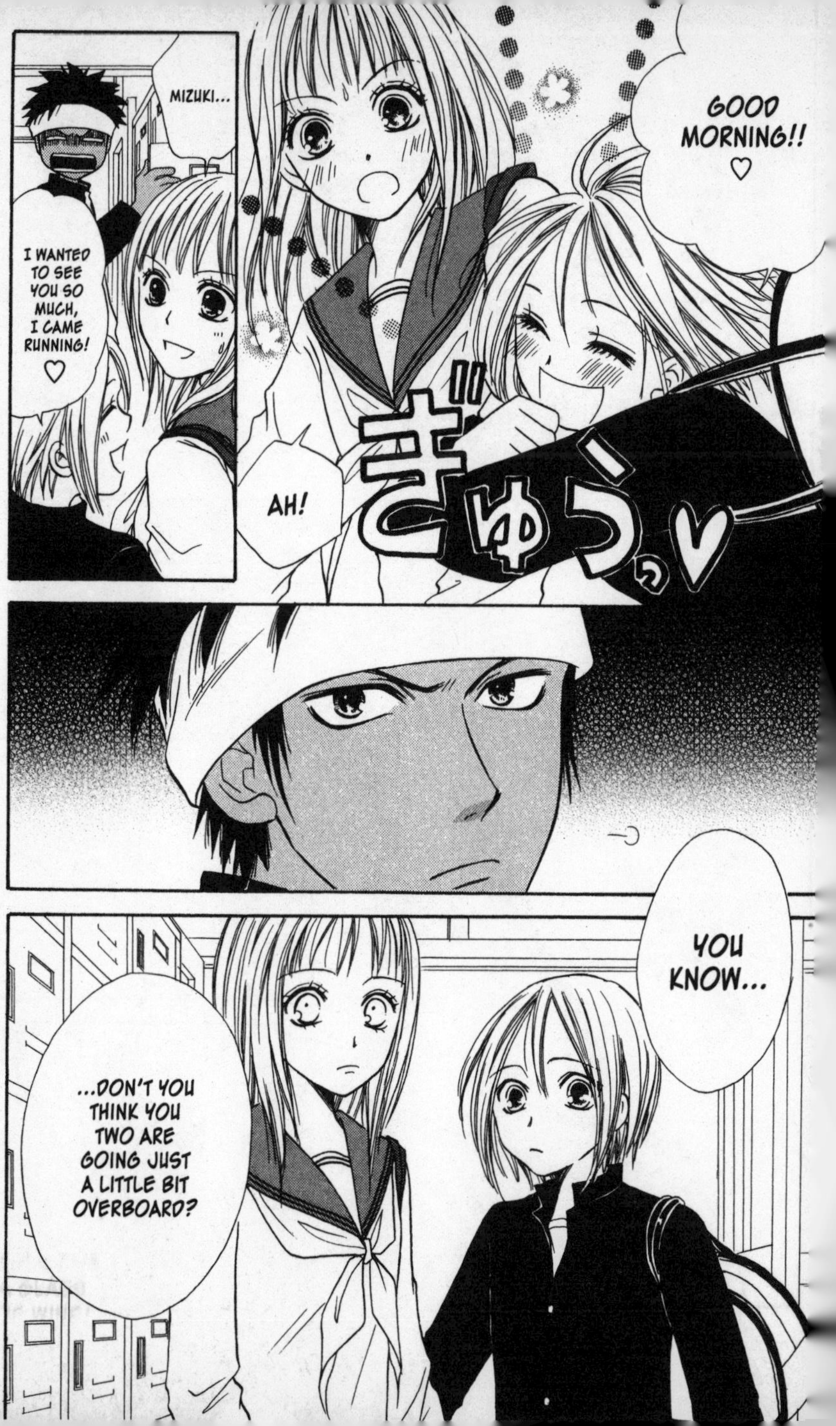
GOOD MORNING!! ♡
ぎゅうっ♡
AH!
MIZUKI...
I WANTED TO SEE YOU SO MUCH, I CAME RUNNING! ♡
YOU KNOW...
...DON'T YOU THINK YOU TWO ARE GOING JUST A LITTLE BIT OVERBOARD?

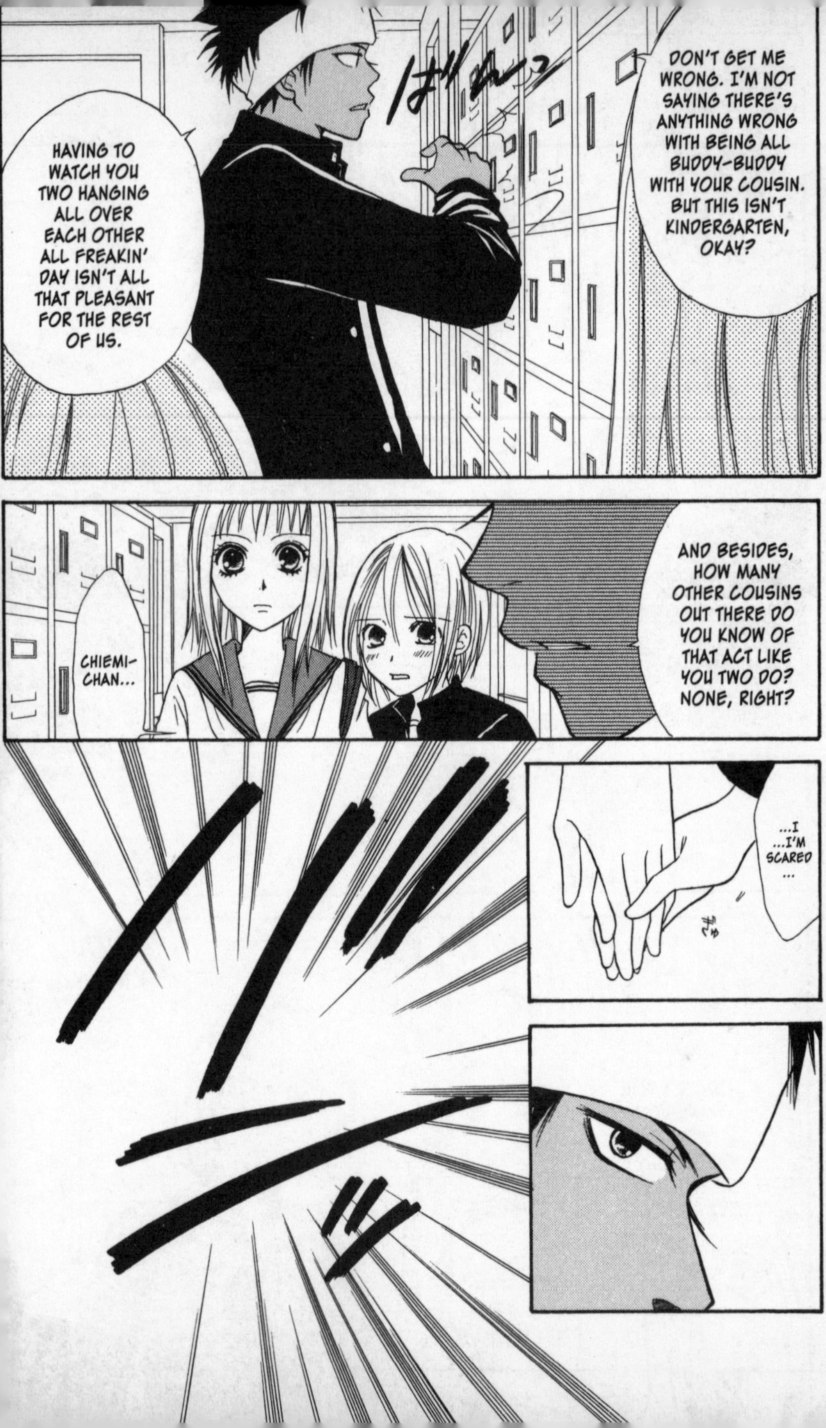
DON'T GET ME WRONG. I'M NOT SAYING THERE'S ANYTHING WRONG WITH BEING ALL BUDDY-BUDDY WITH YOUR COUSIN. BUT THIS ISN'T KINDERGARTEN, OKAY?
HAVING TO WATCH YOU TWO HANGING ALL OVER EACH OTHER ALL FREAKIN' DAY ISN'T ALL THAT PLEASANT FOR THE REST OF US.
AND BESIDES, HOW MANY OTHER COUSINS OUT THERE DO YOU KNOW OF THAT ACT LIKE YOU TWO DO? NONE, RIGHT?
CHIEMI-CHAN...
...I ...I'M SCARED ...

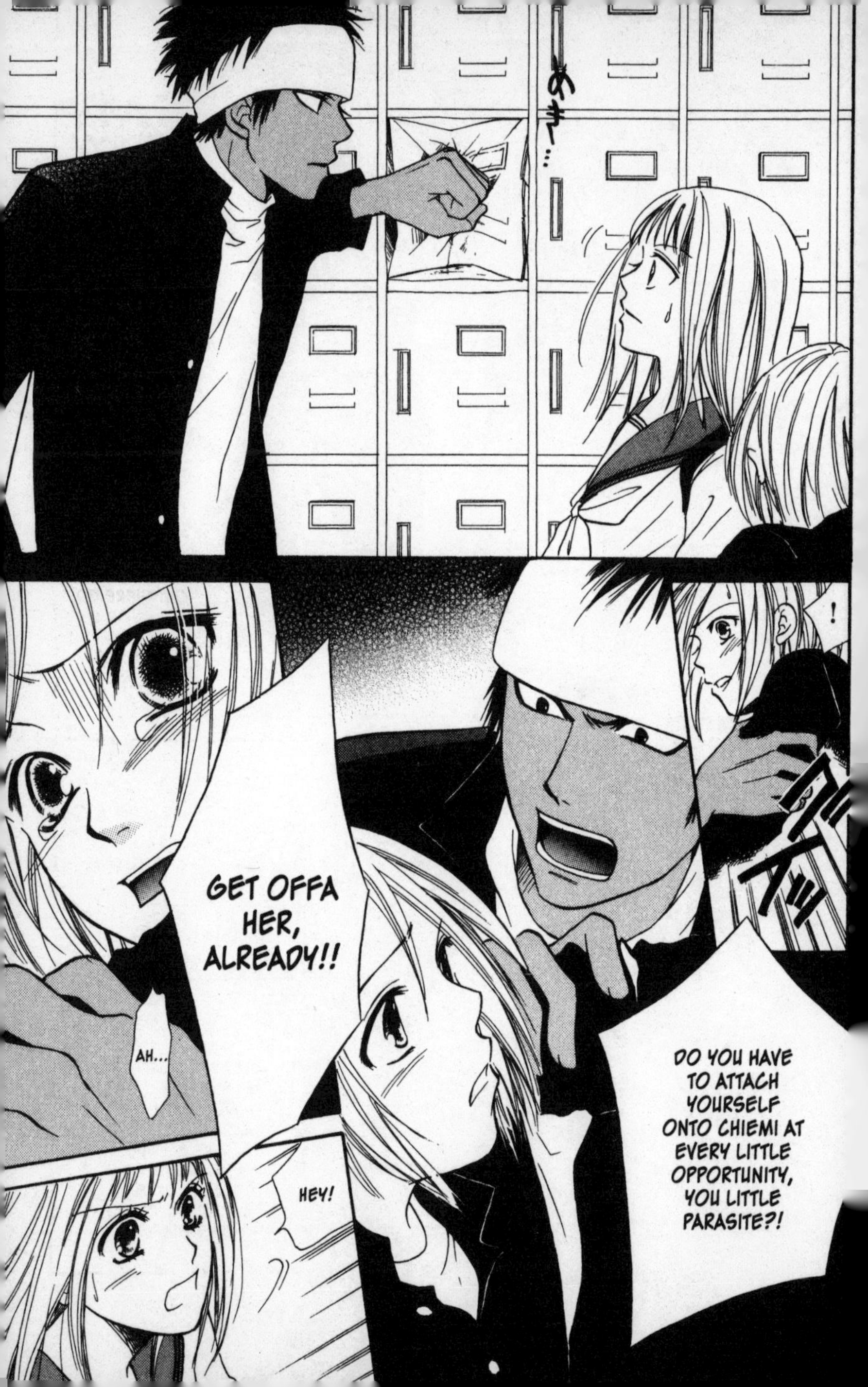
めき…
!
グイッ
DO YOU HAVE TO ATTACH YOURSELF ONTO CHIEMI AT EVERY LITTLE OPPORTUNITY, YOU LITTLE PARASITE?!
GET OFFA HER, ALREADY!!
HEY!
AH...

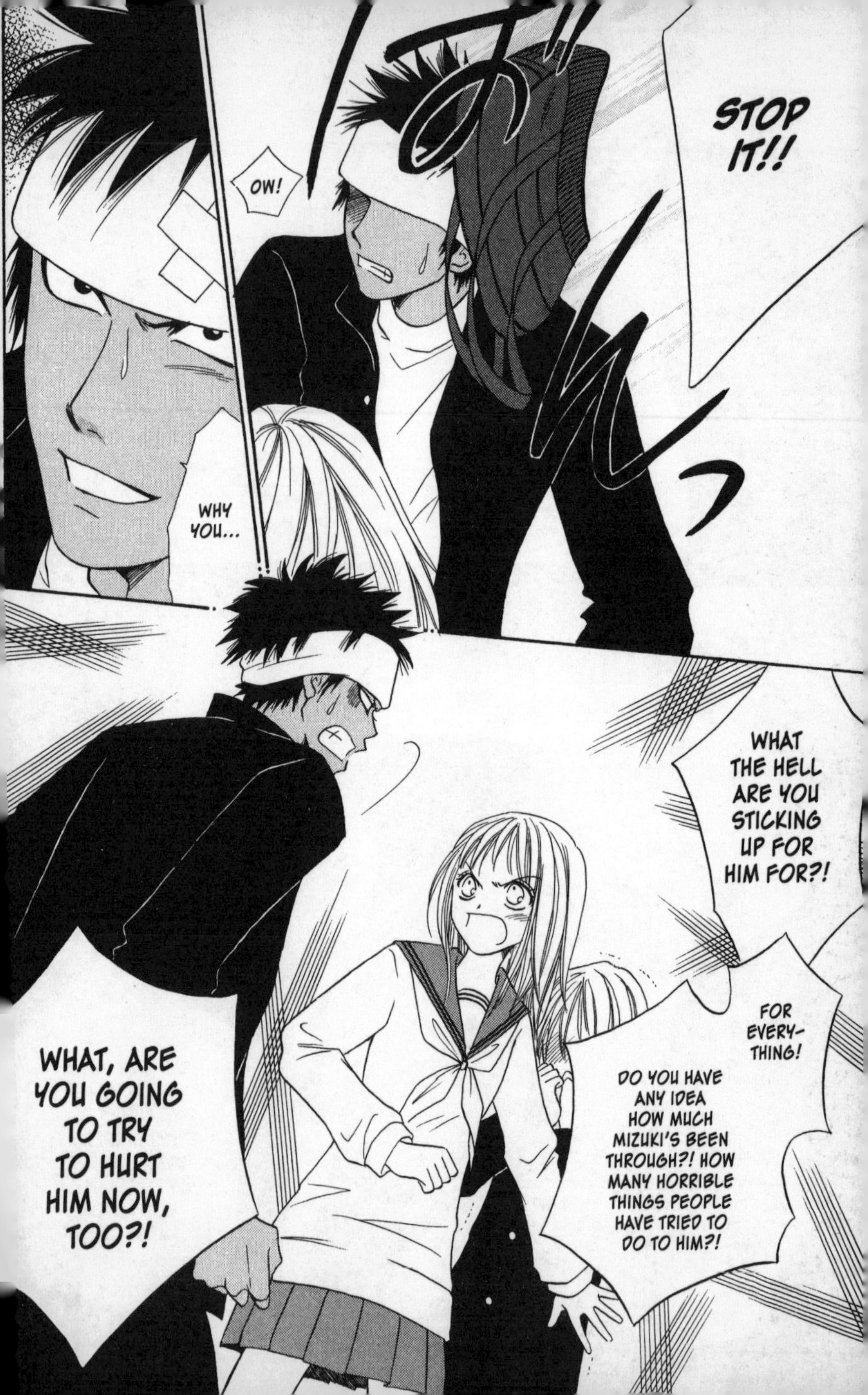
STOP IT!!
OW!
WHY YOU...
WHAT THE HELL ARE YOU STICKING UP FOR HIM FOR?!
FOR EVERY-THING!
DO YOU HAVE ANY IDEA HOW MUCH MIZUKI'S BEEN THROUGH?! HOW MANY HORRIBLE THINGS PEOPLE HAVE TRIED TO DO TO HIM?!
WHAT, ARE YOU GOING TO TRY TO HURT HIM NOW, TOO?!

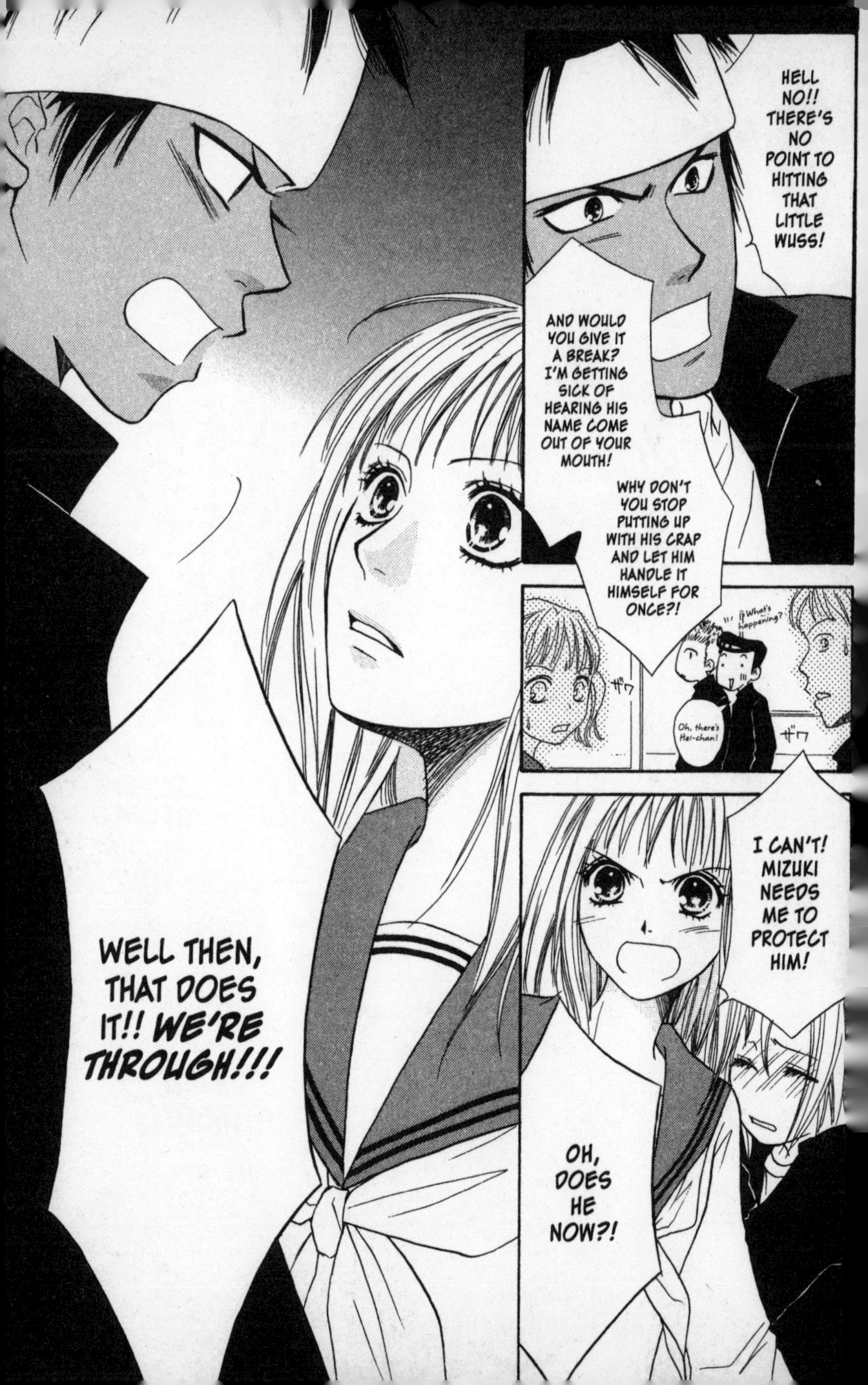

HELL NO!! THERE'S NO POINT TO HITTING THAT LITTLE WUSS!
AND WOULD YOU GIVE IT A BREAK? I'M GETTING SICK OF HEARING HIS NAME COME OUT OF YOUR MOUTH!
WHY DON'T YOU STOP PUTTING UP WITH HIS CRAP AND LET HIM HANDLE IT HIMSELF FOR ONCE?!
What's happening?
ザワ
Oh, there's Hei-chan!
ザワ
I CAN'T! MIZUKI NEEDS ME TO PROTECT HIM!
OH, DOES HE NOW?!
WELL THEN, THAT DOES IT!! WE'RE THROUGH!!!

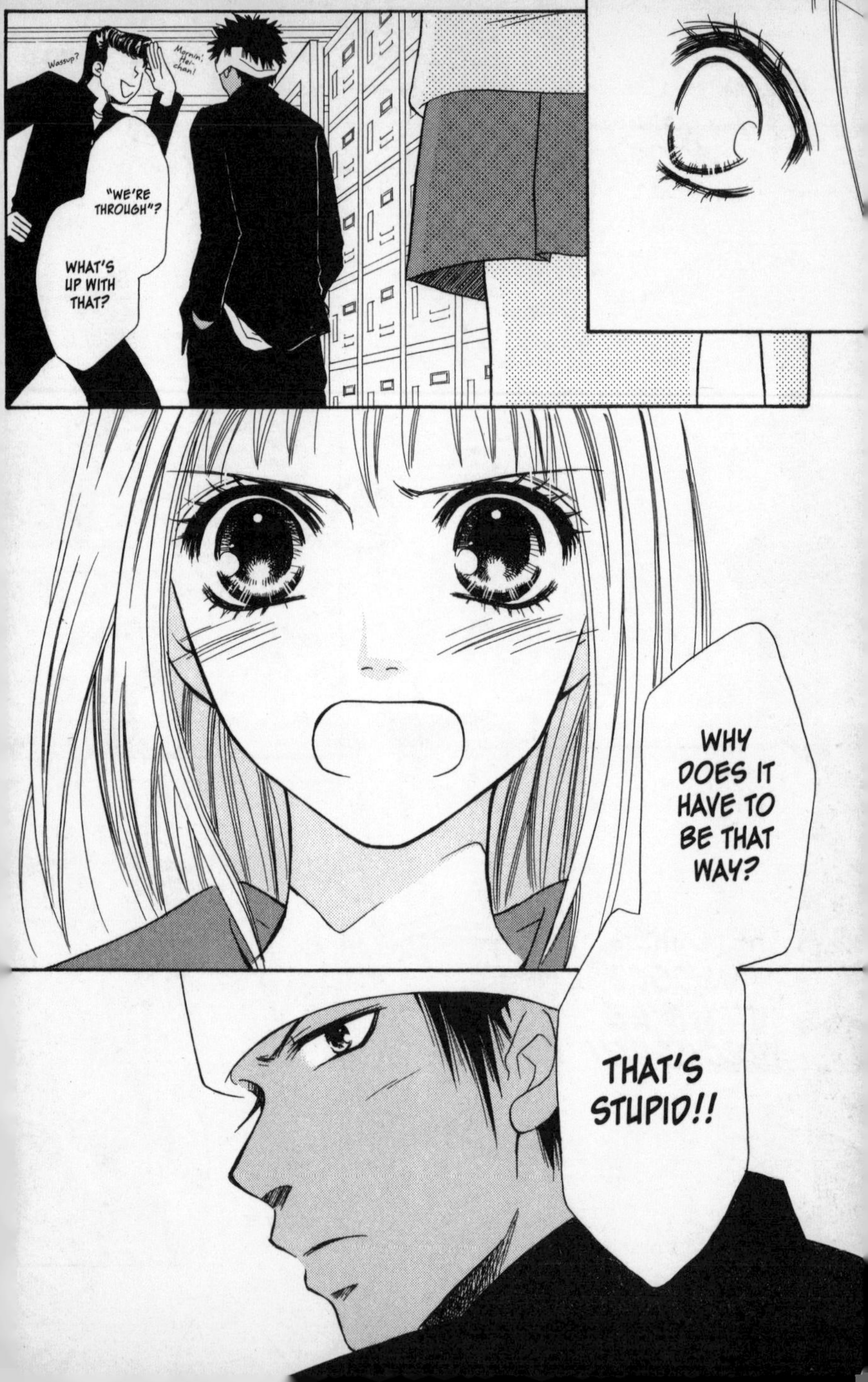
Mornin' Hei-chan!
Wassup?
"WE'RE THROUGH"? WHAT'S UP WITH THAT?
WHY DOES IT HAVE TO BE THAT WAY?
THAT'S STUPID!!

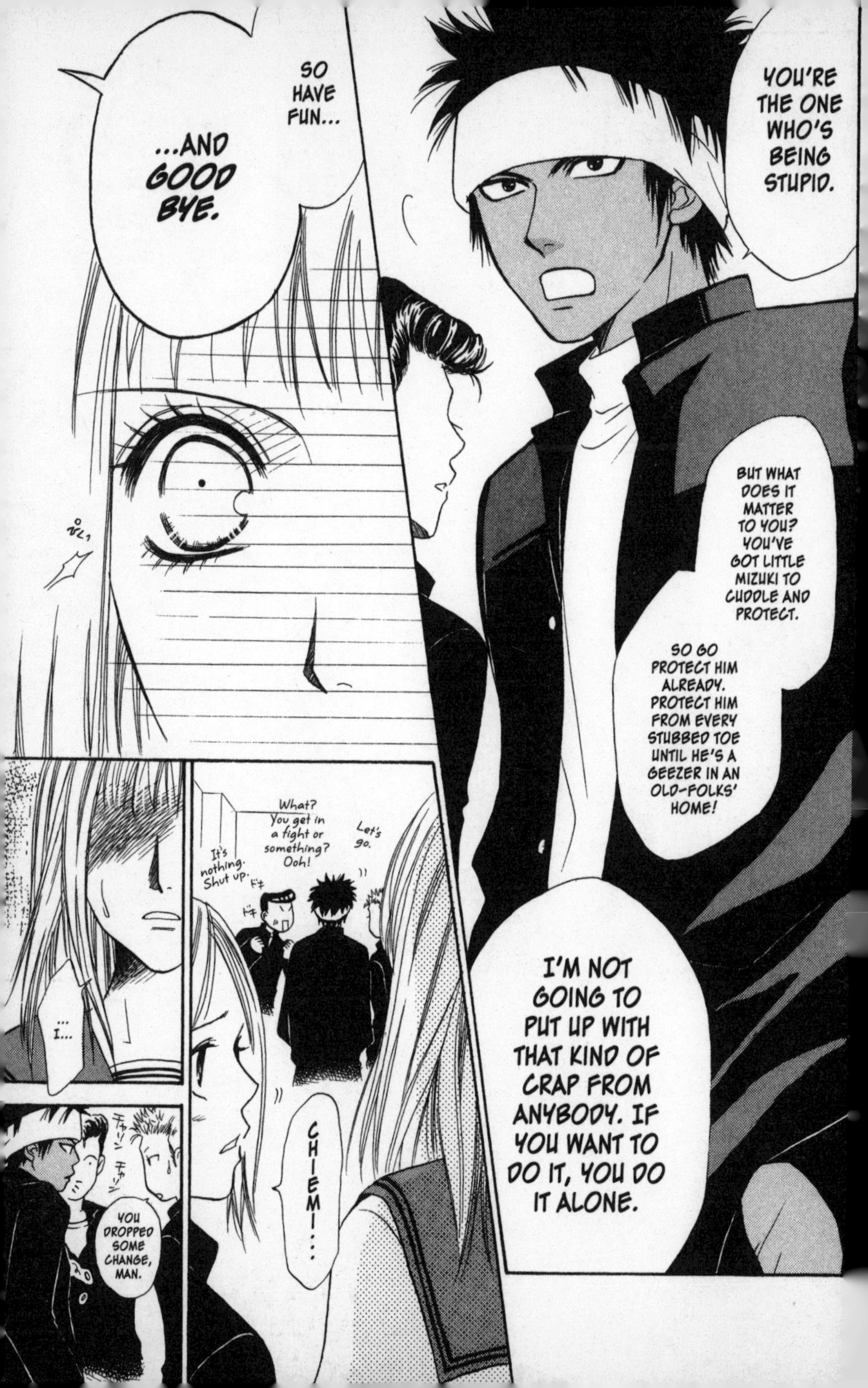
YOU'RE THE ONE WHO'S BEING STUPID.
BUT WHAT DOES IT MATTER TO YOU? YOU'VE GOT LITTLE MIZUKI TO CUDDLE AND PROTECT.
SO GO PROTECT HIM ALREADY. PROTECT HIM FROM EVERY STUBBED TOE UNTIL HE'S A GEEZER IN AN OLD-FOLKS' HOME!
I'M NOT GOING TO PUT UP WITH THAT KIND OF CRAP FROM ANYBODY. IF YOU WANT TO DO IT, YOU DO IT ALONE.
SO HAVE FUN...
...AND GOOD BYE.
What? You get in a fight or something? Ooh!
Let's go.
It's nothing. Shut up.
... I...
CHIEMI!...
YOU DROPPED SOME CHANGE, MAN.

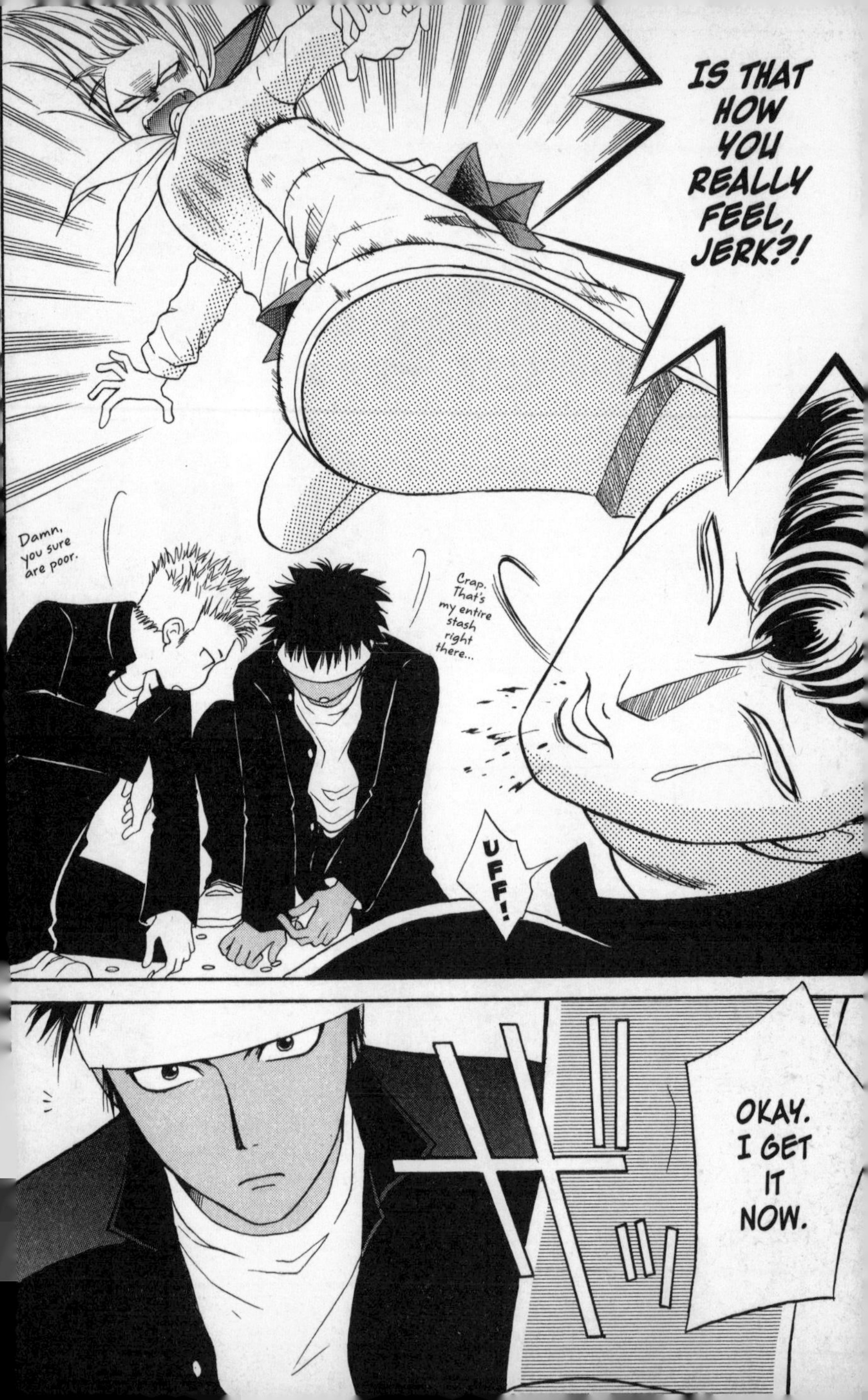
IS THAT HOW YOU REALLY FEEL, JERK?!
Crap. That's my entire stash right there...
Damn, you sure are poor.
UFF!
OKAY. I GET IT NOW.

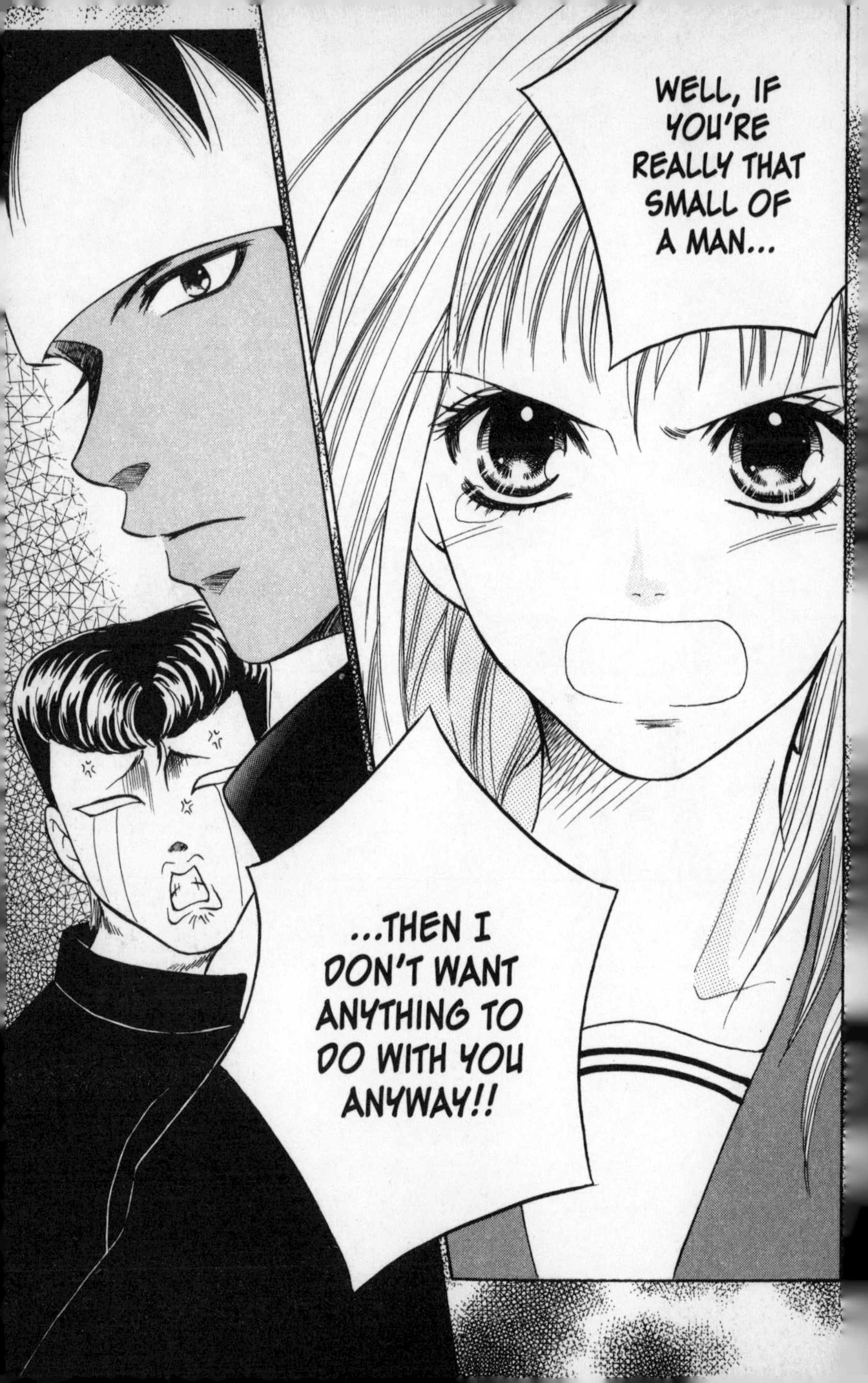
WELL, IF YOU'RE REALLY THAT SMALL OF A MAN...
...THEN I DON'T WANT ANYTHING TO DO WITH YOU ANYWAY!!

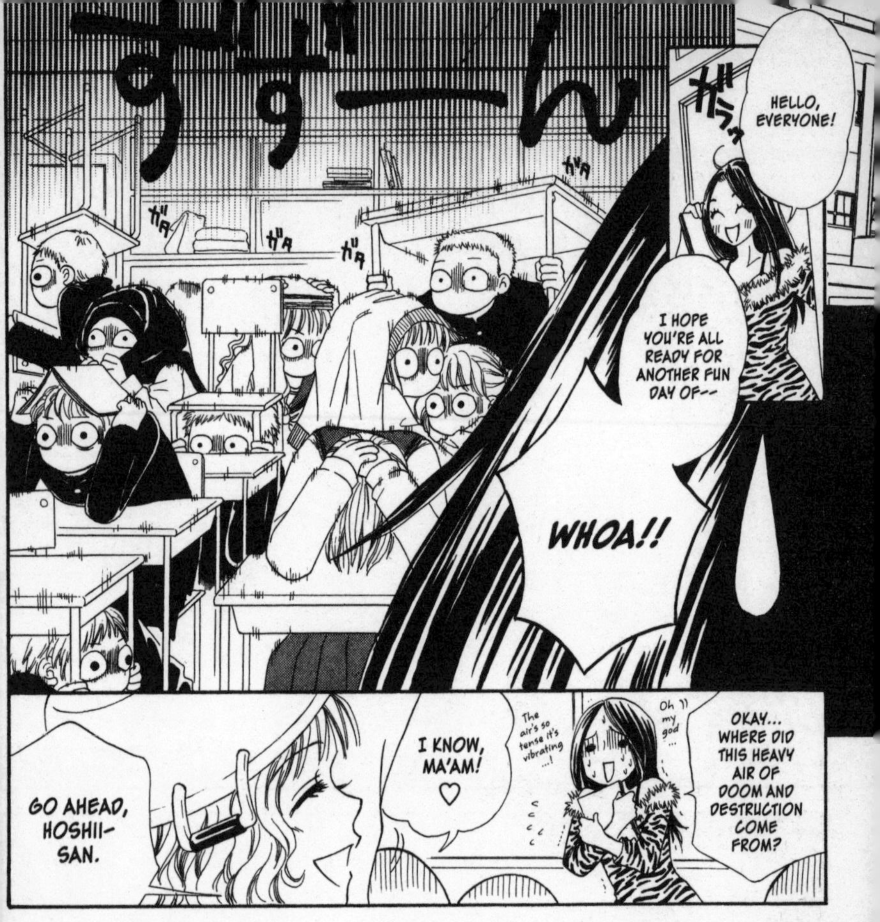
HELLO, EVERYONE!
I HOPE YOU'RE ALL READY FOR ANOTHER FUN DAY OF--
WHOA!!
OKAY... WHERE DID THIS HEAVY AIR OF DOOM AND DESTRUCTION COME FROM?
Oh my god ...
The air's so tense it's vibrating ...!
I KNOW, MA'AM! ♡
GO AHEAD, HOSHII-SAN.

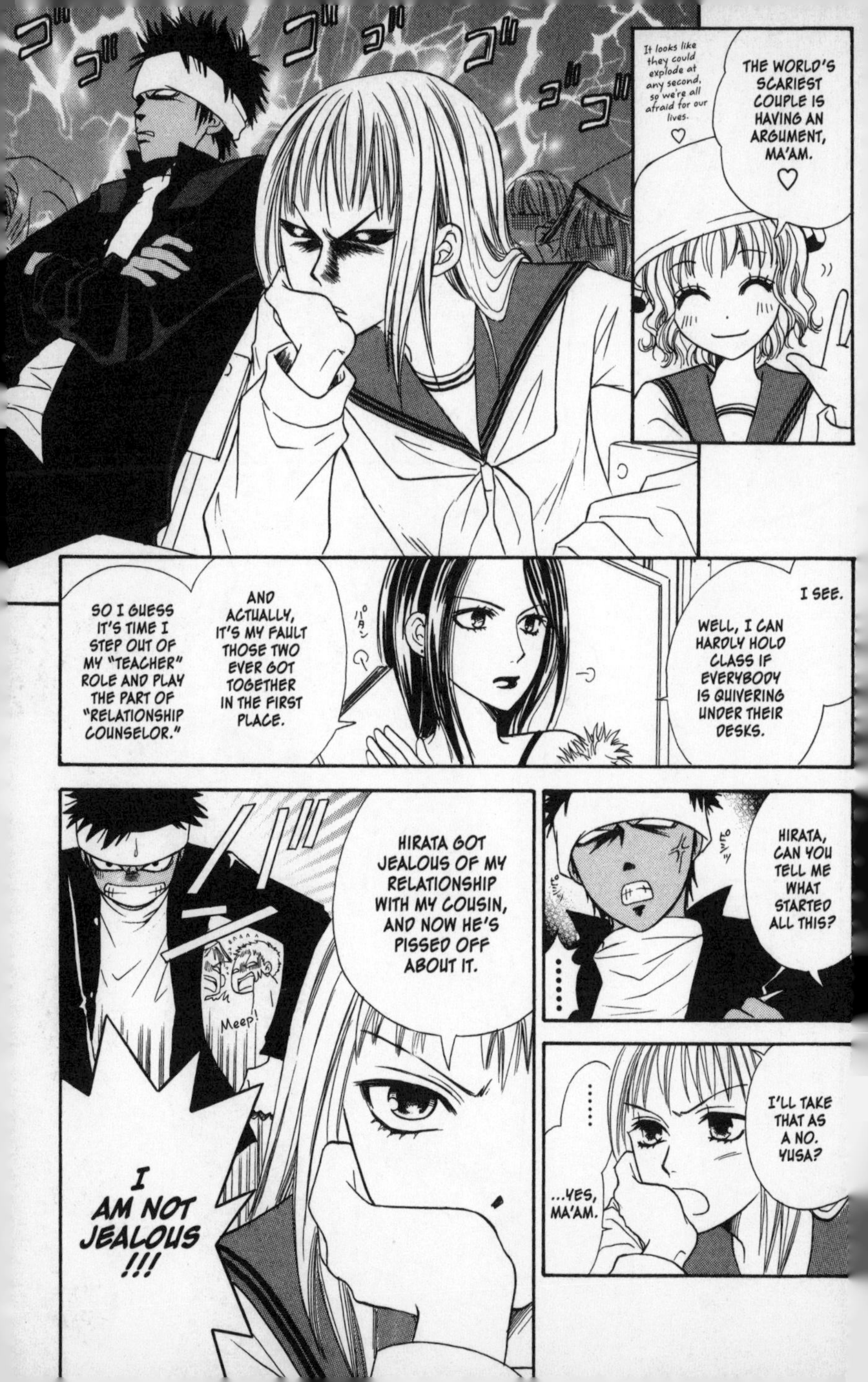
THE WORLD'S SCARIEST COUPLE IS HAVING AN ARGUMENT, MA'AM. ♡
It looks like they could explode at any second, so we're all afraid for our lives. ♡
I SEE.
WELL, I CAN HARDLY HOLD CLASS IF EVERYBODY IS QUIVERING UNDER THEIR DESKS.
パタン
AND ACTUALLY, IT'S MY FAULT THOSE TWO EVER GOT TOGETHER IN THE FIRST PLACE.
SO I GUESS IT'S TIME I STEP OUT OF MY "TEACHER" ROLE AND PLAY THE PART OF "RELATIONSHIP COUNSELOR."
HIRATA, CAN YOU TELL ME WHAT STARTED ALL THIS?
......
I'LL TAKE THAT AS A NO. YUSA?
......
...YES, MA'AM.
HIRATA GOT JEALOUS OF MY RELATIONSHIP WITH MY COUSIN, AND NOW HE'S PISSED OFF ABOUT IT.
Meep!
I AM NOT JEALOUS!!!

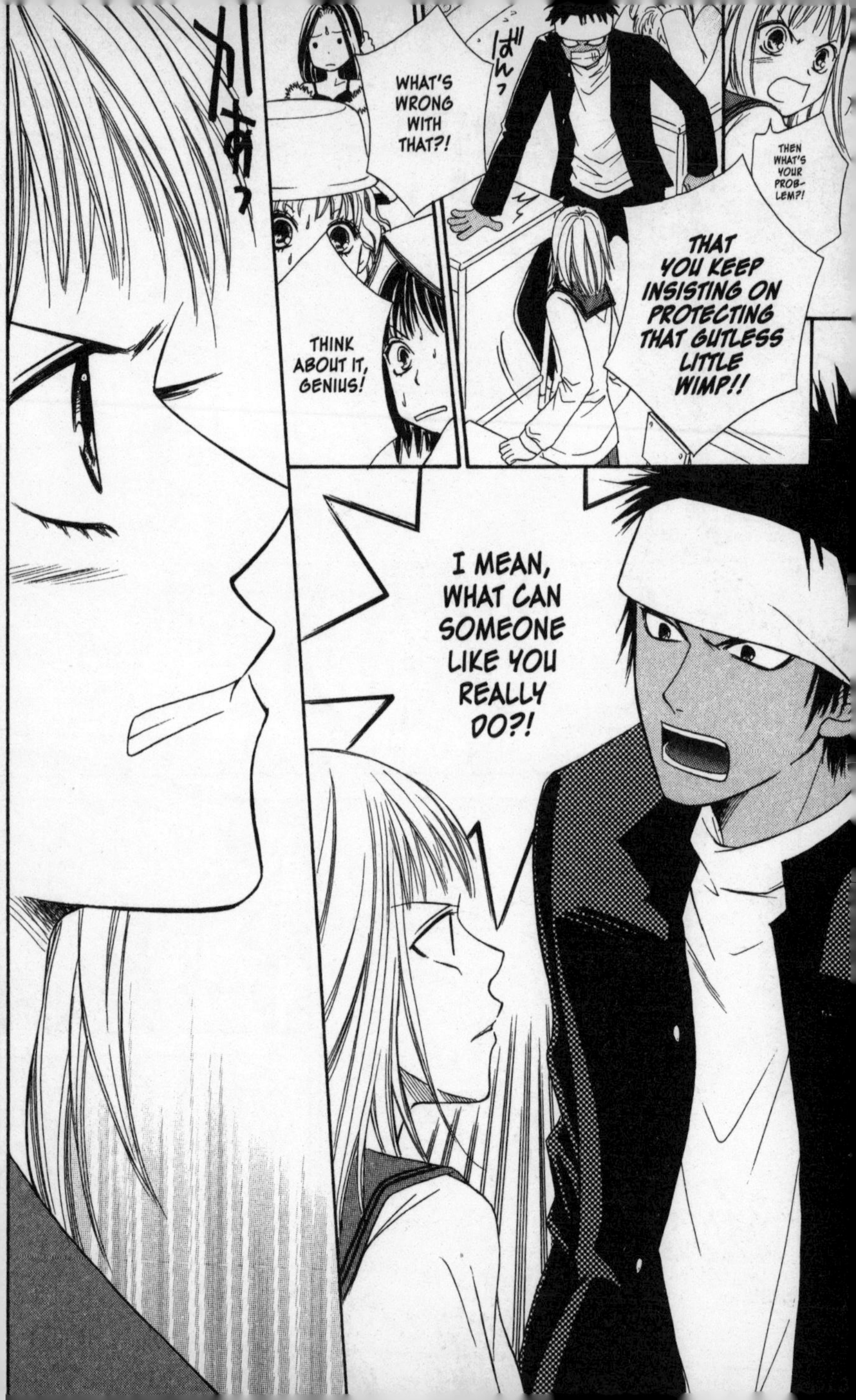
THEN WHAT'S YOUR PROB-LEM?!
ばんっ
THAT YOU KEEP INSISTING ON PROTECTING THAT GUTLESS LITTLE WIMP!!
WHAT'S WRONG WITH THAT?!
THINK ABOUT IT, GENIUS!
I MEAN, WHAT CAN SOMEONE LIKE YOU REALLY DO?!
かあっ

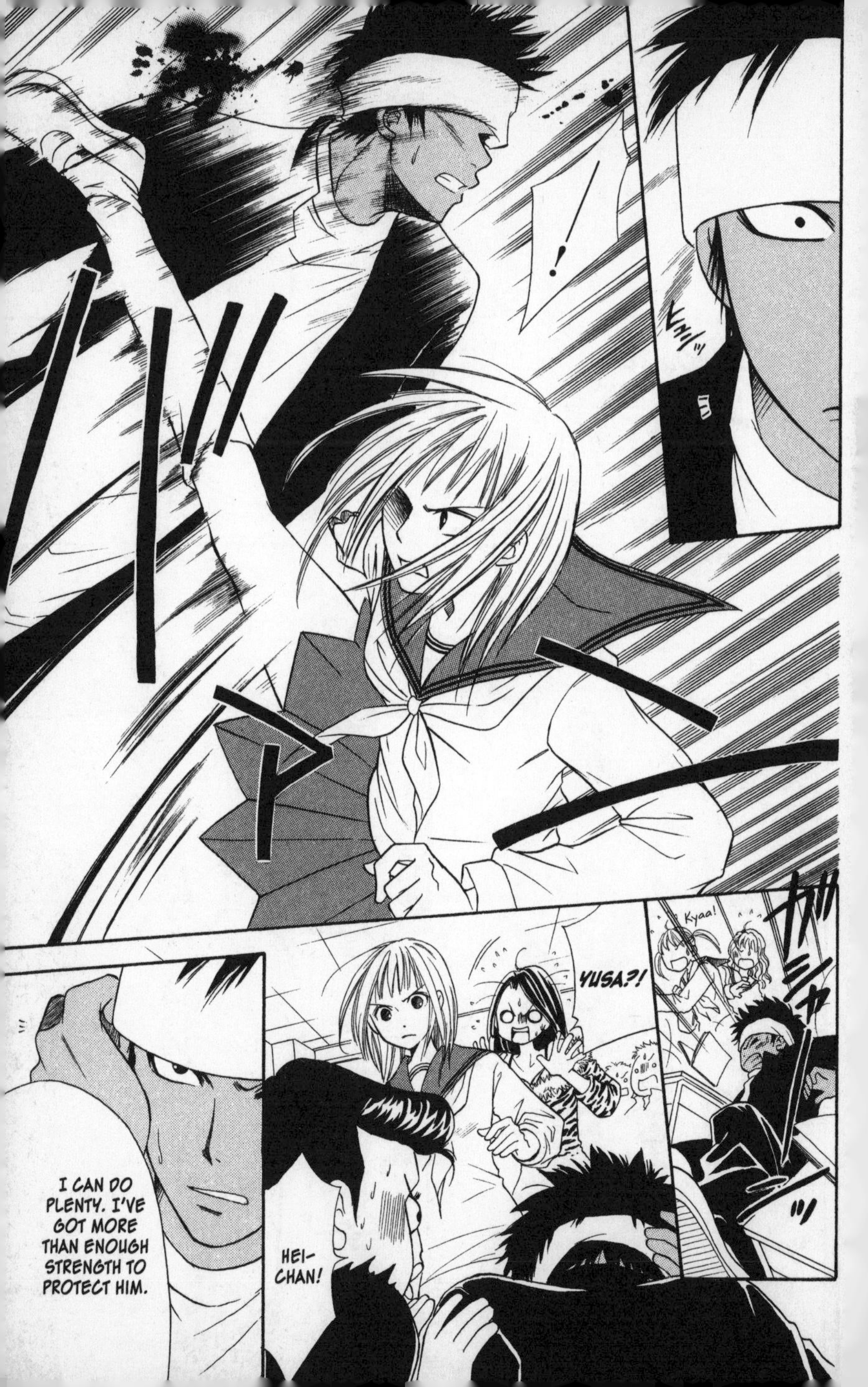
!
Kyaa!
YUSA?!
HEI-CHAN!
I CAN DO PLENTY. I'VE GOT MORE THAN ENOUGH STRENGTH TO PROTECT HIM.

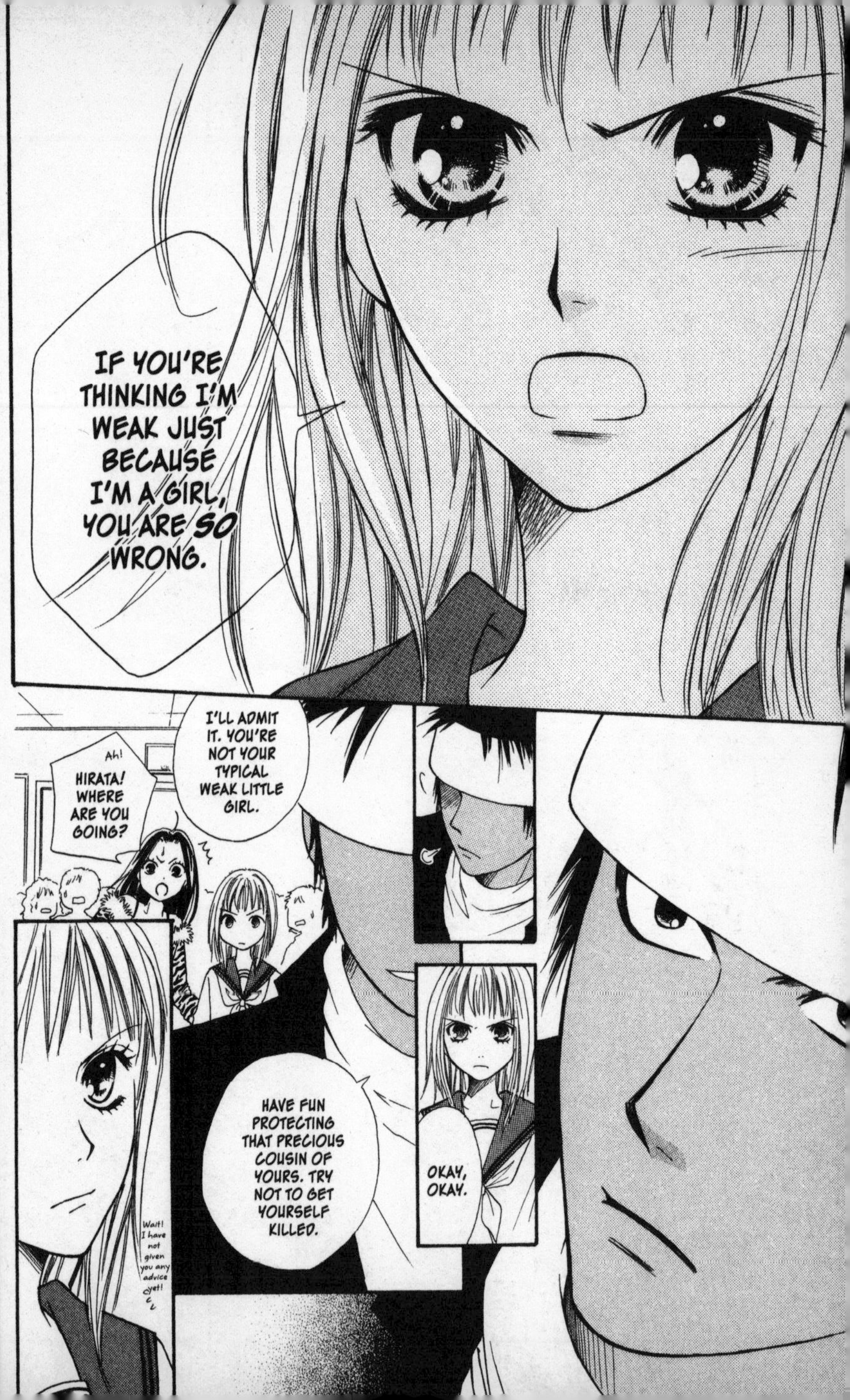
IF YOU'RE THINKING I'M WEAK JUST BECAUSE I'M A GIRL, YOU ARE SO WRONG.
I'LL ADMIT IT. YOU'RE NOT YOUR TYPICAL WEAK LITTLE GIRL.
HAVE FUN PROTECTING THAT PRECIOUS COUSIN OF YOURS. TRY NOT TO GET YOURSELF KILLED.
OKAY, OKAY.
Ah!
HIRATA! WHERE ARE YOU GOING?
Wait! I have not given you any advice yet!

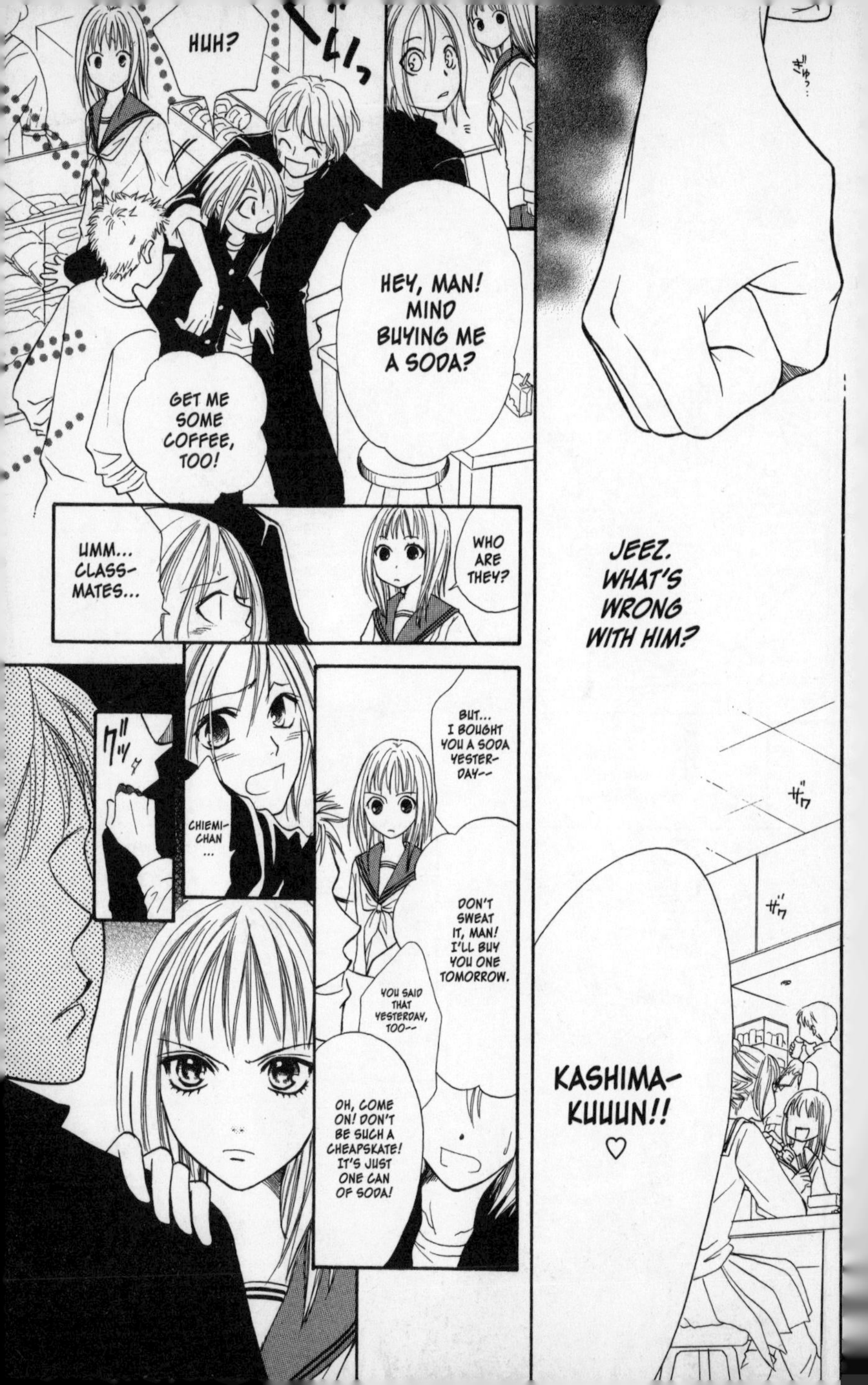
HUH?
HEY, MAN! MIND BUYING ME A SODA?
GET ME SOME COFFEE, TOO!
WHO ARE THEY?
UMM... CLASS-MATES...
BUT... I BOUGHT YOU A SODA YESTER-DAY--
CHIEMI-CHAN ...
DON'T SWEAT IT, MAN! I'LL BUY YOU ONE TOMORROW.
YOU SAID THAT YESTERDAY, TOO--
OH, COME ON! DON'T BE SUCH A CHEAPSKATE! IT'S JUST ONE CAN OF SODA!
JEEZ. WHAT'S WRONG WITH HIM?
KASHIMA-KUUUN!! ♡

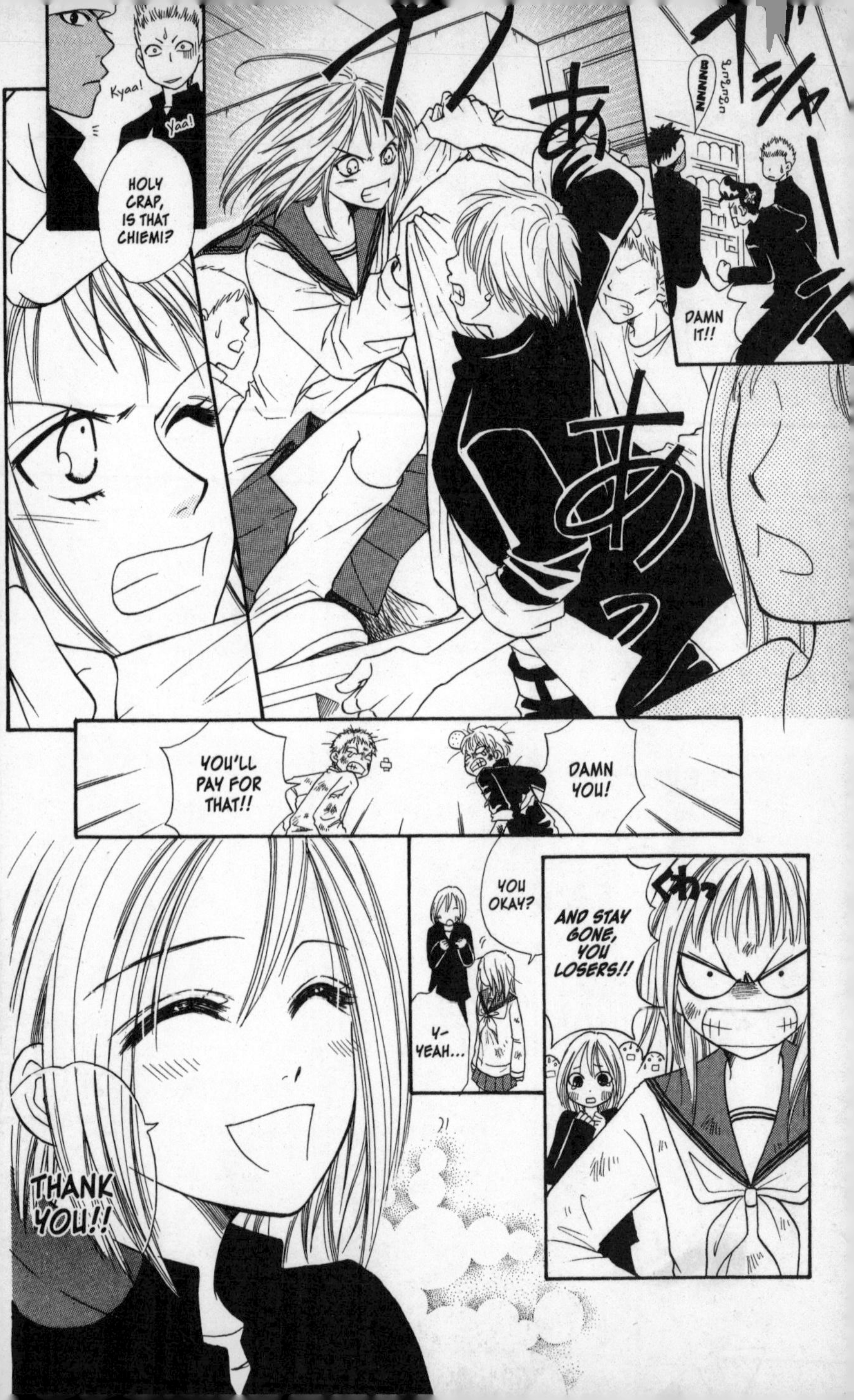
DAMN IT!!
Kyaa!
Yaa!
HOLY CRAP, IS THAT CHIEMI?
DAMN YOU!
YOU'LL PAY FOR THAT!!
AND STAY GONE, YOU LOSERS!!
YOU OKAY?
Y-YEAH...
THANK YOU!!

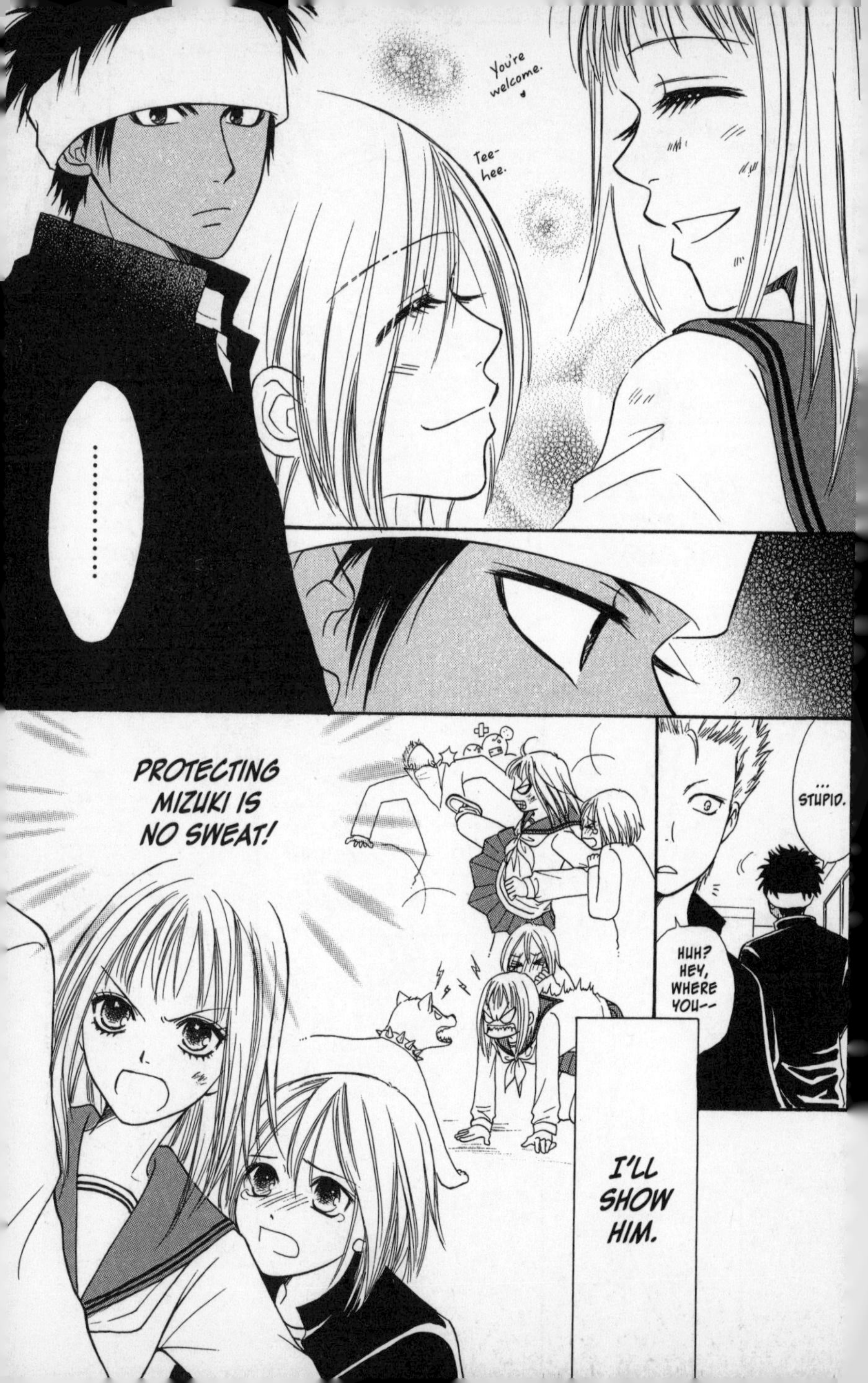
You're welcome. ♥
Tee-hee.
......
... STUPID.
HUH? HEY, WHERE YOU--
I'LL SHOW HIM.
PROTECTING MIZUKI IS NO SWEAT!
...

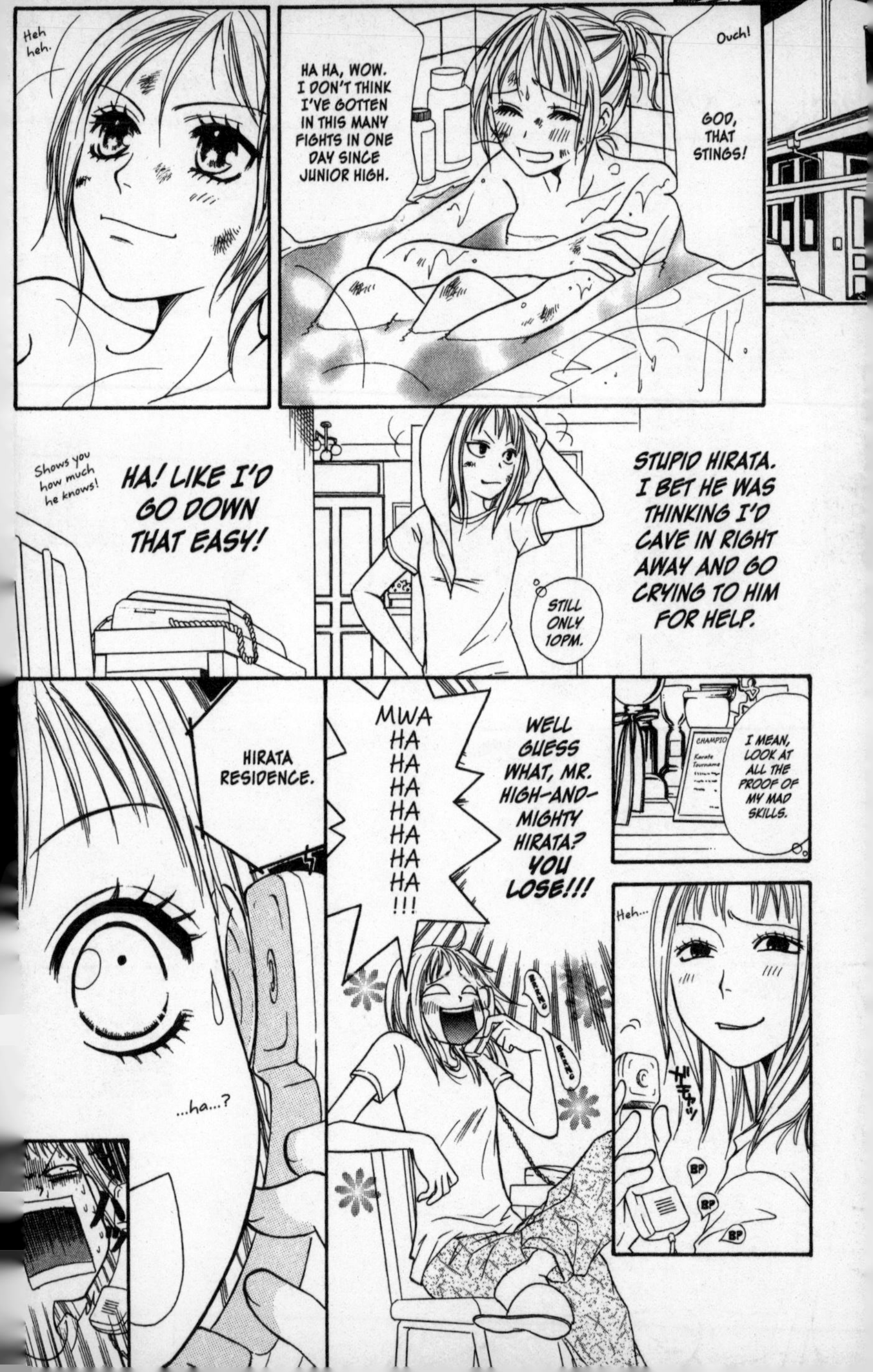
Ouch!
GOD, THAT STINGS!
HA HA, WOW. I DON'T THINK I'VE GOTTEN IN THIS MANY FIGHTS IN ONE DAY SINCE JUNIOR HIGH.
Heh heh.
STUPID HIRATA. I BET HE WAS THINKING I'D CAVE IN RIGHT AWAY AND GO CRYING TO HIM FOR HELP.
STILL ONLY 10PM.
HA! LIKE I'D GO DOWN THAT EASY!
Shows you how much he knows!
I MEAN, LOOK AT ALL THE PROOF OF MY MAD SKILLS.
Heh...
BP
BP
BP
WELL GUESS WHAT, MR. HIGH-AND-MIGHTY HIRATA? YOU LOSE!!!
MWA HA HA HA HA HA HA HA HA!!!
HIRATA RESIDENCE.
...ha...?

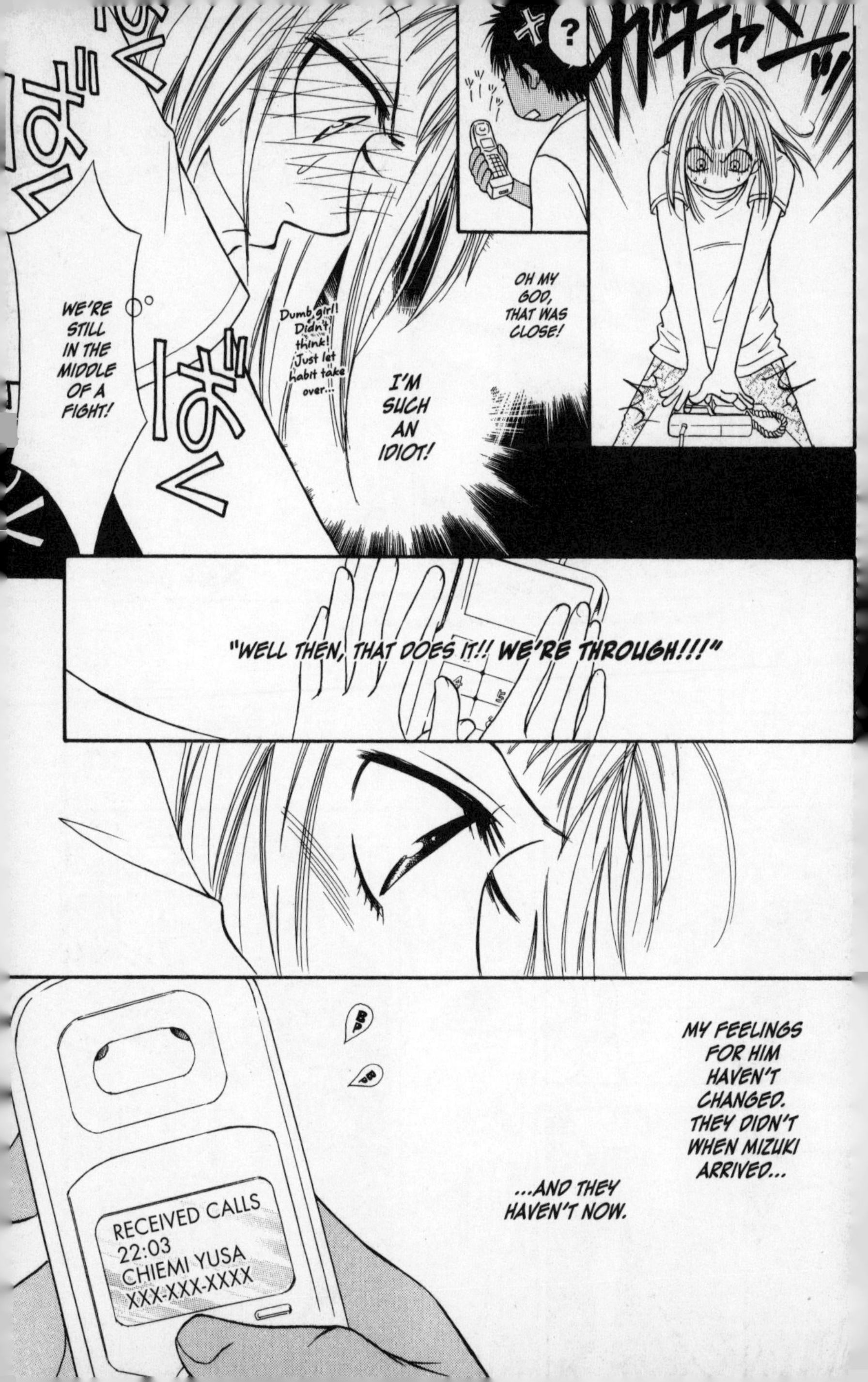
?
OH MY GOD, THAT WAS CLOSE!
I'M SUCH AN IDIOT!
Dumb girl! Didn't think! Just let habit take over...
WE'RE STILL IN THE MIDDLE OF A FIGHT!
"WELL THEN, THAT DOES IT!! WE'RE THROUGH!!!"
MY FEELINGS FOR HIM HAVEN'T CHANGED. THEY DIDN'T WHEN MIZUKI ARRIVED...
BP
BP
...AND THEY HAVEN'T NOW.
RECEIVED CALLS
22:03
CHIEMI YUSA
XXX-XXX-XXXX

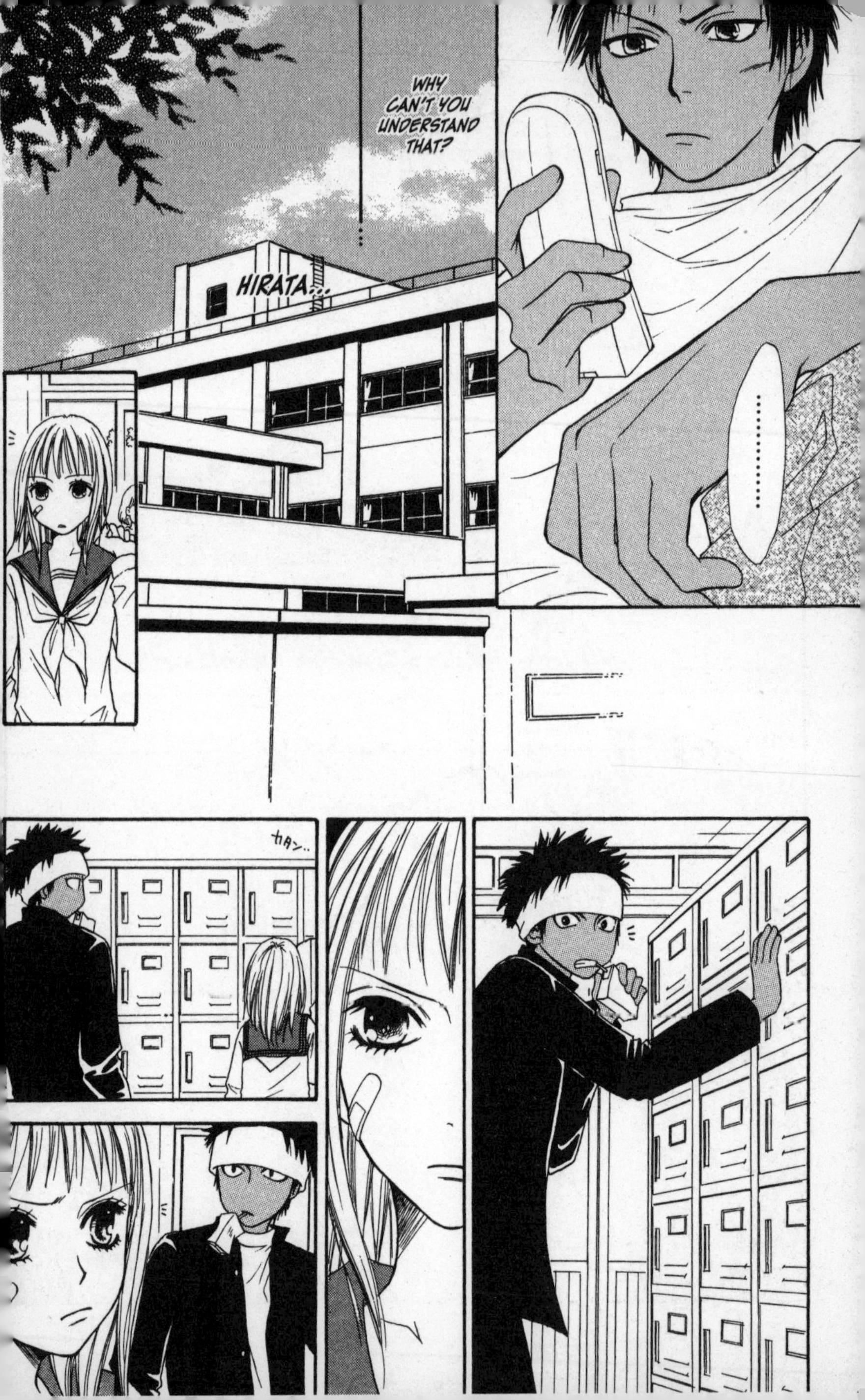
......
WHY CAN'T YOU UNDERSTAND THAT?
HIRATA...
カタン..

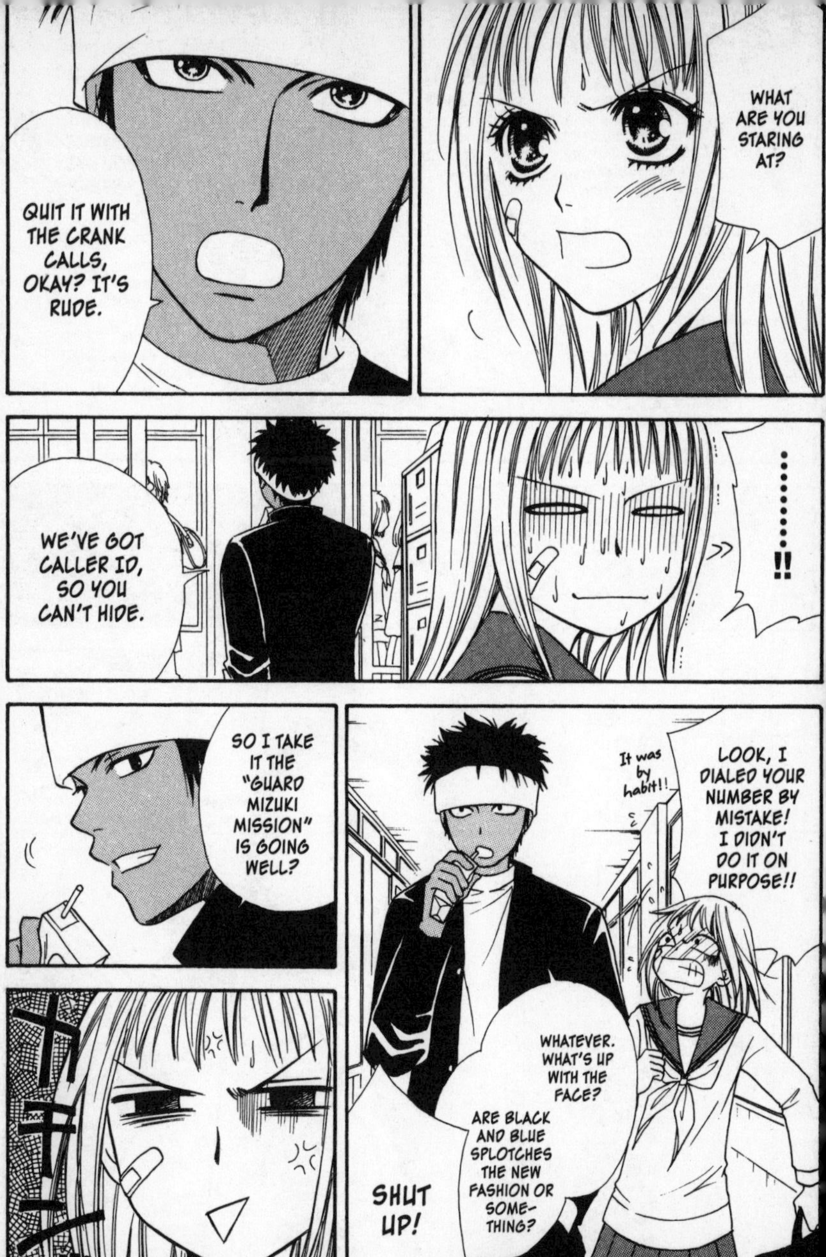
WHAT ARE YOU STARING AT?
QUIT IT WITH THE CRANK CALLS, OKAY? IT'S RUDE.
......!!
WE'VE GOT CALLER ID, SO YOU CAN'T HIDE.
LOOK, I DIALED YOUR NUMBER BY MISTAKE! I DIDN'T DO IT ON PURPOSE!!
It was by habit!!
WHATEVER. WHAT'S UP WITH THE FACE?
ARE BLACK AND BLUE SPLOTCHES THE NEW FASHION OR SOME-THING?
SHUT UP!
SO I TAKE IT THE "GUARD MIZUKI MISSION" IS GOING WELL?

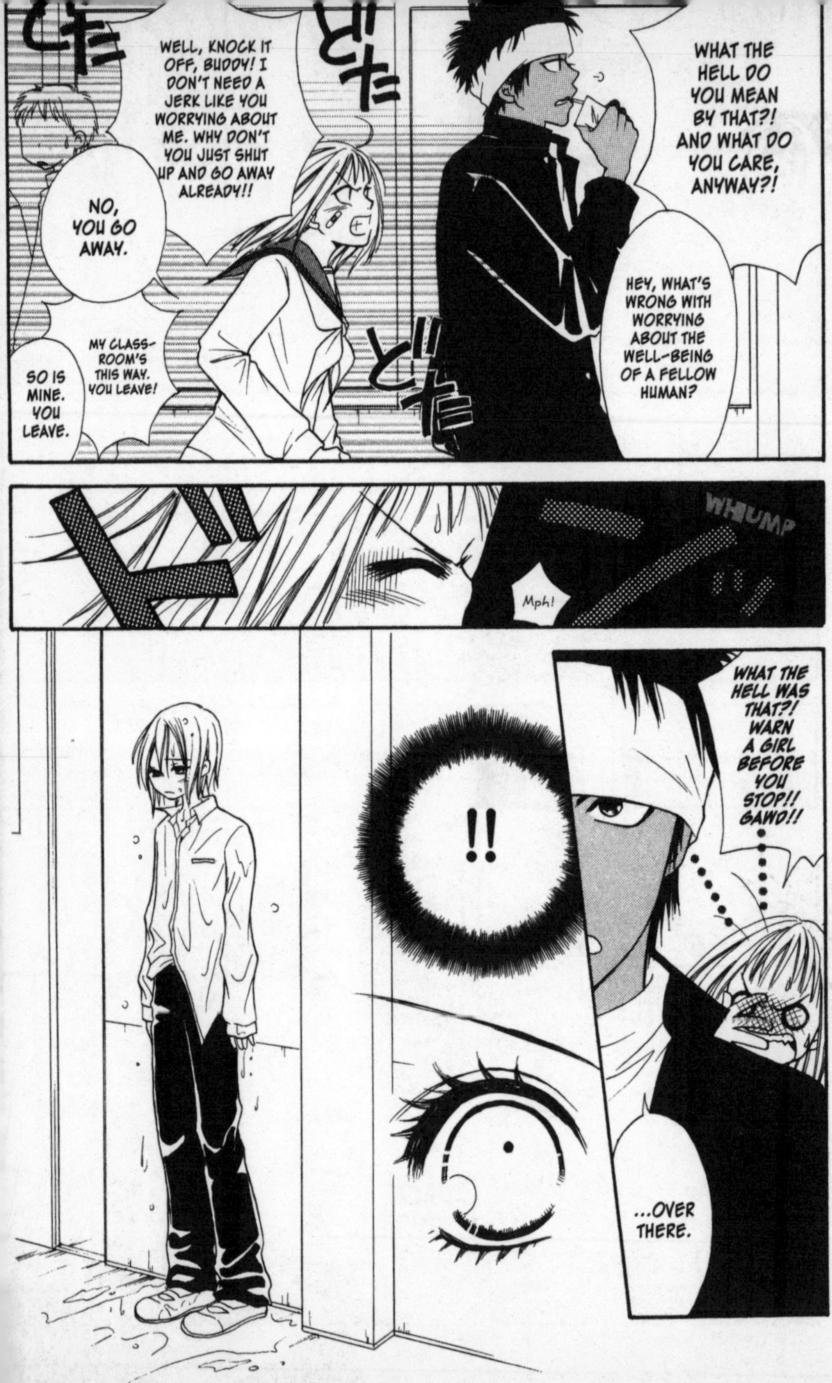
WHAT THE HELL DO YOU MEAN BY THAT?! AND WHAT DO YOU CARE, ANYWAY?!
HEY, WHAT'S WRONG WITH WORRYING ABOUT THE WELL-BEING OF A FELLOW HUMAN?
どた
WELL, KNOCK IT OFF, BUDDY! I DON'T NEED A JERK LIKE YOU WORRYING ABOUT ME. WHY DON'T YOU JUST SHUT UP AND GO AWAY ALREADY!!
NO, YOU GO AWAY.
MY CLASS-ROOM'S THIS WAY. YOU LEAVE!
SO IS MINE. YOU LEAVE.
WHUMP
Mph!
WHAT THE HELL WAS THAT?! WARN A GIRL BEFORE YOU STOP!! GAWD!!
...OVER THERE.
!!

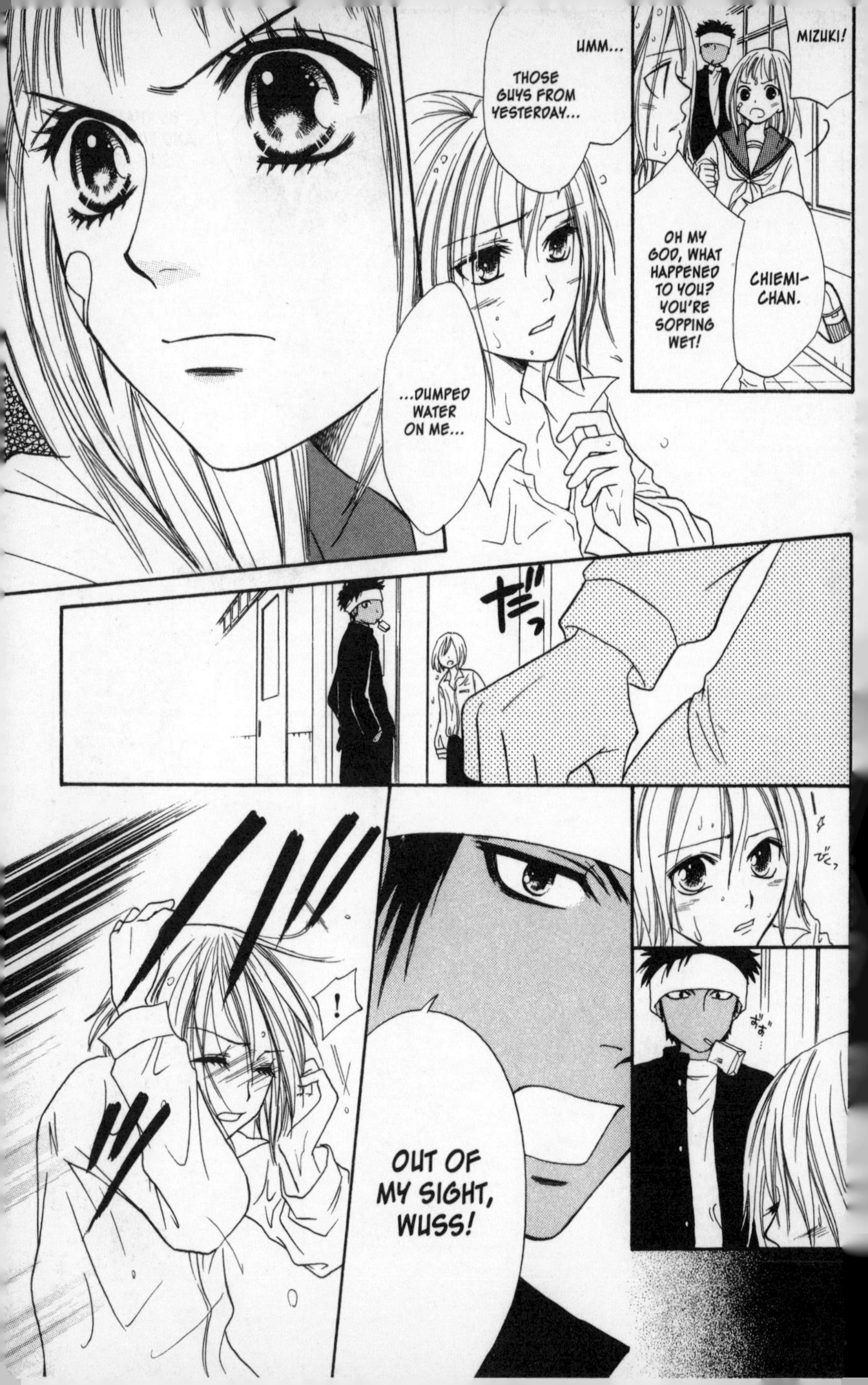
MIZUKI!
CHIEMI-CHAN.
OH MY GOD, WHAT HAPPENED TO YOU? YOU'RE SOPPING WET!
UMM...
THOSE GUYS FROM YESTERDAY...
...DUMPED WATER ON ME...
だっ
びくっ
ずず…
OUT OF MY SIGHT, WUSS!
!

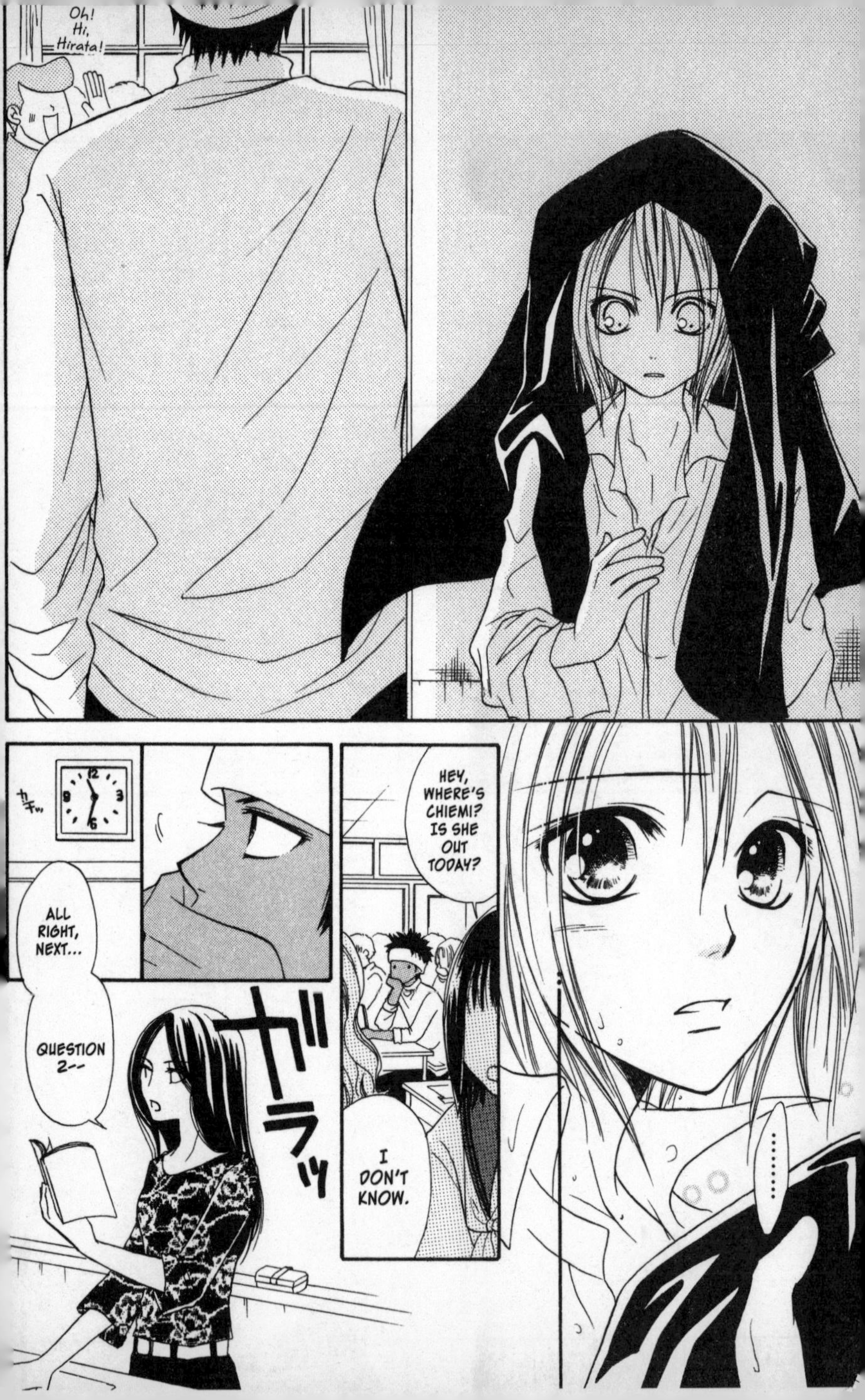
Oh! Hi, Hirata!
HEY, WHERE'S CHIEMI? IS SHE OUT TODAY?
I DON'T KNOW.
カチッ
ALL RIGHT, NEXT...
ガラッ
QUESTION 2--

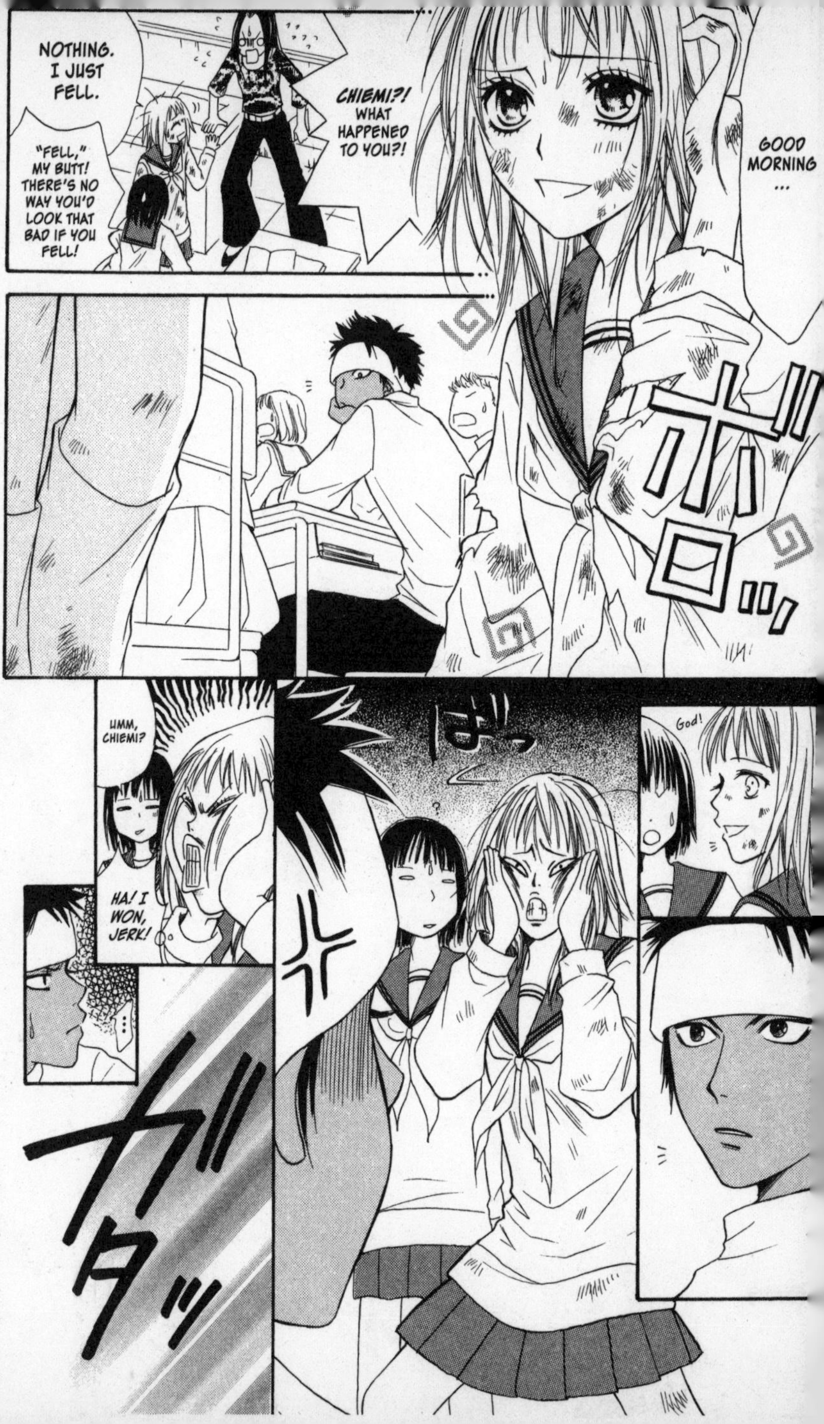
GOOD MORNING ...
CHIEMI?! WHAT HAPPENED TO YOU?!
NOTHING. I JUST FELL.
"FELL," MY BUTT! THERE'S NO WAY YOU'D LOOK THAT BAD IF YOU FELL!
ボロ
God!
UMM, CHIEMI?
HA! I WON, JERK!
...
ガタッ

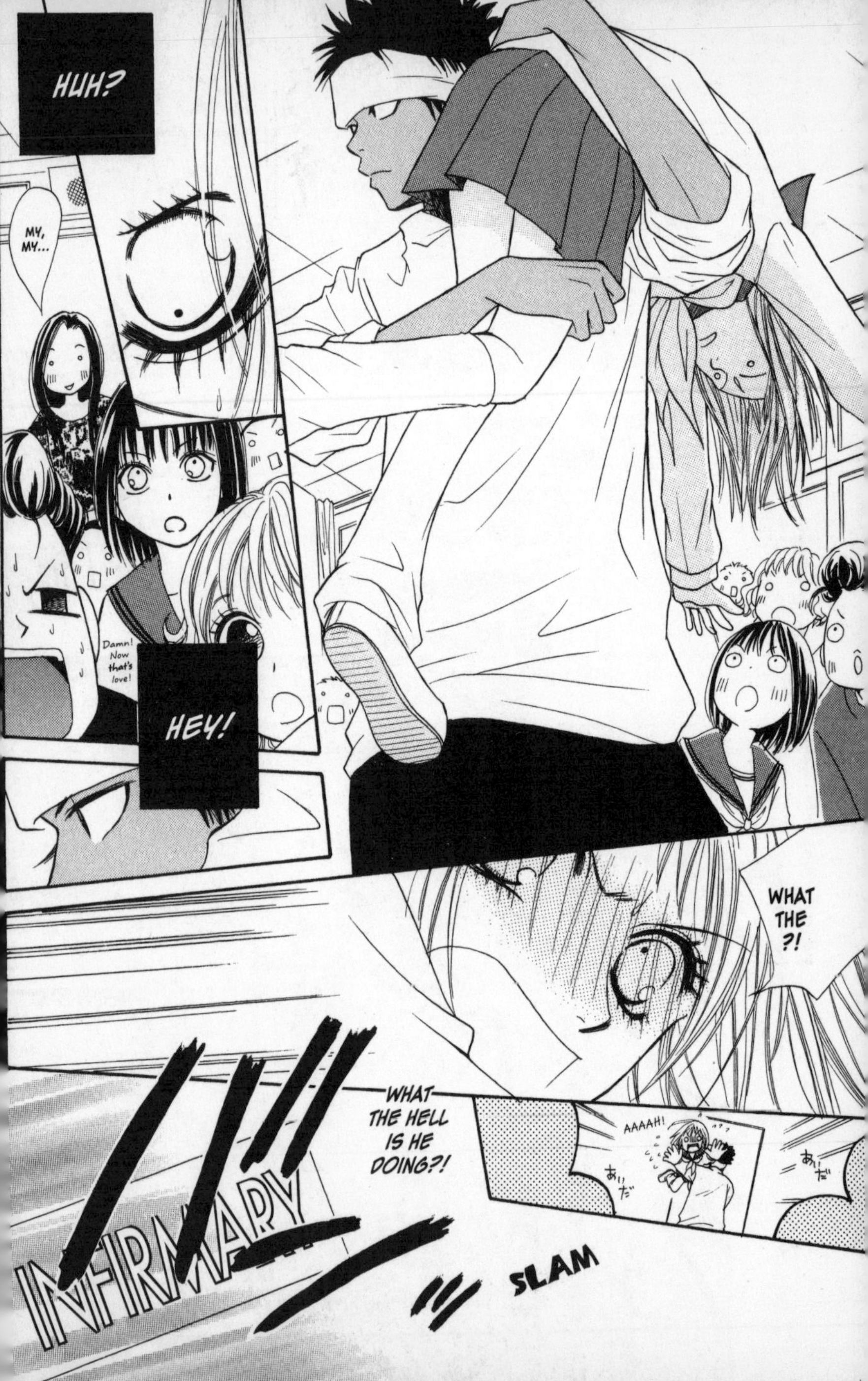
HUH?
MY, MY...
Damn! Now that's love!
HEY!
WHAT THE ?!
WHAT THE HELL IS HE DOING?!
AAAAH!
INFIRMARY
SLAM

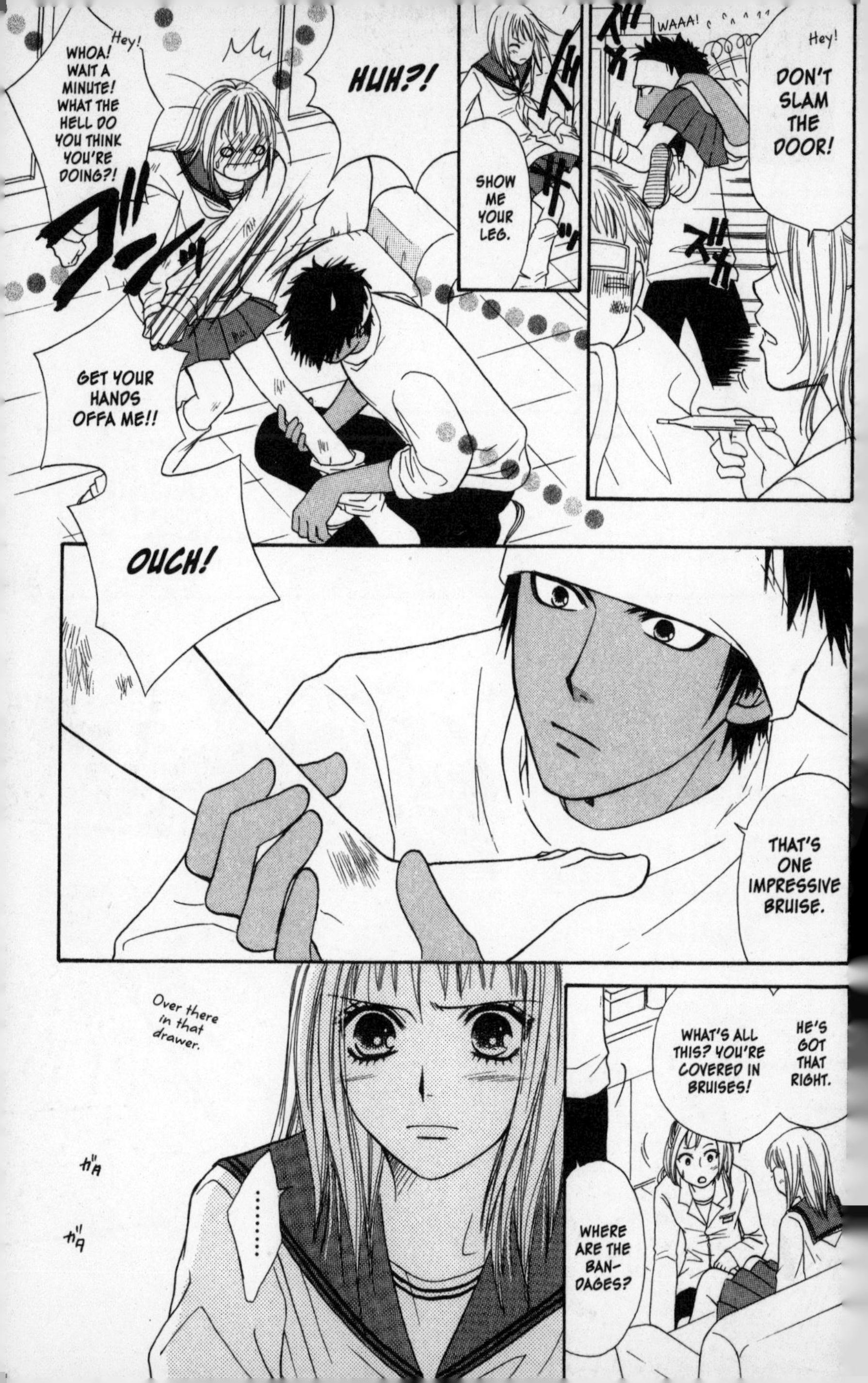
WAAA!
Hey!
DON'T SLAM THE DOOR!
SHOW ME YOUR LEG.
HUH?!
Hey!
WHOA! WAIT A MINUTE! WHAT THE HELL DO YOU THINK YOU'RE DOING?!
GET YOUR HANDS OFFA ME!!
THAT'S ONE IMPRESSIVE BRUISE.
OUCH!
HE'S GOT THAT RIGHT.
WHAT'S ALL THIS? YOU'RE COVERED IN BRUISES!
WHERE ARE THE BAN-DAGES?
......
Over there in that drawer.

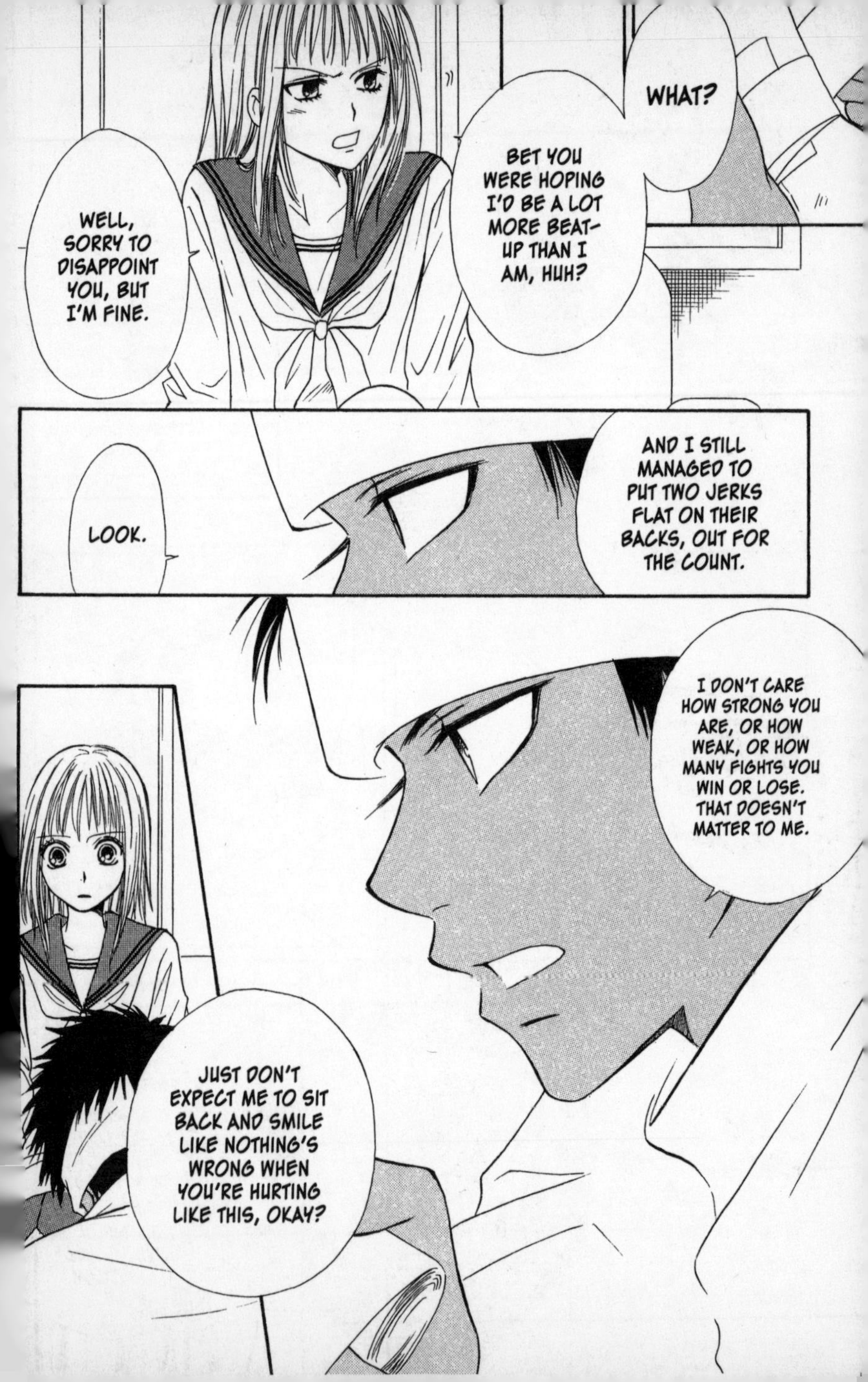
WHAT?
BET YOU WERE HOPING I'D BE A LOT MORE BEAT-UP THAN I AM, HUH?
WELL, SORRY TO DISAPPOINT YOU, BUT I'M FINE.
AND I STILL MANAGED TO PUT TWO JERKS FLAT ON THEIR BACKS, OUT FOR THE COUNT.
LOOK.
I DON'T CARE HOW STRONG YOU ARE, OR HOW WEAK, OR HOW MANY FIGHTS YOU WIN OR LOSE. THAT DOESN'T MATTER TO ME.
JUST DON'T EXPECT ME TO SIT BACK AND SMILE LIKE NOTHING'S WRONG WHEN YOU'RE HURTING LIKE THIS, OKAY?

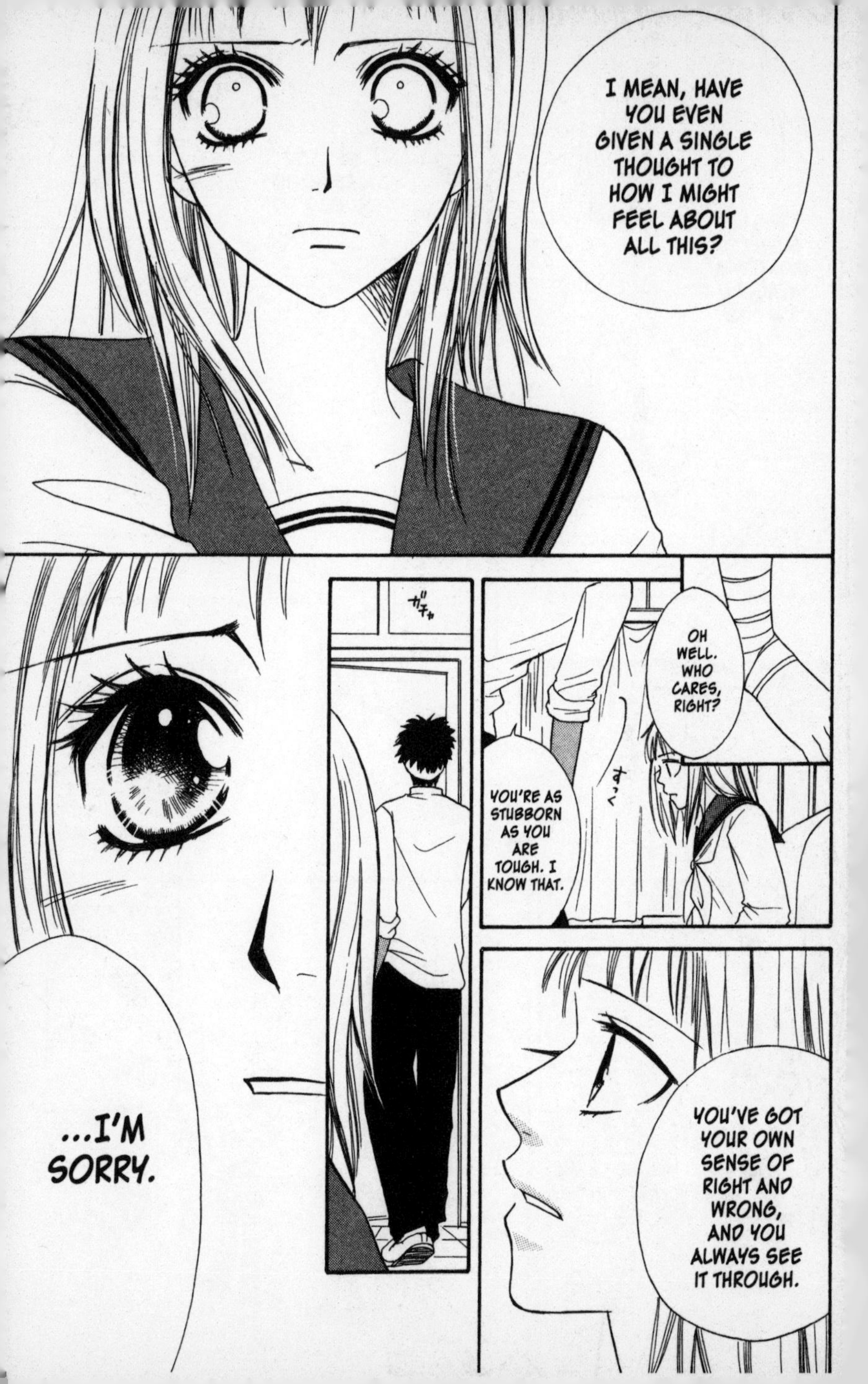
I MEAN, HAVE YOU EVEN GIVEN A SINGLE THOUGHT TO HOW I MIGHT FEEL ABOUT ALL THIS?
OH WELL. WHO CARES, RIGHT?
すっ
YOU'RE AS STUBBORN AS YOU ARE TOUGH. I KNOW THAT.
YOU'VE GOT YOUR OWN SENSE OF RIGHT AND WRONG, AND YOU ALWAYS SEE IT THROUGH.
ガチャ
...I'M SORRY.

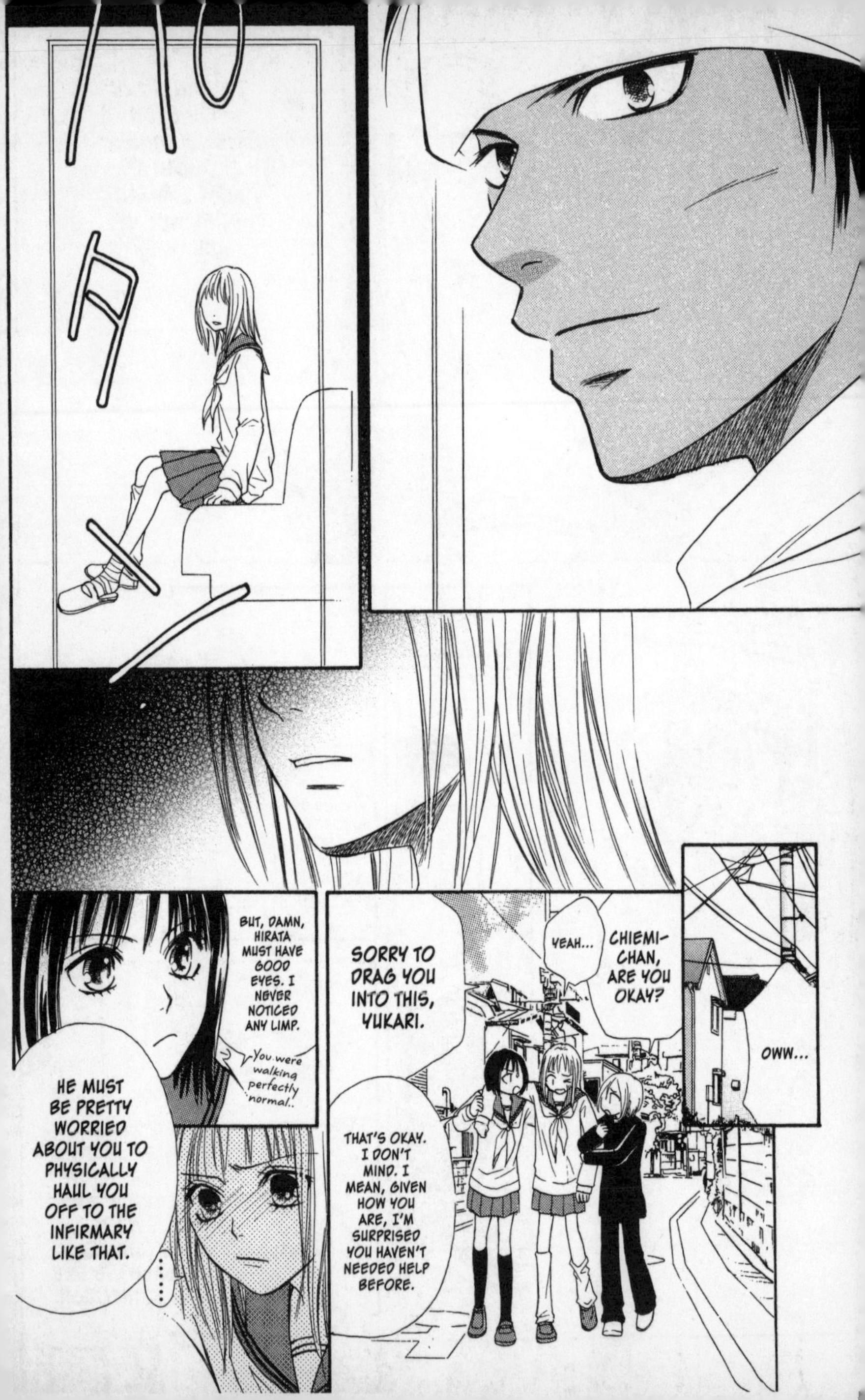
OWW...
CHIEMI-CHAN, ARE YOU OKAY?
YEAH...
SORRY TO DRAG YOU INTO THIS, YUKARI.
THAT'S OKAY. I DON'T MIND. I MEAN, GIVEN HOW YOU ARE, I'M SURPRISED YOU HAVEN'T NEEDED HELP BEFORE.
BUT, DAMN, HIRATA MUST HAVE GOOD EYES. I NEVER NOTICED ANY LIMP.
You were walking perfectly normal..
HE MUST BE PRETTY WORRIED ABOUT YOU TO PHYSICALLY HAUL YOU OFF TO THE INFIRMARY LIKE THAT.
......

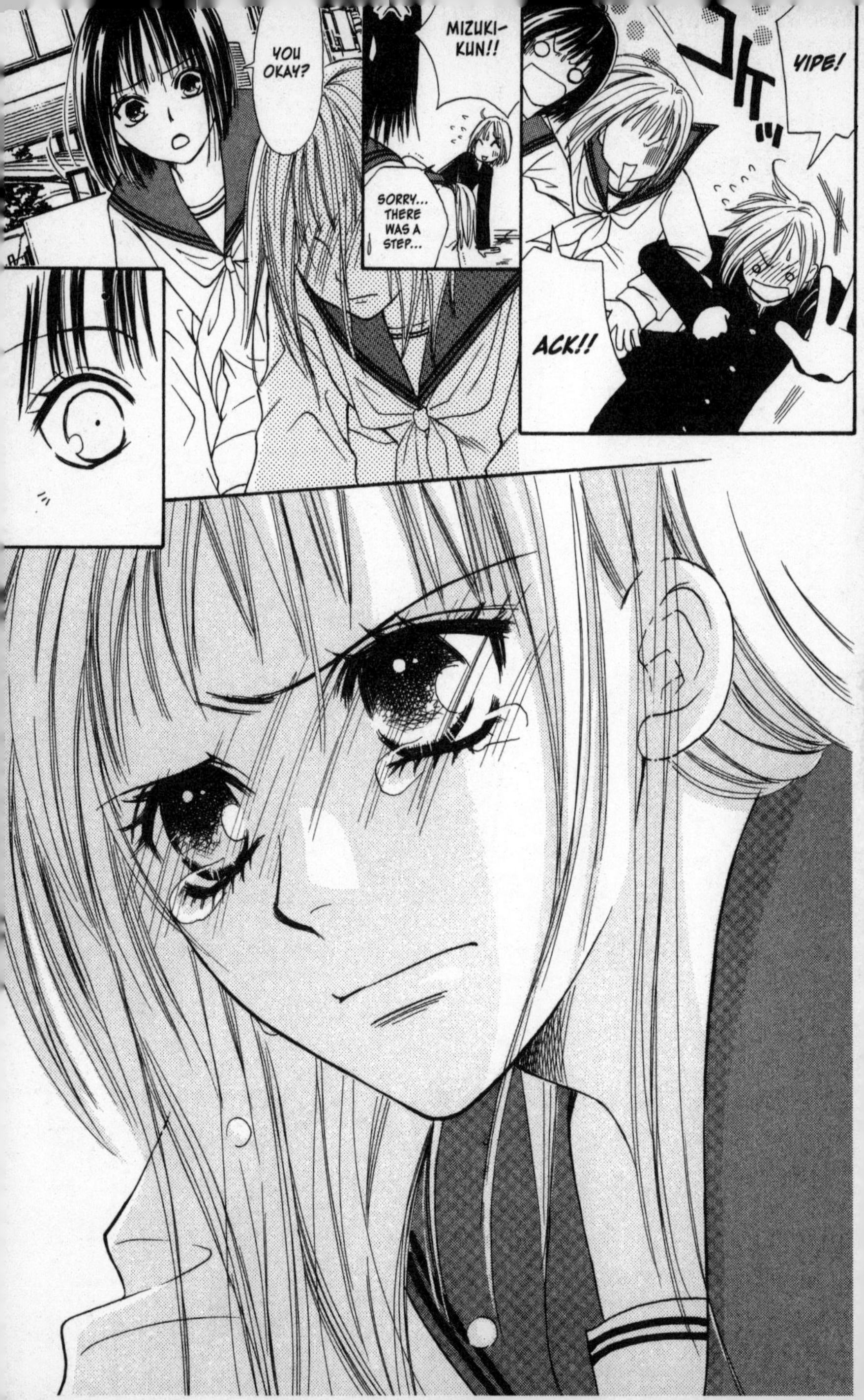
YIPE!
ACK!!
MIZUKI-KUN!!
SORRY... THERE WAS A STEP...
YOU OKAY?

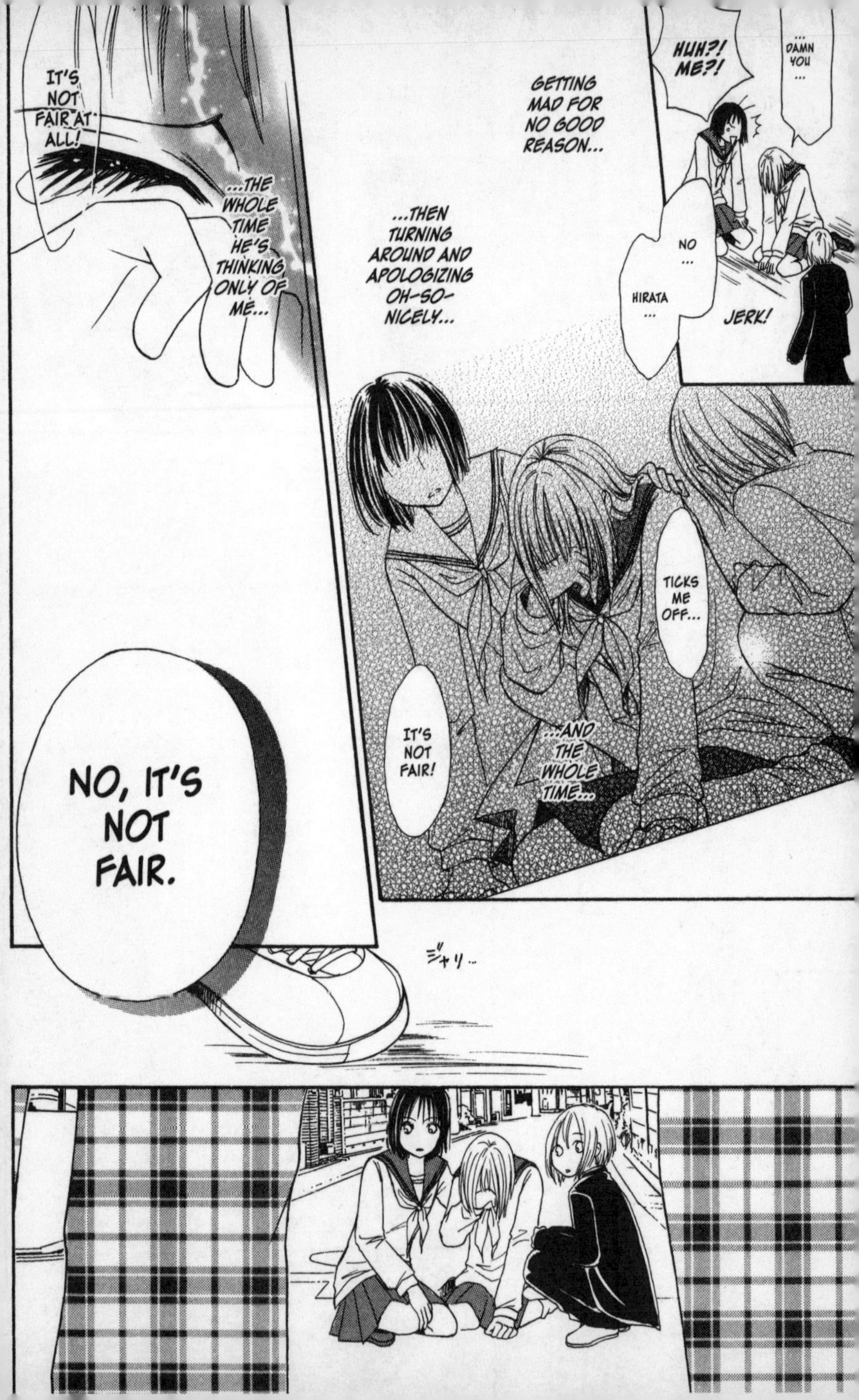

... DAMN YOU ...
HUH?! ME?!
NO ... HIRATA ... JERK!
GETTING MAD FOR NO GOOD REASON...
...THEN TURNING AROUND AND APOLOGIZING OH-SO-NICELY...
TICKS ME OFF...
...AND THE WHOLE TIME...
IT'S NOT FAIR!
IT'S NOT FAIR AT ALL!
...THE WHOLE TIME HE'S THINKING ONLY OF ME...
NO, IT'S NOT FAIR.
ジャリ..

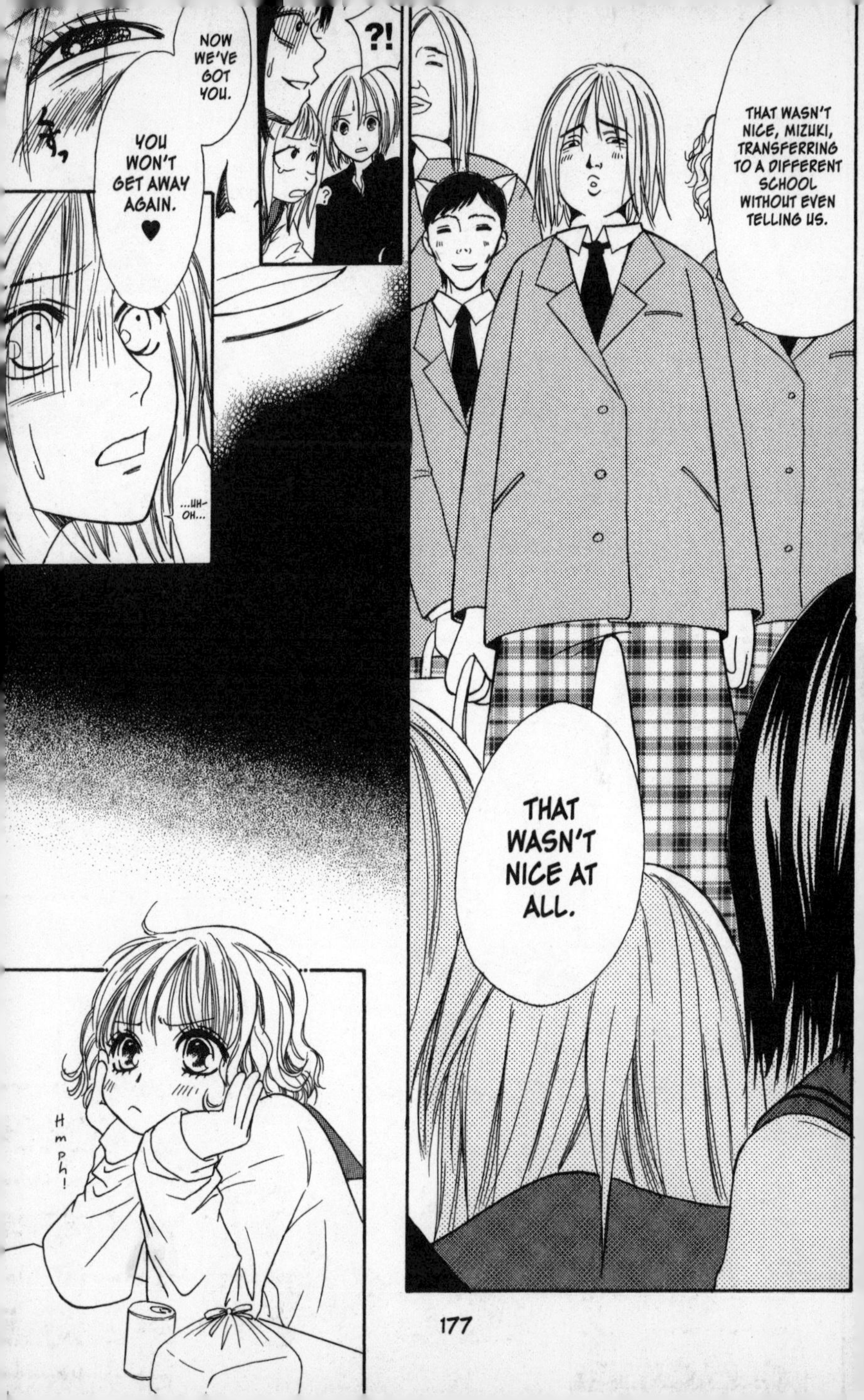
THAT WASN'T NICE, MIZUKI, TRANSFERRING TO A DIFFERENT SCHOOL WITHOUT EVEN TELLING US.
THAT WASN'T NICE AT ALL.
?!
NOW WE'VE GOT YOU.
YOU WON'T GET AWAY AGAIN. ♥
...UH-OH...
Hmph!

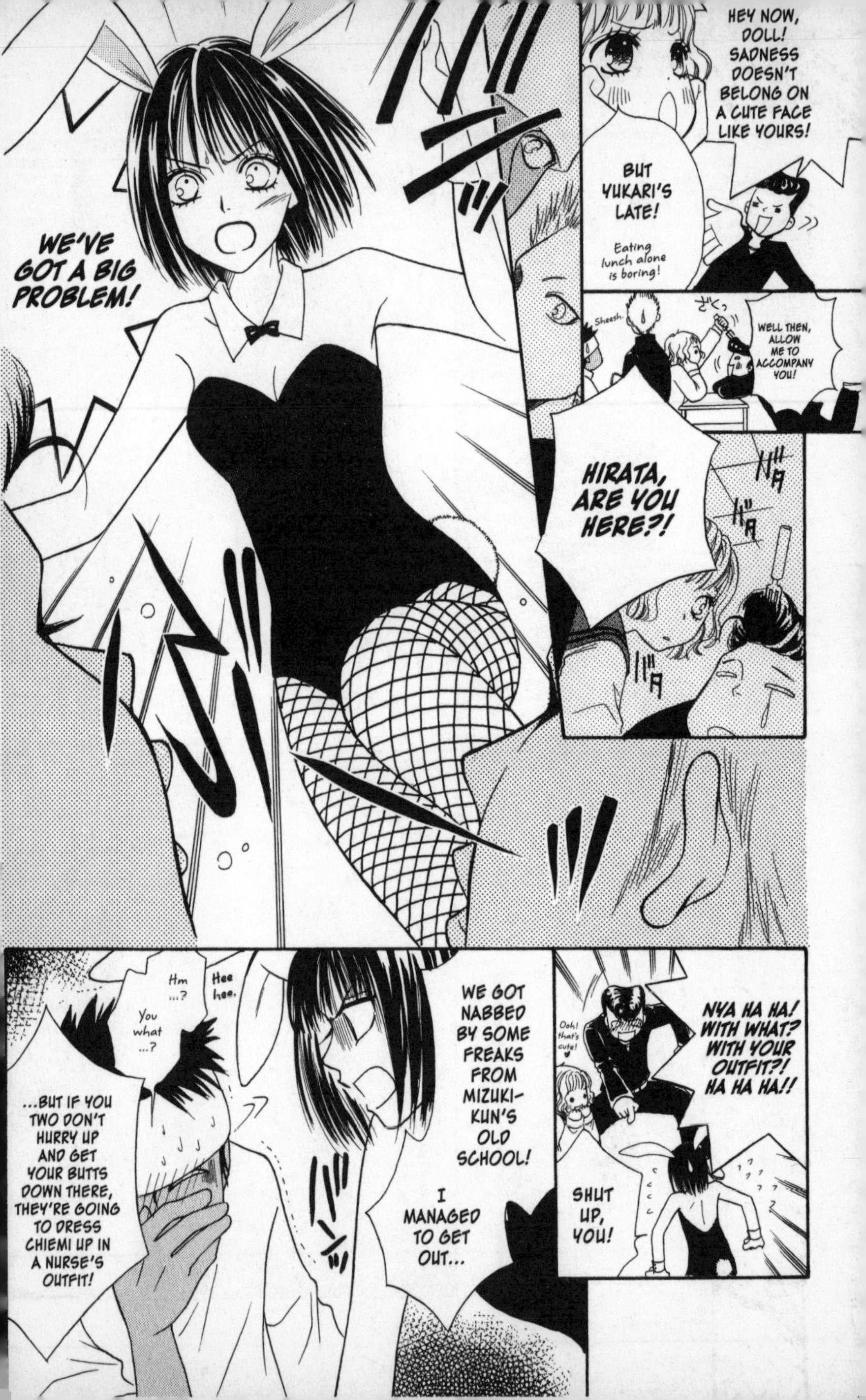

HEY NOW, DOLL! SADNESS DOESN'T BELONG ON A CUTE FACE LIKE YOURS!
BUT YUKARI'S LATE!
Eating lunch alone is boring!
ざくっ
WELL THEN, ALLOW ME TO ACCOMPANY YOU!
Sheesh.
HIRATA, ARE YOU HERE?!
WE'VE GOT A BIG PROBLEM!
NYA HA HA! WITH WHAT? WITH YOUR OUTFIT?! HA HA HA!!
Ooh! that's cute!
SHUT UP, YOU!
WE GOT NABBED BY SOME FREAKS FROM MIZUKI-KUN'S OLD SCHOOL!
I MANAGED TO GET OUT...
Hee hee.
Hm ...?
You what ...?
...BUT IF YOU TWO DON'T HURRY UP AND GET YOUR BUTTS DOWN THERE, THEY'RE GOING TO DRESS CHIEMI UP IN A NURSE'S OUTFIT!

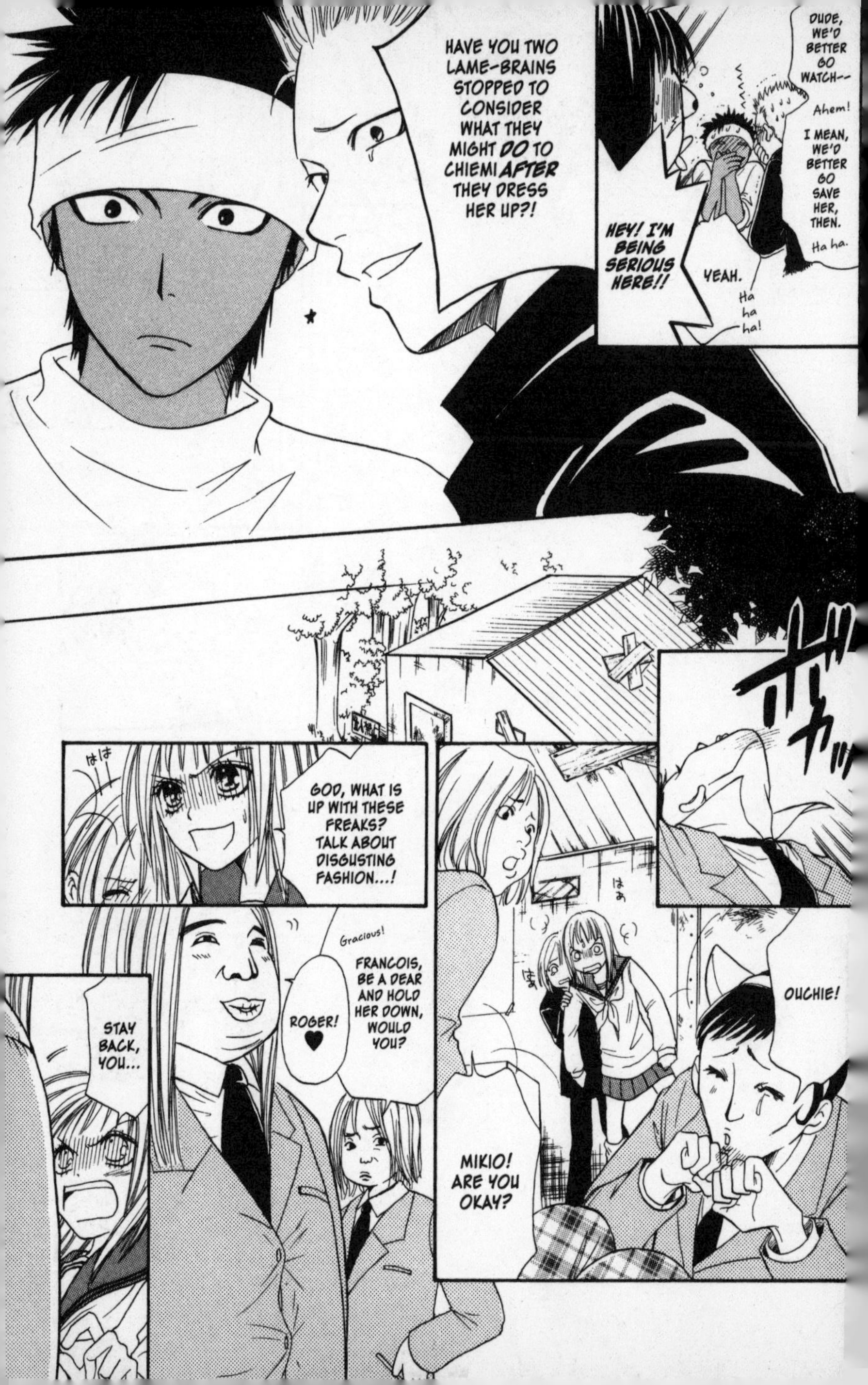
DUDE, WE'D BETTER GO WATCH--
Ahem!
I MEAN, WE'D BETTER GO SAVE HER, THEN.
Ha ha.
YEAH.
Ha ha ha!
HEY! I'M BEING SERIOUS HERE!!
HAVE YOU TWO LAME-BRAINS STOPPED TO CONSIDER WHAT THEY MIGHT DO TO CHIEMI AFTER THEY DRESS HER UP?!
OUCHIE!
MIKIO! ARE YOU OKAY?
GOD, WHAT IS UP WITH THESE FREAKS? TALK ABOUT DISGUSTING FASHION...!
Gracious!
FRANCOIS, BE A DEAR AND HOLD HER DOWN, WOULD YOU?
ROGER! ♥
STAY BACK, YOU...

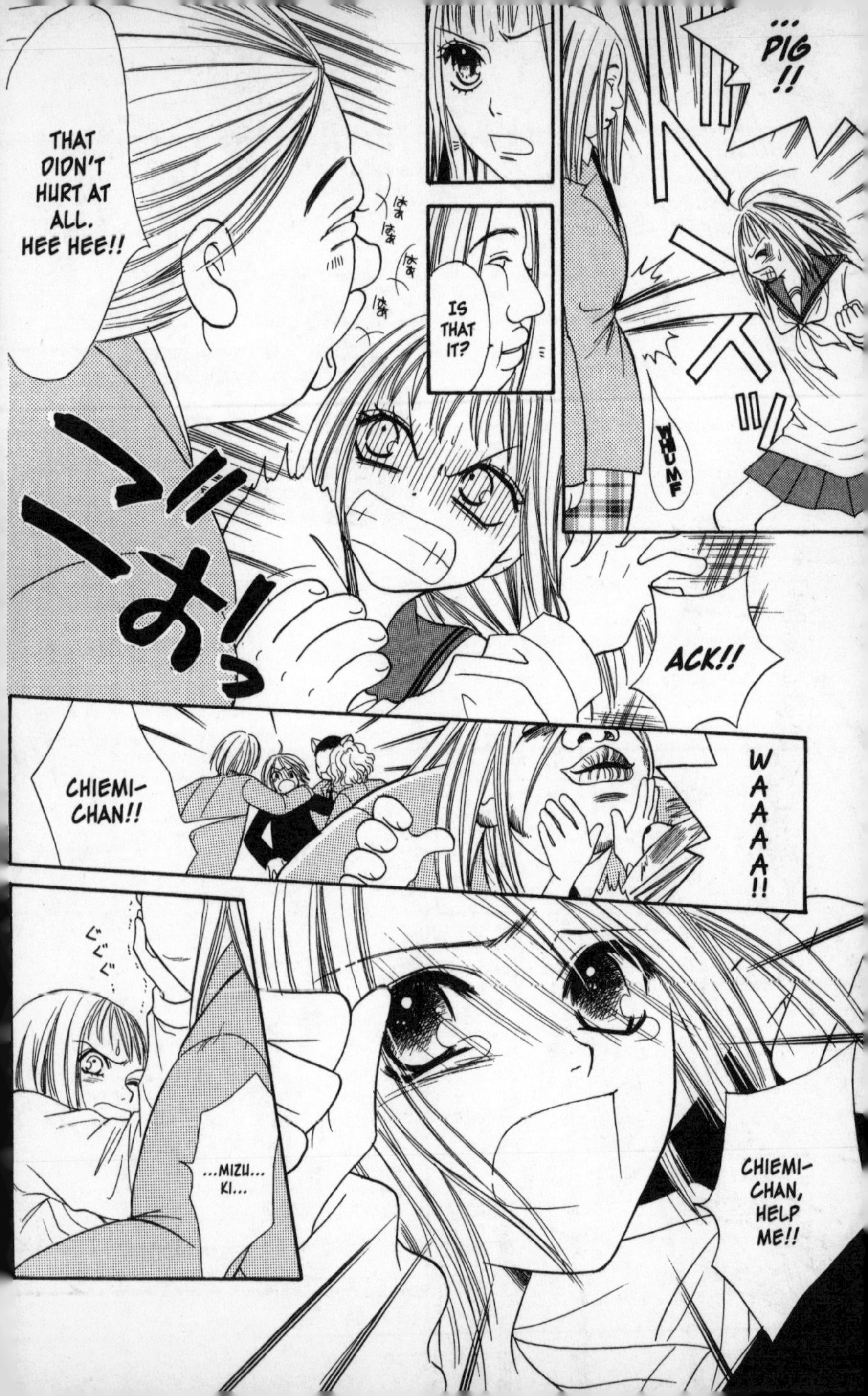
...PIG!!
WHUMF
IS THAT IT?
ACK!!
THAT DIDN'T HURT AT ALL. HEE HEE!!
WAAAAA!!
CHIEMI-CHAN!!
CHIEMI-CHAN, HELP ME!!
...MIZU... KI...

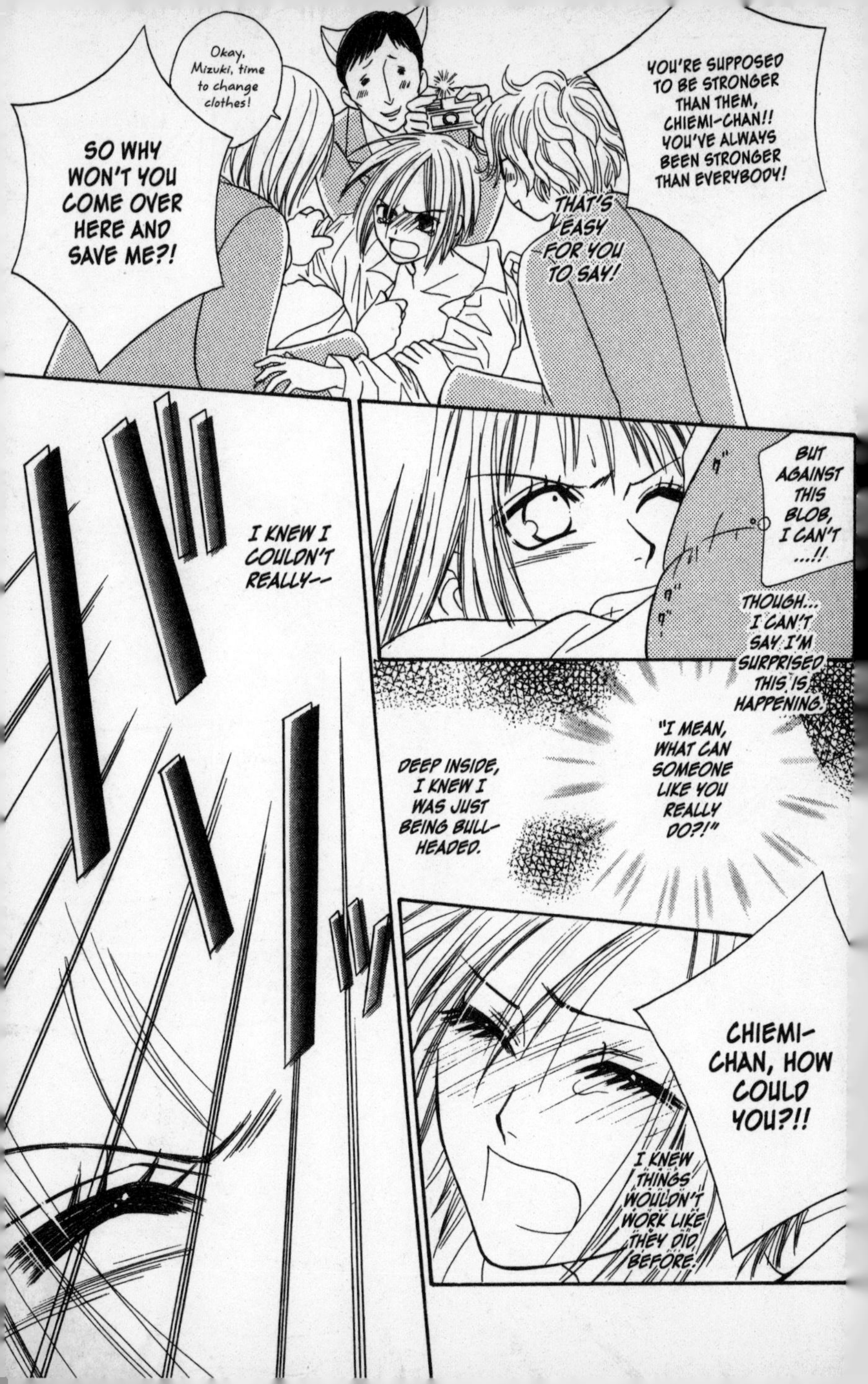

YOU'RE SUPPOSED TO BE STRONGER THAN THEM, CHIEMI-CHAN!! YOU'VE ALWAYS BEEN STRONGER THAN EVERYBODY!
Okay, Mizuki, time to change clothes!
THAT'S EASY FOR YOU TO SAY!
SO WHY WON'T YOU COME OVER HERE AND SAVE ME?!
BUT AGAINST THIS BLOB, I CAN'T ...!!
THOUGH... I CAN'T SAY I'M SURPRISED THIS IS HAPPENING.
"I MEAN, WHAT CAN SOMEONE LIKE YOU REALLY DO?!"
DEEP INSIDE, I KNEW I WAS JUST BEING BULL-HEADED.
CHIEMI-CHAN, HOW COULD YOU?!!
I KNEW THINGS WOULDN'T WORK LIKE THEY DID BEFORE.
I KNEW I COULDN'T REALLY--

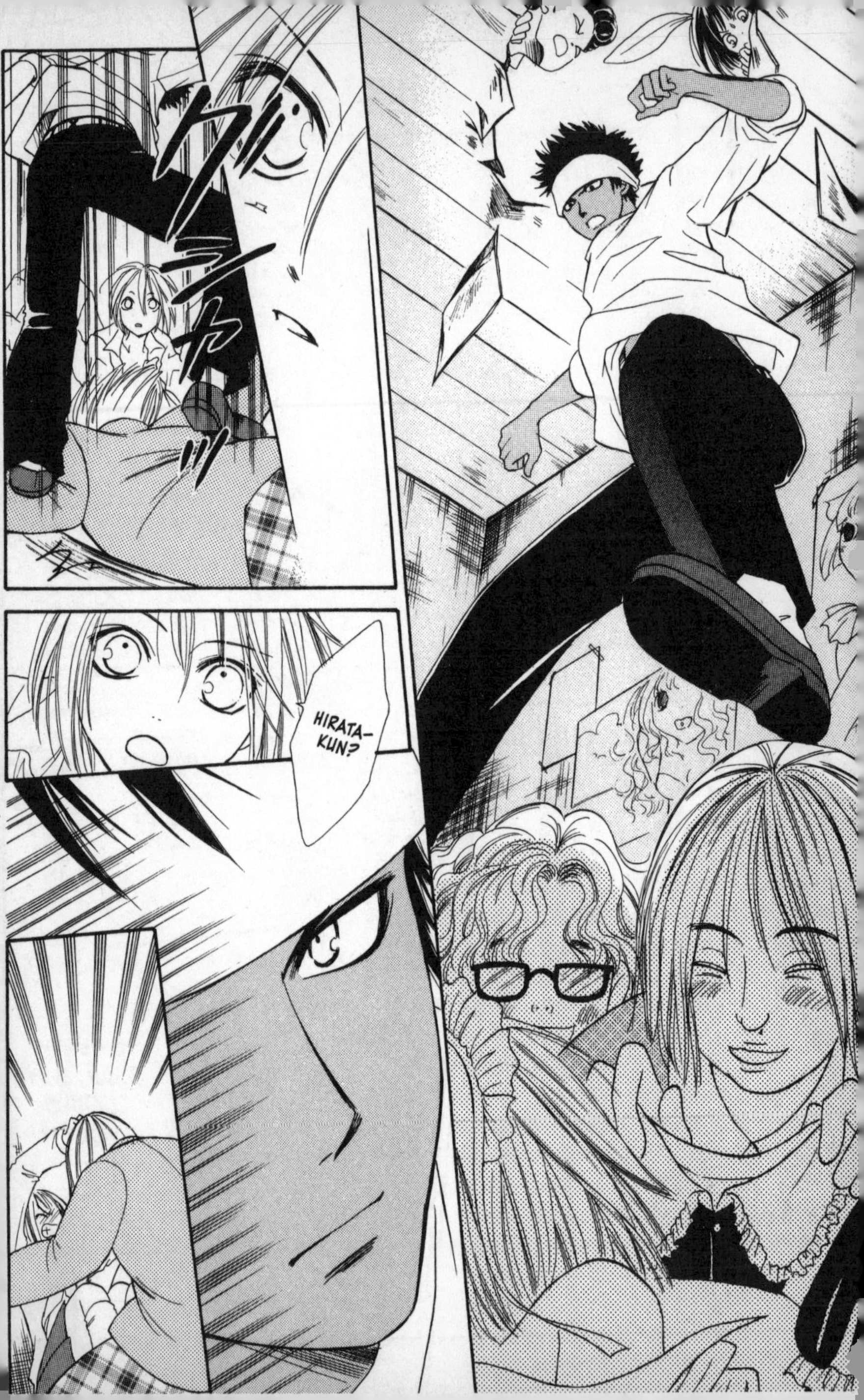
HIRATA-KUN?

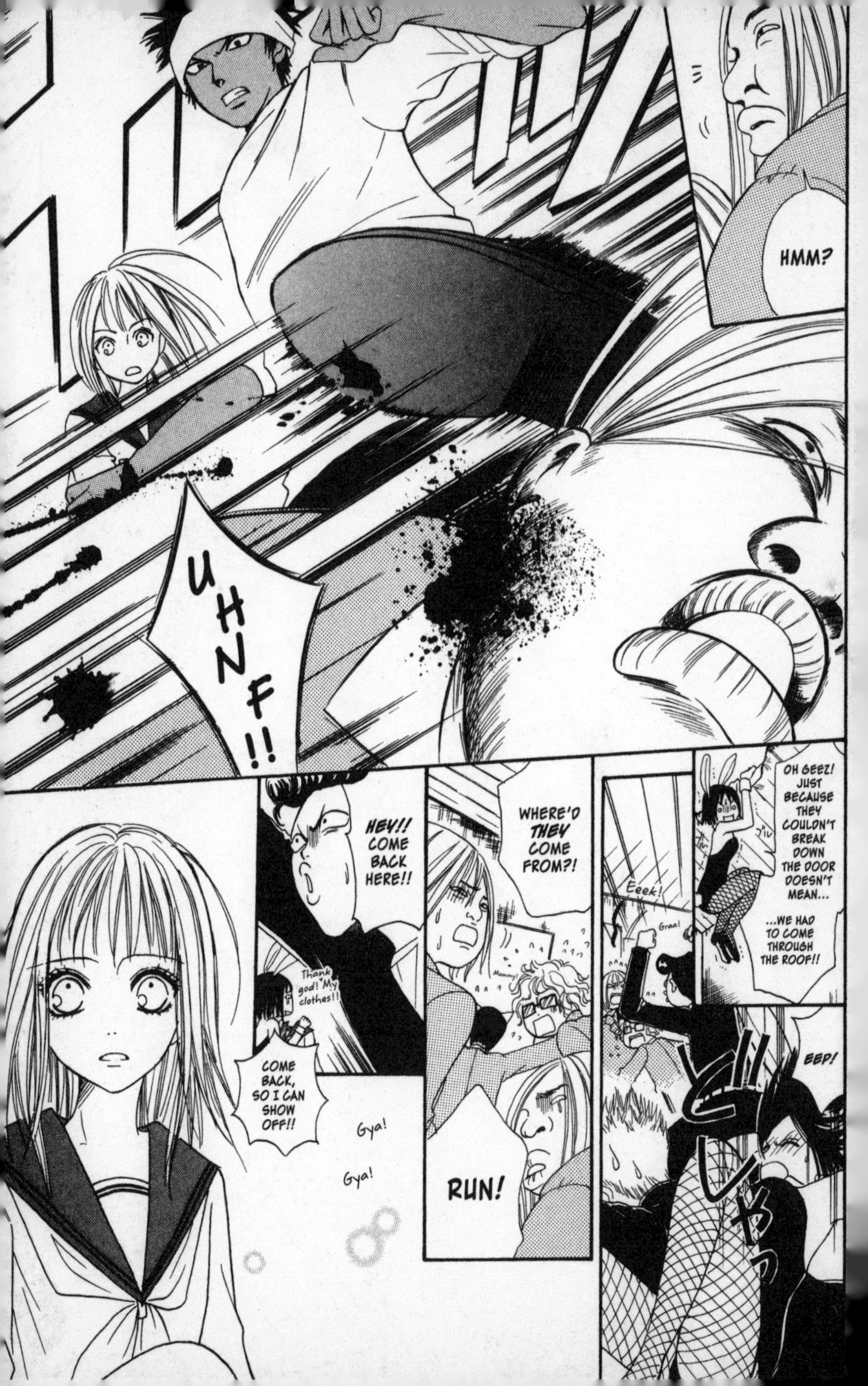
HMM?
UHNF!!
OH GEEZ! JUST BECAUSE THEY COULDN'T BREAK DOWN THE DOOR DOESN'T MEAN...
...WE HAD TO COME THROUGH THE ROOF!!
Eeek!
Graa!
EEP!
WHERE'D THEY COME FROM?!
Mommy!
RUN!
HEY!! COME BACK HERE!!
Thank god! My clothes!!
COME BACK, SO I CAN SHOW OFF!!
Gya!
Gya!

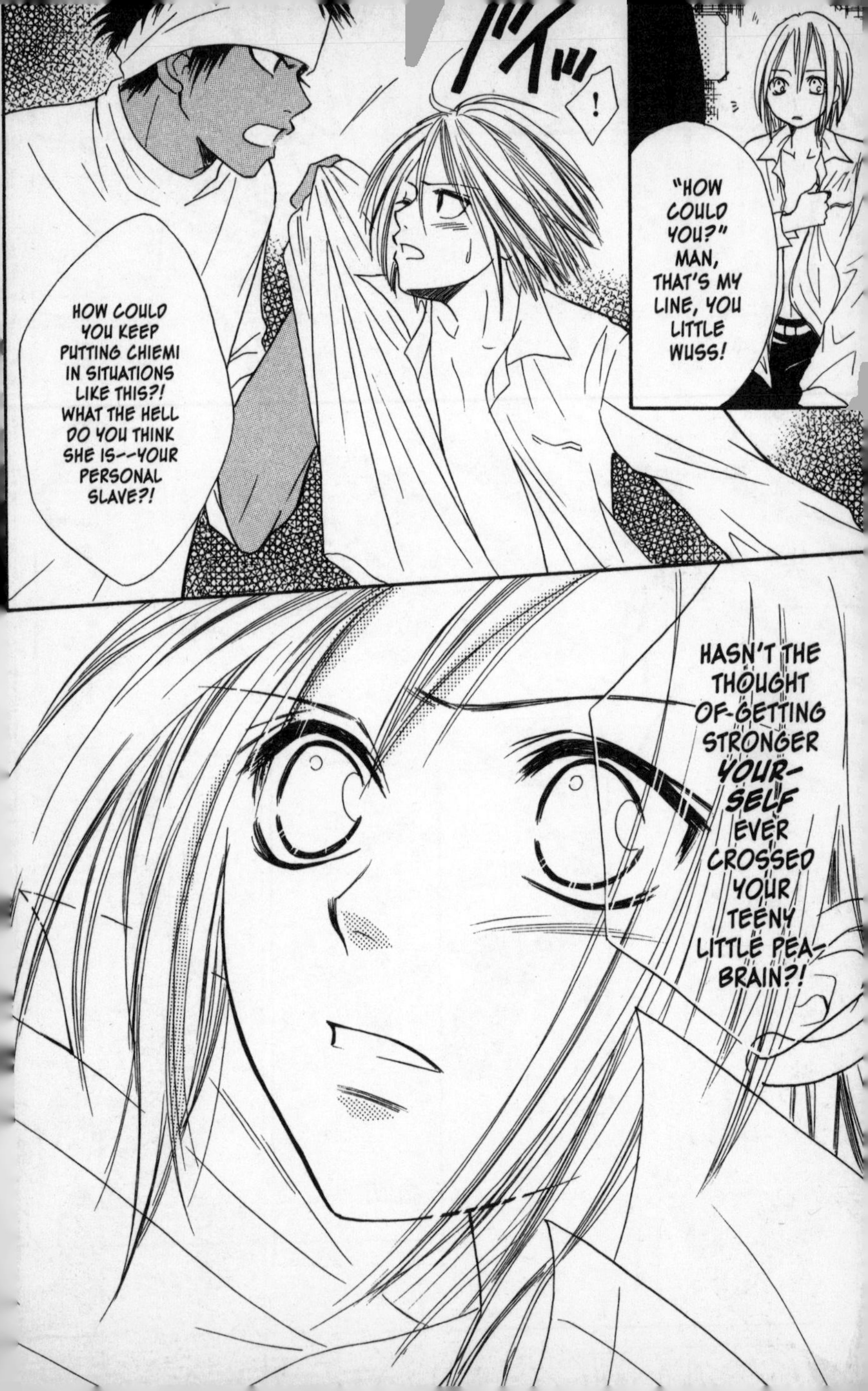
"HOW COULD YOU?" MAN, THAT'S MY LINE, YOU LITTLE WUSS!
!
HOW COULD YOU KEEP PUTTING CHIEMI IN SITUATIONS LIKE THIS?! WHAT THE HELL DO YOU THINK SHE IS--YOUR PERSONAL SLAVE?!
HASN'T THE THOUGHT OF GETTING STRONGER *YOURSELF* EVER CROSSED YOUR TEENY LITTLE PEA-BRAIN?!

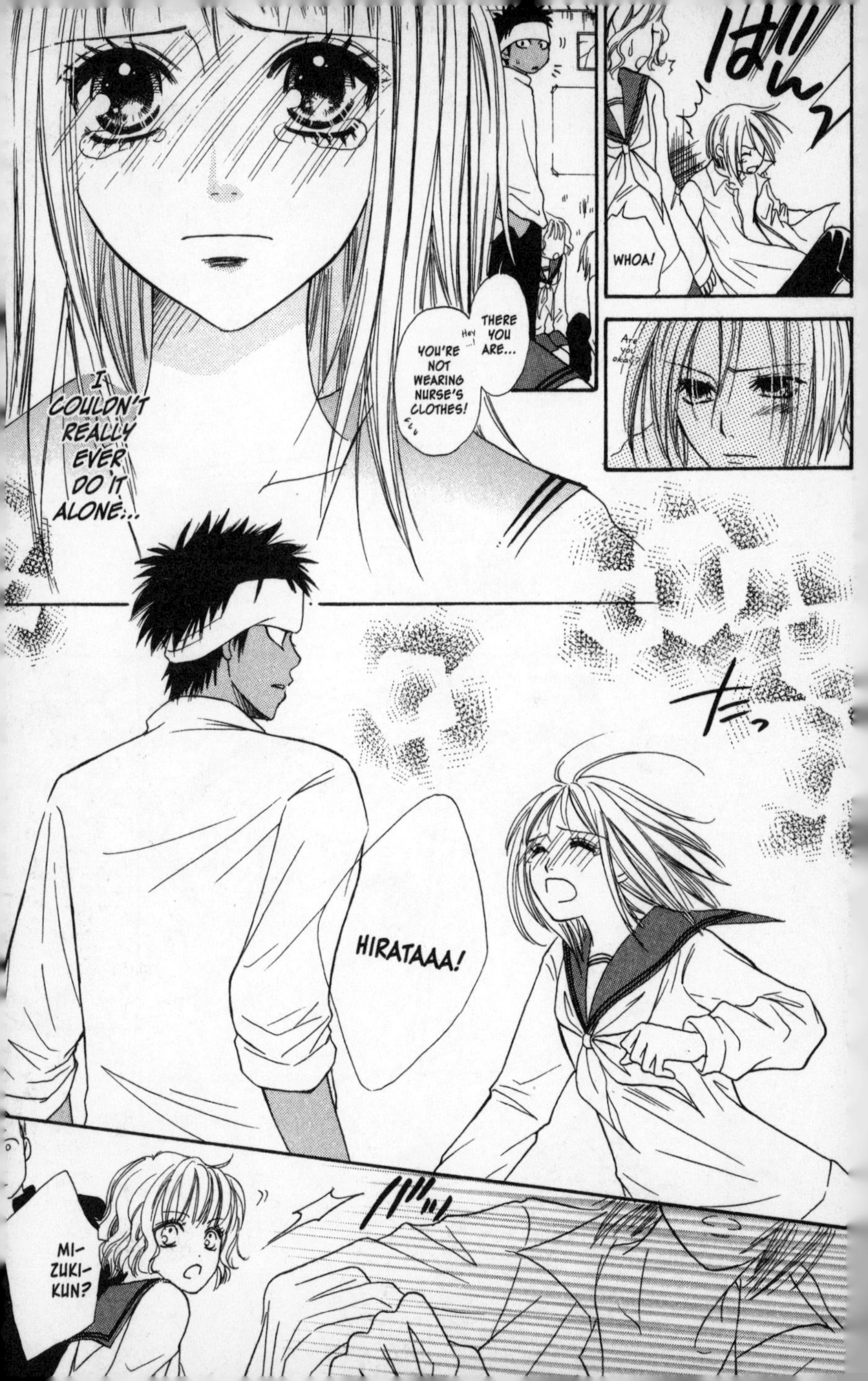
WHOA!
Are you okay?
There you are...
Hey!
You're not wearing nurse's clothes!
I couldn't really ever do it alone...
HIRATAAA!
MI-ZUKI-KUN?

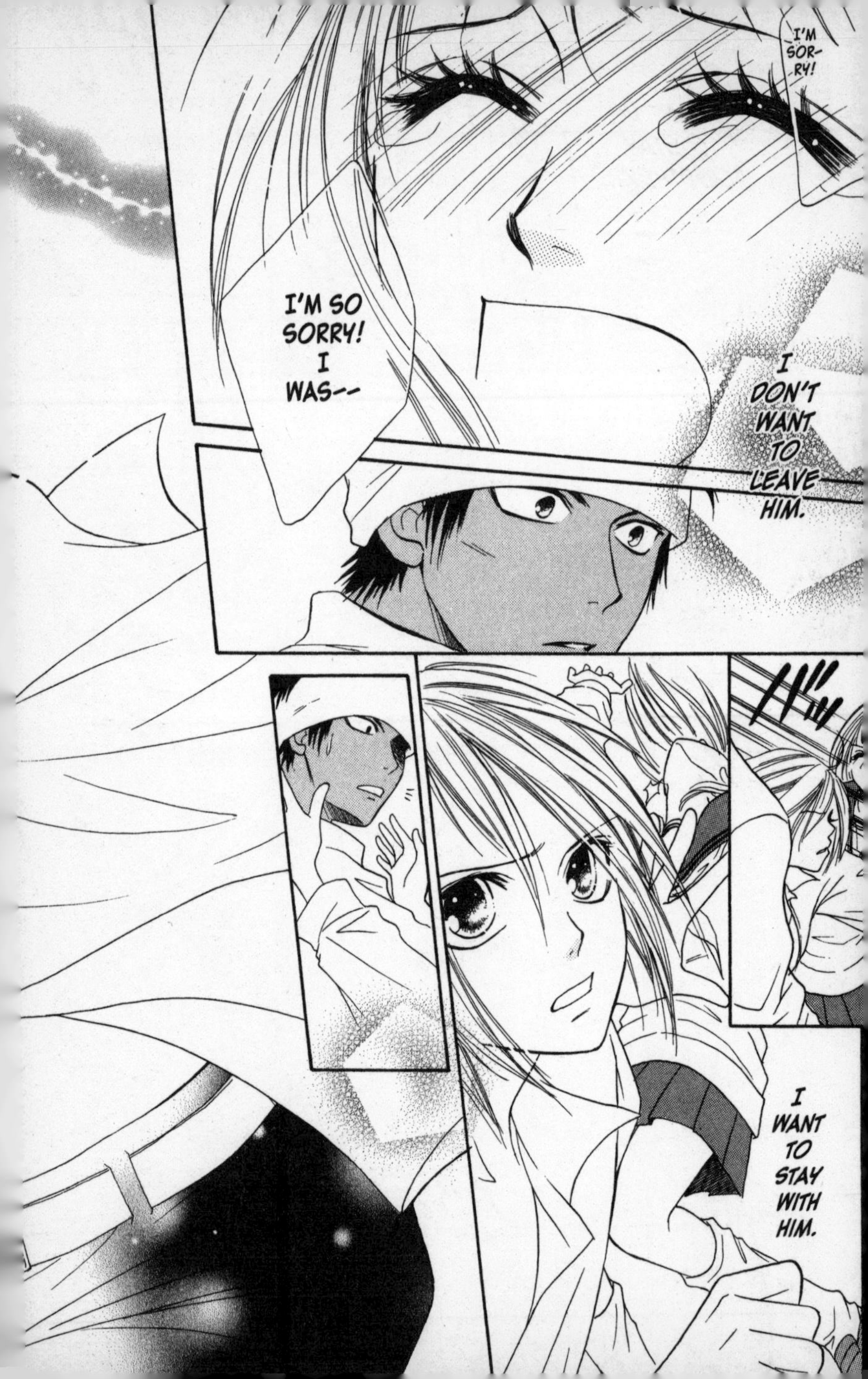
I'M SORRY!
I'M SO SORRY! I WAS--
I DON'T WANT TO LEAVE HIM.
I WANT TO STAY WITH HIM.

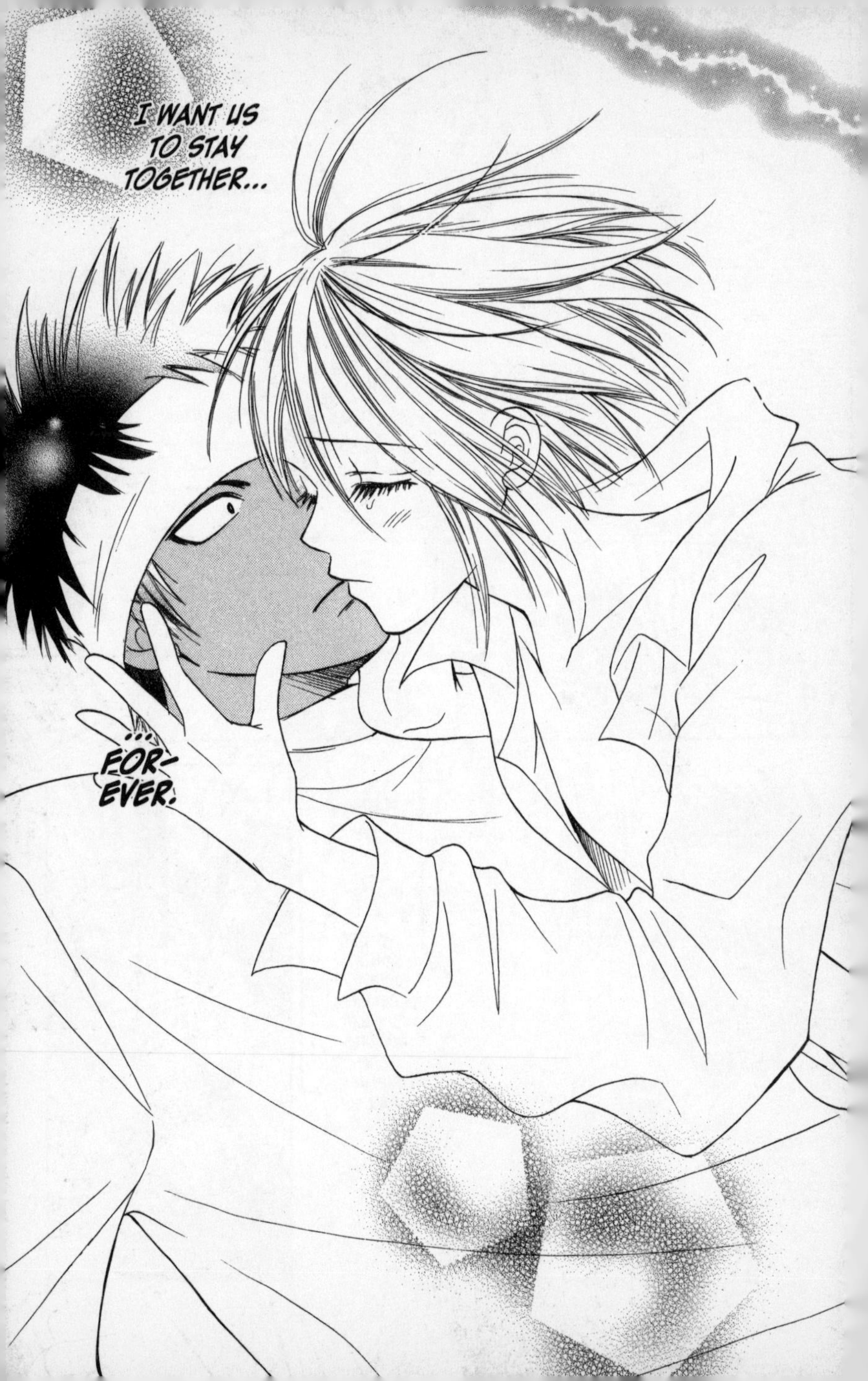
I WANT US TO STAY TOGETHER...
...FOR-EVER.

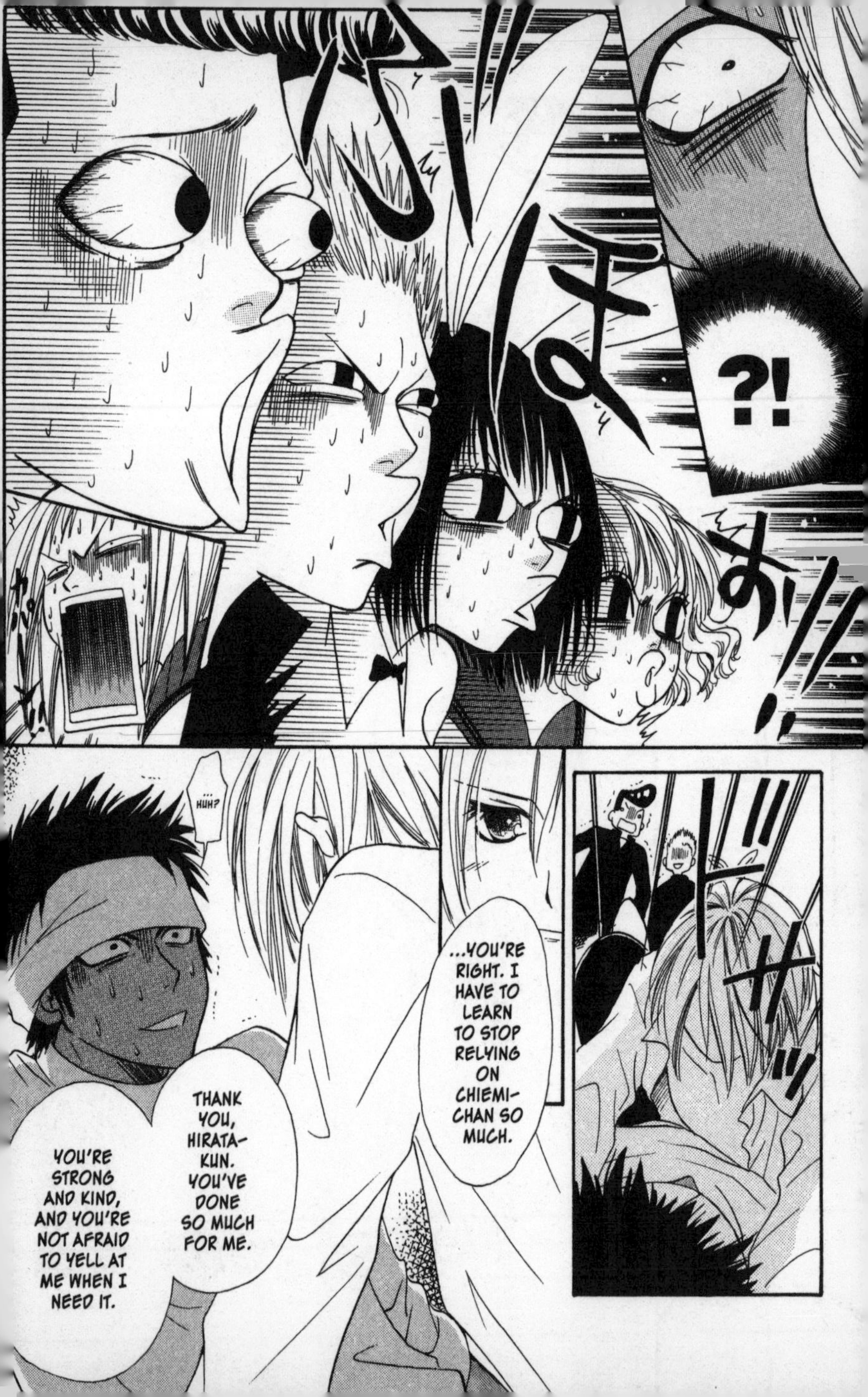
?!
...YOU'RE RIGHT. I HAVE TO LEARN TO STOP RELYING ON CHIEMI-CHAN SO MUCH.
...HUH?
THANK YOU, HIRATA-KUN. YOU'VE DONE SO MUCH FOR ME.
YOU'RE STRONG AND KIND, AND YOU'RE NOT AFRAID TO YELL AT ME WHEN I NEED IT.

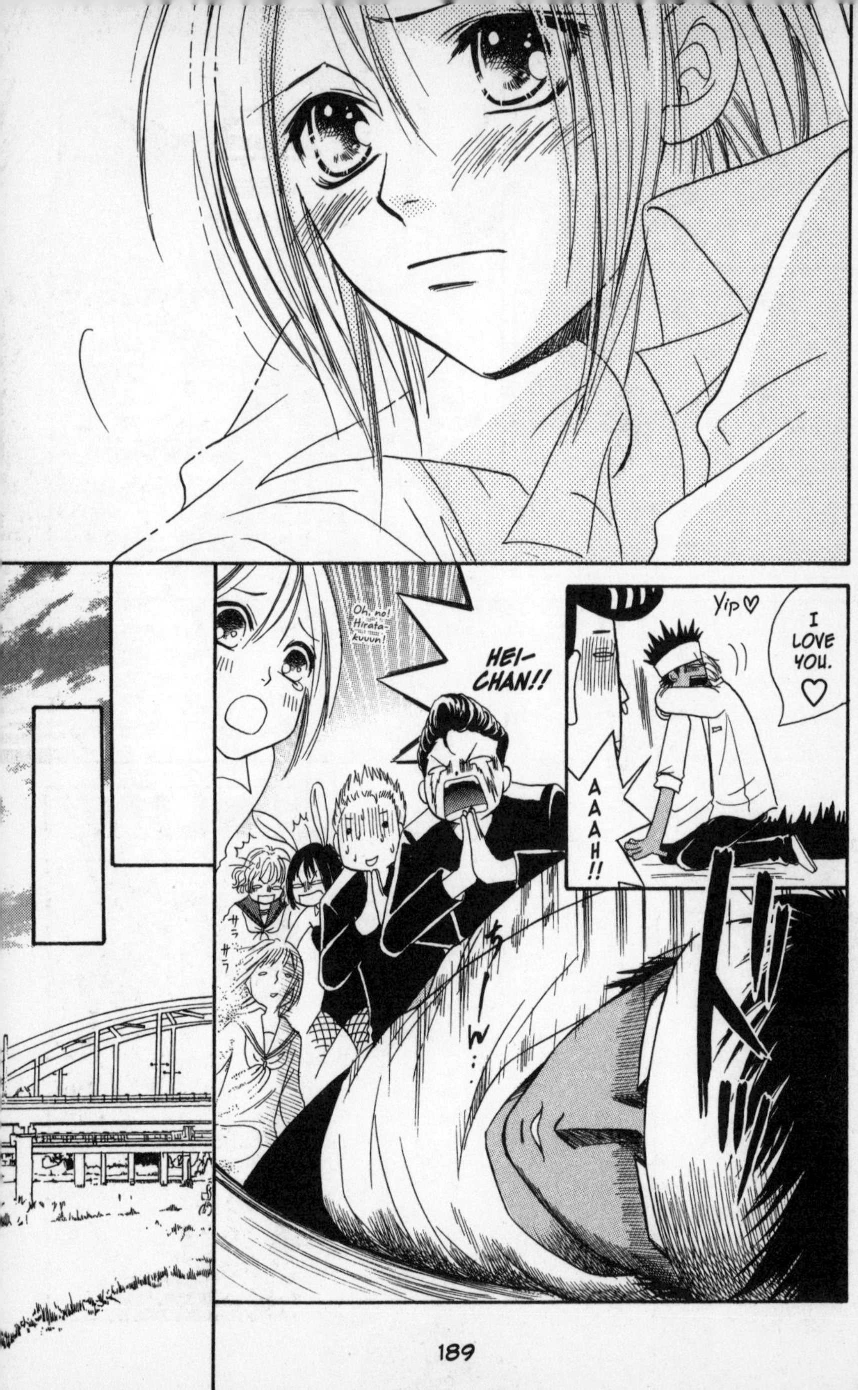

Yip ♡
I LOVE YOU. ♡
AAAAH!!
HEI-CHAN!!
Oh, no! Hirata-kuuun!
サラ サラ

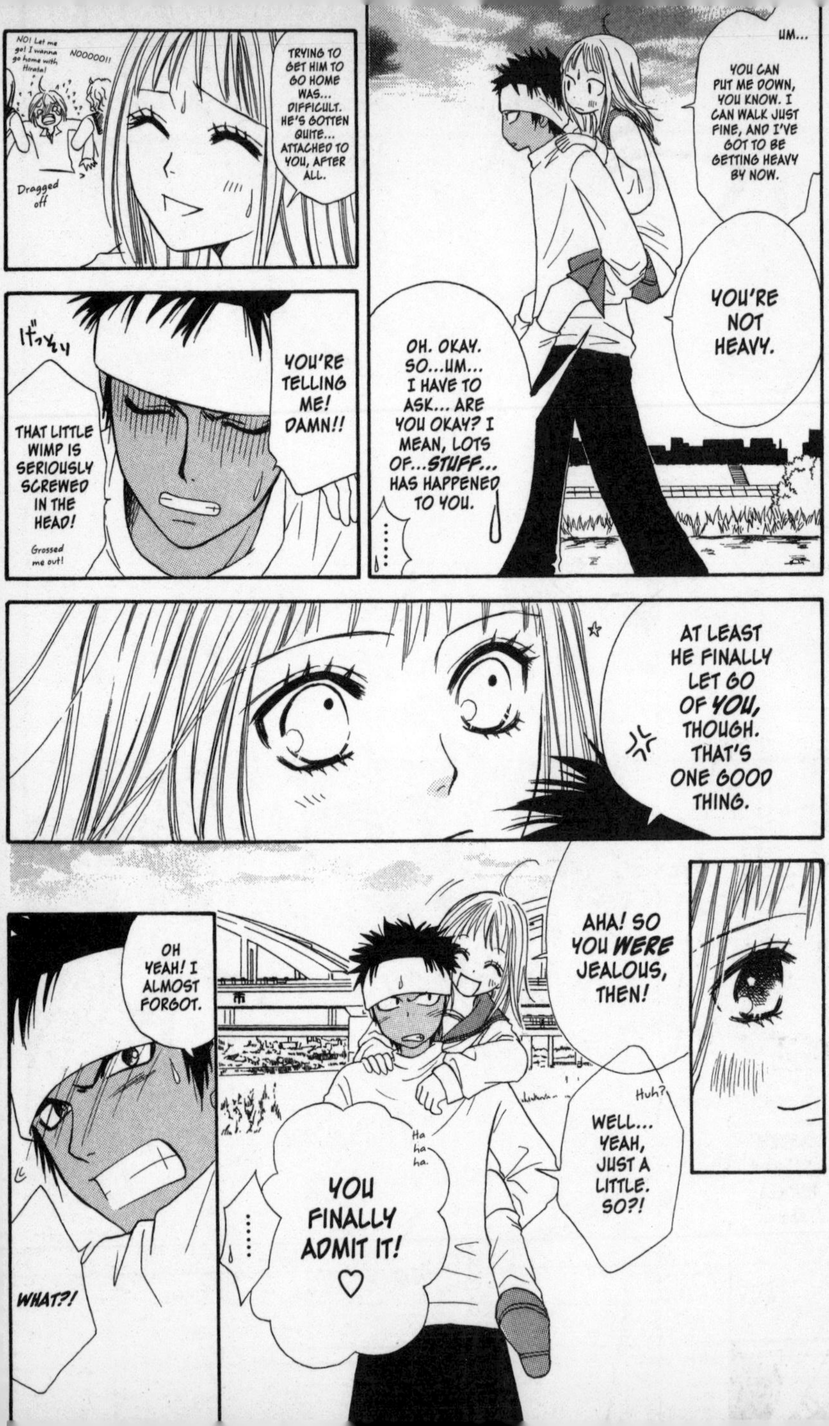
UM...
YOU CAN PUT ME DOWN, YOU KNOW. I CAN WALK JUST FINE, AND I'VE GOT TO BE GETTING HEAVY BY NOW.
YOU'RE NOT HEAVY.
OH. OKAY. SO...UM... I HAVE TO ASK... ARE YOU OKAY? I MEAN, LOTS OF...STUFF... HAS HAPPENED TO YOU.
......
TRYING TO GET HIM TO GO HOME WAS... DIFFICULT. HE'S GOTTEN QUITE... ATTACHED TO YOU, AFTER ALL.
NO! Let me go! I wanna go home with Hirata!
NOOOOOO!!
Dragged off
YOU'RE TELLING ME! DAMN!!
げっそり
THAT LITTLE WIMP IS SERIOUSLY SCREWED IN THE HEAD!
Grossed me out!
AT LEAST HE FINALLY LET GO OF YOU, THOUGH. THAT'S ONE GOOD THING.
AHA! SO YOU WERE JEALOUS, THEN!
Huh?
WELL... YEAH, JUST A LITTLE. SO?!
Ha ha ha.
YOU FINALLY ADMIT IT! ♡
......
OH YEAH! I ALMOST FORGOT.
WHAT?!

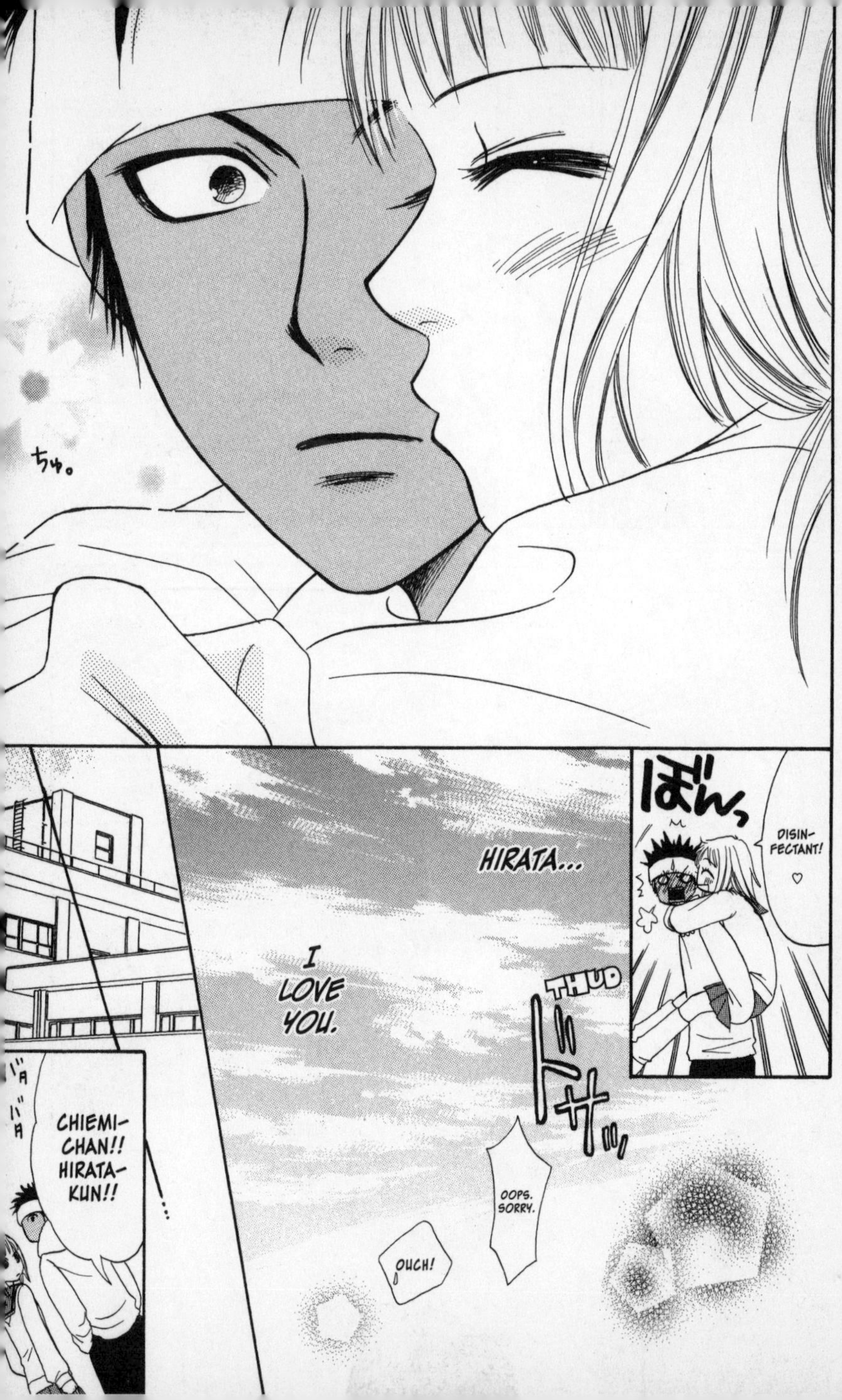
ちゅ。
ぼんっ
DISIN-FECTANT! ♡
HIRATA...
I LOVE YOU.
THUD
ドサッ
OOPS. SORRY.
OUCH!
バタバタ
CHIEMI-CHAN!! HIRATA-KUN!!
...

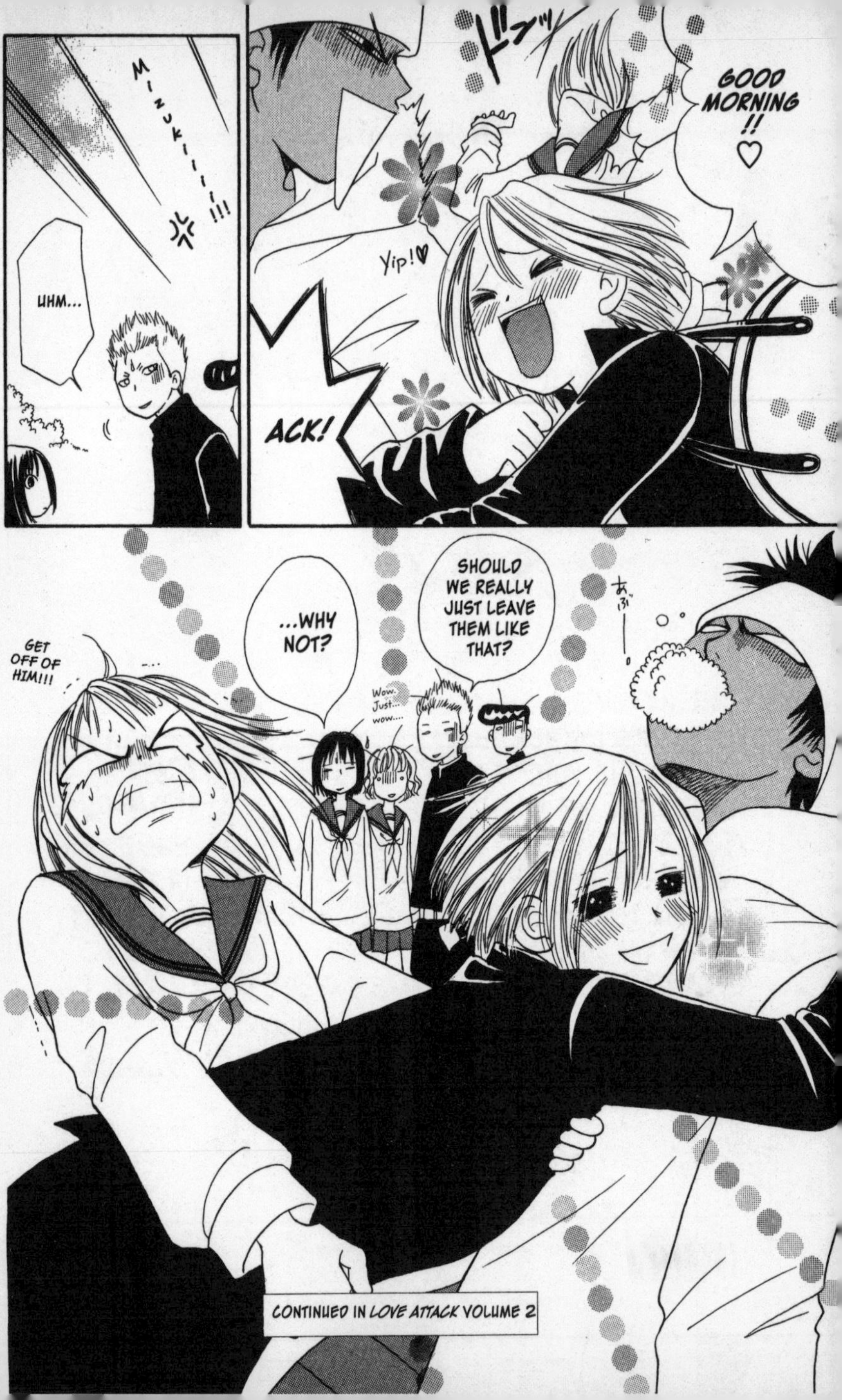
ドブッ
GOOD MORNING!! ♡
Yip!♥
ACK!
MIZUKIIIII!!!
UHM...
あぶ—
SHOULD WE REALLY JUST LEAVE THEM LIKE THAT?
...WHY NOT?
Wow. Just... wow....
GET OFF OF HIM!!!
...
CONTINUED IN *LOVE ATTACK* VOLUME 2

IN THE NEXT...

LOVE ATTACK™

JUNAI TOKKO TAICHO!

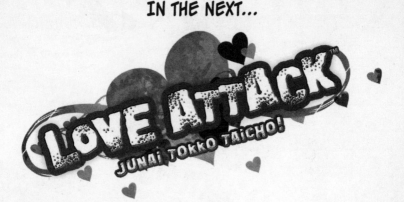

MEETING THE GIRLFRIEND'S FAMILY IS ALWAYS A NERVE-WRACKING EVENT FOR ANY BOYFRIEND, BUT IN HIRATA'S CASE THINGS ARE WORSE. YOU SEE, CHIEMI'S FATHER IS A LEGENDARY PRO WRESTLER, AND ONE WHO'S NOTORIOUS FOR USING DIRTY, ROTTEN TRICKS AT THAT! HIRATA'S MEET WITH THE YUSA FAMILY GOES AS WELL AS ANY SUCH MEETINGS CAN GO UNTIL CHIEMI'S FATHER APPEARS IN HIS FULL-ON WRESTING GETUP, READY TO TEAR HIRATA APART LIMB TO LIMB. HIRATA MUST FIGHT AND WIN TO BE GRANTED THE PRIVILEGE OF DATING HIS DAUGHTER!

DERANGED DEVIL VS. PSYCHO PAPA

COMING IN APRIL OF 2008!

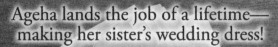

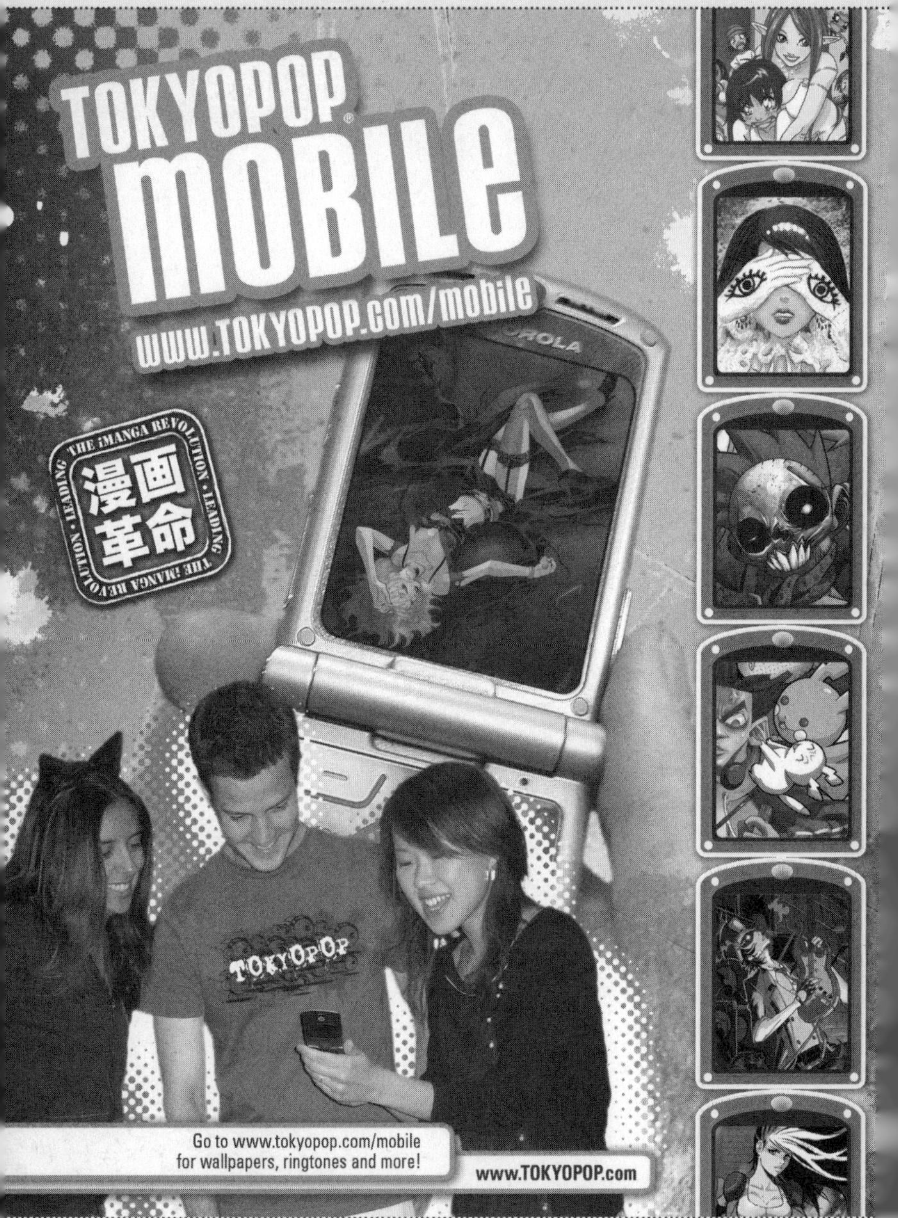
TOKYOPOP
MOBILE
www.TOKYOPOP.com/mobile
THE iMANGA REVOLUTION · LEADING THE iMANGA REVOLUTION · LEADING
漫画革命
TOKYOPOP
Go to www.tokyopop.com/mobile
for wallpapers, ringtones and more!
www.TOKYOPOP.com

FOR MORE INFORMATION VISIT: WWW.TOKYOPOP.COM

HARUKAZE BITTER★BOP™

WELCOME TO THE SCHOOL OF HARD KNOCKS!

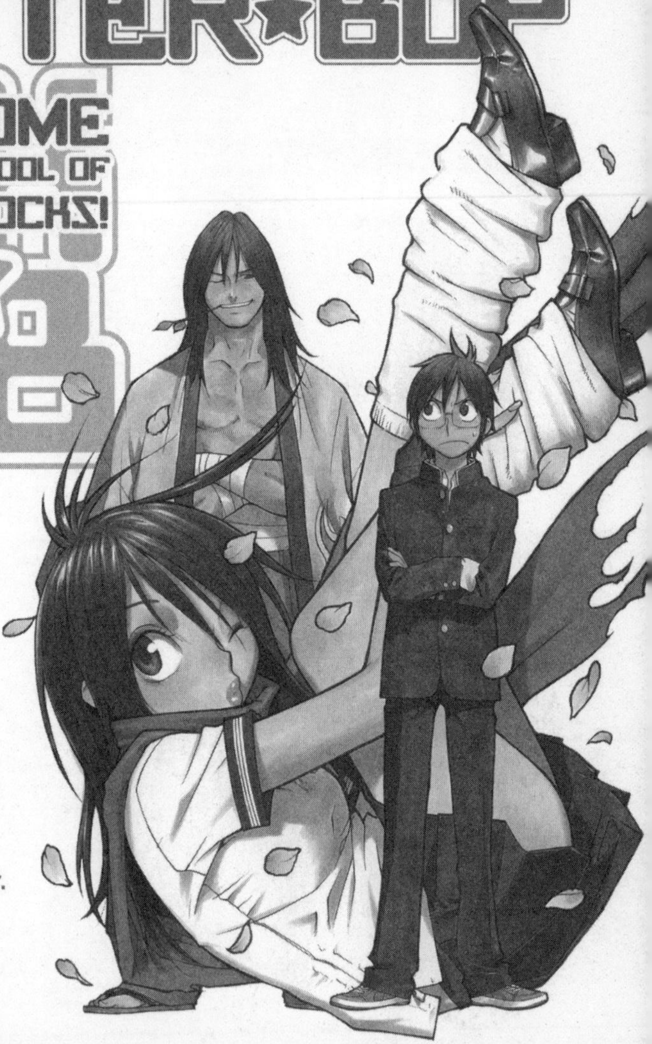

School delinquent Chiyoharu's turned over a new leaf, but the appearance of one amnesiac superhuman and one ditzy self-proclaimed detective isn't about to make his life any easier.

COMEDY

T TEEN AGE 13+

FOR MORE INFORMATION VISIT: WWW.TOKYOPOP.COM

STOP!

This is the back of the book.
You wouldn't want to spoil a great ending!

This book is printed "manga-style," in the authentic Japanese right-to-left format. Since none of the artwork has been flipped or altered, readers get to experience the story just as the creator intended. You've been asking for it, so TOKYOPOP® delivered: authentic, hot-off-the-press, and far more fun!

DIRECTIONS

If this is your first time reading manga-style, here's a quick guide to help you understand how it works.

It's easy... just start in the top right panel and follow the numbers. Have fun, and look for more 100% authentic manga from TOKYOPOP®!